INCARNATIONAL HUMANISM

◆

A Philosophy of Culture for the Church in the World

JENS ZIMMERMANN

REGENT COLLEGE PUBLISHING
Vancouver, British Columbia

INCARNATIONAL HUMANISM

CONTENTS

◆

FOREWORD

♦

Iam honored to write the foreword to this new edition of Jens
Zimmermann's *Incarnational Humanism* at this time of global crisis
when many of the gains made by humanist endeavors over the centuries are at risk. In such times, totalitarianism, nihilism, and rabid
nationalism gain traction, capitalizing on our fears, anxieties, anger,
and disillusionment. Sadly, among them are many Christians who today, as previously, are wary of or simply antagonistic to humanism as
something opposed to Christian faith. It is therefore understandable
that secular humanists regard the notion of Christian humanism as an
oxymoron.

Yet there is a growing conviction even among some secular humanists that the struggle for human rights and, indeed, the survival of
the planet requires spiritual insight and empowerment for the task.
Certainly for Christians, as Dietrich Bonhoeffer observed in his prison
writings, the witness of the church in the modern world depends on
prayer and working for justice in tandem. And the theological foundation for that is undoubtedly, to my mind, what Zimmermann, drawing
deeply on Bonhoeffer's legacy, calls Incarnational Humanism. This
not only provides the basis for Christians to work together with people
of other faiths, but also, as Bonhoeffer discerned, with secular humanists committed to building a more humane and sustainable world.

Unfortunately, since the rise of modernity and the birth of secularism, Christian orthodoxy has been wary of, if not hostile to, any
kind of humanism, largely because of its perceived agnostic or atheist
assumptions. But, as Zimmermann reminds us, long before the birth
of secular humanism during the 18th century, there was a compelling,
even if often sidelined, Christian humanist tradition deeply embedded
in classical Patristic Christology. For if God became truly human in
Jesus Christ, it followed that becoming more fully human in Christ
was the core meaning of Christian formation and the basis for faith
and witness. This also implied that the redemption of the world was
contingent on the birth of a reconciled humanity, one that transcends

divisive and unjust barriers that lead to conflict and anticipates the cosmic redemption and recapitulation of all things in Christ.

This fundamental Patristic premise provided the theological foundation for the Medieval and then Renaissance flourishing of art and science until the synthesis between faith and reason, theology, and science collapsed along with the possibility of creative engagement with Islam. And as the church began to close its mind and harden its heart, so the rich legacy of Incarnational Humanism was pushed to the fringes where it was sometimes recovered by those deemed heretics. The almost inevitable consequence was the birth of secular humanism, followed eventually by Nietzschean anti-humanism which proclaimed the cultural "death of God." Thus, secular humanism, for all its remarkable achievements in the struggle for human rights, began to degenerate into a fractured nihilism in frantic search for meaning and life-giving sustenance. This is by no means the sole fault of humanists who have become secular: it is as much the fault of Christians who have forgotten or ignored their patristic roots and squandered their humanist heritage.

One creative response has been the "post-metaphysical hyper-humanism" of Heidegger, one of Zimmermann's major sparring partners. But his proposal is to recover the legacy of Christian humanism by returning to its biblical and patristic roots. To achieve his goal, Zimmermann introduces into his analysis the contribution of several philosophers who have sought a new foundation for humanism, most notably Gadamer, Levinas, and the Catholic Blondel. But in the end it is Bonhoeffer's Christology that is his major resource in retrieving Incarnational Humanism; and he retrieves it in a way that can fundamentally reshape and inform the life of the Church in the world today as a community in solidarity with the whole of humanity in the search for meaning and the struggle for justice. This is neither triumphalism nor fundamentalism, but exercising a freedom to think, live, and act in the world in a Christian way and, if need be, to suffer for the sake of the re-birth of humanity in the image of the Incarnate God. So, to quote St Augustine, *Tolle lege*!

John W. de Gruchy

PREFACE TO THE SECOND EDITION

◆

This is the second volume of a trilogy on Christian Humanism, taking its place between *Humanism and Religion: A Call for the Renewal of Western Culture* (OUP 2012) and *Dietrich Bonhoeffer's Christian Humanism* (OUP 2019). The latter work showcases Bonhoeffer as a concrete example of what modern Christian Humanism might look like at it is best. In *Incarnational Humanism*, I argue more generally for the engaging and shaping of culture based on a Christian Humanist view of human identity grounded in God's becoming human in Jesus the Christ. This incarnational anthropology follows the lead of the church fathers in maintaining that Christ, who is the true image of God (Heb. 1:3), summed up or recapitulated in himself all of humanity, uniting without confusion the created and uncreated, raising mortal human flesh into the divine and thus into immortality.

Consequently, the vocation of human beings, as those created in Christ's image, is to become fully human by becoming like Christ through participation in his deified humanity. In other words, the human vocation, as articulated by early Christians, is to become *deified* through union with God (John 17:20–3), that is, to become god-like both in moral character by imitating Christ's love of God and neighbour and in our bodily transformation into an "imperishable" state of existence (1 Cor. 15:42). The church, as the new humanity in embryo (Eph. 2:15), ought to reflect the new creation inaugurated by Christ, and therefore is tasked with humanizing culture. In the vein of Jacques Maritain's *Integral Humanism* and Dietrich Bonhoeffer's idea of Christformation in a secular world, this call to humanize culture is issued without nostalgia for Christendom, because both thinkers distinguished clearly between the ideology of *secularism* and the legitimate *secular* realm in which both people of different faiths and non-religious folk must coexist. Both of these theologians renounced any Christian aspiration of turning the world into God's kingdom. Instead, they sought a way to mold secular structures according to the humanistic ideal of Christlikeness. Our task is thus to suffuse culture ever anew with the Spirit of Christ in ways appropriate for the challenges of our time.

Much has changed in Western (and indeed non-Western) cultures since the writing of this book over a decade ago. Or has it? Perhaps what always was has only become manifest in other ways, and longstanding problems have become more obvious than before. *Plus ça change, plus c'est la même chose*! In fact, the loss of Christian roots through increasing secularization and the consequent uncertainty about human identity have become even more apparent in recent years. As Canadian philosopher Charles Taylor rightly argued, secularization is not mainly an emptying of churches or the demise of Christian institutions, but the departure from our embeddedness in a transcendent moral order. Embracing an "immanent frame" as the default starting point for interpreting reality constitutes the main and profound difference between the premodern and the modern world. Such an embrace affects every area of human life and entails the loss of realism.[1]

This loss is complete when the two main reductive moves leading to modernity, the mathematization of reality by Galileo and the subsequent mind-body separation advocated by Descartes, are placed within a physicalist worldview. It cannot be repeated often enough that this move is in no way a scientific and empirical but rather a metaphysical decision based on faith. While this modern materialist and immanentist framework has become inscribed on our perceptive "skin," as it were—and thus equally affects secularists and people of faith—*no experiential data* require us to adopt this framework. Many people still assume that the modern separation of reason and faith, along with its attendant claim that only natural science presents us with true facts while all other knowledge disciplines (theology, philosophy, literature, and the arts) offer mere opinion, is simply common sense. It is not. This position is a historically and culturally trained position that relies on metaphysics—on *faith*—as much as, if not more than, any religious belief.

Although many scholars, whether in the humanities or the natural sciences, have abandoned the modernist worldview described above, the effects of the modern separation between mind and being, together with the unabating reign of scientism in popular culture, have become more pronounced than ever. Current popular imagination, based as it is on Cartesian mind-body dualism, scientific materialism, and the techno-scientific drive to master nature according to our human needs

---

[1] See the important analysis of this loss and philosophical attempt at retrieval by Hubert Dreyfus and Charles Taylor in Hubert L. Dreyfus and Charles Taylor, *Retrieving Realism* (Cambridge, MA: Harvard University Press, 2015).

and desires, has produced a strange world divorced from natural life. This divorce from transcendence and from belief in a natural order of life constitutes the actual loss incurred by the ideology of secularism. *Virtual* reality has become the tragic ruling world picture of our modern age. We increasingly live as if we inhabited a Metaverse in which reality can be bent to the human will through the help of computer technology. Even gender or sexuality are no longer biologically determined but have become subject to personal choice, our now purely material bodies forced to conform to our disembodied desires through the help of surgical technology. Ironically, virtual reality, while ostensibly in service to individualist expressivism and freedom of choice, actually leads to group think, conformism, and enslavement to state administration.

The world-wide overreaction to the outbreak of Sars-CoV-2 powerfully reveals the weakness of cultures uprooted from the actual rhythms of life and unmoored from a Christian view of human identity. Governments worldwide jettisoned longstanding viral outbreak protocols and went into a novel military containment mode. Computing models rather than actual medical research determined the course of events, predicting death tolls that were widely off the mark by orders of magnitude[2] and unnecessarily increased panic. Within the novel bio-security paradigm adopted by governments, human beings were transformed from persons with inherent dignity, freedom, rights, social relations, and responsibilities into "bio-hazards" who needed to be "locked down." In short, political reaction and management of the virus revealed a fundamental anthropological loss.

The redefinition of health during the Covid measures is a good example of this paradigmatic shift toward a reductionist, technocratic view of human beings. Traditionally, health denotes the whole of a person's well-being within the total context of biological and social life. "Health," as Hans-Georg Gadamer explains, drawing on ancient Greek philosophy, "is a being-there, being-in-the-world, being-with-other human beings; health is to be busy with, or joyously fulfilled in one's own life tasks."[3] Health, he notes, is "the rhythm of life," rooted in the biological activities of our metabolism, including breathing, sleeping, and depending on the environment. Yet especially for human beings, health also entails the vital aspects of human sociality that

<hr>

[2]Alberto Boretti, "After Less than 2 Months, the Simulations that Drove the World to Strict Lockdown Appear to be Wrong, the Same of the Policies They Generated," *Health Services Research and Managerial Epidemiology* 7 (2020): 1–11, doi:10.1177/2333392820932324.
[3]Hans-Georg Gadamer, *Die Verborgenheit der Gesundheit* (Frankfurt am Main: Suhrkamp, 2018), 144.

we live out in "familial, societal, and professional life."[4] For the new
bio-security regime adopted to fight a supposed pandemic, this holistic
view of health was abandoned. Health was redefined impossibly as a
virus-free, zero-Covid, functional biological entity, and all other aspects of human health were simply ignored. Without any evidence for
their effectiveness, and despite warnings against their potential harm,
governments imposed military-style lockdowns without any noticeable
effect other than causing unprecedented economic and social damage.[5]

When biosecurity becomes more important than persons, humanism in all its forms, not least Christian Humanism, dies. As the
political philosopher Giorgio Agamben has pointed out, the general
populace's submission to biosecurity is the direct consequence of the
modern fragmentation of the spiritual-corporeal unity of human experience "into a purely biological entity on the one hand, and a social,
cultural, political existence on the other."[6] Irrational fear of the virus,
encouraged by governments worldwide, has shown that "people believe in this abstraction, and they have sacrificed to it their normal life
conditions, their social relations, their political and religious beliefs,
even their friendships and relationships."[7] Once again, the Covid panic
merely crystallized an already extant medicalization and reduction of
human existence to the "bare life" that cultural critics like Ivan Illich
began to point out decades ago.[8]

When Covid was politicized in the name of "science," modernity's
god, most churches stood idly by in silent approval as governments
shut down worship and locked old folks into homes and clinics to die
isolated, undignified deaths. The church's humanistic message is the
unity of humankind as grounded in Christ's recapitulation of humanity. The church abandoned this incarnational message when it failed to
resist these government measures. Some churches went so far as to put
asunder what Christ joined together by excluding unvaccinated persons
from attending church or communion services, thus effectively denying the reality of baptism. Moreover, many churches betrayed their
forgetfulness of the incarnation in embracing digital worship, and even
a digital Eucharist, rekindling the kind of gnostic beliefs in immaterial
salvation Irenaeus so bravely combatted in the 2nd century.

[4]Gadamer, *Die Verborgenheit*, 144 (translation mine).
[5]See the Johns-Hopkins study by Jonas Herby, Lars Jonung, and Steve H. Hanke, "A Literature
Review and Meta-Analysis of the Effects of Lockdowns on Covid-19 Mortality," in *Studies in
Applied Economics* (SAE), no.200 (January 2022).
[6]Giorgo Agamben, *Where Are We Now?: The Epidemic as Politics*, trans. Valeria Dani (Lanham:
Rowman & Littlefield, 2021), 63.
[7]Agamben, *Where Are We Now?*, 63.
[8]Ivan Illich, *Limits to Medicine: Medical Nemesis, the Expropriation of Health* (London: Boyars,
1976).

The public mismanagement of Covid is symptomatic of the deeper cultural malaise of a reductionist anthropology. It is astonishing that many Christians still do not see the anti-humanistic implications of societal behavior that became apparent during the Covid crisis and have continued since. Humanistic culture is based on the dignity of the person, on mutual respect, and on dialogue for the consensual attainment of truth. Christian Humanist education aims at formation into Christlikeness. Christlikeness entails freedom in responsibility for the sake of truthful living. In Christ, truth, freedom, and loving responsibility for one another go hand in hand (John 8:31–3). Hence, humanistic culture requires listening to contrary opinion, respecting difference, and open dialogue, basic features not only of liberal democratic societies but also of universities, originally dedicated to the search for knowledge, truth, and wisdom. Yet what we currently see in universities is uncritical group think motivated by politically correct virtue-signaling and the authoritarian censorship of anyone who does not conform to the accepted mainline narrative. UNESCO is currently working on policies to combat "disinformation" on social media and to erect an "Internet of Trust" cleansed of whatever some censorship committee deems "misinformation, hate speech, and conspiracy theories."[9] As every humanist knows, each time governing authorities propose another "Ministry of Truth," the abolition of humanity is sure to follow.

In fact, we are witnessing the destruction of our humanity through the inevitable combination of technocracy and the loss of proper metaphysical and moral grounding. We are experiencing what C. S. Lewis, in his famous critique of the scientistic-technocratic anthropology of modernity, foresaw as "the abolition of man." It is hard to believe, but recent announcements by Western politicians show that the formerly transhumanist fringe view of a post-human future has now gone mainstream. Government policies in the West now openly embrace bio-digital convergence (merging human biology with computer technology) as the solution to social and environmental issues. For example, the Canadian government think tank "Policy Horizons" boldly proposes that "biodigital convergence" involves a rethinking of biology as providing both the raw materials and a mechanism for developing innovative processes to create new products, services, and ways of being."[10] One would wish that it were indeed merely a childish delusion

---

[9]UNESCO, "Guidelines for the governance of digital platforms: safeguarding freedom of expression and access to information through a multi-stakeholder approach," *UNESDOC Digital Library* (2023), https://unesdoc.unesco.org/ark:/48223/pf0000387339.
[10]The page includes the disclaimer that "Policy Horizons Canada (Policy Horizons) is a strategic foresight organization within the Government of Canada with a mandate to help the Government develop future-oriented policy and programs that are more robust and resilient in

that mortal men now fearlessly reduce the mysteries of biological life to "raw material" for the human "production" of "new ways of being." However, a recent executive order by the current US president on implementing a bio-digital economy makes the abolition of man the official means for solving a nation's most pressing needs. When biological life is reduced to "data," and when one envisions "writ[ing] circuitry for cells and predictably programming biology in the same way in which we write software and program computers," clearly, the mystery of the human person disappears along with the living reality of organic life.[11]

All these rather worrisome recent developments show that the Christian-Humanist appeal to a holistic vision of human identity and the formation of Christians through the Church's liturgical-communal practices are more needed than ever.

If I had the strength and time to revise *Incarnational Humanism*, one major change would entail a greater focus on the concept of *personhood*. I have come to believe that a robust sense of the person is the true counter to the modern reductionist view of human beings. To champion personhood is tricky, however, since the person is more of a mystery and a vocation than an easily identifiable set of characteristics. The Christian view of the person, rooted in the mystery of the Trinity as God's personal self-disclosure, places the person beyond the reach of any quantifiable or measurable characteristics. Nonetheless, as Emmanuel Levinas (who figures prominently in this book) teaches, the way to true humanism lies precisely with the person as the disruption of all that is quantifiable, as the mysterious Other who constitutes a world in himself, a world accessible only through self-revelation beyond all objectification. The human being, as Martin Luther King Jr. once wrote, "is not a thing. He must be dealt with, not as an 'animated tool,' but as a person sacred in himself. To do otherwise is to depersonalize the potential person and desecrate what he is."[12] For pointing us in this direction, I believe, the present version of *Incarnational Humanism* remains a valid effort.

the face of disruptive change on the horizon. The content of this document does not necessarily represent the views of the Government of Canada, or participating departments and agencies." See Policy Horizons | Horizons de politiques, "Exploring Biodigital Convergence," *Policy Horizons Canada*, February 11, 2020, https://horizons.gc.ca/en/2020/02/11/exploring-biodigital-convergence/.

[11]Joseph R. Biden Jr., "Executive Order on Advancing Biotechnology and Biomanufacturing Innovation for a Sustainable, Safe, and Secure American Bioeconomy," *The White House*, September 12, 2022, https://www.whitehouse.gov/briefing-room/presidential-actions/2022/09/12/executive-order-on-advancing-biotechnology-and-biomanufacturing-innovation-for-a-sustainable-safe-and-secure-american-bioeconomy/.

[12]Martin Luther King Jr., "The Ethical Demands for Integration" in *A Testament of Hope: The Essential Writings and Speeches of Martin Luther King, Jr.* (San Francisco, CA: Harper San Francisco, 1991), 117–25 (119).

It is my hope that this reprint will help inform Christian resistance to dehumanizing social practices and policies of our current culture. When do we recognize a human law or practice as dehumanizing? As King so eloquently put it, "a just law is a law that squares with the moral law or the law of God," and "an unjust law is a human law that is not rooted in eternal and natural law. Any law that uplifts humanity is just. Any law that degrades human personality is unjust."[13] In short, whatever relegates human beings to the status of things is to be resisted. King, like Bonhoeffer, believed that nonviolent resistance is required of the Christian when the humanity for which Christ died is trampled underfoot. Also like Bonhoeffer, King urged Christians to combine a "tough-minded," critically-discerning understanding of historical, social, and cultural realities with a tender heart transformed through union with Christ. We need, as King put it, "transformed non-conformists," who realize that resistance to the death-dealing of dehumanizing policies must flow from the death to self that constitutes the true martyrdom of the Christian.

In Christ, who died for the life of the world,
Vancouver, Advent 2023.

---

[13] Martin Luther King Jr., "Letter from Birmingham Jail," in *A Testament of Hope*, 289–302 (293).

PREFACE

◆

Panis angelicus	Bread of Angels,
fit panis hominum;	made the bread of men;
dat panis caelicus	The Bread of heaven
figuris terminum;	The end to all symbols:
O res mirabilis:	A thing wonderful!
manducat Dominum	The Lord becomes our food:
pauper, servus et humilis.	poor, a servant, and humble.
Te trina Deitas	We beseech Thee,
unaque poscimus:	Godhead One in Three
Sic nos tu visita,	That You will visit us,
sicut te colimus;	as we worship You,
Per tuas semitas	lead us through Your ways,
duc nos quo tendimus,	We who aspire to the light
Ad lucem quam inhabitas.	in which You are dwelling.
Amen.	Amen.

—Thomas Aquinas, *Sacris Solemniis*

This book calls for a distinctly Christian philosophy of culture that speaks to the current crisis of reason and identity in Western civilization caused by the loss of its Christian roots. A number of theologians, philosophers and even politicians have agreed with Pope Benedict XVI's claim that we must recover these roots in order to understand the Western legacy of reason, freedom, human dignity and democracy. In developing this Christian philosophy of culture, however, *Incarnational Humanism* seeks not to invent something new but rather to retrieve an ancient Christian humanism for our time in response to the general demand for a com-

mon humanity beyond religious, denominational and secular divides.
Contrary to the current postmodern and pluralist (even relativist) conviction that any particular belief with universal aspirations—let alone religious ones—inevitably leads to oppression and violence, *Incarnational Humanism* asserts that orthodox Christology provides the most promising
source for a common vision of a truly humane society. As the church fathers in both the Eastern and Western traditions have pointed out, the
becoming human of the divine Logos first established the idea of a common humanity. For them, the evangel, the good news, was that Christ had
recapitulated humanity by affirming, judging and redeeming it through
incarnation, death and resurrection in order to restore humanity to its ultimate purpose of communion with God. The church father Irenaeus of
Lyon (death c. 202) was the first theologian to take up and develop the
apostle Paul's conviction that in Christ all of creation had been gathered,
reconciled with God and made new (Eph 1:10).[1] I will deal with this concept of recapitulation and with Irenaeus later on in greater detail. For now
I merely point out that the church fathers grasped fully the import of the
incarnation and its recapitulation of humanity for a unifying and glorious
vision of what it means to be human. The first theologians of the church
were intoxicated with the wonder of the incarnation, and began to unfold
what the faith's deepest mystery—that God had become a human being
while in no way diminishing his utter transcendence of creation—meant
for our understanding of humanity and of the church's relation to the
world. Based on the incarnation and the consequent development of trinitarian theology, Christianity prepared the way for modern conceptions of
freedom, personhood, solidarity and social compassion.

By retrieving this ancient christological source for our vision of what it
means to be human, I want to call Christians to what Henri de Lubac
describes as the "all embracing humanism" of the church fathers,[2] and to
do so in light of pressing current cultural issues. Indeed, *Incarnational Humanism* identifies our modern inability to correlate reason and faith properly as a major cause of the identity crisis of Western cultures and thus of

---

[1]"He, as the eternal King, recapitulates all things in himself" (Irenaeus, *Adversus Haereses* 3.21.9).
[2]Henri de Lubac, *Catholicism: Christ and the Common Destiny of Man*, trans. Lancelot C. Shep-pard and Elizabeth Englund (San Francisco: Ignatius Press, 1988), p. 321.

the philosophical and educational issues discussed in this book. As we shall see, many modern secular societies suffer from a loss of ultimate purpose and meaning because their values have been severed from the transcendent religious sources that gave rise to them. The effects of this separation can be seen in both Christian and non-Christian views on the place of religion in culture. The incarnational humanism of the church fathers did not have this problem. By grounding all human knowledge in the eternal Logos of Christ, early church theologians found a way to unify reason and faith, a way that duly considered both faith's dependence on reason and reason's inability to supersede faith. The church fathers "fully welcomed reason which was open to the absolute, and they infused it with the richness drawn from revelation."[3] By abandoning this healthy correlation of reason and faith, modern Western conceptions of truth continue to suffer from rationalism, relativism and dualism. Rationalism succumbs to the illusion that reason is independent of history, language and tradition. Relativism usually holds the opposite: all truths are historically contingent to the point that none can claim universal validity. In a sense, both of these philosophical positions are species of dualism, that is, attempts to split a complex reality into polar opposites, such as spirit and matter, value and fact, faith and reason, transcendent and immanent, usually favoring one over the other. The motivations for doing so vary greatly, but they ultimately stem from a desire to explain and put in some sort of mental order the world we experience. In our daily experience, however, sober observation and passionate argument, logical thinking and tacit assumptions, mind and matter, thought and language cannot really be separated. Our interaction with reality is not reducible to one particular approach, system or method of explanation. To insist on such clarity and on a particular all-encompassing system to achieve it is futile given human reality.

Christians especially should be wary of dualistic thinking because it fundamentally contradicts incarnational thinking about God and world. In theological terms, *dualism* refers to any unlawful separation of divine revelation from its mediation through beings and things. On the basis of this definition, fundamentalism is also a species of dualism, or at least

---

[3]John Paul II, *Fides et Ratio*, sec. 41, September 14, 1998, Papal Archives, last accessed April 17, 2011, www.vatican.va /holy_father/john_paul_ii/encyclicals/documents/hf_jp-ii_enc_15101998 _fides-et-ratio_en.html.

strongly affected by dualistic tendencies, because fundamentalists usually stress either spiritual or empirical certainty in order to avoid the inevitable messiness of incarnational and integrative thinking. Christian dualism, for example, can range from the neglect of sacramental realities in otherwise nonfundamentalistic denominations all the way to fundamentalism that insists on verbal inspiration of the Scriptures to ensure absolute certainty, and yet interprets the Bible eccentrically to well-established Christian tradition. To overlook the essentially mediated nature of knowledge and meaning is not, of course, limited to Christians or religious people in general. Secular thinkers, especially when they claim the still powerful authority of science as neutral observation, are equally prone to forget that all human knowledge is mediated. The term mediation means that knowledge (rather than individual bits of meaningless information) comes to us through the media of signs and symbols. Not only do we think within language and concepts, but we also have to integrate detailed information into a meaningful whole. But we always do so according to a certain worldview we hold based partially on our own experience but even more so on the inherited views from others. The still powerful myth that we know all things the way we examine bacteria under the microscope, that we just gather the facts dispassionately until some kind of meaning emerges from them, simply does not reflect how we actually perceive and judge realities. We do not encounter meaningless facts in the world, which we clothe afterward with meaning. Rather, we encounter things that are already within a meaningful context. When we see something that seems unrelated to anything we know, we first try to integrate it into our framework of meaning by likening it to something we do know.

It is safe to say that among academics, rationalism—the notion of naked facts to which we give meaning afterward—is mostly passé. Postmodern philosophers, as well as many scientists, have long danced on the grave of scientific and philosophical rationalism.[4] Yet old dualistic habits die hard. Much popular evangelical theology still bears traces of dualism in the opposition of reason and faith, of nature and grace, and of private belief and public policy. All too often such dualisms are justified by the biblical in-

---

[4]Relativism, on the other hand, remains a strong influence in our culture, in part because it is tied to a pervasive cultural sense of tolerance and humility: how dare anyone assert that one culture is superior to another?

junction to be in but not of the world. While not actually a biblical phrasing, this theological maxim derives from passages such as Jesus' prayer in John 17:14-16 ("They are not of the world any more than I am of the world. My prayer is not that you take them out of the world but that you protect them from the evil one") and from the apostle Paul's warning in Romans 12:2 ("Do not conform to the pattern of this world"). By its own remarkable consciousness for social justice, evangelicalism illustrates that these words cannot be taken as simple world denial. But how can we construe properly the relation of Christ and culture? Again, the key is to start from the incarnation to think through this relation in order to avoid dualism.

As we shall see later, even postmodern theologies that strongly denounce rationalistic models of reason often remain highly influenced by dualism in their view of biblical interpretation, tradition and the church because they do not consider sufficiently the philosophical implications of the incarnation. This dualism still characterizes popular discussion both in Christian *and* secular debates over the nature of reason and the purpose of education, two issues very much at the heart of Christian thinking, as Augustine's *De doctrina Christiana* suggests. The failure to correlate reason and faith also unites certain strands of evangelical Christianity and postmodern philosophy that share a dualistic and disenchanted view of the universe, bereft of sacramental portals for the presence of God, and thus prove themselves far removed from the metaphysics that grounded the theology of the early church. At issue is not an uncritical recovery of a certain Christian metaphysics but rather modern Christianity's ignorance of a radically different theological notion of reality, a notion by which earlier Christians achieved a holistic view of the Christian life that neither withdrew from world and culture nor simply endorsed them. The key to this incarnational humanism was the idea that God had become human and thus had truly taken creation and humanity into the divine life. As I suggest throughout this book, Christianity is all about the presence of God with his people, by which he sustains and nourishes them. The great mystery of Christianity is that the "bread of angels" has become "the bread of human beings," as Thomas Aquinas put it in his thirteenth-century hymn *Sacris Solemniis* (see the epigraph). A properly Christian and holistic view of reality derives from this mystery and has implications not merely for Christians but for humanity as a whole.

This holistic view is grounded in Christology. If indeed Christ is the *Logos*, the living active Word and light of God in the world (Jn 1:1-10; Acts 17:28; Col 1:15-20), in whom all things move and have their being, and if this Word took on flesh for the redemption of humanity, how is this unity of all things in the divine Logos reflected in Christian living and thinking? How does this unity form the basis and determine the quality of our common humanity? How does it speak to the separation of reason and faith that is to some degree responsible for the West's identity crisis? Furthermore, if Christ died not simply to save individual souls from hell but to establish a new humanity (Eph 2:15; Acts 5:20; Rom 6:4; 2 Cor 5:17; Col 3:10), how does this new humanity relate to the old? The answer to these questions lies in rethinking salvation as *deification*,[5] and Christian faith as participation in the divine life, by retrieving a high Christology and ecclesiology. In their light, true humanity becomes participation in God's affirmation, judgment and redemption of humanity in Christ; the church as the body of Christ becomes the real presence and foretaste of this new humanity, a *sanctorum communio* nourished by the presence of God in the sacraments.[6] All sacraments, including preaching as the sacrament of the Word that is inseparably tied to the eucharistic representation of Christ's passion and resurrection, are indispensable in transforming Christians into the likeness of God. Incarnational humanism is therefore also a eucharistic humanism, for the Christian lives out the new creational

---

[5]There is considerable debate on what this term means. For a discussion of the differences between a Greek Orthodox doctrine of theosis and a more general theme of theosis within Orthodox Christianity (both East and West, pre- and post-Reformation), see Michael J. Christensen and Jeffery A. Wittung, eds., *Partakers of the Divine Nature: The History and Development of Deification in the Christian Traditions* (Madison, Wis.: Fairleigh Dickinson University Press, 2007). Some suggest that the word *theosis* be reserved for a distinct doctrine indebted to Neo-Platonic categories of participation advocated by Eastern Orthodoxy (see Gösta Hallosten, "Theosis in Recent Research: A Renewal of Interest and Need for Clarity," in ibid., p. 287). However, for the purposes of my discussion, I will use *deification* and *theosis* interchangeably to indicate the broader theme within the Christian tradition of attaining godlikeness. Within the greater Christian tradition, theosis or theopoiesis does not imply a literal divinization or apotheosis, as if human nature became God's nature. Rather, as Thomas Torrance fittingly expressed it, theosis "refers to the utterly staggering fact of God in which he gives himself to us and adopts us into the communion of his divine life and love through Jesus Christ and in his one Spirit, yet in such a way that we are not made divine, but are preserved in our humanity" (*The Mediation of Christ* [Colorado Springs: Helmers & Howard, 1992], p. 64).

[6]For an excellent introduction to a trinitarian, incarnational and participatory model of worship from a reformed perspective, see James Torrance, *Worship, Community and the Triune God of Grace* (Downers Grove, Ill.: InterVarsity Press, 1996).

life of praise and thanksgiving of the eschatological realities of the kingdom that are present in the eucharistic celebration. The church itself as the body of Christ constitutes a sacrament by making present the new humanity whose eschatological outlook on the God-world relation, on society and politics, is shaped by this Christic, ecclesial center.

This book undertakes the retrieval of incarnational humanism as a Christian philosophy of culture in the hope of furthering dialogue not only among Protestants, Catholics and Eastern Orthodox, but also among Christians and secularists, by appealing to a common patristic heritage and to modern Catholic and Protestant theologians. Moreover, the claim that Christianity is the first proper humanism (a claim the remainder of this book will try to explain) also undermines the still prevalent misconception, shared by many Christians and secularists alike, that humanism is equivalent to secular atheism.

In claiming Christianity as the first proper humanism I am not, of course, questioning the sincere desire of secular humanists to improve society. I do believe that Henri de Lubac was right, however, to warn that without God this desire will turn against humanity.[7] While these non-Christian readers are not the intended audience for this text, they should know that this book takes into consideration their unease about the public role of religions. Their worry is usually that any strengthening of dogma leads to dogmatism. Dogmatism, they think, gives rise in turn to either theocratic or separatist aspirations by religious bodies. The central argument for this implied audience will be that the idea of recapitulation provides an intrinsic link between the new humanity inaugurated by Christ and all of humanity. Since Christ summed up in himself, judged, redeemed and glorified humanity, the public role of the church as the body of Christ is defined as being a witness to this new reality. And Christians who participate in Christ through worship are each time shaped in the image of the new humanity and reminded of their public role as witnesses to and ministers of the world's reconciliation with God. The world, as Dietrich Bonhoeffer once put it, "is, as it were, proleptically drawn into the church."[8]

---

[7]Henri de Lubac, *Über Gott Hinaus: Tragödie Des Atheistischen Humanismus*, trans. Edith M. Riley (Einsiedeln: Johannes Verlag, 1984), p. 12.
[8]Dietrich Bonhoeffer, *Dietrich Bonhoeffer Works*, ed. Clifford J. Green, trans. Reinhard Krauss, Charles C. West and Douglas W. Stott, vol. 6, *Ethics* (Minneapolis: Fortress Press, 2005), p. 98. Hereafter, all shortened citations will use the abbreviation *DBWE*.

This belief does not lead to ecclesial imperialism, but to a view of the church as ministering for the common good of society.

In order to establish as much common ground as possible among Christians, people of other faiths and secular humanists, in this book I define humanism in line with Jacques Maritain's idea of "integral humanism" as that which "essentially tends to render man more truly human and to make his original greatness manifest by causing him to participate in all that can enrich him in nature and in history."[9] For the Christian, humanity's original greatness is indicated by the incarnation, death and resurrection of the God-man, Jesus the Christ, who provides the paradigm of true humanity. Indeed, Christians and atheists alike have to acknowledge that historically "the springs of Western humanism are classical and Christian."[10] And since the classical heritage flowered in the West largely as a Christian transformation of Greco-Roman thought, the story of humanism is one of continuous development and later distortion (even by Christians themselves, at times) of these original Christian roots. A large portion of this book will narrate the history of humanism by focusing on the incarnation.

The introductory chapter establishes the current cultural context and concerns that inform our narrative of humanism. This brief sketch portrays contemporary culture as marked by the loss of its Christian roots and the philosophical incoherence resulting from the disappearance of religious sensibilities from public discourse. The secularization of public discourse does not, however, entail the disappearance of religion from Western society and its supposed, and much talked about, return. Religion has not disappeared but merely been relegated by the domination of the scientific method among intellectuals to the private sphere as mere private opinion (along with aesthetics and the human sciences). The postmodern critique of this reductionist method of reflection—especially through hermeneutic philosophy, but also through the realization by scientists themselves that human knowledge, just like the arts, requires imagination and creative integration—has opened up reason once again to the fuller, spiritual dimension of thought. The domination of scientific objectivism and instrumental reasoning has given way to an age of interpretation, that is,

[9]Jacques Maritain, *True Humanism*, trans. Margot Robert Adamson, 6th ed. (London: Geoffrey Bles, 1954), p. xii.
[10]Ibid., p. xiv.

to a basic consensus that any meaningful human knowledge that transcends mere bits of information follows the basic pattern laid down by ancient Christian thinkers of "faith seeking understanding."

After this overview, the second chapter takes us to the Christian roots of humanism in patristic theology. Chapter three interprets medieval and Renaissance cultures as motivated principally by the same Christian humanistic impulse. The Christian roots of humanism share with classical thought the basic presupposition of an intelligible world of rational order in which human consciousness participates. The gradual breakdown of this synthesis between mind and reality explains the subsequent narrative of humanism. The chapter traces the impact of Christian humanism through Giambattista Vico to Wilhelm Dilthey and finally to Hans-Georg Gadamer, whose humanistic, hermeneutic philosophy is indebted to incarnational humanism, especially in his attempt to preserve a participatory ontology through the mediation of truth in the "mid-world" of language.

The fourth and fifth chapters narrate the complete collapse of the onto-theological synthesis that had made possible a Christian participatory ontology. The fifth chapter focuses on the ongoing effects of this loss. Postmodern criticism of instrumental reason has prepared the way for uniting faith and reason once more, but this positive aspect of postmodernity is overshadowed by the inability of postmodern philosophy to recover the synthesis of faith and reason earlier ages possessed. Following uncritically the path laid down by Friedrich Nietzsche, many postmodern thinkers lump together and dismiss Platonic metaphysics and orthodox Christianity as arbitrary impositions of a universal rational order on an irreducibly complex world. Should this world possess any transcendent meaning at all, such meaning cannot be articulated but must remain wholly transcendent (or "other") to escape objectification by oppressive ideologies. When continental philosophy returns within this postmodern intellectual climate to religious resources for the articulation of humanistic themes such as religion, ethics, hospitality and friendship, the result is predictable: God becomes reduced to the human imagination either by claiming dogmatically that nothing substantive may be known about him, or by restricting how God may appear within certain philosophical frameworks.

This God of continental philosophy is highly congenial to a currently popular trend hostile to religious dogma. When the public rejects—usually in the name of peace and tolerance—distinct religious doctrines as dogmatism or fundamentalism, it unconsciously employs two basic intellectual arguments. The first concerns the equality of all religions, and the second, the incomprehensibility of God. The former sees all faiths as equally adequate expressions of the divine because, when abstracted from particular rituals and doctrines, all religions are believed to teach the same ethical values. The latter, the incomprehensibility of God, only strengthens this ethical equality by asserting that religious particularities are all similarly inadequate interpretations of the ineffable divine.

As far as necessary, this chapter will deal in broad and clear fashion with the origins of this thought in German and French Philosophy (Nietzsche, Lyotard, Foucault, Heidegger, Levinas, Derrida) and Vattimo. We will then turn to Hans-Georg Gadamer's hermeneutic philosophy, because while he shares the former thinkers' criticism of scientific objectivism, he provides a less radical humanistic alternative. On account of his theological sensibilities, Gadamer comes much closer to incarnational humanism than do the Derridean strands of continental thought. Influenced by Levinas, Derrida and Gadamer, continental philosophy has for many years now argued for the return of religion to philosophy. John Caputo and Richard Kearney are two of the most vocal proponents of this trend, and we will compare and contrast their two different philosophical approaches to God and culture with incarnational humanism. Richard Kearney's approach will emerge as the more sacramental and hermeneutic way of talking about God. Ultimately, however, the incarnational theology of Dietrich Bonhoeffer provides a much fuller, but still humble, hermeneutic epistemology that enables an interpretive view of the Christian faith without denying God's concrete self-revelation in Jesus the Messiah.

Consequently, the theology of Dietrich Bonhoeffer sets much of the tone for the sixth and final chapter, which provides the basic contours of incarnational humanism by taking seriously the idea of God's presence in the believer, the church and the world. The chapter is essentially a call back to a sacramental, participatory concept of Christian faith and life that posits, with Bonhoeffer, a unified world without a clear division between the sacred and the profane. Rightly understood, the Eucharist, as well as sacraments in general, plays a central role in uniting secular and sacred into the one realm of "Christ-Reality." The key to this unified view of reality is the incarnation. Just as in Christ the transcendent inhabits the immanent without collapsing their differences, so too the sacred is found in the profane without reducing one to the other. The important issue is how Christians can imagine this unified reality, and indeed a unified humanity, without erasing the important differences between church and world. The central insight of Christian humanism so understood is that reality is in effect structured according to the divine self-revelation in Christ as reconciling love. This Christ event is centrally memorialized and *enacted by participation* in the Eucharist. At the very heart of worship, church and world are linked by the reality of the unified, redeemed and glorified humanity of the God-man. On this view, the Christian self is no longer split between a life of public politics and private faith; rather both spheres are unified in their service of humanity, and the Christian life becomes essentially a hermeneutical endeavor of living out the new humanity inaugurated by Christ.

To argue with Bonhoeffer for a this-worldly Christianity in no way denies that the Christian's true home is not the present world but a new creation. One sometimes gets the impression that in their eagerness to join critics of Christianity in denouncing otherworldly tendencies, Christians forget that early Christian's social activism drew its strength from the yearning for another world. Basil the Great, for example, preached and practiced help for the poor to the extent of founding a welfare institution. In what later became known as the *Basiliad*, the poor were fed and provided with free medical services.[11] Yet Basil cites as his motivation, not the creation of heaven on earth, but rather Christ's pattern of becoming poor for our sake and the beautifying of the soul, indeed of the church, for meeting her bridegroom.[12] For Basil, social welfare is a must not because of this world but because of the next.[13] I believe we have much to learn

---

[11]C. Paul Schroeder, introduction to Basil the Great, *On Social Justice* 15-39 (Crestwood, N.Y.: St. Vladimir's Seminary Press, 2009), p. 33.

[12]Basil the Great, *On Social Justice*, p. 87.

[13]"Consider carefully," writes Basil, "I ask you, both the present and the future; do not betray the latter from a shameful motive of profit. The body, your outward manifestation in this life, will forsake you in the end." This "body that has disintegrated in the grave," will, however, "arise and will be reunited with the very same soul from which it was separated by death," and the soul will share in "heavenly glory," and the blessed life, if, and only if, it laid up treasures in heaven by helping the poor (ibid., p. 88).

from the strongly eschatological vision of earlier Christians, who heavily invested in this world because they were captivated by a vision of what creation and human nature will become.

Finally, a word about the intended audience of this book and a word of thanks to all who had a hand in its production. *Incarnational Humanism* is conceived as a companion volume to the earlier book *Humanism and Religion* (Oxford University Press, 2012). Since both works are motivated by the same cultural context, the first and second chapters necessarily repeat already familiar content. Unlike the first volume, which was more philosophical and sought to include a secular audience, this book is more theological in nature, aims predominantly at an evangelical audience and addresses mainly Christian concerns. The section on the incarnational theology of Gianni Vattimo has been partially published before as "Weak Thought or Weak Theology? A Theological Critique of Gianni Vattimo's Incarnational Ontology," in the *Journal of the British Society of Phenomenology* 40, no. 3 (2009): 312-29. I am very grateful that Gary Deddo and InterVarsity Press were intrigued enough by the idea of incarnational humanism to publish this book. As always, many helping hands have contributed to the completion of this work. My thanks to Jillian Snider and Micah Snider for preliminary editing and to Matthew Levering, Hans Boersma and Stephen Dunning for making this a better book by working carefully through the manuscript at various stages. My thanks also goes to my research assistants Nicole Brandsma and Eva Braunstein, for copyediting work and indexing.

1

WITHOUT ROOTS

THE CURRENT MALAISE OF WESTERN CULTURE

◆

Before we begin to explore what incarnational humanism is and how it fits into the tradition of Christian thought, we need to understand why we should even bother thinking about a philosophy of culture and why such a philosophy should be labeled "humanism." In this chapter, I will offer a justification for the recovery of humanism by drawing a map of current Western culture. In referring to the West's current problems as a crisis of cultural identity and purpose, I do not seek to evoke an alarmist reaction but merely to describe what many other commentators have also noted in recent decades. Christians living in the West should clearly understand these "signs of the times" while retaining a global sense of Christianity. As many have observed, Christianity continues to be a dynamic and shaping force of culture, but not necessarily in the Western hemisphere.[1]

The most ancient of human questions about our identity and purpose lie—Who are we and what are we here for?—at the heart of many contemporary cultural conflicts. After all, how a society answers these questions, or refuses to answer them, reveals a people's cultural ethos. And Western culture as a whole seems to have lost the ability to answer these questions of identity and purpose with any confidence. This identity crisis extends from the most basic sense of who we are as human beings to the purpose of "our" Western cultural institutions, from a definition of humanity as such to the social values our schools, universi-

---

[1]See Philip Jenkins, *The Next Christendom: The Coming of Global Christianity* (Oxford: Oxford University Press, 2007). Jenkins also argues more recently that Christianity in Europe may be "less moribund than the formal statistics suggest" (*God's Continent: Christianity, Islam, and Europe's Religious Crisis* [Oxford: Oxford University Press, 2007], p. 58).

ties and courts are to embody. Unfortunately, many Christians share in
this forgetfulness, and thus fail to guard and cultivate the roots of
Western culture that are necessary for current social revitalization. Instead, Christians either withdraw from politics or pursue them in order
to implement a particular brand of right-wing conservatism in the name
of the church.

Is Western culture really as disoriented as I make it out to be? Have
we really lost a sense of human and cultural identity? Many intellectuals and cultural commentators seem to think so. They usually cite two
main reasons for this loss. The first is a lingering postmodern embar-
rassment about universal truth claims, so that talk about common
human values is automatically associated with ideology and hidden political agendas. The second is that in public discussions about ethics,
naturalist definitions of humanity are beginning to replace philosophic
or religious ones. In his book *On the Human Condition*, the French
philosopher Dominique Janicaud argues, for example, that in the absence of traditional religious definitions of our humanity and with the
increasing bio-technical advances in human engineering, Western culture is currently marked by an "unprecedented uncertainty about
human identity."[2]

This loss of human identity is accompanied by a loss of cultural identity. Terry Eagleton's voice is representative of other cultural critics, intellectuals and politicians in his assessment that political pressures force the
West "more and more to reflect on the foundations of its own civilization"
at a time when we have lost the ability to think deeply.[3] According to
Eagleton, postmodernity has rightly criticized naive and oppressive notions of universal reason, but it has also left us without any common
ground for a universal sense of human dignity or purpose. Yet world
events require that we discuss human nature in terms of universal purpose
and ask once again, in all seriousness, "What is the function of human

---

[2]Dominique Janicaud, *On the Human Condition*, Thinking in Action (New York: Routledge,
2005), p. 1. Joel B. Green argues similarly that traditional beliefs about the nature of the
human person have been challenged by scientific discoveries and have blurred the line between
human and nonhuman creatures. See Joel B. Green, *Body, Soul and Human Life: The Nature of
Humanity in the Bible*, Studies in Theological Interpretation (Grand Rapids: Baker Academic,
2008), pp. 36-37.
[3]Terry Eagleton, *After Theory*, Art of Mentoring Series (London: Allen Lane, 2003), p. 73.

beings? What are human beings for?"[4] Eagleton argues that at the very moment when we are forced to think deeply about who we are, our post-modern culture has accustomed itself to shallow thinking. The question of human nature, of course, has a long history, reaching from early Greek thought all the way to recent articulations of our biological and social natures as "dependent rational animals."[5] What emerges from the most recent discussions of human nature is the need to recognize common human dignity and universal moral measures, if the idea of human rights and human flourishing is to make any sense.[6] My point in this book is not, however, to trace the history of the concept of human nature, or to analyze important recent attempts to recover an Aristotelian account of human morality, such as those proposed by MacIntyre and also by Eagelton. My point, rather, is to show that neither Plato nor Aristotle, for all their influence on intellectual history, ultimately shaped the anthropology underlying Western culture, but rather that a specific Christian vision of human nature provided this foundation and thus significantly shaped our cultural horizon. We have to recognize that the religious roots that shaped our basic view of human nature and of Western culture derive from a particular religious tradition. Convinced that all religious traditions roughly say the same thing and are mostly mythological anyway, many no longer look deeply into our own particular religious roots. Yet we cannot answer such weighty universal questions about human dignity or cultural identity in abstract or general terms, even though we aim at universal, enduring values. It is part of our human condition that we can only access universal truths through particular traditions.

The inability to define and to defend Western cultural values is particularly evident in Europe's present struggle to accommodate demands for religious cultural identities within a secular state. Instead of reflecting on the fundamental question of whether religion is indeed essential to human identity, many European intellectuals and politicians still view religion as a problem, and continue to enforce their vision of a society

---

[4] Ibid., p. 120.
[5] Alasdair MacIntyre, *Dependent Rational Animals: Why Human Beings Need the Virtues* (Chicago: Open Court, 2001), p. 5. Contesting Cartesian accounts of rationality, MacIntyre seeks to anchor rational judgments in "pre-linguistic recognitions" based on "vulnerability and afflictions," that is, a basic condition we share with other "intelligent animals" (p. 8).
[6] Roger Trigg, *Morality Matters* (Oxford: Blackwell, 2005), p. 167.

built on secular reason. Not only rapid advancements in biogenetics but also confrontations with foreign beliefs through the increasing number of immigrants from religiously founded cultures, together with growing doubts about the philosophical assumptions behind secularism, are forcing many to rethink their easy dismissal of religion. For example, faced with increasing unease at witnessing native cultural norms questioned by immigrant practices, British prime minister David Cameron and German chancellor Andrea Merkel recently publicly rejected multiculturalism. Cameron merely reasserted a "robust liberalism," thus begging the question concerning the grounds of this political ideal. Merkel went further, however, by rooting Germany's culture in "a Christian view of humanity" and demanded that immigrants accept this basic assumption. I suggest that we can and must learn from Europe's problems because they point to a vital issue for Western culture as a whole: if culture is indeed an expression of our humanity, and if, as we hear increasingly, religious belief is fundamental to being human, then the relation of religion to culture deserves a great deal of attention.

The importance of studying the relation of religion and cultural identity with a focus on our common humanity is not, however, readily appreciated nowadays because sustained reflection on culture does not produce tangible results, nor does it show up on the pie charts worshiped by many institutional administrators and funding agencies. From a Christian perspective this obsession with practical results is itself an indication of cultural decay because it is a regression to the impersonal cosmos of paganism. Greek and Roman philosophy already sought to obtain happiness through attunement to an impersonal logos of natural law or abstract knowledge.[7] The church father Augustine opposed this mindset in the name of the Christian God because the reduction of humanity to natural

---

[7]For a good description of the differences between Greco-Roman attitudes toward wisdom and happiness in contrast with early Christianity's focus on a personal Christ-logos, see Charles Norris Cochrane, *Christianity and Classical Culture* (New York: Oxford University Press, 1957), esp. "Divine Necessity and Human History," pp. 456-516. For someone like Heraclitus, wisdom is found in discovering how the unalterable laws of nature work (p. 459). All attempts to escape this naturalism by positing a realm of ideal forms or other constructs, such as Plato and Aristotle offer, remain in the realm of an impersonal logos. Only Christianity offers a personal, universal and embodied divine Logos, thus laying the ground for history in terms of personality, that is, in terms of real individuality and freedom, thus further inaugurating "an adequate philosophic basis for humanism" (p. 480).

processes and laws betrayed the dignity and personal freedom of human beings, who were made in the image of God. A worldview that reckons only in widgets, numbers and quantities has forsaken the idea that human beings transcend processes and are made for relationality and wisdom. Civilization, in other words, consists in the ongoing effort of a culture or society to answer the question of what it means to be human. We have lost the crucial insight well articulated by the great humanitarian and theologian Albert Schweitzer: culture is civilized to the degree that it reflects and consciously answers the question of what it means to be human. Schweitzer argued that

> to be civilized, means approximately this: that in spite of the conditions of modern civilization, we remain human. Only the most careful concern for everything which belongs to true human nature can preserve us, amid the conditions of the most advanced external civilization, from going astray from civilization itself. It is only if the longing to become again truly human is kindled in the man of today, that he will be able to find his way out of the confusion in which, blinded by the conceit at his knowledge and pride in his powers, he is at present wandering.[8]

Schweitzer clearly recognized the vital connection between civilization and humanism that I want to pursue in this book. He astutely understood that a civilized society requires a common cultural ethos, a basic moral vision for human beings shared by all citizens.[9] For its vibrancy and humane quality, culture depends on the living inspiration of a high ideal of what it means to be human and on the practical implementation of this idea through its institutions.[10]

As many have argued, unearthing foundational ideals for culture entails paying serious attention to religious resources for the dignity and purpose of human life. In order to do this, however, we have to think about the nature of human reason. For understanding the nature of reason is central to our conception of human existence. We have to resist a narrow conception of human rationality that excludes religion as irrational because such a view cripples our ability to analyze correctly the current state of Western culture. As Rodney Stark has argued in his book *The Victory of*

[8]Albert Schweitzer, *Kultur und Ethik* (München: Beck, 1990), p. 334.
[9]Ibid., pp. 116-18.
[10]Ibid., p. 105.

Reason, Christianity's ability to combine faith and reason with a progressive view of human nature laid the foundations for Western science and technological progress.[11] Moreover, as we shall see shortly, building on Judaism, Christianity also allowed for the concepts of human dignity, personhood and individuality that have decisively shaped Western views of society. It is true, of course, that during the cultural period generally known as modernity, scientist rationalism, instrumental reasoning and individualism emerged as unfortunate distortions of the Judeo-Christian heritage. Yet neither the best nor the worst features of modernity are comprehensible without the transformative influence especially of Christianity on Greco-Roman culture.[12]

Without religion, the West would not be what it is, and without understanding the religious roots of Western culture and their continuing influence on Western thought, we lack the self-understanding necessary to address our current cultural crisis. And yet many perceive religion as a cultural weakness rather than a strength. Militant religious fundamentalism, and in Europe this often means open war against Western culture in the name of Islam, attracts so much media attention that we naturally think religion itself is the problem. That, however, is a grave mistake. And the mistake consists in this: the position from which we isolate religion as the single obstacle to peace and progress is itself not neutral or self-evident, but stems from a certain, increasingly contested, view of what counts as self-evident and reasonable.

Pope Benedict XVI has identified correctly the central issue in his reflections on religion and culture: the nature of reason. In his Regensburg lecture, the pope argued that our success in the much-needed interreligious and intercultural dialogue depends on our ability to expand our conception of reason:

> In the Western world it is widely held that only positivistic reason and the
> forms of philosophy based on it are universally valid. Yet the world's pro-

---

[11]Rodney Stark, *The Victory of Reason: How Christianity Led to Freedom, Capitalism, and Western Success* (New York: Random House, 2006), pp. xii-xiii.

[12]Modernity is indeed, as John Thornhill has argued, "Christianity's estranged child," and it retains important developments worth saving, such as the idea of knowledge as a shared project of intellectual inquiry accountable to peer review and rational critique (p. ix), and the idea of emancipation and human progress (pp. 62-63). See *Modernity: Christianity's Estranged Child Reconstructed* (Grand Rapids: Eerdmans, 2000).

foundly religious cultures see this exclusion of the divine from the universality of reason as an attack on their most profound convictions. A reason which is deaf to the divine and which relegates religion into the realm of subcultures is incapable of entering into the dialogue of cultures.[13]

Benedict defines for us one of the two most basic positions on the relation of religion and culture. The first believes religion to be the very heart of culture because without religion society has no identity and purpose. The second considers religion to be the death of culture because, to quote Sam Harris's popular book *The End of Faith*, "religious beliefs are simply beyond the scope of rational discourse" and "intolerance is thus intrinsic to every creed."[14] Yet why should we naively assume, with Harris, that rational discourse is the discourse of scientism?

The only way we can decide between these two opinions is by establishing what counts as reasonable in the first place. When we try to determine the nature of reason, it is important to realize that the exclusion of religion from reason is itself dogmatic, intolerant and, given our current global tensions, in many respects rather unhelpful, even dangerous. The dialogue with religious cultures, which after all make up the majority of the world's population, gets off to a poor start if we tell them that they are infantile and deluded. If we want to address our current cultural issues effectively, religion needs to be part of what counts as rationality.

The remainder of this introductory chapter will provide a brief map of our present cultural geography to explain why the retrieval of Western Christian roots is both necessary and also philosophically possible. To express this necessity and this hope, I will make three preliminary arguments about Western culture, which we will explore in greater detail throughout the rest of the book. The first argument is historical: to exclude religion from what counts as rational thought denies our Western cultural heritage, which was inspired not by secular reason but by Judeo-Christianity. What are these roots and how did we depart from them? A related question is whether we need a theological foundation for Western

[13]Benedict XVI, "Faith, Reason and the University: Memories and Reflections," September 12, 2006, Papal Archives, last accessed April 14, 2011, www.vatican.va/holy_father/benedict_xvi/speeches/2006/september/documents/hf_ben-xvi_spe_20060912_university-regensburg_en.html.
[14]Sam Harris, *The End of Faith: Religion, Terror, and the Future of Reason* (New York: W. W. Norton, 2005), p. 13.

culture and its social values. Do we need religion as the moral and motivational glue that holds society together, or can democratic and humane values sustain themselves?

The second argument is philosophical and has to do with the nature of
human knowledge. If we really want to attempt cultural suicide by excluding religion in the name of secular reason, we should understand that
secularist reason is itself a kind of belief—one that is quickly losing rele-
vance and authority among contemporary intellectuals. How and why is
secular reason disintegrating?

The third argument follows from the second. The exhaustion of secularist
reasoning is accompanied by *the return of religion.* An increasing number of
intellectuals are calling for the return of religion as essential to our humanity
and to the function of society. This indication that the undisputed reign of
secular reason is over and that religious belief is becoming a legitimate part-
ner in public discourse leaves us at an impasse: if religion is essential to our
human and cultural identity, we cannot live without religion, and yet the
social cost of admitting religion with its absolute truth claims and intolerance
seems too high for many. War and terrorism in God's name make us fear
religion. The problem, however, is not religion but fundamentalism, and we
need to retrieve resources from our Christian tradition to establish a common
view of reason that centers on religion but avoids fundamentalism. This common view of reason eschews fundamentalism, paradoxically, precisely because rather than avoiding religious doctrine it focuses on it, namely on the
doctrine of the incarnation. Our discussion of these three points about reason, culture and faith leads us to the conclusion that recovering incarnational
humanism best addresses the cultural issues I have pointed out.

THE WEST'S CULTURAL HERITAGE:
CHRISTIANITY OR ENLIGHTENMENT?

Many people who believe that religion hinders human freedom and cultural development praise Enlightenment values for emancipating people
from backward religious mores. For example, Ayaan Hirsi Ali, in her recent
book *Nomad*, credits the European Enlightenment and its culture of critical
thinking for her liberation from the oppressive male-dominated Islamic
culture of her childhood.[15] This tightly controlled and male-oriented tribal

---

[15]Ayaan Hirsi Ali, *Nomad* (Toronto: Knopf Canada, 2010), p. xviii.

Somali culture favored the collective and had little room for individual development, personality or responsibility.

Yet Enlightenment humanism, with its belief in universal reason and its confidence in the moral progress of humanity, is itself a secular offshoot of a deeper Christian anthropology. As is well known, a single "European Enlightenment" did not exist anyway; rather two fairly distinct branches did: the French, virulently anticlerical and rationalistic version embodied by the Encyclopedists (Denis Diderot, Jean le Rond d'Alembert and Voltaire, among others), and the German, less anticlerical, more theologically oriented, deistic version, represented by Christian Wolff, Gotthold Ephraim Lessing, Johann Gottfried Herder and Immanuel Kant. In Germany, the Enlightenment consisted of an intense discussion between theologians and philosophers, which only after considerable time issued in the rejection of supernatural, divine revelation in favor of a natural religion of reason.[16] In its own way, each of these two Enlightenment strands inverted the original relation of philosophy and religion: up to this point, philosophy had been an important means for unfolding the revealed truths of religion and their import for human life. Now, however, religion was reduced to sanctioning the universal moral truths reason could obtain on its own. This development demonstrates that the Enlightenment is itself a child of Christianity, "a rationalist abstraction of an unacknowledged Christian idea."[17] So-called Enlightenment values, such as social welfare and human rights, with foundational conceptions of human dignity, freedom, agency, rationality and personhood, all go back to Christian roots. By Christian roots I do not mean a general notion of cultural Christianity but specific religious doctrines. Perhaps the most important of these is the Christian doctrine of the incarnation.

The Italian politician Marcello Pera, who is deeply concerned with the loss of Europe's cultural identity and the threat of religious fanaticism, identifies the Christian doctrine of the incarnation as central to Western culture:

> It is true that almost all of the achievements that we consider most laudable are derived from Christianity or were influenced by Christianity, *by the message of*

---

[16]Sabine Roehr, *A Primer on German Enlightenment*, trans. Karl Loenhard Reinhold (Columbia: University of Missouri Press, 1995), p. 68.

[17]Louis Dupré, *Religion and the Rise of Modern Culture*, Erasmus Institute Books (Notre Dame, Ind.: University of Notre Dame Press, 2008), p. 43.

God become Man. In truth without this message, which has transformed all human beings into persons in the image of God, individuals would have no dignity. In truth our values, rights and duties of equality, tolerance, respect, solidarity and compassion are born from God's sacrifice. In truth, our attitude toward others, toward all others, whatever their condition, class, appearance or culture is shaped by the Christian revolution. In truth, even our institutions are inspired by Christianity, including the secular institutions of government that render unto Caesar that which is Caesar's.[18]

It may be more correct to say that Western culture and its institutions *were* inspired by Christianity. For our culture is very much post-Christian, a culture after Christendom. This does not mean that we live in a nonreligious culture, or that Christianity has been abolished and that Christians are a dying breed. Rather, *post–Christian* means that we live "after Christianity" in the sense that Western social, legal and educational institutions are no longer legitimized by the Christian impulses that founded them. It is important that we understand exactly why this rootlessness is problematic. It is not so because the church has lost political power in society. As the Canadian philosopher Charles Taylor points out correctly, secularization, by breaking up Christendom, has often succeeded in implementing Christian principles of human rights and freedoms against church politics.[19]

What is problematic, however, is that secularization's intrinsic tendency to close the world off from transcendence drives a wedge between the transcendent source of Christian beliefs and the secular social values generated by them. Traditional secular humanism is an example of this dynamic. In an immanentizing move that constitutes a "veritable revolution in moral consciousness," modern secular humanism rejects transcendent moral resources and relies on already established moral concepts.[20] Yet without the *living, continuing* inspiration provided above all by the biblical

---

[18]Benedict XVI and Marcello Pera, *Without Roots: Europe, Relativism, Christianity, Islam*, trans. Michael F. Moore (New York: Basic Books, 2006), p. 36.

[19]Charles Taylor, *A Catholic Modernity? Charles Taylor's Marianist Award Lecture, with Responses by William M. Shea, Rosemary Luling Haughton, George Marsden and Jean Bethke Elshtain*, ed. James L. Heft (New York: Oxford University Press, 1999), p. 26. Taylor names specifically human rights and aid organizations as fruits of this positive kind of secularization. Taylor argues that the breakdown of Christendom is not a tragedy but the very mechanism that made it possible for Christian beliefs to become part of mainstream, modern culture. According to him, "the break with Christendom was necessary for this great extension of gospel-inspired actions" (ibid.).

[20]Charles Taylor, *Sources of the Self: The Making of the Modern Identity* (Cambridge, Mass.: Harvard University Press, 1989), p. 94.

teaching that every human being is made in the image of God and thus possesses an inviolable dignity, we have lost both the ground and goal of Western society. In losing a sense of a common human nature and purpose for existence, we have lost, to borrow Charles Taylor's terms, "the horizons of significance"[21] bequeathed to us by Christianity and its cardinal doctrine of the incarnation.[22]

How did we arrive at this identity crisis? Can we no longer argue convincingly the "who and what for" in our culture? In case the label "crisis" for our situation appears a little exaggerated, I would ask the reader to consider that every meaningful aspect of our collective social activities depends on some particular understanding, some ideal even, of the human. Unless we know who we are and what we live for as human beings, how can we define the purpose of education, of justice, of politics, of science or even of business?[23] These disciplines are meant to aid human flourishing, but what does it mean to flourish? How can we define what it means to be fully human and expend energy toward constructing a culture that approximates this ideal unless we know what being human means?

One dominant factor in the forgetfulness of our religious roots was the exclusion of religion from public institutions. This exclusion was in turn based on certain philosophical assumptions about the nature of reason. Due to a number of historical and cultural developments from the sixteenth to the twentieth century, Western ideas of reason and truth were narrowed to a form of rationalism that has become known as *scientific objectivism*. How this definition of reason came about and why this reductive form of human reasoning no longer enjoys universal support takes us to the second major aspect of our analysis of culture, namely the breakdown of secularism as an ideology.

THE EXHAUSTION OF SECULARISM

It is a basic assumption of my argument that our loss of identity and purpose results from too narrow a conception of reason, of what counts

---

[21]Charles Taylor, *The Malaise of Modernity* (Concord, Ont.: House of Anansi Press, 1992), p. 39.

[22]The incarnation and the Trinity are the two central Christian doctrines from which our Western values spring, and they are interdependent. Faced with the historical fact of Jesus' claims to divinity and direct relationality with the Father, the apostles and early theologians developed trinitarian doctrine. See Brian Hebblethwaite, *The Incarnation: Collected Essays in Christology* (Cambridge, Mass.: Cambridge University Press, 1987), p. 23.

[23]John Sommerville, *The Decline of the Secular University* (Oxford: Oxford University Press, 2006), p. 23.

as rational human knowledge. When this narrow conception of reason hardens into a worldview, it becomes secular*ism*. In contrast to the term *secular*, which indicates a shared human rationality without necessary appeal to divine revelation, secular*ism* is an ideology that excludes religion a priori from rational thought. This dogmatic refusal goes back to a now outmoded model of truth within the natural sciences. The rise of science was accompanied by a fascination with the pristine clarity and geometrical purity of mathematical certainty that promised to transcend the murkiness of shifting historical circumstances and the subjective quality of religious truth. Enchanted by this promise of certain knowledge, academics and, later, popular culture identified the rational with the scientific method. It is important to realize that prior to the Protestant Reformation, the scientific revolution and the Enlightenment, reason and faith enjoyed a fairly healthy, reciprocal relation among Western intellectuals. This correlation of reason and faith derived from Christianity's transformation of Greek (Neo-Platonic and Aristotelian) philosophies. The patristic and medieval expression of Christianity through Greek philosophical categories conferred an intellectual advantage especially on the Latin West. The productive correlation of reason and faith prevented Western culture from opposing belief to rational analysis. Instead, reason was seen as a major part of faith. In fact, this combination of reason and faith enabled Western scholars, rather than those of any other culture, to introduce during the Middle Ages the theoretical framework that made systematic science possible. There is little doubt that medieval scholasticism's interest in science was primarily theoretical. Medieval discussions of science were hampered by crude empiricism and philosophical speculation unsustained by empirical evidence. Nonetheless, as we shall see in our brief examination of scholastic humanism, the medieval emphasis on rational analysis and on the intelligibility of nature laid the foundation for modern science by enabling the reign of reason in Western culture.[24]

The real question is why this synthesis of faith and reason fell apart

---

[24]Rodney Stark, for example, shows that crucial scientific Western innovations can be traced "to the unique Christian conviction that progress was a God-given obligation, [and] entailed the gift of reason" (*Victory of Reason*, p. 48). Edward Grant makes a similar point in *God and Reason in the Middle Ages* (Cambridge: Cambridge University Press, 2001), p. 349.

and gave rise to secular*ism*, that is, to the dogmatic exclusion of religious transcendence from rational thought.[25] Answering this question with certainty is difficult, but one thing seems sure: the narrowing of reason occurred within Christianity itself. Christian scholars laid the groundwork for these changes, not atheistic scientists who tried to liberate the world for science by debunking religion. What happened is that, beginning with late medieval theology, a process of "disincarnation" or "disembedding" set in. Prior to modern culture, the human self was firmly embedded in a world inhabited by both higher realities and mundane events. To put it in philosophical language, ontology and reason, nature and supernature, belonged together, and we belonged to both. This "ontological synthesis of faith and reason" began to fall apart in the sixteenth and seventeenth centuries. The human self became isolated from nature and from society; the ground was prepared for individualism and rationalism.

Many scholars agree that late medieval theology laid the groundwork for this development, though few any longer blame "nominalist theology" directly. At the very least, we know that nominalists did not attempt to do away with the church, but argued against all too convenient versions of sacramentalism that shored up arbitrary ecclesial and papal authority. We know that these theologians emphasized human freedom and cooperation with God.[26] Moreover, nominalist theologians such as William of Ockham (1285-1347) emphasized human freedom and cooperation with God to ensure both God's transcendence of creation and the dignity of nature and human nature.[27] And yet it is equally clear that medieval nominalism

---

[25]In this book *secular* and *secularity* are employed to describe the view that rational consensus and a world of common knowledge are possible without insisting on religious revelation. This position can be held by believers and nonbelievers alike. *Secularism*, by contrast, refers to the a priori, dogmatic exclusion of religion from rational thought and public discourse.

[26]William J. Courtenay, "Nominalism and Late Medieval Religion," in *The Pursuit of Holiness in Late Medieval and Renaissance Religion; Papers from the University of Michigan Conference*, ed. Charles Trinkaus and Heiko A. Oberman (Leiden: Brill, 1974), p. 51. Against naive notions of participation, they stressed, in Ockham's case, the idea of "pact or covenant—willed verbal agreements that are no less dependable and certain because they are in origin voluntary" (ibid.). This emphasis on covenant does, of course, constitute a direct link to the rise of federal and covenantal theologies in the Reformation. Clearly, as Courtenay concludes in his authoritative article on nominalism, "the fragmentation of the medieval synthesis can no longer be used as the hallmark of nominalism" (ibid., p. 57).

[27]For a detailed analysis of Ockham's philosophical theology, see Armand Maurer, *The Philosophy of Willian Ockham in the Light of its Principles* (Toronto: PIMS, 1999). Maurer shows that

did set in motion something that negatively affected the former balance of reason and faith, and with it an integrative view of human knowledge. As we shall see in chapter three, an additional factor in the narrowing of reason may have been the excessive passion of Christian medieval scholars for applying Aristotelian logic to theology.

It is hard to pinpoint the exact moment in history when truth became equated with algorithms, but since Galileo is always cited as the champion of scientific freedom against religion, let us cite him for once as a "villain" who reduces reason to mathematics. Galileo proclaims that "philosophy is written in this grand book, the universe, which stands continually open to our gaze." To understand this book, says Galileo, we have to learn its language, and this language is "the language of mathematics, and [the book's] characters are triangles, circles, and other geometric figures without which it is humanly impossible to understand a single word of it; without these, one wanders about in a dark labyrinth."[28] Galileo, who was himself a Christian and who believed his findings strengthened the Christian faith, nonetheless was a major contributor to the modern idea of an immanent universe that functions, more or less, on its own. He is one of many thinkers who ushered in the notion that real truth must be quantifiable and verifiable. According to this view, only that which can be demonstrated experimentally by repeatedly producing the same result counts as "rational." This test-tube epistemology makes short shrift of any human knowledge that does not show up under the microscope or cannot be expressed in mathematical symbols. Since religion, tradition, love and ultimate questions concerning our humanity usually do not show up in a test tube, they do not count as real knowledge. Galileo, along with Descartes, also illustrates the scientific obsession for reducing reality to measurable quantities. Later twentieth-century critics described this reductive view of reality thus: "For Galileo and already before him, Mathematics as the sphere of genuine objective knowledge (and technology under its guidance) constituted the main focus of 'modern' man's interest in a philosophical worldview and rational praxis. . . . And the entire concrete world has to reveal itself as mathematically

Ockham had every good intention to defend Christian orthodoxy, but that his emphasis on the dignity of individual things and on the contingency of creation to safeguard God eventually destroyed the participatory ontology and ontological realism of earlier theologies. See especially pp. 288-92 and 540-47.

[28]Galileo, quoted in Grant, *God and Reason*, pp. 283-84.

objectifiable."[29] It is no wonder that the human sciences have taken a back seat to the supposedly more practical rational or scientific disciplines, such as the natural sciences, economics or whatever else we count as conforming to the ideal of verifiable and calculable knowledge.

The reduction of reason to scientific objectivity, combined with an individualistic understanding of the human self as an island of autonomous consciousness and will, has drawn a sharp line between faith and reason, between science and religion, between fact and value. Religion, moral values and artistic judgments are relegated to the sphere of subjective opinion in contrast to the "real world of facts," things we can calculate and manipulate in the name of impassionate, value-free truth. Religious truth is what you merely *believe*; scientific truth is what you *know* because everyone can know it and access it in the same way.[30] From this distinction stems the division of our society into a secular public realm of administration, law and education on the one hand, and a private realm of religious practices and symbols on the other. Since questions of ultimate purpose and meaning inevitably require religious language, this reductive view of reason excludes them by definition from rational discussion.

Fortunately, the uncontested reign of this narrow secular view of reason is showing signs of decay. In keeping with the broad-brush nature of this first chapter, I will summarize briefly the encouraging insights from this criticism of scientific objectivism, insights that point to the demise or exhaustion of secular reason.

The first insight comes from hermeneutic philosophy, and concerns the nature of knowing as such. Human knowledge is never neutral, dispassionate, timeless or without perspective. Instead, it is always *interpretive*. Interpretation means that we gather the various fragments of knowledge into a more or less meaningful whole through a complex grid of intuitions,

<hr>

[29]Edmund Husserl, *Die Krisis der europäischen Wissenschaften und die transzendentale Phänomenologie: Eine Einleitung in die phänomenologische Philosophie* [The Crisis of European Science and Transcendental Philosophy: An Introduction to Phenomenological Philosophy], ed. Elisabeth Ströker (Hamburg: Meiner, 1996), pp. 39-40.

[30]This notion of access is important, for it reduces the idea of knowledge to information. When this concept enters the technological revolution of the Internet, access to information becomes confused with knowledge because the necessity of personally integrating this knowledge into a meaningful framework, which is hard work, is no longer deemed necessary. With the progressive loss of broadly based education, the mindset and tools for this kind of integration also become ever more scarce.

received ideas, social practice and conventions, likes and dislikes. Interpretation thus always requires personal integration of facts into a framework
of meaning, and this integration requires imagination and narrative. To
make meaning is to tell stories, which is why literature continues to be
central for our cultural memory and outlook. While there remain important differences between knowledge in the human and natural sciences,
the interpretive nature of knowledge is *true for both*.[31]

One fundamental, unquestioned or tacit assumption of science is, for
example, a universe rational enough to make science possible. Such basics
as measurements, computations and algebraic equations require a predetermined framework that the scientist cannot question if he or she wants
to arrive at any knowledge at all. The integration of isolated facts into a
meaningful whole *demands* our *personal* commitment to these tacit frameworks.[32] Hence we may conclude with the philosopher of science Michael
Polanyi that "two functions of the mind are jointly at work from the beginning to the end of an inquiry. One is the deliberatively active power of
the imagination; the other is a spontaneous process of integration which
we may call *intuition*."[33]

In other words, the actual process of how we come to know things itself
denies the bifurcation by secular reason of knowledge into public fact and
private value. As Polanyi observes,

> If personal participation and imagination are essentially involved in science
> as well as in the humanities, meanings created in the sciences stand in no
> more favoured relation to reality than do meanings created in the arts, in
> moral judgments and in religion . . . since the dichotomy between facts and
> values no longer seems to be a real distinction upon which to hang any
> conclusion.[34]

From this first insight into the interpretive nature of truth follows another,
namely, that all human knowing proceeds in a way we normally associate
with religious knowledge, that is, as "a faith seeking understanding."[35] All

---

[31]At least as long as meaning remains a concern for the integration of scientific results.
[32]Michael Polanyi and Harry Prosch, *Meaning* (Chicago: University of Chicago Press, 1996), p. 61.
[33]Ibid., p. 60.
[34]Ibid., p. 65.
[35]Fred Lawrence observes, "Even independently of divine revelation and grace, the human quest for meaning is shaped as 'faith seeking understanding'" ("Gadamer, the Hermeneutic

of us have some basic worldview in place, a pre-understanding of reality and a tacit self-understanding that guides our research and is enriched by it. Research in science and religion proceeds in the same way, by clarifying and modifying an existing worldview as far as possible before yielding to a different framework of meaning.

A third insight that challenges the assumptions of secularist reason has to do with the nature of authority. The postmodern critique of rationalism has helped us see that we do not arrive at conclusions independently but always rely on tradition and authority. While Western individualism is increasingly coming under attack from academics and intellectuals, our culture as a whole still operates on a thoroughly individualistic self-under-standing. We approach knowledge the way teenagers approach parental authority: "no one tells me what to think." Like teenagers, we harbor the illusion of thinking in a context-free vacuum, literally *making up* our minds. Consequently, we lump together tradition, authority and indoctri-nation, equate them with coercion and reject any intrusion on the pure slate of our autonomous minds. This attitude explains not only many first-year students' defiance toward traditional liberal arts subjects they con-sider useless, but also the ridiculous distinction we make between secular and religious orientations in education. According to this distinction, secular public schools are on a neutral fact-finding mission, whereas pri-vate religious institutions are obviously engaging in indoctrination.

Yet this illusion too is crumbling. As the literary critic Stanley Fish argues in his book *The Trouble with Principle*, "Just as you cannot have education without authoritative selection, so you can't have consciousness without authoritative selection, and one you didn't make. . . . The choice is never between indoctrination and free inquiry but between different forms of indoctrination issuing from different authorities."[36] Fish's point is that everyone thinks on the basis of some authority. That is not something we can or even should avoid; that is simply how growing in knowledge and insight works.

Revolution, and Theology," in *The Cambridge Companion to Gadamer*, ed. Robert J. Dostal, Cambridge Companions to Philosophy [Cambridge: Cambridge University Press, 2002], p. 193). In making manifest the ever mysterious nature of human self-understanding in time, Gadamer opens up philosophy to theology and challenges theology to be philosophical.

[36]Stanley Eugene Fish, *The Trouble with Principles* (Cambridge, Mass.: Harvard University Press, 2001), pp. 157-58.

Another sign of the breakdown of secularist reason is the legal system. The attempt to maintain purely secular legal language, purged of all religious connotations, breaks down every time judgments refer to "the sanctity of life" or "human dignity" because these concepts have no traction without their religious roots.[37] This linguistic difficulty illustrates the impossibility of retaining the idea of human values without religion. This "philosophical incoherence" can only stop when the legal profession recognizes its own dependence on implicit faith assumptions.[38]

The same problem has appeared in recent years in European constitutional debates. We recall, for example, the heated discussions about acknowledging the Judeo-Christian roots of Western civilization in the European constitution of 2005. In the end, the term *Judeo-Christian* was assiduously avoided, and the final version referred to European civilization's "inspiration from the cultural, religious and humanist inheritance of Europe, from which have developed the universal values of the inviolable and inalienable rights of the human person, freedom, democracy, equality and the rule of law."[39] This formulation does recognize the important connection between religion, humanism and civilization, but it suppresses the fundamental role Christianity played in forming these values.

The problem with forgetting the West's Christian roots has recently become even clearer in another constitutional debate. German citizens have long been uneasy about the abuse of their generous social welfare system by Germans themselves, but now recently especially by Muslim immigrants—some of whom, instead of integrating into German society, establish parallel societies within Germany. Populist politicians have tried

---

[37]Iain Benson notes the contradictions in the *Rodriguez v. British Columbia* case, when Chief Justice Lamer, in his dissenting judgment, "opined that the court should answer the question of the constitutionality of assisted suicide . . . 'without reference to the philosophical and theological considerations fuelling the debate on the morality of suicide or euthanasia.'" Instead, the judge evoked a "non-religious" sanctity, calling on the sense of the nonreligious as defined by Ronald Dworkin. So Benson asks correctly, "why would a justice of the court choose an important term such as 'sanctity' for key notions—that human life is 'sacred or inviolable' and that there is 'an intrinsic value of human life, and . . . the inherent dignity of every human being' and then promptly attempt to empty it of its settled content?" ("Towards a (Re)Definition of the 'Secular,'" *UBC Law Review* 3, no. 3 [2000]: 524).

[38]Ibid., p. 526.

[39]European Union, preamble to "Treaty Establishing A Constitution for Europe," p. 9, October 29, 2004, last accessed April 14, 2011, http://news.bbc.co.uk/2/shared/bsp/hi/pdfs/09_01_05_constitution.pdf.

to capitalize on this situation by calling for an end to immigration and rejecting Islam as foreign intrusion into German culture; in order to temper such radical voices and yet not alienate her voter base, the German chancellor declared in a widely publicized address that Islam is already—and legitimately—part of German culture, but that German society is constitutionally founded on a Christian view of human nature (*einem christlichen Menschenbild*), and that anyone who does not want to conform to this conception should stay out of the country. Her comment drew responses from atheistic and religious commentators in newspapers and Internet blogs that demonstrate ignorance and ambivalence about Europe's Christian roots. One German legal expert, for example, insisted in his blog that German culture is founded not on Christian anthropology but on a secular humanist one: "No Madame chancellor, I align myself with the image of humanity embraced by humanism and, as 'constitutional patriot,' I am obligated to the constitution's vision of our humanity (*Menschenbild*) and not to that of Christianity."[40] Christianity, the critic avers, has only produced the Inquisition; the Enlightenment, however, produced the free and responsible individual together with an ideal for social progress. This critic opposes Christianity and constitutional democracy to such an extent that he wishes to extract the reference to God in the German constitution from its Judeo-Christian roots and turn it into a nondescript universal cypher in order to protect religious pluralism by inviting the broadest possible interpretation of what "God" may mean.[41] This move indicates that a pluralistic view of religion is still dominant in Western intellectual circles. Even more important for our topic, these criticisms oppose humanism and religion, and thus demonstrate the general ignorance about the Christian religious roots of Western social values. Christian humanism is not the enemy but the very root of secular humanism. The German chancellor is the better cultural histo-

---

[40]Wolfgang Lieb, "Merkel: Wer das christliche Menschenbild nicht akzeptiert, ist "fehl am Platze" in Deutschland," *der Freitag*, October 18, 2010, www.freitag.de/community/blogs/margareth-gorges/merkelwer-das-christliche-menschenbild-nicht-akzeptiert (Zugang am 8.6.2011).

[41]The German constitution preamble states that the German people issued their constitution "in awareness of their responsibility toward God and their fellow human beings" (German Bundestag, preamble to the Constitution of the Federal Republic of Germany, May 23, 1949, as amended by the Unification Treaty of August 31, 1990, www.bundestag.de/dokumente/rechtsgrundlagen/grundgesetz/gg_00.html).

rian for claiming an underlying Christian anthropology for Western social values. Moreover, this debate also illustrates the problem of claiming the self-maintaining nature of such values. Bloggers and commentators seem to forget that the striking introduction of God into the German constitution after World War II stems from the shocking realization that a legal system without a transcendent tether to a loving God who founds human dignity and solidarity can lead to the legal suppression of human rights and freedoms, even to genocide in the name of the law. The German constitution, in other words, recognizes that every constitution requires a higher law that guarantees human dignity beyond any negotiation.[42]

All of these criticisms of secularist reason point to the implosion of secularism. We live not only in a post-*Christian* world but also in a post-*secular* one. As the Italian philosopher Gianni Vattimo has pointed out, grand philosophical narratives of human progress have failed to deliver, thus announcing the end of "modernity," a term usually meant to indicate an unbounded confidence in human reason. Along with this confidence have disappeared the "main philosophical theories that claimed to have done away with religion: positivist scientism, Hegelian and then Marxist historicism. Today there are no longer strong, plausible philosophical reasons to be an atheist, or at any rate, to dismiss religion."[43] The downside of postmodern philosophy is its strong dislike of transcendent claims for universal reason because they militate against the particularism championed by most postmoderns. Any claim to universal reason smacks too much of supremacist ideologies that want to pass off their predilections as universal truths, and then impress this view on everyone. Philosophically, this position derives from Nietzsche's resolute dismissal of *any* transcendence,

---

[42]The reference to human responsibility before God was suggested by the Christian Democrat Süsterhenn during the sixth session on composing Germany's new constitution in 1948. The suggestion found few critics, though there were some. One FDP member suggested this insertion evaded human responsibility and only one SPD member voiced the objection that such a reference was unfitting for a secular state. The insertion of God was prompted by the desire to found human dignity and to delimit the power of the state by rooting them in a metaphysical, transcendent natural law that was in turn anchored in God. The context of the discussion makes clear that the Judeo-Christian deity was implied. See Dieter Murswiek, "Im Bewußtsein seiner Verantwortung vor Gott und den Menschen," in *Bonner Kommentar zum Grundgesetz, Prämbel*, ed. Dolzer, Kahl, Waldhoff and Graßhof (Heidelberg: CF Müller Verlag, 2005), pp. 20-21.

[43]Gianni Vattimo, *Belief*, trans. Luca D'Isanto and David Webb (Stanford, Calif.: Stanford University Press, 1999), p. 28.

and of universal reason as the philosophical equivalent of original sin. Nietzsche argued that the will to power often results in the will to truth, that is, in the desire to impose an eternal order on the world and escape from our finite perspectives. While Nietzsche thus introduces a hermeneutic perspective, his antimetaphysical stance forces us to include him under the rubric of *secularism* because he excludes religion dogmatically as a form of Platonism.[44] Postmodern philosophers have translated Nietzsche's distrust of transcendence into the axiom that universal reason leads inevitably to oppressive ideologies. While this fear is understandable, it is hard to see how a dogmatic rejection of universal notions is any better. For as Husserl already pointed out at the beginning of the twentieth century, a desire for universal reason seems to be hardwired into human beings; thus, suppressing that notion would mean suppressing our humanity. I think we should follow Husserl's intuition that the defeat of Enlightenment rationalism in no way entails giving up on research into universal questions of meaning.[45] On the other hand, postmodernism and hermeneutic theories have greatly helped to debunk the positivistic philosophy behind modern atheism. Atheism both in substance and rhetoric depends on scientific objectivism, but the very idea of truth as neutral fact has turned out to be insufficient to explain our world because we live in a *human* world. Scientific objectivism is wrong because it cannot itself generate the values and interpretive frameworks that sustain its own scientific enterprise and that we require for a human way of being.

Living in a postsecular world means that secularism is no longer the standard for reasonable thought. If indeed it is true that Western culture continues to experience a crisis of identity and purpose, the dogmatic exclusion of sources of transcendent purpose (i.e., religion) seems unwise, to say the least. Such dogmatism is not secular thinking, if *secular* is taken at its root meaning of "this worldly." Rather, the arbitrary exclusion of religion from reasonable discourse is secular*ist* ideology, a fundamentalist rejection of all interpretations of the world, except the materialist one that excludes religion. Thankfully, on account of the developments mentioned previously, secular fundamentalists who still maintain that "nature is all there is" can no longer count on common sense to back them up. The con-

---

[44]I will focus on Nietzsche and his postmodern heirs in chapter four.
[45]Husserl, *Die Krisis*, p. 16.

tinued insistence by secular fundamentalists, such as Richard Dawkins (*The God Delusion*) or Sam Harris (*The End of Faith*), that science holds the key to a better humanity and that religions are the source of all evil in the world begins to sound ever more like a dogmatic religious conviction rather than scientific discovery.[46] It does not help the cause of secularism that this latest installment of atheism consists, as David Bentley Hart puts it, mostly "in vacuous arguments afloat on oceans of historical ignorance, made turbulent by storms of strident self-righteousness."[47]

The German philosopher Martin Heidegger once remarked that "science does not think."[48] When science begins to think, that is, when it moves beyond verification and begins to interpret the meaning of its findings, science takes recourse to philosophy and theology, too often with very little knowledge of either. When scientists such as Richard Dawkins begin to sound like fundamentalist preachers seeking to convert the masses to the belief that matter is all there is and that science is the rational messiah, the epistemological margin between them and the Taliban has narrowed considerably. Heidegger's verdict remains valid: science that seeks to reduce the human spirit and mind to material processes to announce the end of metaphysical thinking cannot actually do so without philosophy— it only ends up doing it poorly. In fact, this kind of "scientism" *is* a religion, and a deeply inhuman one at that. Perhaps the hysterical voices of these authors signal their intuitive recognition of the fading authority of scientific rationalism and the return of religion into public institutions.

Since this book is written for Christians, the main point bears repeating: perhaps the greatest enemy of religion is naturalism, the tendency to reduce human consciousness or the mind to material, biological processes. As Marilynne Robinson recently pointed out, "Whoever controls the definition of mind controls the definition of humankind itself, and culture, and history."[49] Robinson reminds us that science cannot by its nature make absolute statements, because its history testifies to the relative truth

---

[46]Sommerville, *Decline of the Secular University*, p. 26.

[47]David Bentley Hart, *Atheist Delusions: The Christian Revolution and Its Fashionable Enemies* (New Haven, Conn.: Yale University Press, 2009), p. 4.

[48]Martin Heidegger, "What Calls for Thinking," in *Basic Writings: From Being and Time (1927) to the Task of Thinking (1964)*, ed. David F. Krell (New York: Harper & Row, 1992), p. 349.

[49]Marilynne Robinson, *Absence of Mind: The Dispelling of Inwardness from the Modern Myth of the Self*, Terry Lectures (New Haven, Conn.: Yale University Press, 2010), p. 32.

of scientific paradigms. When science oversteps its own methodological boundaries and announces final, nonrevisable truths about human nature on the basis of a momentary stage in scientific discovery, science turns into "parascience."

Parascientific thinkers range from Auguste Comte, the father of positivism, to Freud and the new atheists—all of whom seem to want to explain away the transcendent human mind by dissolving it into impersonal biological processes.[50] Needless to say, everything in the human spirit that transcends matter while being implicated in it would perish with the success of this effort. Religion, humanism, education and much else would become genetically modifiable quantities. It is important to be absolutely clear on this point: such an outcome is nowhere near on the scientific horizon, even though certain groups have a vested interest in wishing it were. Hence the human self, metaphysics and religion are far from dead; they are, in fact as alive and relevant as ever.

THE RETURN OF RELIGION

The implosion of secularism, of the attempt to explain human life without religion, leads me to my final point, the return of religion. The identity crisis of the West and the exhaustion of secular reason have led a number of philosophers and politicians to call for a return to religion. The Italian philosopher Gianni Vattimo, for example, reconciles his postmodern, Heideggerian philosophy of "weak thought" with Christianity by explaining the very progression of history as the kenotic unfolding of God's incarnation in Jesus. According to Vattimo, the process of secularization is itself the outworking of God's self-emptying into history.[51] The German secular philosopher Jürgen Habermas recognizes that we need religious values for social ethics, although he still insists on their translation into secular categories.[52] The prominent Italian politician Marcello Pera is calling for a deconfessionalized Christian civic religion to reverse the cultural decay of Western culture into

---

[50]Ibid., p. 52.

[51]Vattimo, *Belief*, p. 36.

[52]According to Habermas, "under the conditions of postmetaphysical thinking, whoever puts forth a truth claim today must nevertheless translate experiences that have their home in religious discourse into the language of a scientific expert culture—and from this language retranslate them back into praxis" ("Transcendence," in Jürgen Habermas and Eduardo Mendieta, *Religion and Rationality: Essays on Reason, God, and Modernity* [Cambridge, Mass.: MIT Press, 2002], p. 76).

consumerism and relativism.[53] Nicolas Sarkozy, the former French president and minister of internal affairs and culture, insists on religion as an intrinsic part of the state because only religion provides citizens with the transcendence and hope essential for any healthy society.[54] Former education minister of France Luc Ferry calls for a religiously inspired "transcendental" humanism that draws on the Christian idea of the *imago Dei* to introduce a spiritual dimension into secular humanism. Ferry realizes that secular education, art and culture require a sense of the sacred to resist the dominance of instrumental reason, empty professionalism and consumerism.[55] While Ferry refuses to anchor human dignity in an actual particular trinitarian God or any revelation "prior to conscience," his "transcendental humanism" establishes ethics by grounding human worth in the inherent sacredness and transcendence of human beings: "We have to presuppose in [human beings] something of the sacred or accept their reduction to mere animality."[56]

Focusing on higher education, American historian John Sommerville argues further that ethics as a vital part of education requires the inclusion of religion. He warns that the loss of the religious dimension threatens to render secular university education inhumane. Only religious belief, he argues, keeps alive the distinction between nature and humanity, a crucial and foundational distinction for any research. Sommerville explains that "if the point of the secular university was to eliminate the religious dimension, it will eventually find that it has eliminated the human distinction as well, and be unable to make sense of any of its intellectual and professional disciplines."[57] Since religion and spirituality enjoy great public interest, Sommerville concludes that universities will completely lose touch with society unless they can adopt "an intellectual framework that is religiously suggestive."[58] In fact, nowhere is the exhaustion of secularism more evident than in the inability of our universities to articulate education as character formation. Indeed, the very notion of education as character for-

---

[53]Pera's term is *non-denominational Christian religion*, defined as "a *civil religion* that can instill its values throughout the long chain" of social levels but "*without* passing through political parties, government programs and force of states" (*Without Roots*, p. 96).

[54]Nicolas Sarkozy, *La République, Les Religions, L'espérance* (Paris: Cerf, 2004), p. 25.

[55]Luc Ferry, *Man Made God: The Meaning of Life* (Chicago: University of Chicago Press, 2002), pp. 121-43.

[56]Ibid., p. 139.

[57]Sommerville, *Decline of the Secular University*, p. 38.

[58]Ibid., p. 26.

mation and attainment of wisdom that had been important in the university's Christian foundation all but disappeared. As Sommerville puts it, university education is all about making money, but the student no longer learns what is *worth* spending money on.

The so-called return of religion arises because religions offer a language of purpose beyond self-gratification that purely secular, instrumental reason lacks. The notion that religion "returns" is of course only true for a comparatively small elite of Western intellectuals who subscribed to what Charles Taylor has dubbed the "subtraction narrative" of human development. Taylor is highly critical of this account's reductive view of human development. According to this narrative, humanity becomes more mature to the degree that religion diminishes and is displaced by scientific reasoning. This subtraction narrative thus assumes a naive view of reality as something static and impersonal. On this view the naturally secular nature of reality is objectively present, waiting to be discovered, and science has simply subtracted or removed those superstitions that have hitherto prevented reality from shining through. It is a profoundly unhermeneutical narrative, and hence profoundly misguided. To those who live in this secularist subtraction story, religion "returns," the way an alcoholic addiction or immature, primitive drive comes back, and this return instinctively *feels* as though humanity is reverting to the dark, primitive and violent times we should have already outgrown. For the rest of the world, however, religion has always been and always will be an intrinsic part of being human.

It is helpful to recall that in global terms, dogmatic secularism constitutes an anomaly. We cannot dialogue with other cultures when they know we secretly think that all religious people are medieval primitives. At the same time we dare not forget why secularists denounce religion as irrational. I have tried to explain that this rejection of the religious is largely a historically developed belief in a certain kind of reason, in scientific objectivism. Yet this reductive form of reason that excludes religion continues to find adherents because since 9/11 many atheists tend to equate religion with violence. As Sam Harris argues in his diatribe *The End of Faith*, "Adopt too positive an outlook on religion, and the next thing you know is that architects and engineers will start flying planes into buildings."[59]

---

[59]Harris, *End of Faith*, p. 232.

I suggest, however, that fundamentalism, rather than religion itself, is the problem. Fundamentalism in all its forms, whether secular or religious, worships an absolute text and has little or no room for interpretation.[60] It makes little difference whether this text is the King James Bible, the Qur'an or the book of nature and our DNA. Fundamentalism hates complexity, is impatient with ambiguity, remains blind to the historical development of its own position and likes to create totalizing views of reality. Fundamentalism refuses to grant legitimacy to dimensions of human experience that challenge its own worldview, and this mentality is often shared by seemingly opposing camps. In this sense, Terry Eagleton is right to point out in his review of *The God Delusion* that "Richard Dawkins and Oral Roberts have the same [fundamentalist] concept of theology. It's just that Dawkins hates it while Oral Roberts and his unctuous tribe grow fat on it."[61]

Instead of rejecting religion wholesale, and thus signing up with the fundamentalist religion of secularism, I suggest that we retrieve religious resources that are not fundamentalist and are capable of sustaining the best of our Western cultural heritage. To do this we need to study religions' extant and possible contributions to culture. If secularism is itself a faith, we have in effect no "outside," neutral position from which to boil down all religions to their lowest common denominator. No one, not even the secularist, is permitted a godlike stance above the flux of history and development. Since we always argue from within a tradition, we can no longer maintain the comparative religions approach that still influences much of secular thinking about religion, even when secular thinkers invite religion back into public discourse. Religions are not, in fact, all the same, and we cannot compare them by trying to find the lowest common denominator, because determining this denominator assumes a faithless, neutral position that does not exist. As religions scholar Stephen Prothero has put it forcefully in his recent book on world religions, "God is *not* One." Prothero argues that the traditional comparative religions approach, conducted in the name of political liberalism's cardinal virtue of tolerance,

---

[60]Ulrich Körtner, *Wiederkehr der Religion? Das Christentum neuer Spiritualität und Gottvergessenheit* (Gütersloher: Gütersloher Verlag, 2006), p. 151.
[61]Terry Eagleton, "Lunging, Flailing, Mispunching," review of *The God Delusion* by Richard Dawkins, *London Review of Books* 8, no. 20 (2006): 32.

sought to emphasize the fundamental convergence of religions on ethical content and thus to stress the basic sameness of religions. Prothero rejects this assumption as "dangerous, disrespectful, and untrue."[62] Even if this view may be prompted by the laudable desire for religious tolerance, trivializing religious differences and asserting the sameness of religion hardly makes the world safer by allowing ignorance to reign. While world religions do converge on many ethical matters, they "diverge sharply on doctrine, ritual, mythology, experience, and law," and these differences matter greatly to ordinary followers of religion.[63]

Thus instead of excluding religious particularity and conservative religious voices in the name of a tolerance that belittles religion, we must allow each religion to present precisely its positive convictions and then see what kind of human ideal and what kind of faith emerges from it. What do Christianity, Islam, Buddhism and other religions have to say about church-state relations? What concrete notions of personhood, of human dignity and of freedom emerge from these beliefs that can guide our social and environmental policies? To compare even the three monotheistic religions on these questions would go far beyond our limited focus in this book on Christianity. We will limit ourselves to presenting the Christian religion as offering a hermeneutical view of reason that fully accounts for historical development and the cultural forces shaping our identity, while providing a transcendent goal toward which we strive in science, politics and education. Moreover, we will also see that Christianity, precisely because its claim to universality is founded on Christ, can imagine a society that, guided by a Christian humanist ethos, nevertheless shows genuine tolerance for a plurality of faiths.

For Christians concerned with the renewal of Western culture, the resurgent interest in religions as intrinsic to human identity could be very promising. When sociologists like José Casanova criticizes secular Europe for its "fear of religion,"[64] one can hope for a more accurate assessment of Western culture. Casanova castigates Europe's inability to wrestle openly and honestly with its Christian heritage. It is true, he argues, that from a

---

[62]Stephen R. Prothero, *God Is Not One: The Eight Rival Religions That Run the World—and Why Their Differences Matter* (New York: HarperOne, 2010), p. 3.
[63]Ibid., p. 4.
[64]José Casanova, *Europas Angst vor der Religion*, ed. Rolf Schieder, Berliner Reden zur Religionspolitik (Berlin: Berlin University Press, 2009), p. 7.

merely constitutional perspective, European societies do not necessarily require a religious reference point, but constitutional rights do not hold a society together; rather, a common identity does.[65] Casanova concludes that Europe's "inability to acknowledge Christianity openly as one of its constitutive components of [its] cultural and political identity" stands in the way of finally clearing up many common misunderstandings concerning the legitimate public role of religion in a democratic state.[66]

Casanova is one of the few hopeful secular voices that seek to overcome secularist objections to the positive role of religion for society. Yet all too often the newfound interest in religion by secular thinkers expresses itself in merely instrumental terms. They do not really care whether religions express a true reality but rather whether their social values will keep citizens motivated, hopeful and productive. This line of thought is as old as human reflection, and usually entails the partitioning of society into the masses who require religion to maintain law and order from inner conviction and the ruling elite who utilize and control this public religion for the benefit of the state. This position is untenable, not least because those claiming to see through the illusion of religion are themselves beholden to universal assumptions about human existence that derive from something not unlike religious faith. Bruce Sheiman, in his recent and refreshingly honest book *An Atheist Defends Religion*, comes to the same conclusion: "atheism requires faith as much as theism."[67]

Another problem with using religion as an instrument for cultural renewal is the immense role of inner motivation. The Christian faith, particularly with its strong dimension of service to others, cannot be based merely on intellectual convictions. Nietzsche knew this well. Religious faith is more than mental adherence to great ideas; it requires living reality. A few years ago, when Marcello Pera suggested to then Cardinal Ratzinger that the solution to Italy's cultural identity crisis lay in a "deconfessionalized, Christian civil religion," Ratzinger wisely re-

---

[65]Ibid., p. 28.

[66]Ibid., p. 29.

[67]Bruce Sheiman, *An Atheist Defends Religion: Why Humanity Is Better Off with Religion Than Without It* (New York: Alpha Books, 2009), p. 184. Sheiman, in fact, seeks to overcome the reason-faith dichotomy and argues for the coexistence of science and religion, of reason and faith. Reason and faith are for him "two dimensions of one truth; they are *interdependent:* both are necessary components of science *and* religion" (ibid., p. 187).

minded him that Christian ideals cannot be "deconfessionalized" because the confession of a suffering God who gave his life for humanity enables the believer to incarnate this belief in concrete social situations and so shape society and renew culture. And Christian believers are so enabled because they participate in the reality of this God. As Benedict puts it, "something living cannot be born except from another living thing."[68] In other words, societies need a communal moral bond, a moral will, that politics can neither create nor sustain. Such a social ethos begins with the personal decisions and motivations of each individual consciousness, with the internal belief in a transcendent moral reality. It is the church's task and challenge to proclaim and teach this reality, but even the church cannot produce it.[69] Benedict realizes the obvious danger in turning religion into a cultural tool: it becomes too easily identified with nationalism and politics.

Politicians like Marcello Pera turn to religion because they realize that cultural renewal requires universals: it requires big picture, worldview thinking about our cultural ethos; and secular reason, by excluding religion from what counts as rational, cannot itself generate ethics, cannot provide ultimate values about who we are and what we live for. When secular reason claims to possess such values, it merely reveals its own religious convictions, usually derived from Christian roots. Pera is right, of course, to point out that references to human dignity and rights in Western democratic constitutions depend on Christian thought.[70] We do need to recognize, however, that *only religious belief can restore to Western culture the élan and thirst for human improvement from which modernity was born.*[71] And paradoxically this will only happen when religion is not viewed merely as a helpful instrument for social politics, but when a genuinely religious spirit informs a culture's outlook. As the great Albert Schweitzer argued already in 1923, the

---

[68]Benedict XVI and Pera, *Without Roots*, p. 120.

[69]Benedict XVI, *Licht Der Welt: Der Papst, die Kirche und die Zeichen der Zeit: Ein Gespräch mit Peter Seewald,* 2nd ed. (Freiburg im Breisgau: Herder, 2010), p. 64.

[70]Marcello Pera, *Warum Wir Uns Christen Nennen Müssen: Plädoyer Eines Liberalen* [Why We Have to Call Ourselves Christians: A Liberal's Plea] (Augsburg: St. Ulrich Verlag, 2009).

[71]Human progress, of course, is understood here not in its distorted sense rightly condemned by postmodern critics, nor in the legitimate sense of meeting human material needs, but in the eschatological, theological sense of developing divine likeness that we will examine in chapter two.

decay of Western culture can only be reversed if we succeed in renew-
ing a worldview that

> can carry with utmost power the ideals of ethics and of perfecting human-
> ity. Should we succeed in re-establishing a worldview in which ethical af-
> firmation of world and life is once again offered in a convincing way, then
> we will master the present decline of Western culture. Otherwise we are
> condemned to witness the failure of every attempt to stop this degeneration
> of culture. Only when everyone realizes the truth that the renewal of cul-
> ture must come from the renewal of such a worldview, only when a new
> longing for worldview takes hold, do we step onto the right path.[72]

Schweitzer believed that renewal depends on a culture's deep, internalized and living belief in universal ethical values. I have added to
Schweitzer's correct demand for worldview thinking another element:
we have to remain open to religious resources for shaping the meaning
and purpose of human existence, since secularism is philosophically
untenable, and its implicit scientistic or "parascientific" understanding
of human nature cannot generate the humane values a society requires.
Not any religion will do, however, for modern Western society—
accustomed as it is to individual freedom, human rights and secular,
democratic government—cannot brook a religion that is either irrational or theocratic; this is not to say that religion has to conform to contemporary cultural mores, but rather that one should take the philosophical critique of rationalism seriously, and thus insist on the
interpretive nature of truth and its mediation through the human material realities of language, history, social relations and institutions. In
a way, that is nothing less than advocating a sacramental and participatory view of truth.

Where do we find such a worldview? What cultural ethos can we
find in our history that combines reason, faith and science into the
kind of humanism Schweitzer argues for? In this book, I suggest that
incarnational humanism can provide just such a cultural ethos. This
humanism, which began with the patristic theology of the first four
centuries, united reason and faith into a cultural ethos that regarded
education as the restoration of a fallen human nature to the image of

---

[72]Schweitzer, *Kultur und Ethik*, p. 105.

God. I realize, of course, that there are many cultural objections to recovering a Christian humanism, not least from those Christians who have unfortunately followed secular humanists in equating humanism with atheism. This equation has itself historical reasons we will explain after we have first established that Christianity itself is the first proper humanism.

2

THE BEGINNINGS OF INCARNATIONAL HUMANISM

◆

To readers familiar with standard accounts of humanism, the suggestion that Christianity is the deepest root of humanism will seem anachronistic because the term is not employed until the nineteenth century. Yet such technicalities should not prevent the application of this term to the Christian ethos we are concerned with in this book. Much depends, of course, on one's interpretive approach to the term, *humanism,* which may be defined in two ways. One possible approach is a word-based, or "terminal" definition, which limits itself to the first appearance of the label "humanism" in intellectual history. Chronologically, Cicero, the most formative and prominent among Roman philosophers who thought about education, first coined the term *studia humanitatis,* which was later taken up by Renaissance humanists who became known as "umanisti," an Italian term for teachers.[1] Not until the early nineteenth century, however, and probably first in Germany, do we encounter the noun *humanism,* as describing an educational ethos that extols the aesthetic views of the ancient Greco-Roman world and the values they convey.[2] Given this approach, the notion of recovering the true meaning of humanism from Christian roots would be anachronistic foolishness, since the term *humanism,* together with its view of humanity and a certain educational vision, is limited to nineteenth-century Germany. In this limited "terminal" sense, humanism would then

---

[1]August Buck, *Humanismus: seine europäische Entwicklung in Dokumenten und Darstellungen,* (Freiburg: Karl Alber, 1987), p. 26. See also Charles Garfield Nauert, *Humanism and the Culture of Renaissance Europe,* 2nd ed., New Approaches to European History (New York: Cambridge University Press, 2006), p. 12.

[2]Nicholas Mann, "The Origins of Humanism," in *The Cambridge Companion to Renaissance Humanism,* ed. Jill Kraye, Cambridge Companions to Literature (Cambridge: Cambridge University Press, 1996), pp. 1-2.

only refer to the anthropological and theological-philosophical values that were embodied in the German education system by Alexander Niethammer (A.D. 1766-1848) and in the German Enlightenment university founded by Wilhelm von Humboldt (A.D. 1767-1835).

A second, more fruitful approach, however, is to go beyond a narrow terminal definition to one that focuses on substance and content. Obviously, even the ideals of nineteenth-century humanism have a long historical lineage, a lineage whose roots go back to early Christian theology. In this chapter we will explore the ancient roots of Christian humanism, and I will argue that the Christian doctrines of the incarnation and the Trinity radically transformed the antecedent Greco-Roman anthropologies into notions of dignity, personhood, community, freedom and progress that have profoundly shaped Western culture. The Greek concept of education as character formation (*paideia*), for example, is transformed into the Christian ideal of deification, of shaping the image of God inherent in every human being into the likeness of the incarnate God-man. The incarnation has thus greatly exalted and ennobled humanity. Finally, an implicit function of this chapter is to contradict the persistent rumor German scholar Adolf von Harnack started in theological circles that the Greek mindset of early Christian thought distorted the teaching of Jesus, who came merely to kindle "individual religious life."[3] The contrary is the case: Jesus came to found a new humanity and to redeem the cosmos. Moreover, his own claims to direct relationality with the Father, which the apostles and early Christians rightly interpreted as claims to divinity, were the fulfillment of God's promise in the Old Testament to be with his people forever. In short, early Christian thought was thoroughly biblical. That God has become human, has himself taken responsibility for the evil of humanity by defeating sin and death on the cross and risen to inaugurate a new life, was a message that even while being worked out within Greco-Roman culture, transformed its thought patterns "so profoundly that in the end something quite new came into being."[4]

---

[3]Adolf von Harnack, *What Is Christianity?* trans. Thomas Bailey Saunders (Minneapolis: Fortress Press, 1986), p. 11.
[4]Robert Louis Wilken, *The Spirit of Early Christian Thought: Seeking the Face of God* (New Haven, Conn.: Yale University Press, 2003), p. xvii.

GRECO-ROMAN ANTECEDENTS

Greek philosophy originated the idea of education as the realization of one's humanity. The Greeks were "the first to recognize that education means deliberately moulding human character in accordance with an ideal," and thus developed the notion of a "cultured" individual.[5] Regarding the term *individual*, we have to be careful not to read the modern self back into antiquity. The Greek humanistic self is not the autonomous self of secular humanism: "The intellectual principle of the Greeks is not individualism but 'humanism,' to use the word in its original and classical sense. . . . [Humanism] meant the process of educating man into his true form, the real and genuine human nature."[6]

Greek humanism already went beyond pagan animistic or polytheistic cosmologies while retaining a basic theological orientation.[7] While anthropocentric streams of Greek humanism existed,[8] more theologically oriented views of humanity and education eventually dominated Greek intellectual culture. Against both the relativistic excesses of rationalization in the Skeptic philosophies[9] and the pantheistic materialism of Stoic philosophy, a revival of Platonism in the second century (middle Platonism) and third century (Neo-Platonism) rekindled the flame of Greek humanism by intensifying already existing religious tendencies in Plato.[10] For Plato, true education (*paideia*) is conversion from the world of sensual self-deception to the world of true being,[11] the absolute good beyond

---

[5]Werner Wilhelm Jaeger, *Paideia: The Ideals of Greek Culture*, vol. 1, *Archaic Greece: The Mind of Athens*, 2nd ed., trans. Gilbert Highet (New York: Oxford University Press, 1945), p. xxii. The German word *Bildung* recaptures the Greek ideal of character formation according to an ideal image.

[6]Ibid., 1:xxiii.

[7]A. A. Long, "The Scope of Greek Philosophy," in *The Cambridge Companion to Early Greek Philosophy*, ed. A. A. Long, Cambridge Companions to Philosophy (Cambridge: Cambridge University Press, 1999), p. 9.

[8]For example, the sophist Protagoras (c. 490-420 B.C.) and skeptical philosophers generally believed "man" to be the measure of all things.

[9]According to A. A. Long, "the great cosmological issue that will in due course unite Platonists, Aristotelians, and Stoics against the atomistic Epicureans" was "the issue of whether the world is governed by a purposive mind or by purely mechanistic forces" ("Scope of Greek Philosophy," p. 18).

[10]Werner Wilhelm Jaeger, *Early Christianity and Greek Paideia* (Cambridge, Mass.: Belknap Press, 1985), pp. 44-45.

[11]Werner Wilhelm Jaeger, *Humanism and Theology*, Thomas Aquinas Lecture (Milwaukee: Marquette University Press, 1943), p. 53.

being—something Plato calls god.[12] Indeed in the *Republic* and *Theaetetus*, he describes virtue as assimilation to god, a notion later taken up and adapted to their own religion by early Christian theologians.[13]

This basically religious tenor also marked the humanisms of Roman ethical philosophers such as Cicero (106-43 B.C.) and Seneca (4 B.C.-A.D. 65). They assimilated Greek philosophy into an educational program whose ultimate goal was character formation and the welfare of the Roman state. Cicero, the most formative and prominent among them, first coined the term *studia humanitatis* for this educational ideal, which "already contains *in nuce* the program of Renaissance humanism."[14] Roman humanism adopted the Greek emphasis on reason and language (*Logos; Ratio*), which set humans apart from animals. Reason and language allow humans to contemplate and share their lives, thus transcending a merely instinctual life.[15] As Cicero put it, "And it is no mean manifestation of Nature and Reason that man is the only animal that has a feeling for order, for propriety, for moderation in word and deed."[16] Educating the human spirit, not least through literature and poetry, even allows for a new equality that transcends class distinctions toward a "spiritual aristocracy" of the educated humanists.[17] The term *humanitas* thus gains the central double value it was to keep throughout its history: humanistic education is "social virtue as much as an individualistic ideal of education."[18] Cicero learned from the Greek Stoics that "men are born for the sake of men, that they may be able mutually to help one another."[19] For this reason all science and learning should be in service to humanity.[20] For Cicero, the goal of humanistic

---

[12]In Plato *Laws* 4.716c, the character called "Athenian" expresses what is generally true for Plato's entire work as contravening Protagoras's anthropocentric approach: "Now it is God who is, for you and me, of a truth the 'measure of all things,' much more truly than, as they say, 'man.'"

[13]Plato *Theaetetus* 176b. Socrates argues that since evil has no place in the divine world, "we should make all speed to flee from this world to the other, and that means becoming like the divine so far as we can" (ibid.). A good man is one "who is willing and eager to be righteous, and by practice of virtue to be likened unto God so far as that is possible for man" (*The Republic of Plato* 10.613b).

[14]Buck, *Humanismus,* p. 26; *Nauert, Humanism and the Culture of Renaissance Europe,* p. 12.

[15]Buck, *Humanismus,* p. 20.

[16]Cicero, *De Officiis* 1.4.11-14.

[17]Buck, *Humanismus,* p. 18.

[18]Ibid.

[19]Cicero, *De Officiis* 1.7.22.

[20]Ibid., 1.44.56-57.

education is to become truly human through soul formation.[21]

Cicero's opinion that studies of language, art, literature and philosophy are subservient to soul formation and wisdom was upheld by Seneca, another important Stoic philosopher whose thinking was deemed congenial by later Christian humanists.[22] Seneca argued that the goal of moral education is to see the natural unity of humanity and to encourage a morally pure life through which the divinity of the human spirit becomes evident.[23] Marcus Aurelius, Roman emperor and Stoic philosopher (A.D. 121-180), summarized how the monistic pantheism of Stoic philosophy provided a sense of common humanity and common reason: "For there is one Universe out of all, one God through all, one substance and one law, one common Reason of all intelligent creatures and one truth, if indeed the perfection of creatures of the same family and partaking of the same Reason is one."[24] Stoicism's spiritual materialism provided the powerful image of a unifying, all-pervasive reason (logos) that was possibly the most lasting Stoic influence on Christian thought. The apostle Paul established the earliest known Christian use of Stoic philosophy, which he employs in his debate with Athenian philosophers to demonstrate the illusion of idolatry.[25] Early theologians, such as Justin Martyr (c. A.D. 100-165), expanded this critical engagement of philosophy by following Philo of Alexandria's (20 B.C.-A.D. 50) adaptation of the Stoic logos as God's creative, sustaining power of the universe. Drawing on Jewish sources and John's Gospel, Christian theologians replaced the Stoics' materialist principle with the personal eternal Word who became incarnate in Jesus the Messiah.[26] Stoic

---

[21]Buck, *Humanismus*, p. 24; For Cicero, "the cultivation of the soul is the nourishment of 'humanitas': cultus animi humanitatis cibus."

[22]Ibid., p. 28.

[23]Ibid., p. 31.

[24]Marcus Aurelius, *Meditations*, trans. A. S. L. Farquharson (New York: Knof, 1992), p. 45.

[25]Acts 17. Early commentators, such as Clement of Alexandria, still immediately pick up the Stoic reference in Paul. See, for example, Clement of Alexandria, *Stromata, Or Miscellanies* 1.11, in *The Ante-Nicene Fathers*, vol. 2, *Hermas, Tatian, Athenagoras, Theophilus, Clement of Alexandria*, ed. Alexander Roberts and James Donaldson, rev. by A. Cleveland Coxe (Peabody, Mass.: Hendrickson, 2004), p. 311. For a philosopher's analysis of Stoicism in Paul, see Troels Engberg-Pedersen, "Stoicism in the Apostle Paul," in *Stoicism: Traditions and Transformation*, ed. Steven K. Strange and Jack Zupko (Cambridge: Cambridge University Press, 2004). The author, however, does not take sufficiently into account the decisive impact of Christology on Paul's theology, which sets it apart from Philo of Alexandria's thought (ibid., pp. 73-75).

[26]Justin Martyr, *First Apology*, in *The Ante-Nicene Fathers*, vol. 1, *The Apostolic Fathers, Justin Martyr, Irenaeus*, ed. Alexander Roberts and James Donaldson, rev. by A. Cleveland Coxe

philosophy continued to exercise a subtle but constant influence on Christian philosophy from the early church to the Middle Ages and well into the Reformation.[27] John Calvin, no less than Thomas Aquinas, regards Seneca as an important authority on ethics.[28]

The critical engagement of Stoic philosophy by Christians is paradigmatic for how religious and philosophical influences shaped Western culture and its humanistic ideal. Greco-Roman philosophical anthropology was not naively adopted by Christian theologians, but was radically transformed through the biblical story of humanity's Fall and redemption into a finite cosmos, a divine Creator and a trinitarian model of human sociality and selfhood.[29] Moreover, while Roman philosophy was an important influence, it was mostly the Greek ideal of education as formation of true humanity (*paideia*) that shaped Western ideals of civilization. Christian thinkers recognized in Greek culture's aspiration to ennoble humanity, a goal similar to that promised in the Christian gospel. At the time Christian theologians encountered Greek philosophy, that philosophy had completed a circular movement from its pre-Socratic transcendent beginnings

---

(Peabody, Mass.: Hendrickson, 2004), p. 178. For a discussion of this adaptation process, see R. A. Markus, "Faith and Philosophy," in A. H. Armstrong and R. A. Markus, *Christian Faith and Greek Philosophy* (London: Darton, Longman & Todd, 1960), pp. 135-58.

[27]Gérard Verbeke notes the constant influence of Stoic philosophy from the early church to medieval times. Seneca and Cicero were the most often cited thinkers, and the pantheistic materialism that provided a cosmic bond of all living things, but that also clashed with a Judeo-Christian concept of creation, provided endless fuel for discussions of reason, freedom and immortality (Gérard Verbeke, *Presence of Stoicism in Medieval Thought* [Washington, D.C.: Catholic University of America Press, 1983], pp. 23ff., 43ff.).

[28]In his *Summa Theologiae* alone, Aquinas cites Seneca over thirty times. Calvin refers to Seneca about twenty times; see John Calvin, *Institutes of the Christian Religion*, vol. 1, ed. John T. McNeill, trans. Ford Lewis Battles (Philadelphia: Westminster Press, 1960), esp. 1.11.2 and 3.18.4. Even in humanist scholars who intentionally revived Stoicism, as in the case of Justus Lipsius (1547-1606), the result was a Christian version that included Christian Neo-Platonic elements; as John M. Cooper has shown, this iteration nonetheless strengthened human autonomy and increased independence from the ecclesial, ritual elements of religion (John M. Cooper, "Justus Lipsius and the Revival of Stoicism in Late Sixteenth-Century Europe," in *New Essays on the History of Autonomy: A Collection Honoring J. B. Schneewind*, ed. Natalie Brender and Larry Krasnoff [Cambridge: Cambridge University Press, 2004], pp. 13, 24).

[29]For a good start on discussing these differences and also Christian borrowings from Greek philosophy, see A. H. Armstrong and R. A. Markus, *Christian Faith and Greek Philosophy* (London: Darton, Longman & Todd, 1960). Theologian and early church historian Jean Daniélou also argues for the critical use of Stoic philosophy by the early apologists, and for their twofold use of pagan philosophy as "defense and conquest," that is, as showing the rationality of the Christian faith and its universal claim on humanity (Jean Daniélou, *A History of Early Christian Doctrine Before the Council of Nicaea*, vol. 2, *Gospel Message and Hellenistic Culture*, ed. and trans. John Austin Baker [London: Darton, Longman & Todd, 1973], pp. 11, 16).

through a materialist and anthropocentric phase, back to an emphasis on transcendence, mostly on account of Plato's philosophy and, in the Latin West, through Neo-Platonic thought.[30] Thus, Christian humanism begins as the development of Christian anthropology in Neo-Platonic categories, which were radically transformed in this process.[31] One example of this process is Augustine's rejection of the Plotinian graduated triad of the One (One, Intellect and Soul) and of the mind's unaided ascent to God in favor of the Trinity's equality and the mind's dependence on divine grace.[32] The notion of participation in the forms or ideas was adopted by Christian thinkers and reshaped in Christian terms by placing the forms in the mind of God.[33] In short, the Christian apologists from the first to the fourth centuries, well educated in this Hellenistic intellectual world, recognized its possibilities for expressing the claim of the Christian gospel to be the foundation for true humanity.[34]

In light of the mutual openness of Greek and Christian writers to "a common core of ideas," any opposition between supposedly self-enclosed "biblical" and "Hellenistic" worldviews is historically false and philosophically naive.[35] Neither the historical situation nor the fathers' conscious transformation of Greek concepts warrants references to the "underlying

---

[30]Jaeger, *Humanism and Theology*, p. 53. Jaeger controverts the view that Greek culture was "self-sufficient and radically anthropocentric," by suggesting a century-old development in Greek thought toward religious sensibilities that explains the apostle Paul's encounter with long-standing philosophical interest in the divine (ibid., pp. 38-39).

[31]For example, Plotinus's amalgamation of Aristotelian and Platonic elements in his concept of emanation constituted an immediate challenge to the Christian concept of creation by weakening the biblical notion of God's complete freedom from creation. Moreover, Plotinus's attempt to reconcile Platonic transcendence with Aristotle's teleology of gradual development did at times serve to legitimate ecclesial hierarchy, and yet Platonic participation does not necessitate a graduated chain of being, nor does it have to domesticate divine transcendence as some have claimed (see, e.g., Ernst Cassirer, *The Individual and the Cosmos in Renaissance Philosophy*, trans. Mario Domandi [Chicago: University of Chicago Press, 2010], p. 18).

[32]Mary T. Clark, *"De Trinitate,"* in *The Cambridge Companion to Augustine*, ed. Eleonore Stump and Norman Kretzmann, Cambridge Companions to Philosophy (Cambridge: Cambridge University Press, 2001), p. 94.

[33]See Justin Martyr, *Hortatory Address*, in *The Ante-Nicene Fathers*, vol. 1, *The Apostolic Fathers, Justin Martyr, Irenaeus*, ed. Alexander Roberts and James Donaldson, rev. by A. Cleveland Coxe (Peabody, Mass.: Hendrickson, 2004). So congenial to early Christians was Plato's concept of forms as containing the archetypical ideals, that they believed, as did Justin, that Plato must have learned this concept from Moses (ibid., p. 285).

[34]Jaeger, *Early Christianity*, p. 60. Christians "do not deny the value of that [Greek] tradition, but they claim that their faith fulfills this paideutic mission of mankind to a higher degree than had been achieved before" (ibid.).

[35]Ibid., p. 39.

disease" of Hellenic philosophy that pollutes a pure biblical faith in patristic writing.[36] One is tempted to say that the early theologians who sought to express Christianity in the vocabulary of second-century Platonism (Neo- or Middle-Platonism) had more confidence in the transforming power of revelation than modern theologians, who fret about the Hellenization of a more original, and also earthbound, Hebraic Christianity. Scholars have long argued, for example, that the incarnation of God constitutes perhaps the gravest Hellenistic distortion. As we shall see shortly, however, the idea of a preexisting Logos is not a Hellenistic intrusion into biblical thought, but demonstrably an expression in Neo-Platonic vocabulary of Hebraic ideas and traditions, reformulated in light of the incarnation.[37] And based on the divine Logos as seed of all truth, early Christians could afford a generous stance toward culture and adapt the best insights for expressing the gospel.[38] With this confidence in the breadth and depth of divine revelation, the church fathers deliberately sought to engage and transform culture. What Clement of Alexandria (c. A.D. 150-215) begins by making Christ the true educator of humanity, Augustine (354-430) continues by defining his theological humanism as "the ideal of a complete human cul-

---

[36]Colin E. Gunton, *Act and Being: Towards a Theology of the Divine Attributes* (Grand Rapids: Eerdmans, 2003), p. 15.

[37]See, for example, R. G. Hamerton-Kelley, *Son of Man* (Cambridge: Cambridge University Press, 1973), p. 273 and the entire conclusion to this work.

[38]These concepts included, as Jean Daniélou and Frances Young have shown, the adoption of interpretive practices from rabbinic tradition, Hellenized Judaism (Philo) and classical Greek rhetoric. There is no doubt that at times this practice resulted in allegorizing excesses that tended to alter the gospel message; yet as both Daniélou and Young make clear, in the main the early theologians followed a Christological model of the interrelations of the Old and New Testaments, based on typology inherited from Judaism and on the idea of Christ as the fulfillment of divine prophecies about God's people. Patristic exegesis thus "corresponds neither to what is called literal exegesis, namely that which is concerned with the events, characters, and institutions of the Old Testament itself, nor to allegorical exegesis, which covers the many possible uses to be made of Scripture considered as a complex of symbols. It deals with the historical interrelation of any two given moments in the divine plan; and the exegetical method which establishes the theological affinities between these two moments in order to elucidate the laws of God's action is known, in accordance with patristic use, as typology" (*Gospel Message and Hellenistic Culture*, p. 198). Young ascribes the same Christological center to patristic exegetes who sought to discern "the mind of scripture," that is, the Scripture's "underlying coherence, its unitive testimony to the one true Son of God." In interpreting on the basis of this assumed unifying christological key, patristic exegesis is neither literal nor allegorical (as we understand the term today); Frances concludes that "the categories usually used to discuss patristic exegesis are inadequate to the task" (Frances Young, *Biblical Exegesis and the Formation of Christian Culture* [Cambridge: Cambridge University Press, 2007], p. 35).

ture consecrated to the service of faith" that it attempts to embody.[39]

Of course, Christianity is not the only religious movement with humanistic elements. Beginning with Judaism, all three Abrahamic, monotheistic religions introduced the novel idea of a transcendent source of being who is entirely independent from the cosmos itself. This idea of the world's radical contingency creates room for human freedom and creativity without which none of the later humanistic developments in either Western or Eastern thought would have been possible.[40]

Yet the Christian idea of the incarnation as the restoration and fullest unfolding of the *imago Dei* provides a conceptual and existential tool for correlating immanence and transcendence, or, to say it theologically, nature and grace, that is less prominent in Jewish (and virtually absent from Islamic) philosophy. Unlike Western philosophy, Islamic reasoning could not take recourse to an incarnational concept, and hence faced greater difficulty in relating faith and reason.[41] Already in early Christian writings the idea of *ex nihilo* creation is qualified by the eternal word, the divine wisdom that became incarnate as the God-man within a specific time and history (Col 1:15-20). The mediation of God's transcendent being in concrete and personal terms endows Christianity with a unique concept of far-reaching philosophical and ethical consequences.

PATRISTIC HUMANISM

Christology and the incarnation. Thus far, I have explored the Greco-Roman categories that the church fathers adapted to their own means. Now I would like to consider how the incarnation is central to this adaptation. This will help us understand later why God's becoming human is central to a true and vital understanding of humanism. In contrast to its sister religions of Judaism and Islam, Christianity begins with the correlation of transcendence and immanence by uniting God's immanence in the incarnation with the Jewish concept of a personal but transcendent God. The importance of the incarnation as the central mystery of the Christian

---

[39]Armstrong and Markus, *Christian Faith*, p. 149.

[40]Robert Sokolowski, *The God of Faith and Reason: Foundations of Christian Theology* (Washington, D.C.: Catholic University of America Press, 2006), pp. 19-23. For an overview of Islamic creation theology and its philosophical implications, see Oliver Leaman, *Introduction to Classical Islamic Philosophy*, 2nd ed. (Cambridge: Cambridge University Press, 2002), pp. 74ff.

[41]Fazlur Rahman, *Major Themes in the Qur'an* (Minneapolis: Bibliotheca Islamica, 1989), p. 169.

faith is evident already in the New Testament and the earliest creeds.[42] One of the clearest formulations of this doctrine is found in the tradition's summation by Athanasius (c. A.D. 296-373), who carefully correlates divine transcendence and God's enfleshment. The incarnation is an affirmation of creation and of God's deep involvement with it, but this in no way compromises the distinct difference between God and his creation.

> At one and the same time—this is the wonder—as Man He was living a human life, and as Word, he was sustaining the life of the universe, and as Son He was in constant union with the father. Not even his birth from a virgin, therefore, changed Him in any way, nor was He defiled by being in the body. Rather, He sanctified the body by being in it. For His being in everything does not mean that He shares the nature of everything, only that he gives all things their being and sustains them in it.[43]

Athanasius alludes to the sustaining, mediating function of the incarnate, divine Word and thereby already typifies the Christian transformation of the Platonic idea of participation. Plato's doctrine of participation (*methexis*) was his answer to Greek materialism and skepticism. Plato agreed that human knowledge begins with sense perception, but since sense perception is subject to temporality, objects of sense perception could be intelligible only by their participation in unchanging ideas, which lent them stable and identifiable characteristics. An object's participation in the form of beauty, for example, allows us to identify something as beautiful.[44] This in turn required the mind's knowledge of the forms. The real problem of this theory, which Plato kept modifying throughout his career, was how temporal, mutable objects can participate in the forms whose immutability demands that they exist in total separation from sensible things. Plato, lacking the kind of incarnational mediation Christology provided, never really solved this problem.[45] Early

---

[42]It is on account of the incarnation that the second central mystery of Christianity, the Trinity, had to be formulated. See J. N. D. Kelly's classic study of the creeds. He affirms that trinitarian theology is not a later accretion to a more biblical monotheism, but a qualification arising from the New Testament's claim that the historical, human figure of Jesus is Lord. J. N. D. Kelly, *Early Christian Creeds* (London: Longmans, Green, 1950), pp. 9, 13-14.

[43]Athanasius, *On the Incarnation: The Treatise De Incarnatione Verbi Dei* (Crestwood, N.Y.: St. Vladimir's Seminary Press, 1998), pp. 45-46.

[44]Plato, *Phaedo* 100b-101c.

[45]See Kenneth M. Sayre's painstaking analysis of Plato's attempt to solve this issue from his middle to late dialogues by seeking to correlate forms and sensible things (*Plato's Late Ontology:*

Christian theologians, attracted by Plato's transcendent vision of the Good, thought they had found a solution. When Augustine writes that Plato's forms reside in the mind of God, he stands on the shoulders of a long line of theologians who had solved Plato's riddle.[46] One such thinker was Justin Martyr, one of the most philosophical and creative early theologians, who was likely influenced by the Hellenized Jewish philosopher Philo of Alexandria.[47] Philo had combined the Stoic idea of a universal, immanent reason with Plato's transcendent ideas to form the concept of a "seminal logos" (*logos spermatikos*) to describe the generative and ordering principle of the universe, a notion easily adapted by Christian thinkers like Justin Martyr to formulate a doctrine of the Christian Logos.[48] Justin was well aware, however, of the important philosophical advantages the incarnation afforded Christian theology. As is usually the case with patristic theology, Justin used Greek idioms to express a distinctly Christian idea through the christological, trinitarian interpretation of the Old Testament. He identifies the incarnate Christ, "being Lord, and God the Son of God," with God's wisdom and operative power encountered in various theophanies throughout the Old Testament.[49]

Justin's incarnational theology already shows the interrelation of participation, reason and the *imago Dei*. For Justin, Jesus the Messiah is the incarnation of God's eternal Word through whom all things were created. It follows that all those created in the image of God also in some sense participate in the mediation of the eternal Word insofar as their being is sustained by it. Every human being thus possesses the "seed of reason,"[50] and thus every human being, Christian or not, reflects divine reason when

A Riddle Resolved [Princeton, N.J.: Princeton University Press, 1983], p. 255).

[46]Augustine, *Concerning the City of God Against the Pagans* 8.6, trans. Henry Bettenson (New York: Penguin Books, 1984), p. 307.

[47]H. Chadwick, "Justin's Defense of Christianity," *Bulletin of the John Rylands Library* 47 (1965): 296-97.

[48]For a good analysis of Philo's engagement with Plato's cosmology, see Jaroslav Pelikan, *What Has Athens to Do with Jerusalem? Timaeus and Genesis in Counterpoint* (Ann Arbor: University of Michigan Press, 2000), pp. 74ff.

[49]Justin Martyr, *Dialogue With Trypho*, chaps. 77-79, in *The Ante-Nicene Fathers*, vol. 1, *The Apostolic Fathers, Justin Martyr, Irenaeus*, ed. Alexander Roberts and James Donaldson, rev. by A. Cleveland Coxe (Peabody, Mass.: Hendrickson, 2004), pp. 263-64.

[50]Justin Martyr, *The Second Apology of Justin*, chap. 8, in *The Ante-Nicene Fathers*, vol. 1, *The Apostolic Fathers, Justin Martyr, Irenaeus*, ed. Alexander Roberts and James Donaldson, rev. by A. Cleveland Coxe (Peabody, Mass.: Hendrickson, 2004), p. 191.

he or she utters truth.[51] The Stoics and Plato only grasped parts of the truth; hence they contradicted themselves and distorted the meaning of human existence because the whole Word of God as embodied in Christ had not been revealed to them.[52] Nonetheless, for Justin all human beings share in the Logos, and pagan philosophers often recognized a particular aspect of the whole Word of God and thus spoke at least partial truth. This also explains to Justin why such reasonable thinkers often encounter hatred from others, for enmity toward reason goes back to demonic hostility to Christ himself.[53] For all his extolling of reason, Justin does not promote a merely rational faith but asserts the need for the incarnation, in which "Christ, who appeared for our sakes, became the whole rational being, both body and reason, and soul"[54] to free humanity from the effects of sin.[55] It is the incarnate Word of God, who "becoming man according to His will . . . taught us these things for the conversion and restoration of the human race."[56]

The doctrine of the incarnation is unique to Christianity and allows early theologians to overcome certain Greek philosophical problems.[57] At the same time, their consequent conviction that Christianity was the fulfillment of Greek humanism ensured the ongoing validity of Greco-Roman wisdom. This view, however, did not blind them to profound differences between biblical and classical wisdom, such as a radically different understanding of being. The church fathers' belief in a creation from nothing (*creatio ex nihilo*) established God's utter freedom from creation and allowed them to reject the Greek eternal universe and Stoic fatalism.[58] By replacing an eternal universe with a contingent one, and by affirming a personal God as the paradigm of being, patristic theology asserted the

---

[51]"For whatever either lawgivers or philosophers uttered well, they elaborated by finding and contemplating some part of the Word" (ibid., chap. 10, p. 191).
[52]Ibid.
[53]Ibid.
[54]Ibid.
[55]Justin Martyr, *First Apology*, chap. 50, p. 179.
[56]Ibid., chap. 23, p. 171.
[57]Emil Brunner, *The Mediator: A Study of the Central Doctrine of the Christian Faith*, trans. Olive Wyon, Lutterworth Library (Philadelphia: Westminster Press, 1947), p. 330.
[58]Justin Martyr affirms against Stoicism the superiority of God as Creator of all things (*First Apology*, chap. 20, p. 169). Athanasius defends God's freedom against Plato, who "said that God had made all things out of pre-existent and uncreated matter, just as the carpenter makes things only out of wood that already exists" (Athanasius, *On the Incarnation* 1.2, p. 27).

freedom and responsibility of human beings as made in God's image.[59] This teaching transformed all prior concepts of being, all antecedent images of reality. By defining ultimate being in personal and communal (trinitarian) terms, Christianity revolutionized humanity's outlook by placing the ideas of freedom and hope at the heart of Western civilization. As Emil Brunner put it in his lectures on Christianity's determinative influence on civilization, "The personal Gods of mythology are not absolute, and the Absolute of Greek philosophy is not personal. There is but one alternative to fatalism or determinism—the idea of God being almighty, sovereign, Lord, Whose freedom is above everything that exists," but whose freedom is also irrevocably expressed in his affirmation of creation and love for humanity in the incarnation.[60]

The Christian doctrines of creation and incarnation establish the world as purely contingent gift, but also assure its relative order and stability through God's affirmation of creation and his identification with humanity through his enfleshment. For the fathers, this was the greatest mystery Christianity possesses. The second-century theologian Irenaeus of Lyon marvels at the fact

> that His offspring, the First-begotten Word, should descend to the creature (*facturam*), that is, to what had been moulded (*plasma*), and that it should be contained by Him; and, on the other hand, the creature should contain the Word, and ascend to Him, passing beyond the angels, and be made after the image and likeness of God.[61]

Even taking into consideration differences in patristic authors' Christologies and in their interpretations of the *imago Dei*, Irenaeus's anthropology does represent the patristic consensus that a high view of humanity depends on a high Christology. The eternal Word and Wisdom of God, through whom and for whom all things were made, became human, so that humanity could attain true humanity. This christological anthropol-

---

[59]Justin Martyr claims: "Unless the human race have the power of avoiding evil and choosing good by free choice, they are not accountable for their actions, of whatever kind they may be" (*First Apology*, chap. 43, 177).

[60]Emil Brunner, *Christianity and Civilization*, vol. 2, *Second Part: Specific Problems*, Gifford Lectures (New York: Scribner's, 1949), p. 23.

[61]Irenaeus, *Irenaeus Against Heresies* 5.36.3, in *The Ante-Nicene Fathers*, vol. 1, *The Apostolic Fathers, Justin Martyr, Irenaeus*, ed. Alexander Roberts and James Donaldson, rev. by A. Cleveland Coxe (Peabody, Mass.: Hendrickson, 2004), p. 567.

ogy is the heart of patristic, indeed of Christian, humanism.

Yet there has been a longstanding tradition regarding patristic high Christology as the result of injecting foreign Hellenistic philosophy into biblical thought patterns. As a result, the argument goes, the idea of an actual enfleshment of God and its ensuing trinitarian theology have obscured Jewish monotheism and its more earth-bound, Old Testament categories. In different ways, this argument has been advanced by theologians such as Joseph Priestly, Adolf von Harnack and all the way to modern proponents of a more narrative, Jewish Christianity, such as Brian McLaren in his recent book *A New Kind of Christianity*. The Unitarian priest and natural philosopher Joseph Priestly (1733-1804) in England and Adolf von Harnack (1851-1930) in Germany were two influential fathers of the idea that patristic anthropology distorted an initially Jewish, more earthbound worldview with abstract and escapist Hellenic theology. Priestly, for example, attributes the divinity of Christ to Christian philosophers like Justin Martyr, Clement and Irenaeus, who he believes mistakenly identified the Logos in John's prologue with the Greek idea of logos and then attributed it to Christ as the eternal Word, thus ascribing divinity to the Christ.[62] Adolf von Harnack follows a similar line of thought when he argues that "The most important step that was ever taken in the domain of Christian doctrine was when the Christian apologists at the beginning of the second century drew the equation: the Logos=Jesus Christ."[63] This identification

---

[62]See Joseph Priestly, *A History of the Corruptions of Christianity* (London: British and Foreign Unitarian Association, 1781). Priestly believed that primitive apostolic Christianity adhered to strict monotheism and did not proclaim the divinity of Christ. This only changed during the late first century under the influence of Hellenistic thought: "Later Christians, however, and especially those who were themselves attached to the principles of either the Oriental or the Greek philosophy . . . began to raise the dignity of the *person* of Christ, that it might appear less disgraceful to be ranked among his disciples" (p. 8). These Christians tried to mitigate the offence of the cross by inventing, as it were, the divinity of Christ (p. 10). According to Priestly, the Platonic notion of the Logos was adopted eagerly by these "Christian philosophers" in order to falsely identify in John's prologue the Logos with Christ, "in direct opposition to what he really meant, which was that the *Logos*, by which all things were made, was not a being, distinct from God, but God himself, being his attribute, his wisdom and power, dwelling in Christ, speaking and acting by him" (p. 11). Apparently Priestly was unaware of the patristic argument that this view makes Christ no different than an inspired prophet. At any rate, Priestly claims that "we find nothing like *divinity* ascribed to Christ before Justin Martyr, who, from being a philosopher, became a Christian, but always retained the peculiar habit of his former profession" (p. 11).

[63]Adolf von Harnack, *What is Christianity?* trans. Thomas Bailey Saunders, 2nd ed. (New York: Putnam's Sons, 1901), pp. 202-3.

was "the determining factor in the fusion of Greek philosophy with the apostolic inheritance,"[64] and was inspired, according to Harnack, by trying to recast the Jewish ideas of the Messiah and redemption in Hellenistic terms.[65] Especially the Greek idea that mortality itself was the greatest evil and eternal life the greatest blessing prompted patristic theologians to radically alter the Jewish idea of redemption as "forgiveness of sins, release from the power of the demons, and so on." Hellenizing theologians reconceived redemption in Greek terms as "*redemption from death and therewith as elevation to the divine life, that is to say, as deification.*"[66] In Harnack's view, this desire for an ontological transformation of human nature required the invention of the incarnation. Such a transformation of human nature could no longer be satisfied, as original Christianity supposedly was, with a mere moral connection between God and Jesus, but had to stipulate "the complete *unity* of the divine and the human in the Redeemer." Hence it is Greek rather than truly Christian logic that gave us the incarnation: "Only when the divine itself bodily enters into mortality, can mortality be transformed. . . . The Logos, then, must be God Himself, and He must have actually become man. With the satisfying of these two conditions, real, natural redemption, that is to say, the deification of humanity, is actually effected."[67] The very essence of incarnational humanism is thus unacceptable for Harnack because such a radical transformation does not suit his own conception of Christianity as primarily a personal and ethical religion.

The notion that the influence of Platonism, and indeed of philosophy in general, has distorted a purer biblical language is still very much alive. To cite a popular example, Brian McLaren suggests in *A New Kind of Christianity* that Christians ought to liberate themselves from the Greco-Roman paradigm that has enslaved the Christian imagination with such conventional notions as "the Fall" and "original sin."[68] That these terms aren't even found in the Bible indicates to McLaren that the authentically

---

[64]Ibid., p. 204.

[65]Greek Christians, Harnack claims, found the Jewish notion of a Messiah "quite unintelligible" (ibid., p. 231).

[66]Ibid., p. 232; italics original. Harnack admits to a starting point of this idea in the gospel but not in such a way as to require the actual incarnation of God himself.

[67]Ibid., p. 233.

[68]*A New Kind of Christianity* (San Francisco: HarperOne, 2010), p. 34. McLaren's slogan for this reading is to read the Bible "frontward," that is, beginning with its Jewish roots. The Christian tradition clearly reads the Bible christologically, and in this sense "backward."

Jewish biblical story line from which Jesus emerged was lost on account of Greek philosophy: "[the church] unwittingly traded its true heritage through Jesus from Judaism for an alien heritage drawn from Greek philosophy and Roman politics."[69] One wonders if McLaren's suggested return to a more Jewish narrative also includes abandoning the Trinity, a concept we also don't find stated as such in the Jewish story.

McLaren's suspicion that traditional Christianity, as handed down to us by patristic theology, is little more than Platonism has a strong philosophical pedigree. Both Nietzsche and Heidegger identified Christianity as Platonism for the people, and their judgment that Christianity adopts the static, ahistorical and world-denying nature of Platonic teaching is remarkably similar to McLaren's complaint. For Nietzsche, Christianity has fallen into the trap of Plato's hero Socrates, the archvillain of intellectual history, who imposed on the exciting primordial Dionysian nature of an ever-changing world the stifling ideal of permanence. For Heidegger, Plato's forms freeze-framed the mysterious open dynamism of being into an artificial, fixed measure, and thus ushered into Western thought the manic obsession with truth as verifiable objectivity that has ruined our more authentic stance toward being. Metaphysics and onto-theology are the respective catch-all terms for these developments, and Christianity itself is allegedly so implicated in this deterioration of human self-understanding that only a thorough revision of our world-view can save humanity. Needless to say, philosophy alone can accomplish this and has now become, if not our savior, then the new mediator which can clear the way to a truer experience of God. I mention these fathers of anti-Platonism in order to make the point that the effort to free a more original Christianity from its Platonic distortions is itself a historical construct from which we have to free ourselves. This is obvious historically but also theologically.

Historical research into Jewish and patristic Christianity shows a continuity of major themes from Jewish to Hellenistic phases of doctrinal development, including the divinity of Christ and the importance of the

---

[69]Ibid., p. 41. It is telling that the only footnote evidence advanced for this claim is McLaren's own book *The Secret Message of Jesus*. McLaren suggests that we should return to the Jewish story, reading the Bible "frontward for a while, to let it be a Jewish story that, through Jesus, includes all of humanity" (ibid., p. 45).

church.[70] Moreover, even a cursory survey of patristic texts demonstrates that Christianity's supposed distortion by Platonism is actually a conscious transformation of Greek concepts in light of God's self-revelation in Christ. Even if patristic theologians do not always strip theology of every possible problematic Platonic notion, their intent is clearly to follow Scripture rather than Plato. In Gregory of Nyssa's words, "even if the truth could be sufficiently demonstrated by the secular philosophy . . . we always use the holy Scripture as the canon and rule of all our doctrine. So we must necessarily look towards this standard and accept only that which is congruent with the sense of the writings."[71] When we look with a generous mind at patristic anthropology, we actually find very little of what the fathers are accused of. Instead of onto-theology that argues its way from being up to God, we find an insistence on creation's dependence on God as the mysterious, incomprehensible but personal, all-encompassing ground of being. Similarly, instead of a static metaphysics pretending to have comprehensive knowledge that objectifies human and divine nature, we find assertions of the ultimately apophatic nature of both God and man. If "humans are the image of God they must be, as Gregory of Nyssa affirms, an incomprehensible image of the incomprehensible."[72] Nor do we find a flight from the world of matter into the Platonic heaven of disembodied forms, but an eschatological understanding of a renewed creation in which, as Irenaeus assures us, "neither the substance nor the essence of

---

[70] According to the study of early Jewish Christian texts by Jean Daniélou, there is "little room to doubt that in all major features the Christian faith in its most archaic expression was even then what it always has been." *The Development of Christian Doctrine Before the Council of Nicea* 1, "The Theology of Jewish Christianity" (Chicago: The Henry Regent Company, 1964), p. 408.

[71] Following this reasoning, Gregory (rhetorically Macrina in this dialogue) seems himself forced "to abandon the Platonic chariot and the pair of horses yoked to it, which pulled unequally, and the charioteer controlling these horses, through all of which Plato presents symbolically a philosophy concerning these faculties in relation to the soul. We shall leave behind also whatever the philosopher who followed him set forth, he who skillfully observed the phenomena and examined carefully the subject which concerns us now, inferring that the soul is mortal." Gregory of Nyssa, "On the Soul and Resurrection," in *Gregory of Nyssa: Dogmatic Treatises*, vol. 5 of *Nicene and Post-Nicene Fathers*, Second Series, ed. Philip Schaff and Henry Wace, trans. William Moore and Henry Austin Wilson (Peabody, Mass.: Hendrickson, 1994), p. 50. However, the difficulty for a true adherence to Scripture is evident. Not only does Gregory later draw on the very analogy he here rejects (57), but he also defines the image of God as the soul, whereas the text declares man as a whole made in the image of God. Thus Irenaeus's anthropology is closer to the mark.

[72] Tanner, *Christ the Key* (Cambridge: Cambridge University Press, 2010), p. 54; she refers to Gregory's statement in "On the Making of Man," chapter 11, section 4, p. 396 in *PNF*.

creation is annihilated."[73] Ironically, it is the detractors of patristic theology, both ancient and modern, who remain entrapped by a false opposition between earthly, storied and Jewish Christianity on the one hand, and later Platonic distortions on the other. Their imagination remains shackled by this paradigm, because they disregard the centrality of the incarnation for patristic thought.

Frequently, Hellenism and high Christology are seen by modern theologians as barriers to a radical Christianity deeply concerned with social justice. Certain Protestant theologians, interested in retrieving the political implications of Jesus' life, have stated that patristic theology failed to include Jesus' earthly life in their highly abstract, metaphysical Christology. This is not the place to answer this criticism in detail.[74] In general, however, one could argue that high Christology is precisely what makes early Christian theologians champions of social justice. In our introduction we have already mentioned Basil the Great, who founded in Caesarea of Cappadocia a welfare center that provided food and medical service for the poor. He urged his parishioners "to follow Christ, the Good Counselor who loves you. He became poor for us so that he might make us rich through His poverty."[75] High Christology was not a hindrance to social justice but its very foundation, because it encouraged Christians to follow in the footsteps of the human-divine philanthropist.

Moreover, biblical scholarship has shown that neither high Christology nor the incarnation is a foreign imposition of Christian Platonic categories on the Old Testament. In the 1970s, for example, Charles Moule, following the lead of Oscar Cullmann and Martin Hengel, argued against the traditional higher critical scholarship and history of religions school, which had proposed an evolutionary christological model. According to this model, attributions of preexistence, divine sonship and fulfilled mes-

---

[73] *Against Heresies, ANF,* 5.26.1, p. 566.

[74] John Howard Yoder expresses this worry. In his essay "The Christological Presuppositions of Discipleship," he opposes the "logological" Christology of patristic theologians (whose influence he senses behind Dietrich Bonhoeffer's equally abstract Christology) to a "Jesulogical" approach that incorporates the "whole career" of Jesus' life into Christology. For Yoder, "Not 'becoming man' but 'becoming *that* man' is then the wonder and the scandal of the incarnation." John Howard Yoder, "The Christological Presuppositions of Discipleship," in *Being Human, Becoming Human: Dietrich Bonhoeffer and Social Thought,* ed. Jens Zimmermann and Brian Gregor (Eugene, Ore.: Wipf & Stock), p. 145.

[75] Basil the Great, *On Social Justice,* trans. C. Paul Schroeder (Crestwood, N.Y.: St. Vladimir's Seminary Press, 2009), p. 57.

sianic expectations in Jesus were later and essentially foreign additions by Christian theologians under the influence of Hellenistic savior cults to the much more mundane figure of a Palestinian rabbi.[76] On the basis of textual evidence, Moule suggests instead a "developmental model," which assumes that "the words and practices of Jesus himself, together with the fact of the cross and of its sequel, presented the friends of Jesus, from the earliest days, with a highly complex, multivalent set of associations" that allowed an organic development of Christology based on an embryonic substance.[77] Contrary to the evolutionary model, later christological insights are thus not departures from a more originary historical Jesus caused by borrowings from Hellenistic outside sources, but subsequent developments of an already existent substance, namely, the experience of Jesus by the early Christians.[78] In a similar vein, New Testament scholar Richard Bauckham, for example, has argued more recently that incarnation and high Christology follow logically from the Old Testament framework. The key to recognizing this continuity is personal categories of identity rather than the metaphysical abstractions of nature and essence. The Old Testament relational categories of divine identity are God's relation to Israel and God's relation to the world. Once we apply these to Jesus, "God's own identity is revealed in Jesus, his life and his cross, just as truly as in his exaltation, in a way that is fully continuous and consistent with the Old Testament and Jewish understanding of God, but is also novel and surprising."[79] Bauckham rightly believes that a Christology of "divine identity" is already a high Christology. On the basis of this conclusion, he also argues for continuity between the New Testament and patristic Christology. The fathers did not develop a new christological vision "so much as transpose it into a conceptual framework constructed more in terms of the Greek philosophical categories of essence and nature."[80]

---

[76]Charles F. D. Moule, *The Origins of Christology* (Cambridge: Cambridge University Press, 1977), p. 2.

[77]Ibid., p. 31.

[78]Ibid., p. 9.

[79]Richard Bauckham, *God Crucified: Monotheism and Christology in the New Testament*, Didsbury Lectures (Grand Rapids: Eerdmans, 1999), p. viii.

[80]Ibid., p. viii. "This Christology of divine identity is not a mere stage on the way to the patristic development of ontological Christology in the context of a trinitarian theology. It is already a fully divine Christology, maintaining that Jesus Christ is intrinsic to the unique and eternal identity of God" (ibid.).

Patristic theology is essentially a continuation of the Jewish belief that the Messiah is God's representative who will defeat sin and evil and renew humanity. Indeed, as we will see in greater detail later, the whole point of patristic humanism is that partaking in that identity, in his suffering and resurrection, will restore the divine image in Christ's likeness.[81] Patristic Christology is thus a continuation of New Testament Christology rather than a radical departure from it. When we recognize the central theme of humanity's restoration to its divine image in the Old and New Testaments, a real case can be made for the biblical, specifically Pauline, origins of patristic humanism. The work of N. T. Wright has been helpful in uncovering the neglected theme of a new humanity in Pauline epistles. Paul extols Christ's incarnation, death and resurrection for the sake of a new humanity (*deuteros anthropos*) and of the restoration of creation.[82] By interpreting the central Pauline term of "God's righteousness" as his covenant faithfulness to humanity, Pauline scholars have affirmed Karl Barth's verdict that Paul's theology highlights God's faithfulness to his creature: "The true God did not forget humanity."[83] Barth follows an authentically Pauline lead, and also agrees with many patristic theologians when he reinterprets the exodus narrative christologically as the liberation from the distorting slavery of sin toward true humanity.

In light of this recovered biblical theme of a new humanity, patristic theology with its emphasis on restoring the image of God sounds sur-

---

[81]As Steenberg points out, for this reason the fathers conducted theology as anthropology "straight across the board," discerning God through the human in the perfect divine image of the incarnate Son of God (M. C. Steenberg, *Of God and Man: Theology as Anthropology from Irenaeus to Athanasius* [London: T & T Clark, 2009], p. 191).

[82]For this theme, see especially the work of N. T. Wright, who argues that Israel's election, covenants, Torah, the prophetic tradition and the divine invective against pagan idolatry, as much as against oppression of the needy, were expressions of God's plan for a full humanity, which eventually happened in Jesus. See, for example, N. T. Wright, "The Letter to the Romans: Introduction, Commentary, and Reflections," in *The New Interpreters Bible: A Commentary in Twelve Volumes*, ed. Leander E. Keck (Nashville: Abingdon, 2009), 10:466, 488, 524 (on Christ as second Adam and new humanity, and Jesus as true Adam and the true Israel); and 10:548 (on Exodus as liberation narrative toward true humanity). See also N. T. Wright, *What Saint Paul Really Said: Was Paul of Tarsus the Real Founder of Christianity?* (Grand Rapids: Eerdmans, 1997), p. 136; N. T. Wright, *Paul: In Fresh Perspective* (Minneapolis: Fortress Press, 2005), pp. 92-93; and N. T. Wright, *Justification: God's Plan and Paul's Vision* (Downers Grove, Ill.: IVP Academic, 2009), p. 104 (on God's people summed up in Christ); pp. 108-9 (on new humanity).

[83]"Der wahre Gott hat den Menschen nicht vergessen," in Karl Barth, *Der Römerbrief* (Zurich: TVZ Verlag, 1999), p. 18.

prisingly modern. Its incarnational theology and concern for humanity do indeed incorporate humanistic elements from Greco-Roman culture, but it grows essentially from the messianic hopes of the Jewish Old Testament narrative that God would rescue humanity from the destructive power of sin, whose ultimate effects were spiritual and physical death.[84] In emphasizing the restoration of the divine image in human beings, the church fathers followed the apostle Paul in interpreting the incarnation, death and resurrection of the expected Messiah in light of the Genesis account: humanity had been created in the image of God, and in Christ, this image had been fully revealed; Israel's messianic hopes are identical with the universal hope of humanity to be liberated from the power of death and restored to the fullness of being in communion with God. The christological interpretation of the *imago Dei* concept in patristic theology is thus intrinsically connected to the Old Testament narrative of liberation. The coming of the Messiah, embodied in Jesus, meant neither the fulfillment of nationalistic hopes nor primarily the salvation of disembodied souls, but inaugurated the restoration of humanity to its godlikeness. In his treatise *On the Incarnation*, Athanasius pertinently summarizes this theme: "Therefore he assumed a human body, in order that in it death might once for all be destroyed, and that men [i.e., human beings] might be renewed according to the Image [of God]."[85] The incarnation makes possible the attainment of true humanity through achieving godlikeness or deification—this is really the heart of incarnational humanism, which we will now explore in the next two sections. The fathers argued that the incarnation revealed for the first time in history the true nature of the divine image and therewith the destiny of human existence.

The **imago Dei.** Christian humanism begins with the christological interpretation of Genesis 1:26-28. For New Testament and patristic authors, the meaning of humanity's being "made after the image and likeness of God" is determined by the Word become flesh. The incarnation determines Christian anthropology in a unique way. Judaism and Islam share

---

[84]Jaroslav Pelikan, *Christianity and Classical Culture: The Metamorphosis of Natural Theology in the Christian Encounter with Hellenism* (New Haven, Conn.: Yale University Press, 1993), p. 318. Pelikan reminds us not to underestimate the inner biblical coherence and motivation of patristic theology.

[85]Athanasius, *On the Incarnation* 3.13, p. 41.

with Christianity the concept of the *imago Dei*,[86] but as Irenaeus of Lyons points out, only the incarnation actually *shows* concretely what humanity is to be. In the incarnation, Irenaeus sees God's affirmation of and identification with humanity to an unprecedented extent:

> And then, this word was made manifest when the Word of God was made man, assimilating Himself to man, and man to Himself, so that by means of this resemblance to the Son, man might become precious to the Father. For in times long past, it was *said* that man was created after the image of God, but it was not [actually] *shown*; for the Word was as yet invisible, after whose image man was created. Wherefore also he [man] did easily lose the similitude. When, however, the Word of God became flesh, He confirmed both these: for He both showed forth the image truly, since he became Himself what was his image; and He re-established the similitude after a sure manner, by assimilating man to the invisible Father through means of the visible Word.[87]

While the terminology of divine image and likeness was common among Greek philosophers from the Stoics to Plato,[88] Irenaeus's defini-

---

[86]On Judaism, see Norman Russell, *The Doctrine of Deification in the Greek Patristic Tradition*, The Oxford Early Christian Studies (Oxford: Oxford University Press, 2004), pp. 53-78. He shows that Philo, most likely following Antiochus of Ascalon (died 69 B.C.), already placed Plato's forms into the mind of God and identified them with the Logos, the creative wisdom of God (ibid., p. 59). On Islam, see Hans Küng, *Der Islam: Geschichte, Gegenwart, Zukunft* (Munich: Piper, 2004), p. 118. Man's creation in God's image is mentioned not in the Koran, but in a Hadith (the recorded sayings by and traditional accounts of Mohammed's deeds and sayings), and retains the Jewish ethical aspect of dignity (see www.al-islam.org/fortyhadith/40.htm). The Sufi tradition has especially emphasized the image of God as the sacred or spiritual dimension man has received from God, something we must work to regain. As the Sufi writer Seyyed Hossein Nasr explains: "The sacred, precisely because it comes from God, asks of us all that we are. To sacralize life and to reach the sacred we must become ourselves sacred, like a sacred work of art. We must chisel the substance of our soul into an icon which will reveal us as we really are in the Divine Presence, as we were when we were created, the imago Dei; for as the Prophet of Islam has said, 'God created man upon his Image'" (*Islam and the Plight of Modern Man* [Chicago: ABC International Group, 2001], p. 81). Islamic theology rejects, however, any attempt to connect the image of God to a human incarnation and thus to imply the identification of Jesus the man with God the creator (Rahman, *Major Themes in the Qur'an*, pp. 168-69). For the same reason, some Islamic thinkers offer an almost evangelical rejection of humanism as Promethean aspiration to Godhood. They reject Renaissance and Baroque art and architecture as "worldly and unspiritual," as "a reflection of the revolt against Heaven embedded in Renaissance humanism, which succeeded in destroying in the West the traditional concept of man as the imago dei" (Nasr, *Islam and the Plight of the Modern Man*, p. 196 n. 6).

[87]Irenaeus, *Against Heresies* 5.16.2, p. 544.

[88]Eric Francis Osborn, *Irenaeus of Lyons* (Cambridge: Cambridge University Press, 2001), p. 211.

tion of the *imago Dei*, like most patristic concepts, transforms this language by drawing upon New Testament teaching. In keeping with the resolutely christological exegesis of the fathers, Irenaeus interprets the *imago Dei* language of Genesis through the incarnation and its purpose of drawing humanity into the divine life. He sets the tone for subsequent patristic theology by insisting that "the human person is only rightly comprehended as a mystery of the material creation wrought into communion with the divine life of God, through the incarnational activity of the Son with the Spirit."[89] For Irenaeus, the incarnation reveals that the *imago Dei* always indicated relationality and its ultimate goal of communion with God. For him, this reading was clearly warranted by Scripture. The apostle Paul already speaks of Christ as the "image of the invisible God" (Col 1:15) and links the language of image and likeness to human participation in God.[90] Through the incarnation, fallen humanity has been reconciled to God, and through the work of God, humanity is being healed and restored to its original glory. Irenaeus takes Paul to mean that humanity is not created in God's image in a general sense, but specifically in the image of the Son, who is revealed in the incarnation.[91] The redemptive work of Christ, who is the archetypical image and perfect human being, restores to humanity "what we had lost in Adam—namely, to be according to the image and likeness of God."[92] This distinction between *image* and *likeness* is important. While he is not always consistent in his use of these terms, Irenaeus generally refers to the natural physical and intellectual qualities as "image,"[93] in distinction to the "likeness," which comes from the Son and Spirit.[94] This differentiation between image and likeness, which we also find in other fathers,[95] is important

---

[89]Steenberg, *Of God and Man*, p. 52.
[90]"Just as we have borne the likeness of the earthly man, so shall we bear the likeness of the man from heaven" (1 Cor 15:49). I owe this insight to Steenberg, *Of God and Man*, p. 8. On Paul and participation, see Wright, "Letter to the Romans," p. 539. Michael J. Gorman also highlights the participatory understanding of faith in the apostle Paul (*Inhabiting the Cruciform God: Kenosis, Justification, and Theosis in Paul's Narrative Soteriology* [Grand Rapids: Eerdmans, 2009], pp. 41-45).
[91]Irenaeus, *Against Heresies* 5.16.2, p. 544; see Steenberg, *Of God and Man*, p. 37.
[92]Irenaeus, *Against Heresies* 3.18.1, p. 446.
[93]Ibid., 5.10.2, p. 536.
[94]Ibid., 5.6.1, p. 531.
[95]Tatian, in his Address to the Greeks, links image to the material and likeness to the transcendent part of the human nature (Tatian's *Address to the Greeks*, in *The Ante-Nicene Fathers*, vol. 2,

because it attributes to human beings a common rational ability and freedom. Not the image (freedom and reason) but the likeness (immortality and moral perfection in loving God and human beings) was lost in the Fall. This distinction preserves human freedom and rational ability (albeit subject to death and corruption), which is the divine breath that sets human beings apart from the animals. Reason is assumed to be a common endowment that requires training and schooling for its perceptive unfolding of truth. It is no surprise, therefore, that early theologians recommend philosophical training as necessary for deepening theological understanding, while also arguing that divine revelation and faith shed light on philosophy and its ultimate goal of self-understanding by revealing the human self most fully in light of its intended communion with God. Already a hermeneutical circle is at play, in which faith seeks understanding and understanding pursues faith. As we will see shortly, for the fathers, salvation consisted not in the mere salvation of the soul apart from the mind or body, but in the training of the entire human being toward the perfection of Christ's humanity.

The distinction between image and likeness also establishes the free will of every human being as constitutive of the *imago Dei*. Hence the Christian gospel's invitation to full humanity appeals to human beings' God-given freedom, placing before each individual the choice of life with or without God: "It is manifest that His Father has made all in a like condition, each person having a choice of his own, and a free understanding; and that he has regard to all things, and exercises a providence over all 'making His sun to rise upon the evil and the good, and sending rain upon the just and unjust.'"[96] God, in other words, offers his grace of restoration

Hermas, Tatian, Athenagoras, Theophilus, Clement of Alexandria, ed. Alexander Roberts and James Donaldson, rev. A. Cleveland Coxe [Peabody, Mass.: Hendrickson, 2004], chap. 12, p. 70). Clement makes a similar distinction between image as natural endowment and likeness as the holiness, wisdom, and righteousness of Christ (*Exhortation to the Heathen*, in *The Ante-Nicene Fathers*, vol. 2, Hermas, Tatian, Athenagoras, Theophilus, Clement of Alexandria, ed. Alexander Roberts and James Donaldson, rev. A. Cleveland Coxe [Peabody, Mass.: Hendrickson, 2004], chap. 12, p. 206); see also Clement of Alexandria, *Instructor*, in *The Ante-Nicene Fathers*, vol. 2, Hermas, Tatian, Athenagoras, Theophilus, Clement of Alexandria, ed. Alexander Roberts and James Donaldson, rev. A. Cleveland Coxe (Peabody, Mass.: Hendrickson, 2004), chap. 12, pp. 234-36. Clement argues that Christ alone is fully made in the image and likeness of God, while "the rest of humanity is created merely in His image" (ibid.).

[96]Irenaeus, *Against Heresies* 5.27.1, p. 556.

to all human beings; therefore, punishment for refusing the life and healing of human nature offered through the incarnation is, so to speak, self-
inflicted. God does not punish the rejection of his offer out of wounded
pride, but the punishment lies in deliberately refusing the fullness of life
for which human being is intended.[97]

Among patristic interpretations of the *imago Dei*, Irenaeus's includes
the physical body in the image, thereby showing the most conscious distance from Greek thought. In distinction from the Alexandrine fathers,
who define *image* in more spiritual terms,[98] Irenaeus does not confine the
imago Dei to human rationality or to the mind, but includes the body.
Neither image nor likeness can be saved alone, but together require transformation into the true image of God. This transformation is a gift of
grace by which the whole person is brought into communion with God,
and, by the power of the spirit, begins the transformation into the likeness
of the "pristine nature of man—that which was created after the image
and likeness of God."[99] Most likely because of his world-denying, Gnostic
audience, Irenaeus insists that the flesh too is God's excellent handiwork,
animated into a living thing through the soul.[100] The complete human
being consists of the union of all three,[101] for this is the model of the perfect human being advanced by God in the incarnation: "For the perfect
man consists in the comingling and the union of the soul receiving the
spirit of the Father, and the admixture of that fleshly nature which was
molded after the image of God."[102]

In contrast to any philosophers who seek a disembodied, "pure" spirituality, Irenaeus insists that Christian spirituality does not require the flesh to be
"stripped off and taken away."[103] In this case, we would only have "the spirit

---

[97]Ibid., 5.27.2, p. 556. "But communion with God is life and light, and the enjoyment of all the
benefits which he has in store. But on as many as, according to their own choice, depart from
God He inflicts that separation from Himself which they have chosen of their own accord.
But separation from God is death, and separation from light is darkness; and separation from
God consists in the loss of all the benefits which He has in store" (ibid.).

[98]Osborn, *Irenaeus of Lyons*, p. 215.

[99]Irenaeus, *Against Heresies* 5.10.1, p. 536.

[100]Ibid., 5.6.1, pp. 531-32.

[101]Irenaeus's anthropological thought is remarkably nondualistic and also refuses the notion of
incorporeal spirits when exploring the resurrection. Life, both mortal and immortal, depends
on God's sustaining power (ibid., 5.4.1, p. 530).

[102]Ibid., 5.6.1, p. 532.

[103]Ibid.

of a human being" but not a "spiritual *human* being."[104] In the same way, he who has merely an animated body possesses only the image of God, but not the likeness or "similitude through the Spirit."[105] Spirit, soul or body have no value by themselves, and cannot in isolation establish what human being is in completeness. Rather, "the comingling and union of all these constitutes the perfect man."[106] Since the Bible promises the salvation of the complete human being, Irenaeus sees in the resurrection of the incarnate Christ, who "rose in the substance of the flesh," the promise of a new creation, a new humanity.[107] Perhaps the best illustration of this embodied faith is Irenaeus's reading of Paul's claim that "flesh and blood cannot inherit the kingdom of God" (1 Cor 15:50). Irenaeus believes that Paul's meaning does not repudiate "the substance of flesh but show[s] that into it the Spirit must be infused."[108]

In Irenaeus's concept of recapitulation, which he developed from Paul's *anakephalaiōsis* in Ephesians 1:10, the full breadth of the patristic vision for humanity becomes apparent: "God recapitulated in himself the ancient formation of man, that He might kill sin, deprive death of its power, and vivify man."[109] Even though humanity has fallen into sin, God restores rather than completely recreates his handiwork. God's becoming human in the likeness of sinful flesh shows his determination that "the very same formation should be summed up [in Christ as he had existed in Adam], the analogy having been preserved."[110] To preserve the analogy of God and man, a human being was needed who was both divine and human, the perfect human being who unites in himself the workmanship of God but also the image and likeness of God.[111] Out of love for the human race, God in the incarnation "caused human being (human nature) to cleave to and become one with God."[112] Irenaeus brings out the full depth of God's identification with human nature by arguing that Christ "passed through every stage of human life, restoring all to communion with God."[113] Not

---

[104]Ibid., emphasis added.
[105]Ibid.
[106]Ibid.
[107]Ibid., 5.7.1, p. 532.
[108]Irenaeus, *Against Heresies* 5.10.2, p. 536.
[109]Ibid., 3.18.7, p. 448.
[110]Ibid., 3.21.10, p. 454.
[111]Ibid., 3.21.9, p. 454; 3.18.7, p. 448.
[112]Ibid., 3.18.7, p. 448.
[113]Ibid.

only every stage of life, but he "has summed up in Himself all nations dispersed from Adam downwards, and all languages and generations of men, together with Adam himself."[114] Christ thus sums up in himself "the long line of human beings," to restore what had been lost, "namely to be according to the image and likeness of God."[115] For Irenaeus, the incarnation draws into itself *all* of humanity, offering to the Father true humanity, the true *imago Dei*.[116]

Even if other fathers do not follow Irenaeus's exact definition of the image,[117] he implanted in the Christian tradition an indelible appreciation of creation and the body that is everywhere evident. Augustine, for example, equally rejects both naturalist philosophies that deny transcendence and religions that deny the body.[118] There is, in short, a broad consensus in patristic discourse about viewing the human being holistically, as an integral being whose salvation consists in the transformation of one's whole being into the immortal, incorruptible humanity of Christ. The church fathers routinely defend the incarnation against pagan philosophers by referring to the value of material creation. Created by God, none "of the elements that contribute to animal life, is liable to the charge of being worthless or wicked."[119] If the commonly held prejudice against patristic theology as world-denying, contemplative Platonism was true, the strong emphasis of the fathers on ethics as evidence of being transformed toward true humanity would remain an inexplicable oddity. If, however, the incarnation proved that true humanity could be understood only as the

---

[114]Ibid., 3.22.3, p. 455.

[115]Ibid., 5.18.1, p. 446.

[116]Irenaeus argues that the Christ ascended to heaven, "commending to his Father that human nature (*hominem*) which had been found, making in His own person the firstfruits of the resurrection of man." In Christ all those who are members of this new body, this new humanity, will find a place in heaven when rising again (ibid., 3.19.3, p. 449).

[117]Tertullian, for example, defines the *imago Dei* without substantial reference to the incarnate Christ (Steenberg, *Of God and Man*, p. 79), which does not at all mean, however, that he denigrates the body, but like Irenaeus sees it as becoming transformed into "a thing joined to God" (ibid., p. 74).

[118]On transcendence, see Augustine, *City of God* 7.26, p. 287. On account of the incarnation, true spirituality, for Augustine, follows the incarnation in which Christ the mediator "showed us, for our salvation, . . . [a truth] of the greatest importance: that the true divine nature cannot be polluted by the flesh" (ibid., 9.17, p. 364).

[119]Gregory of Nyssa, "The Great Catechism," in *Gregory of Nyssa: Dogmatic Treatises*, vol. 5 of *Nicene and Post-Nicene Fathers*, Second Series, ed. Philip Schaff and Henry Wace, trans. William Moore and Henry Austin Wilson (Peabody, Mass.: Hendrickson, 1994), p. 497.

mystery of material creation in communion with the divine life of God, and if Christ exemplified this life and made possible our participation in it,[120] then the emphasis on transformed conduct fits into the larger picture of a holistic anthropology. Indeed, patristic theology *is* necessarily also anthropology. The incarnation of the Son of God "forms the whole basis" and unifying core of this patristic theology, because theology is "the articulation of God encountered in the human."[121]

The fathers' incarnational theological humanism indicates a paradox we must keep in mind. Modern critics of Christianity have argued that this religion devalues the human (Nietzsche), fails to change human conditions (Marx) and weakens human responsibility by detracting attention from this world (new atheists). The fathers' incarnational humanism contradicts all these claims: the *more* we emphasize the transcendent origin and ground of humanity in the incarnation and Trinity, the more we value human beings. Humanity is elevated to the extent that it is grounded in the personal, transcendent divine. Nowhere is this more evident than in the most important concept of patristic humanism, namely, the idea of deification. Irenaeus's claim that the incarnation's purpose was the assimilation of humanity to the "invisible Father through the means of the visible Word" takes us to the heart of patristic theology: the idea of healing the divine image in human beings and of drawing them up to the noble height for which they were created.

The paradox of human elevation through the subordination of God has its root in the unique kenotic act of the Christian God. In Athanasius's words, it is "on our account that He is dishonoured, so that we may be brought to honour."[122] The unique spiritual and moral impact of the incarnation within its historical context and also in comparison to the world religions is difficult to appreciate from our modern vantage point. For early Christians, the conviction that God had become flesh had implications for what it means to be human that shook the ancient world and should still fill us with awe. On the most general level the incarnation indicates that "the material is not alien to the spiritual, but that the body is to be seen as the vehicle of the spirit."[123] More specifically, the incarna-

---

[120]Steenberg, *Of God and Man*, p. 52.
[121]Ibid., p. 191.
[122]Athanasius, *On the Incarnation* 6.34, p. 66.
[123]Hebblethwaite, *Incarnation*, p. 43.

tion, without reducing God to our understanding, nevertheless reveals God to us on a human level. Jesus, as God in *person*, allows a knowledge of God that has an "intelligible, personal human focus."[124] In the incarnation, "God overcomes the vagueness and dread that limit the experience of God, which elsewhere and otherwise people can and do enjoy."[125] Yet in this very concreteness God confronts us with the mystery of divine love and reveals himself as the wholly other God. This is precisely the stumbling stone, the scandal of the incarnation: the encounter with God's infinite love in a concrete personal address disallows any vague religious sentiments of cosmic spirituality and reveals our own self-love.[126] It remains one of the great paradoxes of the Christian faith that we are free to respond to this love, but that we can do so only because of the very love extended to us by God. In becoming human, God himself constitutes the perfect human response to divine love, and we are able to respond by participation in this response. The novelty within the history of religions is that this concrete, personal and historical self-revelation of God in the human being Jesus cannot be reduced to mythical terms. God's self-communication in Jesus of Nazareth means that "the world of myth has been forever left behind."[127] It is equally important that the incarnation not be reduced to God's activity in or through the man Jesus, so that he becomes merely one religious guru or divine exemplar among others. Especially modern theologians have been tempted to reduce the scandal of the incarnation by adopting functional categories in Christology (what God is doing in and through the man Jesus) rather than ontological ones (that Jesus' being incarnates God).[128] It is important for the church's faithful witness to God's love for humanity to retain on positive grounds the idea that in Jesus the personal, triune God lives out a real human life without compromising his deity. This is a mystery, to be sure, but this mystery arises from the concrete experience related to us in Jesus's prayers to the

---

[124]Ibid., p. 23. As Hebblethewaite points out, this insight is lost if we suppose that Jesus is only one of many other possible incarnations of the divine.

[125]Ibid.

[126]Hans Urs von Balthasar, *Love Alone Is Credible*, trans. D.C. Schindler (San Francisco: Ignatius Press, 2004), p. 73.

[127]Ibid., p. 80.

[128]Hebblethwaite names liberal Protestantism and Hans Küng as representatives of functional Christologies (*Incarnation*, pp. 87-88).

Father.[129] New Testament and patristic Christology is not the arbitrary imposition of Greek concepts on God, but employs their help to come to terms with Jesus' claims, such as "don't you believe that I am in the Father, and that the Father is in me?" (Jn 14:10) and with many similar passages of personal indwelling.[130] Moreover, the humanity of Christ mediates God to us in concrete, personal form, not only through the witness of the Gospel accounts and New Testament letters, but also through God's incarnate presence in each believer and the church. The importance of this personal, sacramental presence for Christian belief cannot be stressed enough, and will be discussed in a later chapter.

Another important aspect of the incarnation is that it reveals God as a trinitarian relation of love. To put it more precisely, the doctrine of the Trinity arises within Jewish monotheism from the necessity of interpreting the Son's intimate relation of love with the Father as reported in the New Testament accounts, and of defining the role of the Holy Spirit as equally divine in pouring out God's love into the heart of believers (Rom 5:5).[131] The Trinity as utterly free communion of love reveals the self-sufficient creator God whose love for us is indeed a gift, for he *is* love in his eternal being, irrespective of his love for us. Within the Trinity, Christ, the incarnation of the eternal Word, is the true image of God. Since we are made in this image, we may infer that human personhood and relations are inherently social and ideally based on reciprocal love. As we shall see shortly, incarnation and Trinity gave rise to a concept of personhood and especially of community hitherto unknown in the ancient world.

Finally, the doctrine of the incarnation provides a tremendous moral force by revealing a unique way of confronting the world's evil. God *himself* takes on the responsibility for evil in the life, death and resurrection of Christ. And because God, on the cross, bore our sorrows, he identifies with human suffering, and we can find Christ in every suffering human being. Nor is suffering something to be transcended by some form of detachment, for the incarnate God on the cross reveals the utmost seriousness and reality of suffering, but also transforms it by taking it up into the

---

[129]Ibid., p. 65.
[130]For a list of such sayings indicating that in Jesus God himself lived out a human life from within the very center of the internal Godhead, see C. F. D. Moule, *The Origins of Christology*, p. 64.
[131]Hebblethwaite, *Incarnation*, p. 136.

glorious hope of a new creation, where neither death nor suffering will impede human life on earth. All these notions become mere sentiments and ideas, however, unless God *really* did become human and remains present in the world.[132] An older argument against the incarnation that still holds some power criticizes the orthodox claim that God actually took on human form in order to avoid any possible identification of God with human ideologies and political structures. Theologians such as Don Cupitt feared that "the assertion that deity itself and humanity are permanently united in the one person of the incarnate Lord suggests an ultimate synthesis, a conjunction and continuity between things divine and things of this world."[133] The church's history, according to Cupitt, shows us that the incarnation gives Christology too much anthropocentric weight and tends to "validate this-worldly sovereignty and to politicize the transcendent."[134] Yet one cannot have it both ways. Without God's actual *real* humanity, without the claim that the Jesus who walked on Palestinian soil *was* and *still is* God, all of the moral values we just named fall flat. The original impact of Christianity on ancient culture derived from the conviction that God *is* with us, Emmanuel. This belief in humanity's communion with God allowed early Christian theologians to distance themselves from Greek anthropology with its emphasis of salvation through knowledge. Christians emphasized the personal cosmological aspect of sin as separation from God and the reinstating of human beings into communion with God through the incarnation and resurrection. Christ died and rose for the liberation of humanity from sin and for the healing of humanity from its residual effects.[135]

---

[132]This entire paragraph is heavily indebted to Brian Hebblethwaite's essay "The Moral and Religious Value of the Incarnation," in *Incarnation*, pp. 27-44.

[133]Don Cupitt, "The Christ of Christendom," in *The Myth of God Incarnate*, ed. John Hick (London: SCM Press, 1977), p. 140. Jesus himself, by contrast, always emphasized divine transcendence and "the disjunction of things divine and human" (p. 145). For Cupitt, the gravest consequence of the incarnational error is Constantinian Christianity, that is, an institutionalized church, its hierarchical order and political power.

[134]Ibid., p. 145.

[135]Irenaeus, *Against Heresies* 5.7.2, 5.8.1, p. 533. This language is common to most fathers. See Justin Martyr: "He became man for our sakes that becoming a partaker of our sufferings, he might also bring us healing" through our participation in the divine (*Second Apology*, chap. 13, p. 193). Clement also mentions the restoration of humanity's soul and reason: "healing their souls and enlightening them and leading them to the attainment of truth" ("Who Is the Rich Man That Shall Be Saved," *Stromata*, chap. 1, p. 590). See also Augustine: "We might have despaired, thinking your Word remote from any conjunction with human kin, had he not

The heart of patristic humanism: Deification. The key to early Christian anthropology is the idea of deification, of being made like God. This theme of *theosis*, the deification of the human as God's redemptive plan for a fallen race, initiated through God's becoming human, is dominant among the church fathers. Even if Christians cannot quite agree on the exact meaning of the term "theosis," this does not call into question the centrality among patristic theologians of the idea that God became human to deify and restore humanity. This theme is not confined to the Eastern Church but is equally present in the Latin tradition,[136] and describes the fathers' common view of the divinely intended goal of human existence.[137]

As with image terminology, so the language of deification was fairly common in the Greco-Roman world[138] and eventually became a handy

---

become flesh and made his dwelling among us" (*The Confessions*, trans. Maria Boulding [New York: New City Press, 1997], 10.43.68, p. 283).

[136]At the conclusion to a recent study of *theosis* in the Christian tradition, Gösta Hallonsten cautions wisely against too broad a conception of *theosis* as roughly meaning "union with God." She urges that one needs to distinguish between a general theme and the more comprehensive and distinct Eastern doctrine (Gösta Hallosten, "Theosis in Recent Research: A Renewal of Interest and Need for Clarity," in *Partakers of the Divine Nature*, ed. Michael J. Christensen and Jeffery A. Wittung [Madison, Wis.: Fairleigh Dickinson University Press, 2007], p. 287). Yet as Norman Russell points out, *theosis* in the sense Athanasius understood it, as the deification of the human being and as restitution to original humanity, is clearly present in Augustine, who preaches in a recently recovered sermon that God not only wishes to make us alive but even to deify us. Augustine silences any objections to this idea by saying that "[i]f God can become man, then surely he can deify mortals" (Henry Chadwick, article on Augustine's doctrine of deification, *Revue des Sciences Religieuses* [forthcoming], quoted in Russell, *Doctrine of Deification*, p. 331). On Augustine's view of deification in his exposition of the Psalms, including Psalm 81, see Robert Puchniak, "Augustine's Conception of Deification Revisited," in *Theōsis: Deification in Christian Theology*, ed. Stephen Finlan and Vladimir Kharlamov, Princeton Theological Monograph Series (Eugene, Ore.: Pickwick, 2006).

[137]Stephen Finlan and Vladimir Kharlamov, eds., *Theōsis: Deification in Christian Theology*, Princeton Theological Monograph Series (Eugene, Ore.: Pickwick, 2006). *Theōsis*, p. 1.

[138]Plato already spoke of deification and even linked deification, as the alignment of the soul with the eternal forms (and especially the good), to beneficial social effects. Plato taught deification, but that "the nature of the god to whom one is to assimilate oneself is not presented very clearly" (John M. Armstrong, "After the Ascent: Plato on Becoming Like God," *Oxford Studies in Ancient Philosophy* 26 [summer 2004]: 174). For Plato, becoming like god is not an "unremitting flight from the world" but "the good human life involves the application of one's knowledge to the world of change, creating harmonious mixtures of limited and unlimited as an intelligent craftsman" (ibid.). In this way, souls "become like God by becoming measured" (ibid., p. 181), thus stressing the transformative nature of deification. Stoic belief that the human *logos* is a fragment of the divine *Logos* lent itself to this language (Marcia L. Colish, *Stoicism in Classical Latin Literature*, vol. 1 of *The Stoic Tradition from Antiquity to the Early Middle Ages* [Leiden: Brill, 1985], p. 35).

political tool in promulgating the emperor cult of Rome.[139] The Christian idea of deification uses the existent vocabulary to express its own concept of deification based on a christological interpretation of the Old Testament.[140] Justin Martyr, for instance, reads Psalm 82 in this light to argue that "all men are deemed worthy of becoming 'gods,' and of having power to become sons of the Highest," which is what Christ offers to human beings.[141] Irenaeus expounds Psalm 82 in similar fashion, but with a different aim; Justin had tried to show that Christians, rather than Jews, were the true sons of God. Irenaeus, in contrast, argued—against the epistemological elitism of the Gnostics—that incorruption could be attained by all believers rather than by a select spiritual elite.[142] Irenaeus also advances beyond Justin's concept of deification by linking it to the Pauline notion of "adoption," thus strengthening the participatory element. God became human so that "man, having been taken into the Word, and receiving the adoption, might become the son of God."[143] Irenaeus marvels at what he calls the "great exchange," that God "became what we are in order to make us what He is himself."[144] Christian theologians used the term *godlikeness* deliberately to prevent any confusion of the creaturely human and the divine nature. Becoming like God precisely did not mean to become God by sharing his substance, but to become like God by participating in the divine life. The fathers are careful to distinguish between the human subject who participates in the divine life and the divine object of participation.[145]

Eastern theologians especially, such as Clement of Alexandria, interpret *theosis* as the Christian fulfillment of Plato's ecstatic model of the soul's progress toward divinity by assimilating to the forms through ac-

---

[139]Russell, *Doctrine of Deification*, pp. 18ff.

[140]Russell makes the point that Christians like Clement of Alexandria could use the Greek language in this way after it had become secularized and referred to men rather than Homerian gods (ibid., p. 18).

[141]Justin Martyr, *Dialogue with Trypho*, chap. 124, p. 262. I prefer Norman Russell's translation, which makes clearer the idea of restoration to rational and moral ability: "and will be judged and condemned on their own account like Adam and Eve" (Russell, *Doctrine of Deification*, p. 99).

[142]Russell, *Doctrine of Deification*, pp. 105-6.

[143]Irenaeus, *Against Heresies*, 3.29.1, p. 448.

[144]Ibid., 3.29.5, p. 526; Russell, *Doctrine of Deification*, pp. 106ff.

[145]Vladimir Kharlamov, "Rhetorical Application of *Theosis*," in Christensen and Wittung, *Partakers of the Divine Nature*, p. 122.

quiring knowledge by means of rational inquiry.[146] Standing in this tradition, Clement enriches the Christian idea of deification with his typical emphasis on knowledge: "And knowing God, [the Christian] will be made like God." As Clement puts it elsewhere: "Yea, I say, the Word of God became man, that you may learn from man how man may become God."[147] This idea may sound strange to our modern ears, but early theologians, both Eastern and Western, were enamored with the notion that God's descent into human nature allows the human ascent to the divine. So when Athanasius summarizes the orthodox teaching on the incarnation in the fourth century, he can draw on a longstanding tradition of interpreting Christian salvation as our restoration to the image of God, the image as it had been perfected in the God-man Jesus: "He indeed assumed humanity that we might become God. He manifested Himself by means of a body in order that we might perceive the mind of the unseen Father. He endured shame from men that we might inherit immortality."[148]

It is difficult to convey in a few pages the breathtaking scope of the patristic vision for humanity. We are confronted with a comprehensive program for elevating humanity to its rightful place of godlikeness. As Clement put it, "the greatest and most regal work of God is the salvation of humanity." Salvation meant the renewal of human being toward "all that pertains to love of truth, love of man, and love of excellence."[149] For the fathers, Christ had died so that true humanity could become possible. Patristic humanists answer the two questions of "who am I" and "what am I living for," the two crucial elements not only of individuality but also of genuine personhood, by pointing to the original purpose of human beings: to be in communion with God. For the fathers, communion with God was not merely a mystical experience but the comprehensive plan of God to lift his human creatures above irrational behavior to their true rational and relational image in Christ. According to the fathers, Christ's message to the entire human race is his "desire to restore you according to the original model, that ye may become also like Me."[150] This ideal of deification had

[146]Michael Morgan, "Plato and Greek Religion," in *The Cambridge Companion to Plato*, ed. Richard Kraut (Cambridge: Cambridge University Press, 1992), p. 232.
[147]Clement, *Exhortation to the Heathen*, chap. 1, p. 174.
[148]Athanasius, *On the Incarnation* 8.54, p. 93.
[149]Clement, *Instructor*, chap. 12, p. 235.
[150]Clement, *Exhortation to the Heathen*, chap. 1, pp. 172-73.

a number of far-reaching consequences for Western culture. I will name
three to show the foundational importance of Christianity for humanism:
the correlation of reason and faith, the idea of a common humanity, and,
finally, the ecclesial foundation of human solidarity.

The correlation of reason and faith. Humanism has always emphasized
the importance of reason. Reason, of course, already played an important
part in Greek and Roman philosophy. We recall Socrates' famous dictum
that the unexamined life is not worth living and the Stoics' identification
of reason both with the spark of divinity in man and with natural law. It
was not until Christianity, however, that right reasoning became identified with the image of God *as embodied in the incarnation.* For classical
thought, reason was the means by which one ascended from nature to the
divine. Especially Platonism had assumed that the disciplined mind could
withdraw from the sensible world to attain pure knowledge through apprehending the pure reality of the forms. This view also gave rise to the
Gnostic heresy of two worlds, a lower sensible sphere and a higher intellectual one that only elite philosophers perceived.[151] The fathers argued,
however, that in the incarnation, the very ground of reality, the cosmic
principle of order and substance of the Father, had become flesh and accessible to all who cared to look. Christianity thus inverted the direction of
the pagan search for truth: instead of approaching the meaning of God
through nature, they interpreted the meaning of nature through God's
self-revelation in Christ.[152] The incarnation indicated not only that there
was only one world, shared by all, but also that access to the cosmic *ratio*
of this world was no longer a matter of intellectual ascent toward a mystery
reserved for the initiate. Rather, eternal truth was concretely embodied in
the historical figure of Jesus the Messiah,[153] and access to this truth was
no longer intellectual but relational, no longer primarily *cognitio* but *communio*, not an ascent of the mind but participation in the divine life through
a personal encounter with the risen Christ. Hence, for the first time in
ancient philosophy, reason was intrinsically shaped as ethics, because the
Logos itself had embodied divine love within history for human beings,

---

[151]Charles Norris Cochrane, *Christianity and Classical Culture: A Study of Thought and Action
from Augustus to Augustine* (New York: Oxford University Press, 1957), p. 238.
[152]Ibid., p. 237.
[153]Ibid., p. 236.

love that pursued its object to the point of death. If the eternal Logos became human and set the pattern for our full humanity, then reason is intrinsically concerned with love for other human beings. So much, then, for
the misconception that Christianity is otherworldly and irrational. Moreover, as we shall see in this and the following sections, many patristic humanists defy the stereotype that they are arguing for a supposedly Platonic, disembodied spirituality.[154] Christian humanism begins with the
incarnation returning humanity to the course it was created for: to become
fully human through communion with God and the right use of reason.[155]

Deification, the human ascent to God, does not bypass reason but, on
the contrary, heals reason through participation in the divine Logos. Reason and faith are closely related for patristic humanists because the rational
image is geared not primarily toward logical analysis but toward relation
and communion with the divine. Athanasius explains:

> How could men be reasonable beings if they had no knowledge of the Word
> and Reason of the Father, through Whom they had received their being?
> . . . [A]nd why should God have made them at all, if He had not intended
> them to know Him? But, in fact, the good God has given them a share in
> His own Image, that is, in our Lord Jesus Christ, and has made even them-
> selves after the same Image and Likeness. Why? Simply in order that
> through this gift of Godlikeness in themselves they may be able to perceive
> the Image Absolute, that is, the Word Himself, and through Him to ap-
> prehend the Father; which knowledge of their Maker is for men the only
> really happy and blessed life.[156]

Faith is not contrary to reason but is its very source and its fulfillment.
Made in God's image, human beings are endowed with reason, and reason's true source and home is the divine Logos, "the Word Himself." Reason is thus ultimately relational and inseparable from the body and its final
destiny of becoming immortal like God.[157]

---

[154]Origen is perhaps the least successful, but his tendency to push for an incorporeal spirituality
(see for instance his contorted explanation of Paul's view that the corruptible will be swal-
lowed up by the incorruptible as disembodied resurrection in his *Commentarii in Epistolam ad
Romanos*) is far outweighed by the more incarnational theologies of Augustine and Irenaeus
(*Commentarii in Epistolam ad Romanos: Origenes Römerbriefkommentar* [Freiburg: Herder,
1990], 4:51-17).
[155]Augustine, *City of God* 12.6, p. 477.
[156]Athanasius, *On the Incarnation* 3.11, p. 38.
[157]Irenaeus, *Against Heresies* 5.29.1, p. 558.

The crucial idea emerging from patristic anthropology and its understanding of deification (taken in a broad way) is that adoption into the new
humanity sets one on the path to restoring one's human image and likeness
of God through spiritual and moral advancement. Since what is spiritual
is always equated in the church fathers with reason and knowledge, we
find here the very roots of humanism's passion for education as the restoration of knowledge and character. The theological roots of this passion lie
in the doctrine of the perfectibility of human being once taken up into the
divine life: "Those, then, are the perfect, who have had the Spirit of God
remaining in them, and have preserved their souls and bodies blameless,
holding fast the faith of God, that is, that faith which is [directed] towards
God, and maintaining righteous dealings with respect to their
neighbours."[158]

This notion of moral and spiritual progress closely follows Paul's admo-
nition to "by the Spirit . . . put to death the misdeeds of the body" (Rom
8:12-14). Patristic theologians did not think that Paul encouraged some
form of dualism with this statement. Rather, in light of Paul's additional
remark about the Holy Spirit's presence with the Christian as deposit of
the future immortal life, they thought he talked about the present beginnings of the future perfect human being.[159] We find no opposition to reason in this theology of Spirit. On the contrary, the presence of the Spirit
enables human being, or the "spiritual being," to walk according to the
light of reason (Logos); "spiritual" human being does not indicate the
flight of the soul from some corporeal prison or the world, but "the union
of flesh and the spirit of God," and the ascent of the whole being (body,
soul, and spirit) to the full image and likeness of God.[160]

The Christian life is thus seen as a transformative enterprise in which
no experience is lost, but by "putting on the new humanity," this life anticipates already the recapitulation of all things in Christ. The new human
being, with its animal nature now infused with the Spirit of life, is en-

[158]Ibid. For the contours of this "divine paedagogy," see also J. L. Kovacs, "Divine Pedagogy and
the Gnostic Teacher According to Clement of Alexandria," *Journal of Early Christian Studies*
9, no. 1 (2001).
[159]Irenaeus, *Against Heresies* 5.7.1, p. 533.
[160]"And again, those persons who are not bringing forth the fruits of righteousness, and are, as
it were, covered over and lost among brambles, if they use diligence, and receive the word of
God as a graft, arrive at the pristine nature of human being—that which was created after the
image and likeness of God" (ibid., 5.10.1, p. 536).

gaged in the vivifying of body and soul through moral exertion with the Spirit's help until only the new human being remains in the kingdom of God after the final resurrection.[161] Patristic humanists like Irenaeus thus emphasize the continuity between this life and the life to come, in part because they see a much deeper continuity of nature and grace between this world and the next than some modern theologies are often willing to grant. Irenaeus's main categories for describing the Christian existence are "life" and "true humanity," offered to all in the dynamic of exchange inaugurated by the incarnation through which God brings to perfection "His handiwork, confirmed and incorporated with His Son."[162]

The destiny of human being is, to use another patristic term, assimilation to God, the training of reason, emotions and conduct to reflect the perfect humanity of Christ. Far from disparaging reason, this view adopted and transformed the Platonic (and Stoic) idea of subordinating the passions to reason. Clement, for example, transforms Plato's famous chariot analogy for the rational person[163] to a Christian version of self-control; reason as the governing principle or "pilot" of the soul is the human's participation in the divine Logos by faith.[164] Asserting the fulfillment of Greek philosophy's desire for knowledge in Christ, Clement claims that true philosophy and true *gnosis* are the results of deification *already at work* in the Christian. The goal of this participation is assimilation to God, which, on account of God's love for humanity, should result in the pursuit of the personal, but also of the common, good. Right reasoning, as be-

---

[161]Ibid., 5.35.2, p. 566.

[162]Ibid., 5.36.3, p. 567.

[163]See Plato, *Phaedrus* 246a-254e. In order to explain the inner conflict between reason and passion, Plato describes the soul as "a team of winged steeds and their winged charioteer" (246a). Reason is "the soul's pilot" (247c), whose progress toward union with the beautiful (and hence with virtues) is hindered by the discord between the "steed of wickedness, who wants to pull down the chariot toward earthly things (247b), and the willing steed of rational love, of "temperance and modesty" (253d). When this uneven team is disciplined and balanced, allowing the philosopher to draw near the divine but not in irrational intoxication, then "the higher elements of the mind" become the guide "into the ordered rule of the philosophical life." The days of those who attain this way of life "will be blessed with happiness and concord, for the power of evil in the soul has been subjected, and the power of goodness liberated; they have won self-mastery and inner peace" (256a-b).

[164]"Our knowledge, and our spiritual garden, is the Saviour himself into whom we are planted, being transferred and transplanted, from our old life, into the good land. And transplanting contributes to fruitfulness. The Lord, then, into whom we have been transplanted, is the Light and the true knowledge" (Clement, *Stromata* 6.1, p. 480).

comes clear from the following citation, is always ethical, and self-control is ultimately for the benefit of society:

> He is the [true] Gnostic, who is after the image and likeness of God, who imitates God as far as possible, deficient in none of the things which contribute to the likeness as far as compatible, practicing self-restraint and endurance, living righteously, reigning over the passions, bestowing of what he has as far as possible, and doing good both by word and deed. "He is the greatest," it is said, "in the kingdom who shall do and teach;" imitating God in conferring like benefits. For God's gifts are for the common good.[165]

God's gifts are for the common good! These words capture the cross-shaped result of deification: love of God and love of fellow human beings. All this is not divorced from reason but flows from participation in the divine Word, the creating and sustaining power of the cosmos. Jesus the Christ is the embodiment of the divine Logos, the perfect, physically embodied interpretation of the divine *nous*, of the mind of God. The incarnation prevents Christian contemplation of the divine reason from lapsing into the passive quietism of pagan mystery religions and philosophical wisdom schools. On account of the incarnation, the restoration of one's being encompasses far more than the salvation of one's soul or spiritual reorientation. Early Christian theology speaks of God's bodily involvement with the world for the purpose of liberating creation and humankind, enabling the latter's ascent to full humanity in the likeness of God. Without this initial impulse to view salvation as becoming fully human, a process already beginning in *this* world, the enthusiasm of Christian humanism for this world, such as the later enthusiasm of scholasticism for the unity of knowledge, remains incomprehensible. Patristic humanism's wide conception of rationality provides the basic foundations for the kind of faith in an intelligible world, in human dignity and human progress that characterized Christian humanism and enabled a culture marked by its unique passion for reason, science and education.

In light of modern discussions concerning faith and reason, some fathers furnish surprisingly sophisticated philosophical arguments for the dependence of reason on faith. As I outlined in chapter one, modern hermeneutic philosophy has reintroduced a notion that, albeit in a different

---

[165]Ibid., 2.19, p. 369.

historical context, was already known to Christian humanists: all reasoning requires faith. Naturalism and rationalism, the two primary sources for denying an interpretive dynamic of truth, are not new. They have ancient philosophical roots in atomist and Stoic philosophies, and Clement's contention about the basic faith structure of all human knowledge anticipates certain elements of modern hermeneutic philosophy, which also combat modern forms of rationalism. From Plato and Epicurus, Clement learned that what modern philosophy calls "fore-understanding" is basic to all human knowing. He concludes, "If, then, faith is nothing else than a preconception of the mind in regard to what is the subject of discourse, and obedience is so called, and understanding and persuasion; no one shall learn aught without faith, since no one [learns aught] without pre-conception." Hence all knowledge conforms to the biblical dictum "unless ye believe, neither will ye understand."[166]

Faith in this primary, "nonreligious" sense is necessary for knowledge in the proper sense of understanding something. There is, Clement concedes, also a kind of knowledge bereft of understanding, namely, "the knowledge of individual objects, in which not only the rational powers, but equally the irrational share." Yet apprehension is not actual knowledge, for "that which *par excellence* is termed knowledge, bears the impress of judgment and reason."[167] Judgment and reason, therefore, require *understanding*, that is, an integration of information into an interpretive framework that itself forms a set of convictions or "first principles" that are themselves incapable of verification by empirical proof. Such first principles "are incapable of demonstration; for they are known neither by art nor sagacity."[168] Knowledge of facts, argues Clement, can be established by simple demonstration. But the higher form of knowledge as understanding is "faith," that is, the integration of facts into a preconceived framework of meaning. He rightly insists that meaning only comes about when material facts are interpreted in light of that which is itself "indemonstrable" and nonmaterial.[169] Clement, in other words, already knows about the mediation of truth; he asserts what philosophical hermeneutics, beginning with Heidegger, have carried

---

[166]Ibid., 2.4, p. 351.
[167]Ibid., 4.1, p. 480.
[168]Ibid., 2.4, p. 350.
[169]Ibid.

forward from Greek thinking into our time: faith is "a preconception of the mind," and "without preconception, no one can either inquire, or doubt, or judge, or even argue. How can one without a preconceived idea of what he is aiming after, learn about that which is the subject of his investigation?"[170]

According to Clement, faith, not yet understood as *religious* faith but as tacitly held preconceptions, is also intrinsic to education; for learning, after all, requires skill not only from the teacher but also from the student:

> As then, playing at ball not only depends on one throwing the ball skillfully, but it requires besides one to catch it dexterously, that the game may be gone through according to the rules for ball; so also is it the case that teaching is reliable when faith on the part of those who hear, being, so to speak, a sort of natural art, contributes to the process of learning. . . . For there is no good of the very best instruction without the exercise of the receptive faculty on the part of the learner.[171]

A learner's receptivity to what is taught, in other words, depends on his or her *faith*, however feeble, in the basic plausibility of the teacher's material. For Clement this analogy to learning shows that faith, as intrinsic to human knowing, is inseparably connected to free choice and to hope. For faith is "the voluntary supposition and anticipation of pre-comprehension," expressing confidence in the truth of the received information, and expectation (i.e., hope) of its future value, "the expectation of the possession of the good."[172]

Because Clement structures human knowledge on faith and free choice, he demonstrates not only that belief is reasonable but that the fiduciary structure of knowledge points to the divine. Religious faith is merely a higher form of what all understanding requires. Faith is not something "simple and vulgar," only for the weak, but since it is ubiquitous, Clement

---

[170]Ibid., 2.5, p. 351.

[171]Ibid., 2.6, p. 353. I note in passing Clement's use of the ballgame analogy for learning through entering the play of interpretation, a comparison that returns in Ranier Maria Rilke and Hans-Georg Gadamer. Gadamer cites Rilke's poem on play at the beginning of *Truth and Method*, trans. Joel Weinsheimer and Donald G. Marshall, 2nd rev. ed. (London: Continuum, 2004), p. v (hereafter all shortened citations will use the abbreviation TM); see also Gadamer's use of the ballgame in *Die Aktualität des Schönen: Kunst als Spiel, Symbol u. Fest* (Stuttgart: Reclam, 1977), pp. 23-24.

[172]Clement, *Stromata* 2.6, p. 353. Anticipation of completeness remains an important hermeneutical element in Gadamer's hermeneutic philosophy.

affirms that faith, "whether founded in love or in fear, . . . is something divine."[173]

Clement ties his observations about an essentially hermeneutic episte-mology to the humanistic theme of self-understanding. Philosophy, in opening the self toward transcendence, embodies and rightly focuses the human quest for self-knowledge: "It is, then, as appears, the greatest of all lessons to know one's self."[174] Self-knowledge, of course, also depends on faith in basic principles, for, as Clement already knows, understanding moves in an interpretive circle: "it is not possible to know the parts without the essence of the whole."[175] For Clement, this hermeneutic circle requires understanding the purpose of human existence in the light of a holistic cosmology within which human existence finds its particular meaning. For without a theory concerning the genesis of the universe and humans' role in it, self-knowledge is impossible.[176]

The origin, destiny and meaning of the cosmos are determined, how-ever, by the particular event of the incarnation. Truly meaningful knowl-edge of the world thus begins with faith, that is, with participation in the divine life through Christ. The incarnation as the embodiment of divine wisdom is therefore the fulfilment of every other philosophy. The quest for truth and careful reasoning is the essence of philosophy, wherefore philosophy is "a preparatory discipline" to religious belief, not, however, as a handmaiden, but as the guardian of general truth. "Hellenic philosophy does not," argues Clement, "by its approach make the [Christian] truth more powerful," for the Christian faith cannot be deduced from philoso-phy, nor do its essential truths depend on it. Yet Greek philosophy in its pursuit of knowing truth and the good, at its best, renders "powerless the assault of sophistry against truth," and thus "is said to be the proper 'fence and wall of the vineyard.'"[177] Clement, of course, sees in all of this God's providential hand: "The Greek preparatory culture" already pointed to

---

[173]Ibid., 2.6, p. 354.

[174]Clearly Clement draws here on the Platonic notion of self-knowledge as found in Socrates and Plotinus, which already combined self-knowledge with *phronēsis* and tied both self-under-standing and wisdom to the knowledge of the divine. See the chapter titled "The Delphic Commandment as Philosophical Propaedeutic," in Gerald J. P. O'Daly, *Platonism Pagan and Christian: Studies in Plotinus and Augustine* (Surrey: Ashgate, 2001), p. 11.

[175]Clement, *Stromata* 1.14, p. 314.

[176]Ibid.

[177]Ibid., 1.20, p. 323.

divine truths Christ was to reveal more fully. The early theologians' belief that Jesus was the embodiment of God himself, the very Word that
had created and still sustained all things, emboldened them to make "a
supersessionary claim in relation to all of culture."[178] This audacious
"take-over bid" by Christianity was fueled by the conviction that Christ
most fully revealed the best of what ancient wisdom had to say about a
transcendent everlasting good and the way to attain it.[179] As the historian
Jean Daniélou explains,

> for Justin [Martyr] and Clement of Alexandria alike there is but one truth,
> revealed in the beginning, preserved in Judaism and grossly obscured else-
> where, and finally manifested in its fullness in Christ. It is on this basis that
> they claim the right to appeal to the sages of Greece, and to the philoso-
> phers who were their legatees, for those portions of the truth which they
> have preserved.[180]

Seen in this light, Plato was no more than a "Moses speaking in attic
Greek."[181] It is ironic that while today the church fathers are accused of
Hellenizing Christianity, they themselves held that Plato had learned
from the Hebrews and that Christianity was the actual true heir and com-
pletion of Moses' teaching.[182] Early Christian theologians interpreted
Christianity in direct opposition to many Enlightenment and Post-
Enlightenment thinkers. Enlightenment philosophy has bequeathed to

---

[178]Francis Young, *Biblical Exegesis and the Formation of Christian Culture*, p. 49. What is little
known, however, is that this claim, to which belongs the common assertion among the fathers
that Plato's greatest insights derived from his reading of Moses, employs a strategy that was
common among intellectual writers in the culture wars of antiquity. By common consensus,
innovations were bad and evoking ancient traditions was good. Thus the Christian argument
that Plato's greatest insights derived from his reading of Moses was not so much an appeal to
new revelation, but to an ancient wisdom known to ages long before Plato. Christians claimed
that Moses was the more ancient representative of a "primitive, unitive wisdom known to
ancient Brahmans, Jews, Magi and Egyptians which Plato had learned from them" (ibid., p.
53). The point was that Platonism was newer and thus less trustworthy than the Scriptures,
and that this ancient wisdom had become most fully known in Christianity. Jean Daniélou
confirms that early Christian writers aimed "to show that, though Plato echoes an earlier
tradition, it is in a distorted form, and that the authentic version is that given by Moses" (*A
History of Early Christian Doctrine*, vol. 2, *Gospel Message and Hellenistic Culture* [Philadelphia:
Westminster Press, 1973], p. 113).
[179]Ibid., 1.17, p. 318.
[180]Daniélou, *Gospel Message and Hellenistic Culture*, p. 134.
[181]Clement of Alexandria, quoting the Pythagorean philosopher Numenius in *Stromata* 1.22,
2:334.
[182]Ibid., 1.27, p. 340, "It is He [the Savior] who truly shows us how we are to know ourselves."

the European consciousness the powerful image of religious faith as an infantile stage of human development, so that any suggested return of religion must necessarily be a regress to more primitive superstition. Early Christianity, however, operated on the opposite assumption. Greek and Roman philosophy at their best were merely fragmented insights into the truth of human existence that were more fully expressed in Judaism and Christianity. The Old and New Testaments were the two principal "phases in the education of mankind,"[183] one looking forward to the incarnation and the other unfolding the implications of humanity's recapitulation in Jesus the Messiah. Humanity and human progress are measured by the Christ event, and any other view of humanity, at least in the fathers' eyes, regresses from this apex.

According to this view, Greek philosophy lacked the moral strength of the gospel, but still prepared the way for its teachings by attuning the mind to the reception of God's revealed truth.[184] Given this preparatory role of philosophy, Clement picks up the Platonic idea of assimilation to the divine forms and claims to find in Paul's theology the common goal of philosophy and faith: "Assimilation to God, so that as far as possible a man becomes righteous and holy with wisdom, [Paul] lays down as the aim of faith."[185] The theme of becoming godlike has a long history in Greek stoicism and Platonic philosophy. Already in Plato there are strong ethical connotations to this idea, and assimilation to the forms or the good beyond being is not merely an escape from this world, but also entails benefiting one's neighbor.[186] Yet, characteristically, Clement's notion of deification derives its content from the biblical idea of a personal God and his incarnation.

---

[183]Daniélou, *Gospel Message and Hellenistic Culture*, p. 170.

[184]Ibid.

[185]Ibid., 2.22, p. 377. Clement refers to Plato's doctrine of assimilation in various places. For example: "Now Plato, the philosopher, defining the end of happiness, says that it is likeness to God as far as possible" (ibid., 2.19, p. 369). The logic of assimilation follows the conviction that knowledge entails the participation of the object in the subject, and that such participation is achieved to the highest degree in the Christian's union with God (even though such union does not entail the actual comprehension of God). Clement cites Plato's *Timaeus:* "You must necessarily assimilate that which perceives to that which is perceived, according to its original nature; and it is by so assimilating it that you attain to the end of the highest life possible by the gods to men, for the present or the future time" (ibid., 5.14, p. 467).

[186]For a fuller analysis of and possible influences of Platonic conceptions about man as divine image and of deification on the apostle Paul, see Georg H. VanKooten, *Paul's Anthropology in Context*, Wissenschaftliche Untersuchungen zum Neuen Testament 23 (Tübingen: Morh Siebeck, 2003), pp. 93ff.

The difference, of course, is that in the "true philosophy communicated by the Son" assimilation is not to impersonal forms but to the likeness of God as revealed in the person of Christ. The restoration of humanity consists in participation in the divine Logos, ordering the self toward God and others. Already striking a note we will hear again in Renaissance humanism, Clement argues that self-restraint and control of one's passions are major goals of the new humanity. Salvation—and Clement is merely one example of this general tendency in patristic theology—is not merely the salvation of an individual soul but the restoration of the soul to life and a reincorporation into God's restored creation.

The best analogy Clement can find for this humanist faith is a musical one he takes from the Psalms.[187] The incarnation, the Word incarnate, is like a "new song," the manifestation of the Word that was in the beginning and before the beginning, by whose becoming human our full humanity is restored: "Behold, the might of the new song! It has made men out of stones, men out of beasts. Those, moreover, that were as dead, not being partakers of the true life, have come to life again, simply by becoming listeners of this song."[188]

The fruits of reason: Education as transformative participation in the divine Word. Within early Christian theology's remarkable portrayal of a participatory, incarnational and humanistic theology, education takes on a central role.[189] Clement's musical analogy of "the new song" captures the cosmic nature of the patristic vision of the transformative power of participation in the divine Word. For Christ, the new song, "has also composed the universe into melodious order, and tuned the discord of the elements to harmonious arrangement, so that the whole world might become harmony."[190] The human being is this universe "in miniature," now once again attuned to the divine Logos, to the Word. God had created the human being as "a beautiful breathing instrument of music, after his own image." The Word through whom all things were created now calls "the rational creatures of the Word of God" into participation with this "original harmony."[191] The Christian life is training for an eternal vocation

---

[187]Ps 33; Ps 40; this choice indicates once more the christological hermeneutic of the fathers.
[188]Clement, *Exhortation to the Heathen*, chap. 1, p. 174.
[189]Ibid.
[190]Ibid., chap.1, p. 173.
[191]Ibid., chap.1, p. 172.

through education by God himself. Since God himself has now appeared as man, Christians by him are "taught to live well" and "sent on our way to life eternal."[192] God, to take up a previous citation, "became man that [we may] learn from man how to become God."[193]

Education is thus defined by early Christian writers as assimilation to God, a process initiated by God's gift of life and energized by the indwelling of the Holy Spirit, but nevertheless a process that requires cooperation with the divine Spirit for a truly human life. For the church fathers, a truly human life was one in which both body and spirit controlled the passions, not just by repressing them but also by orienting them in light of God's love for humanity. Indeed, we will misunderstand patristic talk about "sinful passions" unless we regard them within the greater context of the *imago Dei* theology we discussed earlier. Human reason is an important part of the divine image in us because free choice reflects divine sovereignty. In contrast to the pagan understanding of fate, patristic anthropology insists on genuine freedom of choice to shape one's destiny. Internally, at least, in our moral choices, we are "free from necessity and not bound by any natural power, but have decision in our own power as we please."[194] God has endowed the human being as the image of God with reason and will. Christian education is to exercise this will with God's help, in order to regain the likeness of God. As Gregory of Nyssa put it, "purity, freedom from passion, blessedness, alienation from all evil, and all those attributes of the similar kind that help to form in men the likeness of God: with such hues as these did the Maker of His own image mark our nature."[195] Patristic anthropology does not consider matter or passions evil.[196] Patristic statements on the passions have to be taken in the context of humanity's original angelic destination. Even when someone like Gregory of Nyssa states that the image of God in Adam before

---

[192]Ibid., chap. 1, pp. 172-73.

[193]Ibid., chap. 1, p. 174.

[194]Gregory of Nyssa, "On the Making of Man," in *Gregory of Nyssa: Dogmatic Treatises*, vol. 5 of *Nicene and Post-Nicene Fathers*, Second Series, ed. Philip Schaff and Henry Wace, trans. William Moore and Henry Austin Wilson (Peabody, Mass.: Hendrickson, 1994), p. 405.

[195]Ibid., p. 391.

[196]The patristic scholar John Behr concurs that for the fathers, "the sinfulness of the passions does not lie in the materiality of the body but in the manner in which the mind uses and abuses the body, its impulses and appetites" (*The Mystery of Christ: Life in Death* [Crestwood, N.Y.: St. Vladimir's Seminary Press, 2006], p. 162).

the Fall in his "archetypal beauty" was "without passion in his nature," he is not sliding back into some Greek notion of blessedness as passivity of soul, as *apatheia*. How can this be, when the fundamental relation of God in himself, of God to mankind, and of mankind to God is one of *love*? Rather, the passions are equated with anything that pulls against the human destiny of becoming like God. Not passion but misdirected passions are the problem, enslaving passions[197] that indulge "self-love," rather than yearn "for God alone."[198] The Christian life is training in virtue toward the goal of being Christlike.[199]

The Christian life is education in love of God, through the pursuit of virtues that heal the fallen nature and aid its restoration to angelic life.[200] This exercise in Christlikeness through the self's turning away from its self-centeredness toward God was thought to include, by definition, love of neighbor. It is important to realize that human freedom, reason and human progress were thus framed within the context of human solidarity. Human thinking and acting become Logos-centric in the patristic *paideia*. The purpose of education is to complete the inborn image of God, our natural abilities of reflection and knowledge, by attaining Godlikeness: "as you have that which is according to the image through your being rational, you come to be according to the likeness by undertaking kindness."[201] Indeed, so natural is the intrinsic connection of freedom, reason and deification in patristic humanism that it defines Christianity. Basil of Caesarea asks "What is Christianity?" and answers "Likeness to God as far as is possible for human nature."[202] Basil advances the same theological argument for deification as Irenaeus does by interpreting Genesis 1:26 ("Let us

---

[197]Gregory of Nyssa, "On the Making of Man," p. 403.

[198]Maximus the Confessor, "Letter 2: On Love," in *Maximus the Confessor*, ed. Andrew Louth, Early Church Fathers (London: Routledge, 1996), p. 87.

[199]Gregory of Nyssa, "On the Making of Man," p. 405.

[200]Gregory of Nyssa speculates that God, in foreseeing the Fall, created man as "the mean between Divine and incorporeal nature, and the irrational life of brutes," and included gender to ensure the reproduction of human beings after the Fall (ibid.). Gregory's point is easily misunderstood if one neglects his exegetical starting point in Christ's revelation that in the new creation, human beings, like angels, will no longer be defined by sexual relations (ibid., p. 407). He does make clear, however, that this is not doctrine but "theoretical speculation" (ibid., p. 406).

[201]Basil the Great, *On the Human Condition* 1.17, trans. Nonna Verna Harrison, Popular Patristics Series (Crestwood, N.Y.: St. Vladimir's Seminary Press, 2005), p. 45.

[202]Ibid.

make man in our image, in our likeness") to mean that the image of God entails the endowment of reason and relationality, but it is by our free will in the pursuit of divine virtues that we pursue the "likeness of God."[203] Christians, by God's power, are "artisans of the likeness to God," whose work is to love humanity as God did in Christ: "If you are brother-loving and compassionate, you are like God." Christian education is thus apprenticeship in the craft of true humanity, for this is what the creation story in Genesis indicated: true humanity is "an education in human life,"[204] according to the image of God in Christ. The disciplining of one's passions and moral conduct toward a perfect humanity had far-reaching consequences for Western culture. Today, the only way to address the crisis of Western educational institutions from the ground up is to return to this fundamental insight of incarnational anthropology: Deification, becoming truly human by pursuing Godlikeness, laid the foundation for the Western ideal of education as character formation.

Western intellectuals have largely forgotten these Christian roots for the ideal of education as character formation, which remained the main goal of humanistic or liberal arts education well into the twentieth century. The church father Augustine is a key figure in this process and represents many of its main elements.[205] Augustine, whose writings have decisively shaped the curriculum of what we now call the liberal arts, described the Christian life as the training of one's soul and body in the service of God, a process meant to reverse the effects of the Fall, a striving to fit ourselves for the "fellowship of angels."[206] The task for those who are in Christ is thus to reshape the image of God: "the image," says Augustine, "now needs to be refashioned and brought to perfection, so as to become close to him in resemblance."[207] On account of the Fall, the body and passions tend to control the soul and the will rather than the other way around. "Becoming like God," for Augustine, entails regaining true freedom from slavery to one's

---

[203]Ibid., 1.16, p. 43.
[204]Ibid., 1.17, p. 44.
[205]Cochrane, *Christianity and Classical Culture*, p. 399.
[206]Augustine, *City of God* 5.20, p. 214. Many other passages also attest to the idea of moral progress in deification: "For in the individual man, as I have said, the base condition comes first, and we have to start with that; but we are not bound to stop at that, and later comes the noble state towards which we may make progress, and in which we may abide, when we have arrived at it" (ibid., 15.1, p. 596).
[207]Ibid., 11.26, p. 459.

lower instincts through the right ordering of body, soul, mind and will in light of God's love.[208] Education in the right order of love for the purpose of deification is thus the main impulse behind Augustine's famous distinction between enjoyment and use (*uti et frui*).[209] Education is training in Christian virtue defined as prioritizing one's entire life in light of God's love. Everything in creation, Augustine argues, is good, but we love things in the right way when we subordinate their use to our love for God. This "proper order" of love becomes especially difficult in the case of items that truly deserve our love. Augustine insists that this proper order must be kept so "that there may be in us the virtue which is the condition of the good life. Hence, for Augustine, a brief and true definition of virtue is 'rightly ordered love.'"[210] Education, in a sense, is remedial, reversing the effects of sin. Love of God and love of neighbor are the basic goals of education in *agapē*, to which our passions and material enjoyment ought to be subordinate.

Augustine's foundational and immensely influential treatise on education, *De Doctrina Christiana*, is a guide on how to learn the truths of Christianity from Scripture and also a manual for teaching these truths to others.[211] Yet what are these teachings but a call toward the same kind of artisanship in humanity Basil called for? After all, the sum of the Scriptures is love of God and neighbor.[212] The book is really about faith, hope and charity, that is, about an education in Godlikeness. Faith is the beginning of this "arduous journey,"[213] hope sustains it, and the result is love of God and neighbor, a hermeneutic of charity.[214] Augustine's lessons retained their influence all the way into Renaissance humanism. Erasmus, for example, passes on this very advice of rightly ordered love to his friend, a successful industrialist and merchant:

You love the arts and sciences. That is good if you do so because of Christ. If you love them, however, for knowledge's sake, then you stop where one

[208] Augustine, *De Doctrina Christiana: Teaching Christianity*, ed. John E. Rotelle, trans. Edmund Hill, Works of Saint Augustine: A Translation for the 21st Century (New York: New City Press, 1990), pp. 117-19.
[209] See also Augustine's highly influential "right order of love," with its distinction between use and enjoyment of things in *De Doctrina Christiana* 1.26-40, pp. 117-26.
[210] Augustine, *City of God* 15.22, pp. 636-37.
[211] Mario Naldini, introduction to Augustine, *De Doctrina Christiana*, p. 12.
[212] Augustine, *De Doctrina Christiana* 1.35, p. 123.
[213] Ibid., 1.34, p. 123.
[214] Ibid., 14.22-15.23, pp. 178-79.

should proceed. But if you desire the arts and sciences, because they help you to see Christ more clearly, who is hidden in the mysteries of the holy scriptures, and if you want to enjoy your love and knowledge of Christ and share it with others, so prepare for studying them. But only pursue these studies to the extent that they further, in good conscience and to your knowledge, a good attitude (*bonum mentem*). . . . [I]t is better to know less and to love more than to know much and not love.[215]

The Augustinian *uti et frui* distinction between love and enjoyment is not at all a hindrance to fully enjoying friendships, nor does it undermine human solidarity, but actually protects it by anchoring intrahuman love to its transcendent source and model. Within incarnational theology it makes no sense whatsoever to oppose God as the goal of human devotion to the love of family and neighbor. Rather, the formula is as follows: the more you love God, the more you love others. For the supreme reward, as Augustine put it, is that "we should enjoy Him and that all of us who enjoy Him should also enjoy one another in Him."[216]

The foundation of a common humanity. From its beginnings in the New Testament, Christian humanism expressed a fundamental ontological unity of all human beings in the divine Logos become flesh. Stoic philosophy already knew about the connection of all human beings through a universal, immanent logos.[217] Platonic philosophy countered this cosmic monism with the archetypical form of human being, a spiritual ideal which, however, cannot give full value to the physical body. Christian anthropology, by contrast, affirms both human physical nature and transcendent spirit by establishing human nature christologically. The apostle Paul has set the pattern for this Christian anthropology; the two reference points are Adam and Christ: "From the first earthy man has sprung a multiplicity of earthy beings, all bearing the physical mortal characteristics of the ancestor," and in Christ, the second Adam, humanity has been renewed and the destiny of this perfect humanity is revealed.[218] In the incarnation, with its unique union of human and divine, of the particular and the transcendent, of

[215]See Desiderius Erasmus, "Enchiridion militis Christiani," in *Ausgewählte Schriften*, ed. Werner Welzig (Darmstadt: Wissenschaftliche Buchgellschaft, 1967-80), 1:173.

[216]Augustine, *De Doctrina Christiana*, pp. 122-23.

[217]Colish, *Stoicism in Classical Latin Literature*, pp. 23-27.

[218]C. K. Barrett, *Paul: An Introduction to His Thought* (Louisville, Ky.: Westminster/John Knox Press, 1994), pp. 12-13.

the historical and the eternal, of the cultural ethnic and the collective human race, a common humanity becomes possible.[219] For in Christ every person attains an individual identity grounded in personal transcendence, but is also linked to humanity as a whole. And yet, following the mystery of incarnation and Trinity, this totality does not compromise individuality.

For the first time in Occidental philosophy, a proper correlation of a common humanity *and* individuality is introduced by what the twentieth-century French Catholic theologian Henri de Lubac called the "all embracing humanism" of the fathers' incarnational theology. The idea of individual personhood began with the theological reflections of the Nicene Creed, that is, with the trinitarian controversies of the fourth and fifth centuries, and the notion of a common humanity united in a transcendent source likewise originates in trinitarian theology. Lubac argues that the incarnation first made the concept of a common humanity possible by the paradoxical affirmation of the person and humanity as a whole. Christology thus resolves the opposition of individual and collective. The individual exists only in the context of humanity as a whole, which is itself united and defined by the transcendent God in his unique humanity as the God-man Jesus the Christ. Thus, any human interpretation of our common humanity is itself always relativized by the ideal human being, the incarnate Word. This simultaneous affirmation of individual and collective offers a possible answer to the ethical dilemma of postmodern thought expressed in the work of Levinas and Derrida: how to protect uniqueness against totalizing sameness and yet retain a common humanity.

The incarnation and our consequent union with the personal, triune God combine the "know yourself" of Greek philosophy with "you are known by God," and incorporate the individual into humanity unified in Christ. The participation grants the individual a personal depth of the self hitherto impossible. The two novelties introduced into philosophy at this point are the "I" and the "I"-as-part-of-a-common-humanity. Lubac writes, "By revealing the Father and by being revealed by him, Christ completes the revelation of man to himself. By taking possession of man, by seizing hold of him, and by penetrating to the very depths of his being, Christ makes man go deep down within himself, there to discover

---

[219]Henri de Lubac, *Catholicism: Christ and the Common Destiny of Man*, trans. Lancelot C. Sheppard and Elizabeth Englund (San Francisco: Ignatius Press, 1988), p. 340.

in a flash regions hitherto unsuspected. It is through Christ that the person reaches maturity, that man emerges definitively from the universe, and becomes conscious of his own being." Here lies the birth of full human dignity, and here, says Lubac, "the wise man's precept 'know thyself' takes on a new meaning. Every man who says 'I' gives utterance to something that is absolute and definitive"[220]—definitive because called and individuated by the absolute, and absolute because incorporated into humanity as affirmed, recapitulated and restored by Christ. As Lubac puts it,

> Henceforth the idea of humanity is born. That image of God, the image of the Word, which the incarnate Word restores and gives back to its glory, is "I myself"; it is also the other, every other. It is that aspect of *me* in which I coincide with every other man, it is the hallmark of our common origin and the summons to our common destiny. It is our very unity in God.[221]

And so for the fathers of the early church, the deepest mystery of our union with the Trinity defines our humanity: "We are fully persons only within the Person of the Son, by whom and with whom we share in the circumincession [mutual co-inhabiting] of the Trinity."[222]

Patristic theology, inspired by the incarnation, transformed the Old Testament notion of *imago Dei* into what Hans Urs von Balthasar has called *Imago Trinitatis*.[223] The notion of ultimate being as a personal, transcendent deity existing in communion profoundly changed philosophical anthropology. The Greek idea of personhood exhausted itself in the definition of person as individual substance of a rational nature. This individual is differentiated from others by its role or *persona*, but not by a personal calling. The uniqueness we moderns associate with the concept of person, "the uniqueness that fully identifies *who* this individual is" beyond mere self-awareness requires more, for "a person is not just a subject, but a subject commissioned with a particular role that gives it its identity."[224] Personal identity, as Lubac puts it, depends on being looked at by another

---

[220]Ibid.

[221]Ibid.

[222]Ibid., p. 342.

[223]Hans Urs von Balthasar, "Person und Geschlecht," in *Homo Creatus Est*, Skizzen zur Theologie 5 (Einsiedeln: Johannes Verlag, 1986), p. 99.

[224]Robert Sokolowski, *Eucharistic Presence: A Study in the Theology of Disclosure* (Washington, D.C.: Catholic University of America Press, 1994), p. 128.

person, for only then does personhood transcend subjectivism in a way that founds a personal identity.[225]

Yet at the same time, vocation or identity cannot merely come from another human being or from the collective as a whole, for this would undermine the subject's personal interiority, his or her sense of transcending social relations. Lubac summarizes the difficulty:

> But we can no more follow the upholders—if there be any—of such personal atomism than we can those who, in reaction against attributing an excessive value to the human person . . . would make the end of the person subordinate to some other, supposedly higher, end: for it is possible to sacrifice the individual to the species or to require of a man the sacrifice of this earthly life for the community, or even for the good of the universe.[226]

As Dostoevsky's Ivan Karamazov already knew, if the stability of God's universe requires that some should be damned, it ought to be rejected.[227] Lubac finds in the theology of the church fathers a spiritual unity of humanity in a personal, trinitarian God, by whom both the individuality and unity of all human beings in God are established without compromising either universal unity or individual personhood: "He creates in man new depths which harmonize him with the 'depths of God,' and he projects man out of himself, right to the very end of the earth; he makes universal and spiritualizes, he personalizes and unifies."[228]

This unity is not an abstract function that can be captured by a proposition or formula, nor is there any prior, deeper foundation for reality. In the trinitarian, communal being of God, this paradoxical unity of individual and humanity *is* ultimate reality and exceeds any conceptual objectification. Christian anthropology is founded on participation in this reality, through the existence of an incarnate Logos. Christologically founded individuality and humanity thus provide a way to imagine a common humanity that avoids the danger of individualism, on the one hand, and totalitarian or monistic concepts that absorb human being into a totality, on the other. Based on the incarnation, the church fathers held that we are

---

[225]Monistic philosophies can argue that the whole transcends the human part, but this transcendence is impersonal and cannot found a personal identity without a transcendent other who also knows and thus forms a connection to all others.

[226]Lubac, *Catholicism*, p. 335.

[227]Fyodor Dostoevsky, *Brothers Karamazov* (New York: Bantam, 1981), p. 307.

[228]Lubac, *Catholicism*, p. 339.

thus fully persons and share in an ontologically real humanity only when we share, through Christ, in the trinitarian communion.

Christianity thus introduces novel concepts of personhood and communion into classical thought. As Hans Urs von Balthasar argues, the incarnation and Christology make a distinctive contribution that has fundamentally shaped our conceptions of what it means to be human:

> The Christian difference begins and ends with the revelation that the eternal God loves the individual human being with unending love, which expresses itself in the fact that he dies the death of redemption (i.e., the death of a sinner) for this loved "Thou" in the form of humanity [*in Menschengestalt*]. Who "I" am is not evident to me from the general *gnosi seauton* and *noverim me*,[229] but from the effect of Christ's deed which tells me two things at once: how valuable I am to God and how far lost from him I had been.[230]

Real knowledge of self as personal identity rather than mere instantiation of a universal archetype is thus a unique Christian gift to Western civilization.[231]

Balthasar suggests that the Christian doctrine of a personal God who is deeply involved with his creation without depending on it has decisively shaped modern conceptions of individuality, sociality and freedom. Christianity's incarnational-trinitarian view of God establishes the social nature of the self and its meaningful participation in a greater "drama of love." Without denying the individual self, Christian anthropology ensures that human relations and love constitute the heart of reality and the deepest meaning of being (*der Ursinn des Seins*). Balthasar concludes that the mystery of the Trinity becomes the inevitable requirement for the existence of the world, that *between* God and world the drama of love is enacted, and that this drama *internally* fulfills the world as encounter of "I" and "Thou." Such an encounter is ontologically impossible without Christianity (and thus involves Christian dogma in its entirety).[232] Only within this frame-

---

[229]Greek for "know yourself" and Latin for "know myself."

[230]Hans Urs von Balthasar, "Krisis: Gott begegen in der heutigen Welt," in *Spiritus Creator,* Skizzen zur Theologie 3 (Einsiedeln: Johannes Verlag, 1967), p. 274.

[231]Once again Augustine is the main influence for this view in the West. He establishes this theme in his *Soliloquies* (2.1), an imagined dialogue with reason, and uses this theme to frame his more intimate dialogue with God in the *Confessions* (see 1.1.1, 10.5.7).

[232]Balthasar, "Krisis," p. 274. Étienne Gilson affirms a similar significance of trinitarian doctrine for the concept of personhood in medieval philosophy: "Indeed almost all that we know of the philosophy of personality is found in the mediaeval thinkers in the questions they de-

work, Balthasar believes, does the value of the individual human dignity remain preserved. The paradox is that while this theological impulse has defined our perception of personhood and human dignity, it remains inaccessible to philosophy without a firm grasp of Christian ontology, which, in turn, depends on the belief in God's love.[233]

As the German philosopher Robert Spaemann has shown, the Christian view of humanity has profoundly shaped Western conceptions of humanity.[234] Doctrines, however, seldom change the face of reality unless they are taught through tangible symbols and social practice. Christian concepts of human solidarity influenced culture because they became enshrined in the sacramental theology and liturgical practices of the church. The Christian sacraments of baptism and the Eucharist, for example, are essentially about entering into and maintaining participation in the new humanity inaugurated by Christ.[235] Since patristic Christology insisted that all of humanity was summed up in the incarnation, ecclesial practice encouraged in Christians a strong sense of solidarity with every human being.

Eucharistic humanism and human solidarity. For the apostle Paul and for his patristic interpreters, the *sanctorum communio*, the church, was "God's redeemed humanity, the new mode of what it meant to be human."[236] As the New Testament insists, the imperative of the gospel meant, above all, the unity of the human race.[237] Paul's theology especially stresses the unity of the human race in Christ because being called into communion with God provides a personal and family identity that supersedes (while not eradicating) national, racial and even gender distinctions (Gal 3:28).[238] The incarnational theology of the church fathers also clearly views the church as the new humanity, as the body of Christ who is also

---

vote to the theology of the Trinity" (*The Spirit of Mediaeval Philosophy* [Notre Dame, Ind.: University of Notre Dame Press, 1991], p. 204).

[233]Balthasar, "Krisis," p. 274.

[234]Robert Spaemann, *Personen: Versuche Über Den Unterschied Zwischen "Etwas" Und "Jemand"* (Stuttgart: Klett-Cotta, 1996), pp. 25-42. Spaemann argues, for example, that "what we call 'person' today, would have remained unnamable without Christian Theology" (ibid., p. 27).

[235]Jean Daniélou, *The Bible and Liturgy* (Notre Dame, Ind.: University of Notre Dame Press, 1956), p. 53: "A whole theology is thus expressed in this symbolism, the theology of the New Adam."

[236]Wright, *Paul*, p. 165.

[237]Ibid.

[238]See also John 11:52 and all of Romans for Paul's vision of nations in God.

Lord over creation. Irenaeus has expressed in his cosmic vision of Christ the basic integration of church and world through the incarnation:

> The Word becoming man, recapitulates all things in Himself, so that just as the Word of God is foremost in things super-celestial, spiritual, and invisible, so also in things visible and corporeal He might have the primacy; and so that, in taking the primacy to Himself, and in constituting Himself the Head of the Church, He might at the proper time draw all things to Himself.[239]

The incarnation as the recapitulation of all of humanity also required early Christian humanists to think through the relation of the new to the old humanity, that is, the relation of church and world. Without question, the church was seen as the place in which the new humanity was trained.

But was not the identification of the supremacy of Christ over all things and of the church as his body a sure recipe for theocracy? At some points in its history the church gave in to this temptation. At other points the church has fallen into the opposite extreme by becoming sectarian, renouncing a common humanity and forming a Christian counterculture. Patristic humanism, however, offers us a more promising conception of what it means to be in and yet not of the world. The early church did not understood itself simply as a self-contained entity in contrast to the world. Rather, the church's self-understanding as the new humanity, and as the body of Christ, included an intrinsic link to humanity as a whole through Christ who had summed up in himself all of humankind.

In the early church of the first four centuries, this important link between the new humanity (comprising the individual and the community), as embodied by the church, and humanity as a whole is often discussed when theologians expound the meaning of the Eucharist. The Eucharist is the central sacrament of the church because it expresses its nature as the restored humanity, the Christian "we" in which everyone's individuality is properly founded and maintained. The Eucharist is the sacramental event by which each local, particular church expresses its nature as a new, united humanity, namely, "to be a gathering of human diversity in Christ, who

---

[239]Irenaeus, *Against Heresies* 3.16.6, pp. 442-43.

reconciles [the church] with the Father and reconciles its members with one another."[240]

A careful study of the eucharistic sermons of the first four centuries makes clear that the common Christian heritage of both Eastern and Western traditions is a *eucharistic humanism*. The central theme of this humanism is humanity's restoration to communion with God, defined as participation, following the Pauline notion of *en Christo*, of being in Christ.[241] This participation in the divine life determines the "new self" of restored humanity as sociality. As Tillard puts it,

> At its source, the Christian way of life is radically, in virtue of God's very self, the absolute negation of any form of self-sufficiency, of any sort of self-absorption. The relationship with the other—this other who is first of all God but God grasped within the unity between brothers and sisters in Christ Jesus—is intrinsic to the Christian way of life. It constitutes it.[242]

The Christian life is thus inherently, in its very "being-in-Christ," ontologically structured as being with and being for others. Already in the New Testament, exhortations concerning the Christian life "insist much more on the glorification of God and the behavior to adopt toward *others* than on an ethics centered on the individual."[243]

It seems that already in the apostle Paul's writings, this intrinsic unity and incarnational solidarity are celebrated and experienced in the Eucharist. Paul criticizes the Corinthian church mainly for perverting a celebration of communion with God and one another by turning this event into an individualistic affair, in which "each one takes his own supper" (1 Cor 11:21 NASB). New Testament scholars suspect that at this central celebration of Christian unity and solidarity, of being one in Christ, social or other hierarchies began to determine the execution of the Communion meal, so that some gorged themselves while others remained hungry.[244] If indeed the meal was regarded as "communion because through it we com-

---

[240]J. M. R. Tillard, *Flesh of the Church, Flesh of Christ: At the Source of the Ecclesiology of Communion,* trans. Madeleine Beaumont (Collegeville, Minn.: Liturgical Press, 2001), p. ix.
[241]Ibid., p. 3.
[242]Ibid.
[243]Ibid., p. 1.
[244]For a discussion of the various options of reading this difficult passage in Paul (1 Cor 11:21-34), see Gordon D. Fee, *The First Epistle to the Corinthians*, New International Commentary on the New Testament (Grand Rapids: Eerdmans, 1987), pp. 539-45.

municate with Christ, both by partaking of his flesh and divinity and by communicating with and being united to one another through it," then violations of this solidarity hurt the very essence of the new humanity and the spiritual equality of its new order.[245] Latin Christianity and Western culture inherited this concept of human solidarity from Augustine, who clearly refers to the living source of participation in the incarnate Logos. In his commentary on Psalm 101, Augustine offers us a representative example of divine communion as participation, which establishes an ontological link not only between the individual and Christ or between Christ and the church, but also between the church and humanity as a whole. Augustine sees the church not as the sum of its baptized members but rather as one body with a common life rooted in communion with God:

> Within Christ's body, let us sing of these things. Christ is singing about them to us. If the head were singing alone, the song would be about the Lord but would not belong to us; but if Christ is a whole, head and body, you must be among his members and cleave to him by faith and hope and charity. Then you are singing in him, and rejoicing in him, just as he labors in you, and thirsts in you, and hungers in you, and endures tribulations in you. He is still dying in you as you have already risen in him.[246]

In early Christian theology, the Christian self was thus socially constituted as participating in the Trinity. And this participation is the central meaning of God's presence in the eucharistic elements. For the early Christians, the Eucharist was an event of fellowship with God through the incarnate and risen Christ, a mystical communion through which the participants were reminded of and reoriented toward their true humanity. The Eastern Church in particular has retained the concept of the Eucharist as "vision" of God's in-breaking kingdom of which Christians already partake. The Eucharist is "a journey of the Church into the dimension of

---

[245]John of Damascus, "Expositions of the Orthodox Faith" 4.13, in *Nicene and Post-Nicene Fathers*, Second Series, vol. 9, *Hilary of Poitiers, John of Damascus*, ed. Alexander Roberts et al. (Peabody, Mass.: Hendrickson, 1994), p. 84, quoted in Tillard, *Flesh of the Church*, pp. 53-54: "Participation is spoken of; for through it we partake of the divinity of Jesus. Communion, too, is spoken of, and it is an actual communion, because through it we have communion with Christ and share in His flesh and His divinity; yea, we have communion and are united with one another through it."

[246]Augustine, *Psalms 99-120*, ed. Boniface Ramsey, trans. Maria Boulding, vol. 5 of *Exposition of the Psalms*, Works of Saint Augustine: A Translation for the 21st Century (New York: New City Press, 1990), pp. 32-33.

the Kingdom," an "ascent to heaven" from whence participants, after entering Christ's presence and receiving a glimpse of the world to come, are sent out into the world as witnesses of God's love.[247]

The sacramental communion with God did not, however, allow separation from the world but, in following God's example, entailed sacrifice in service of the world. Consequently, a crucial element of eucharistic humanism for Western culture is its civic dimension. The universal, indeed cosmic, significance of the incarnation as the assumption of humanity by the divine endows the Christian religion with an intrinsic impulse toward universal solidarity. Participating in God was to participate in a transcendent reality that was essentially relational, communal and charitable, the very foundation of human solidarity. For this reason, Christian humanism argues that solidarity's true inspiration lives first within the body of Christ. After all, if the "real man within us is spiritual, philanthropy is brotherly love to those who participate in the same spirit."[248]

This internal communion of the saints, however, is complemented by an equally intrinsic bond with all of humanity. Participation in Christ does not separate the church from the rest of humanity, because Christ recapitulates humanity as a whole. Without lapsing into a Stoic or Neo-Platonic panentheism, the church fathers could nonetheless affirm that eucharistic participation in the incarnation links the Christian in Christ to all of humanity. At the very heart of the church, in the encounter with the incarnate Word of God through preaching and the Eucharist, the Christian is called to participate in Christ's humanity, which is ontologically structured as *being for* others. The incarnate Logos of Christianity correlates words and deeds, faith and reason, according to the incarnational logic of philanthropy, of love for humanity. Love for the common good is thus also a mark of deification.[249]

---

[247]Alexander Schmemann, *For the Life of the World: Sacraments and Orthodoxy* (Crestwood, N.Y.: St. Vladimir's Seminary Press, 2004), pp. 23-35. For Eastern eucharistic mysticism as vision of God and participation in a new reality, see John Zizioulas, *Communion and Otherness: Further Studies in Personhood and the Church*, ed. Paul McPartland (London: T & T Clark, 2006), pp. 296-98. Zizioulas explains the difference between incarnational humanist and Greek conceptions of friendship: the participant is freed from self-affirmation and from any rational, aesthetic or moral causality to love even the unpleasant "others" (ibid., p. 304).

[248]Clement, *Stromata* 2.9, p. 357.

[249]Clement, *Exhortation to the Heathen*, chap. 2, p. 178. At times Clement restricts philanthropy to Christians (*Stromata* 2.9, p. 357), but in other places links it clearly to the common good of society (ibid., 4.17, p. 429).

In his summary of the first four centuries of Eastern and Western eucharistic theology, J. M. R. Tillard explains that in the church as the new humanity, God's

> salvation through *agapē* and communion is realized in this: in his historical work, the Son assumed *everything* in the human condition (by taking it on himself); at the same time, since the resurrection, he continues to live in his members the human tragedy in all its truth and all its reality. What this means is not a "continued incarnation" but the fulfillment (*teleiōsis*) of the work of the incarnation, in the power of the Spirit.[250]

He concludes that "the church is grafted onto the great pain-ridden body of humankind. And the graft is but a fragment taken from the reconciling power of the cross."[251] According to this theology, the Eucharist models the "melting of individuals into one new human being."[252]

Far from separating church and world, the christological humanism of the church fathers teaches that on account of the central importance of the incarnation, the sacraments and the liturgy form an intrinsic link between church and world. There are not two radically separate cities, the city of God and the city of man; rather, the new humanity presented in Augustine's *Civitas Dei*, this "city of living stones," is connected through the incarnation ontologically with all of humanity. By virtue of this link, the Christian is called to labor for the good of humanity and to suffer with humanity in its common problems, not, however, to create heaven on earth, but to proclaim the new humanity in Christ.[253] Augustine explains this more fully when describing the inhabitants of the City of God, whose good deeds for the commonwealth are sacrificial, for "sacrifice, even though made or offered by a human being, is a divine thing, as those who called it *sacrifice* wanted to show. Hence the one consecrated in the name of God and vowed to God is in himself a sacrifice inasmuch as he 'dies to

---

[250]Tillard, *Flesh of the Church*, p. 54.
[251]Ibid., p. 138.
[252]Benedict XVI, *Die Einheit der Nationen: Eine Vision Der Kirchenväter* (Salzburg, Munich: Pustet, 2005), p. 35.
[253]Tillard writes, "In virtue of its sacrificial nature, the church cannot be [simply] a servant of the world. It is the priest of the love of God in and for the world. Because the Spirit of the Lord Jesus, the priest of God, dwells in it, it offers 'in Christ,' in its life, the sacrifice of humanity to the glory of the Father" (*Flesh of the Church*, p. 133). The church is a living eschatological mystery of union, not, however, an ethical program for global unity and peace (ibid.).

the world' so that he may 'live for God.'"[254] And so participation in God requires the sacrifice of self-control, the disciplining of the body "by temperance" in order to train one's body in the service of the new humanity.[255]

The Christian life, then, is essentially self-sacrificial, for in this other-oriented life consists God's "image of immortal beauty" into which the believer is being transformed.[256] In light of the incarnation and God's redemptive work, celebration of the Eucharist is nothing less than immersing oneself in this other-oriented sense of unity: "This is the sacrifice of Christians, who are 'many, making up one body in Christ.' This is the sacrifice which the Church continually celebrates in the sacrament of the altar, a sacrament well-known to the faithful where it is shown to the Church that she herself is offered in the offering which she presents to God."[257] This theology of participation in the incarnation is a powerful, motivating force toward character formation and care for others. The notion of charity or *agapē* love is not just "a feeling, an attitude of sympathy and affection toward the other, but also . . . the motivation for actions as concrete as the sharing of goods, hospitality, service, mutual forgiveness."[258]

Augustine's description of the Christian life strongly implies that Christians should not be sectarian fundamentalists who draw a clear line between the City of God and non-Christians. God, after all, is concerned with humanity, and the City of God must bear in mind that among the unbelievers "are hidden her future citizens; and when confronted with them she must not think it a fruitless task to bear with their hostility until she find them confessing their faith."[259] And unlike Luther, who infamously lost patience with the Jews for not converting to Christianity fast enough, Augustine advocates a long-range view in which the "two cities are interwoven and intermixed in this era, and await separation at the last judgment."[260]

---

[254]Augustine, *City of God* 10.6, p. 379.
[255]Ibid. Augustine refers here to Rom 12:1: Therefore "I urge you, brothers, in view of God's mercy, to offer your bodies as living sacrifices, holy and pleasing to God—this is your spiritual act of worship."
[256]Augustine, *City of God* 10.6, p. 379.
[257]Ibid.
[258]Tillard, *Flesh of the Church*, p. 24.
[259]Augustine, *City of God* 1.35, p. 46.
[260]Ibid.

CONCLUSION

The theological origins of humanism planted in Western consciousness a profound sense of human dignity, solidarity, freedom and social responsibility based on a reasonable faith. I hope that this brief glimpse at patristic anthropology has been sufficient to justify the label "incarnational humanism" for early Christian theology. Secularists have claimed humanism as a term to indicate the importance and autonomy of the human; Christian critics of this label have disparaged it for the same reason. It should have become clear, however, that the most ecstatic exclamations of humanity's glorious dignity and singular importance stem from patristic humanists. Moreover, a proper notion of human personhood balancing individual integrity and social responsibility also grew on Christian soil. Incarnational theology leaves us with the paradox Augustine fully understood: only by anchoring human dignity in a personal, transcendent and loving source can the true dignity of humanity be upheld against totalizing political or intellectual systems. I have also tried to show that the patristic idea of deification, along with a contingent, yet ordered and stable universe, laid the foundation for education as character formation in Western culture.

3

THE FURTHER DEVELOPMENT
OF CHRISTIAN HUMANISM

◆

This chapter provides a brief overview of the further development of incarnational humanism. I could also simply speak of Christian humanism, since the incarnation will always remain central to any properly Christian humanism. Nonetheless, since the centrality of the incarnation for Christian humanism is often neglected, I continue to use the term *incarnational humanism* to remind us of what makes Christianity intrinsically a humanism: God became man, so that man could become like God, that is, attain to the fullness of divinely ordained humanity as exemplified in Christ. The main purpose of this chapter is to show the *continual* importance of humanism during the next two formative cultural periods: the Middle Ages and the Renaissance. Reading Western culture through the lens of incarnational humanism, with its distinctive emphasis on deification, will force us to abandon a number of familiar clichés about medieval and Renaissance cultures.

Contrary to popular prejudice, medieval scholasticism does not consist merely in irrelevant mental gymnastics that end up undermining both faith and Christian humanism. Rather, Scholasticism is a continuation of Christian humanism, with its own distinct humanistic emphasis on reason and knowledge for the restoration of humanity to its original, divinely mandated greatness. Similarly, Renaissance culture is not simply the Promethean turn toward human autonomy, a kind of protosecularism that extols the independence of human creativity from God. On the contrary, Renaissance philosophy as a whole builds on the Christian ideas of the *imago Dei* and deification. Therefore, Renaissance talk about the greatness of humanity and becoming godlike can be interpreted as faithfulness to prior Christian roots rather than as their subversion.

MEDIEVAL HUMANISM

The essential contribution of medieval humanism to Western culture was its elaboration of the church fathers' view of humanity as God's rational, restorative agent, of the human person as the "uniquely endowed, conscious and co-operating link between the created universe in space and time, and the divine intelligence in eternity."[1] Scholastic humanism, and medieval theology in general, continued the church fathers' emphasis on knowledge and self-understanding as assimilation to God, insofar as faithful reasoning, embedded in the pursuit of a life obedient to the Christian Logos, was thought to approximate, in a fallen world, the image and likeness of God. In other words, the patristic and Neo-Platonic motif of *theosis* and its furtherance by some form of *gnosis* continued in scholastic humanism.

The ideal of scholastic humanism takes up the concept of the restoration of human being to the *imago Dei* from the church fathers by seeking to repair the fragmentation of knowledge occasioned by humanity's fall from divine grace. Scholastics aimed at "restoring to fallen mankind, so far as was possible, that perfect system of knowledge which had been in the possession or within the reach of mankind at the moment of Creation."[2] Within the boundaries of human finitude, scholastic humanists were confident about achieving knowledge for a proper view of God, nature and human conduct sufficient to restore society to as close a resemblance to the original endowment of its first parents as was possible for fallen humankind.[3] They did not believe that everything knowable would be known, but rather that "at least all reasonably obedient and well-disposed members of Christendom would have access to a body of knowledge sufficient for achieving order in this world and blessedness in the world to come."[4]

Besides a basic trust in the intelligibility of the world and in the progress of knowledge that provided the foundation for the Enlightenment,[5]

---

[1]R. W. Southern, *Foundations*, vol. 1 of *Scholastic Humanism and the Unification of Europe* (Oxford: Blackwell, 1995), p. 44.
[2]Ibid., p. 5.
[3]Ibid., p. 10.
[4]Ibid., pp. 5-6.
[5]Edward Grant, *God and Reason in the Middle Ages* (Cambridge: Cambridge University Press, 2001), p. 356.

scholastic humanism also bequeathed to Western culture the basic exegetical character of knowledge acquisition that shaped the liberal arts well
into the nineteenth century.[6] Scholasticism did not strive so much to discover new knowledge as to systematize received knowledge, to clarify, sift,
organize and ready for practical application the body of knowledge already
made available by existing authoritative texts.[7] In this effort, reason and
revelation were seen to work hand in glove. The basic pool of knowledge
to be systematized consisted of two "texts." The first was the prophets and
apostles who had prepared and conveyed the revelation of God: Old Testament prophets, New Testament writers and the church fathers. The second textual resource was the great scholars of pagan antiquity who had
explored the world of human behavior and natural phenomena. From this
abundance of knowledge, the schoolmen sought to produce a single system
of assured and well-ordered knowledge. Such an undertaking required the
aid of every known science.[8]

Like every cultural accretion of the Christian faith, scholastic humanism contains problematic elements. Two of these are especially important for our retrieval of incarnational humanism. The first has to do
with the relation between religion and politics. Scholasticism enor-
mously affected Western culture because it developed an effective administrative method for the organization of a society that was growing
ever more complex. Monastic culture had played a key role in Christianizing European tribes right up to the eleventh century. After pagan Europe had become predominantly Christian, however, religious needs
shifted from Christianizing to organizing society along Christian lines.
Monastic culture and its rituals could no longer adequately serve the
increasing administrative needs of a growing society that sought "doctrinal and disciplinary sources of help."[9] Scholasticism provided trained
experts with the necessary knowledge of Latin, the new universal administrative language, and with argumentative and reasoning skills to
serve as clerks, lawyers and courtly administrators.

The downside of this expansion, however, was an unprecedented

---

[6]"Medieval university education was based upon authoritative texts" (ibid., p. 103).
[7]Southern, *Foundations*, 6.
[8]Ibid., p. 7.
[9]Ibid., p. 140.

strengthening of the church's political power in Europe, especially through the application of the scholastic method to law. The tremendous power of the scholastic humanistic method to organize society and shape culture is evident from the first compendium of canon law, compiled by the Benedictine monk Gratian in the middle of the twelfth century. In combining the theoretical principles and legal procedures of the existing Roman law code with the content of ecclesial canon law, Gratian provided the first basic, universal textbook in response to the growing need for the legal administration of emerging Christendom. This compendium of canon law, however, turned every dispute that involved a breach of orthodox Christian doctrine into a possible subject of legal action. By making the pope the final arbiter in these proceedings, Gratian centralized and enhanced the church's legal authority, mixing political with spiritual power. Gratian's work "did more than any other single instrument to make the papal court the ordinary court of appeal for the whole of western Europe."[10]

A second ambivalent aspect of scholastic humanism was its tremendous trust in the power of reason. Scholasticism inherited and cultivated the patristic synergy of faith and reason based on the incarnation.[11] On the positive side, the Judeo-Christian idea of creation assumes the inherent intelligibility of nature, of a rational universe. The Christian doctrine of the incarnation affirms creation, but even beyond that postulates friendship between the human and the divine; the combination of these teachings had a profound impact on the rational structures of European thinking through "an increasing concentration on the resources within the human mind in progressing towards the knowledge of God. The significance of this for the future lay in its making the exploration of the human mind, and of human nature generally, an integral part of the growth in knowledge."[12]

Based on this incarnational theology, medieval humanism also continued the patristic tradition by viewing the desire to explore human nature as a reflection of God's image.[13] The "image of God," wrote Thomas Aqui-

---

[10]Ibid., p. 309.

[11]Josef Pieper, *Scholasticism: Personalities and Problems of Medieval Philosophy*, trans. Richard Winston and Clara Winston (New York: McGraw-Hill, 1964), p. 150.

[12]Southern, *Foundations*, p. 26.

[13]Gilson comments that "no one can study the medieval texts from this standpoint without

nas, "is found in the soul according as the soul turns to God."[14] The image
of God is not a static possession, but is realized in the pursuit of knowledge
as participation in the creative power of God.[15] Thus, as in patristic anthropology, for medieval humanism the pursuit of self-knowledge remains an
ascent to God and is valid only in this context.[16] Self-knowledge remained
intimately connected to the transcendent, personal God who had become
human and thus allowed and encouraged the progression of thought from
the natural to the supernatural.[17] This progression formed the basic principle not only of monasticism but also of the twelfth-century schools.[18] The
concept of the incarnation as God's reconciliation with creation and his
most intimate fellowship with humanity wove nature, humanity, reason
and religion into a meaningful tapestry of ennobling purpose that was central to medieval theology from the twelfth century onward.[19] These religious developments "brought the universe within the reach of human understanding," but also disclosed God as the "friend of mankind."[20] In the
words of Aquinas, "by willing to become man, God clearly displayed the
immensity of his love for men, so that, henceforth, men might serve God,
no longer out of fear of death, which the first man had scorned, but out of
the love of charity."[21] No other humanism before Christian humanism had
postulated the friendship of God or elevated human dignity to the role of
"co-operators" with God.[22] Assured of God's love, the intelligibility of creation and the trustworthiness of human reason, the scholastics were energized to restore the fullness of knowledge to humankind. Faith and reason
were seen as interdependent aspects of human knowing. Without diminishing the need for grace for the vision of God, Scholastic theologians, on

being struck by the extreme importance attached to the question of self-knowledge." Étienne
Gilson, *The Spirit of Mediaeval Philosophy* (Notre Dame, Ind.: University of Notre Dame
Press, 1991), p. 223.

[14]Thomas Aquinas, *Summa Theologiae* 1.93.9, ed. Thomas Gilby, trans. Jordan Aumann (Cambridge: Cambridge University Press, 2006), p. 500.

[15]Gilson, *Spirit of Mediaeval Philosophy*, p. 205: "To be a person is to participate in one of the
highest excellences of the divine being."

[16]This too reveals the influence of Boethius on medieval thought (ibid., p. 204).

[17]Pieper, *Scholasticism*, pp. 18-19.

[18]Southern, *Foundations*, p. 28.

[19]Ibid., p. 29.

[20]Ibid., p. 30.

[21]Thomas Aquinas, *Shorter Summa: St. Thomas Aquinas's Own Concise Version of His Summa
Theologica*, trans. Cyril Vollert (Manchester, N.H.: Sophia Institute Press, 2002), p. 230.

[22]Gilson, *Spirit of Mediaeval Philosophy*, p. 144.

the whole, did not regard the natural and the supernatural as separate but as interpenetrating aspects of human knowing. This relative congruence of nature and grace constituted "the culmination of scholastic humanism," which recognized the relative autonomy of nature while never forgetting the need for that which is above nature.[23]

Scholasticism's faith in reason was based on the same theological foundation as in patristic teaching. Since the divine Logos was both creator and sustainer of human and cosmic nature, God's relationship to creation could be explored within the limits of fallen human nature. Systematization and belief in the increase of knowledge as part of God's restorative plan for creation provided Western culture's powerful drive for learning and exploration. Indeed, Scholasticism's strong emphasis on reason was institutionalized in Europe's Christian universities and their liberal arts curriculum. Through educating generations in philosophy, logic, theology and law, Christian universities laid the foundation for Western culture during the formative period from around 1100 to 1500, giving birth to "a deep-rooted scientific temperament" within Europe, to which we owe the rise of modern science.[24] Indeed, without scholastic humanism, secular humanism with its belief in the power of human reason could never have developed.[25] Rather than denigrating medieval Scholasticism as irrational obfuscation, secular humanism should especially honor the schoolmen of the twelfth and thirteenth centuries as its direct ancestors.[26] Without abandoning a Christian conception of creation, scholastic humanists opened the door to a world in which objects were no longer mere symbols of the divine but became concrete beings with their own proper natures.[27] One could even say that Scholastic humanism is more truly the

---

[23]Southern, *Foundations*, p. 43. See also Henri de Lubac, who, in *The Mystery of the Supernatural*, shows that the congruence of nature and grace was prevalent in the Middle Ages until the sixteenth century. In contrast to modern philosophy, the idea of "pure nature," was unknown to medieval theologians. Henri de Lubac, *The Mystery of the Supernatural*, trans. Mary Sheed, Milestones in Catholic Theology (New York: Crossroad, 1998), p. 12.

[24]Grant, *God and Reason*, p. 3. Grant explains that "a major feature of the new European society was an extraordinary emphasis on the use of reason to understand the world and to solve problems, both practical and theoretical" (ibid., p. 8).

[25]This is one of Grant's main arguments: "Without the momentous events that unfolded in the Middle Ages, during the period from approximately 1100 to 1500, the seventeenth-century version of the Age of Reason could not have occurred" (ibid., p. 15).

[26]Southern, *Foundations*, p. 18.

[27]Gilson, *Spirit of Mediaeval Philosophy*, p. 101.

progenitor of scientific humanism than of the literary humanism that marked the Renaissance. By recognizing the intrinsic rather than solely sacramental value of nature, Scholastic humanism of the twelfth and thirteenth centuries laid the groundwork for the scientific developments of the nineteenth and twentieth centuries.[28] Indeed, the true beginning of the age of reason, if ever there was one, lies in the Middle Ages, for "the use of reason in a self-conscious manner began in the twelfth century and has continued, without interruption, to the present. The Middle Ages was itself an Age of Reason and marks the real beginning of the intense, self-conscious use of reason in the West."[29]

And yet scholasticism's emphasis on reason was not without its problems. Early on, monastic critics, such as Bernard of Clairvaux (1090-1153), challenged the Scholastic confidence in reason to explain Christian doctrine. Bernard had no time for philosophers, neither for Aristotle nor for the inroads his logic and syllogistic reasoning made into the scholastic expositions of Christianity, because they merely fed idle curiosity and pride.[30] The twentieth-century historian of theology Henri de Lubac, who greatly appreciated Scholasticism and did not easily oppose revelation to reason, provided a more nuanced critique. He argued that Scholastic dialectal reasoning undermined the sacramental ontology with its synthesis of transcendence and immanence on which divine mysteries, and thus the church, depend. Scholastic dialectics were "capable of dissociating a reality that was believed to have been united by those geniuses of ontological symbolism, the Fathers of the church."[31] Yet this danger was only a tendency within Scholastic theology. Lubac shows in numerous citations from Scholastic theologians that medieval masters generally upheld the participatory theology inherited from the church fathers. Like the fathers, these theologians used the language of *imago Dei* and participation to indicate the supernatural end for which humanity was destined from inception. Here the synthesis between reason and faith was fully upheld: "na-

---

[28]Southern, *Foundations*, p. 21.

[29]Grant, *God and Reason*, p. 291.

[30]Étienne Gilson, *Reason and Revelation in the Middle Ages* (New York: Charles Scribner's, 1938), p. 12.

[31]Henri de Lubac, *Corpus Mysticum: The Eucharist and the Church in the Middle Ages: A Historical Survey*, ed. Laurence Paul Hemming and Susan Frank Parsons, trans. Gemma Simonds (Notre Dame, Ind.: University of Notre Dame Press, 2007), p. 226.

ture and the supernatural are thus united, without in any sense being confused."[32] Yet according to Lubac, medieval theology did not always preserve the fullness of the sacramental ontology it inherited from the church fathers. Lubac's concern is specifically Christ's eucharistic presence in the church and the Christian's participation in this presence through the sacraments.

There is, however, no reason to believe that medieval humanism replaced mystery with dry rationality and thus departed essentially from the participatory ontology of patristic humanism. As we can see in the thought of Thomas Aquinas, for example, the theological premise that God was known according to an analogy with being in no way precluded divine mystery and otherness.[33] On the contrary, the analogy of being assumed the radical otherness of God and his mystery. Yet the analogy also allowed for a limited knowledge of God, even while confessing that he exceeds any human comprehension. Aquinas is still able to say that through faith as participation, the believer is "united to Him [God] as to one unknown," and yet rational knowledge of God remains possible, not equivocally (and certainly not univocally) but analogically. So, for example, the term *wise*, while capturing a recognized value, "is not applied in the same aspect to God and to man." The same goes for other terms. Hence no name "is predicated univocally of God and of creatures."[34] Nonetheless, "affirmative propositions" can be made about God as long as it is understood that God himself remains incomprehensible and always exceeds them.[35] The intention behind analogy, in other words, is the preservation of God's incomprehensibility and otherness. Aquinas still echoes the church fathers' insistence that knowledge of God comprises participation in divine reason *and* that human reflection tries to unfold what this participation means. Moreover, meaning is intimately connected with both the intellect *and* conduct; in this way, knowledge of God and self-knowledge are intrinsically ethical, if ethics means not primarily a set of rules but an other-oriented comportment. Understanding is

[32]Lubac, *Mystery of the Supernatural,* pp. 98-99.
[33]The *analogy of being* means simply that since God is unknown in his essence, whatever labels we use to describe him from our human world are at best analogous (rather than univocal) since his divine reality is above our comprehension and itself the measure of all things. Aquinas carefully develops this argument, for example, in *Summa Theologiae* 1.13.4, 5, pp. 59-67.
[34]Ibid., 3.13.6, p. 67.
[35]Ibid., 3.13.12, pp. 74-75.

thus intimately related to wisdom because "to understand is in a certain way to live."[36]

Nonetheless, in some later developments medieval humanism did endanger the balance of faith and reason in two ways. The first is the saturation of revelation with natural philosophy. As the example of Aquinas shows (and numerous others could be mentioned), medieval theologians consciously separated theology and natural philosophy, and they always thought within the boundaries of the Christian faith. At the same time, however, their often bold application of logic and natural philosophy to the deepest mysteries of the Christian faith, such as the Trinity and the Eucharist, eventually had a deadening effect on theology. "Inexorably, . . . theology was transformed into a highly analytical pursuit," which ended up "empt[ying] theology of its spiritual content."[37]

As a result of this tendency, the sacramental worldview inherited from patristic Christianity became threatened, especially in fourteenth-century theological proclivities now summed up under the umbrella of "nominalism." Along with Platonic philosophy, Christianity held to the foundational idea of our participation in a transcendent reality as "an ontological core in which all things share and which intrinsically links them to one another."[38] Without such an ontological synthesis, language, art, poetry, indeed all the human disciplines of knowledge, lose the vital link that makes them truthful expressions of reality.

The breakdown of this medieval synthesis of reason and transcendent reality is complex, and its exact progress is not easily determined. The traditional view is that late medieval nominalists, such as William of Ockham and Gabriel Biel, "attacked metaphysics, ethics, and even scientific methodology, thus undermining and destroying the major achievements of high scholasticism."[39] Nominalism, so the story goes,

---

[36]Ibid., p. 75.
[37]Grant, *God and Reason*, pp. 278-79.
[38]Louis Dupré, *Religion and the Rise of Modern Culture*, Erasmus Institute Books (Notre Dame, Ind.: University of Notre Dame Press, 2008), p. 116.
[39]William J. Courtenay, "Nominalism and Late Medieval Religion," in *The Pursuit of Holiness in Late Medieval and Renaissance Religion; Papers from the University of Michigan Conference*, ed. Charles Trinkaus and Heiko A. Oberman (Leiden: Brill, 1974), p. 27. Courtenay details the traditional account of nominalism as consisting of "(1) atomism, particularism, or individualism; (2) excessive stress on the omnipotence of God; (3) voluntarism; (4) skepticism; and (5) fideism" (ibid.).

initiated the separation of appearance and reality. Formerly, mostly based on the Neo-Platonic ideal of form, phenomena were believed to appear in an orderly and meaningful way on account of the mind's participation in their reality; now nominalism, with its focus on the particular, becomes a kind of medieval structuralism, positing the impossibility of knowing things "in themselves," as Kant put it. It laid the ground, on this view, for empiricism on the one hand and transcendental philosophy on the other. In short, nominalism severed the tie between the knowing mind and external reality. Nominalists believed "that only the individual was real and that common nature was a figment of the imagination. Moreover, logic concerned the interrelation of mental concepts, not external reality, and thus logic was the study of terms . . . rather than things."[40]

It is often claimed that nominalism made science possible because reality was no longer determined by religiously interpreted universals, thus unchaining research from the fetters of theological ideologies. Yet if nominalism as the solvent of metaphysics makes science possible, its secondary implication also poses a problem: without any universals at all, the very idea of patterns and prediction becomes impossible. The metaphysical and theological implications of this separation are equally grim: reason and faith become separated, to be bridged only by irrational fideism.

Far from being mere academic trivia, the issues raised in the nominalist debates directly concern current debates about religion, culture and fundamentalism. Of key importance for this discussion are the nominalist terms *potentia absoluta* and *potentia ordinata*. This distinction between the absolute and ordained powers of God originated in the late eleventh century, and attempted to differentiate between God's ability to act and his desire to act.[41] This definition is often misunderstood to mean that God is not bound by his ordained creation order and could, therefore, in combination with the possibility of direct divine intervention in the created order, possibly deceive the knower, by producing an intuitive cognition of an object

---

[40]Ibid., p. 28.

[41]William Courtenay offers this definition: "Simply put, the distinction meant that according to absolute power God, inasmuch as he is omnipotent, has the *ability* to do many things that he does not *will* to do, has never done, nor ever will do. By viewing God's intellect and will from the temporal standpoint and by attributing to God a distinction between the ability to act and the desire to act, theologians acknowledged an area of initial possibility for divine action, limited only by the principle of contradiction, out of which the things God did do or is going to do were chosen" (ibid., p. 37).

or concept that does not actually exist. Pope Benedict XVI, for example, refers to this danger, which he detects jointly in nominalism and Islamic theology.[42]

Benedict subscribes to the traditional narrative that nominalism has destroyed the medieval synthesis of reason and faith. This standard view has, however, undergone some revision during the last forty years,[43] with the result that we can no longer locate the birth of modernity clearly in late medieval theology. It is not clear to what extent nominalism is responsible for destroying the participatory ontology of the church fathers and thus for breaking up the medieval correlation of reason and faith. The distinction between God's absolute and ordained will, for example, has been shown not to refer to "possibilities and avenues of divine action," but to continue the longstanding theological tradition of what the medievalist Étienne Gilson had called "the metaphysics of Exodus."[44] In other words, the nominalist distinction between absolute and ordained power is another way of expressing creation's dependence on God. The emphasis is not on divine action but on the nonnecessity of the created order and its status as divine gift.[45] The origin of this distinction was not an undue stress on God's radical transcendence, thus aligning Christian theology with Greco-Arabian views of ultimate reality as inscrutable and necessary. On the contrary, the Scholastic distinction was meant to combat "Greco-Arabian necessitarianism by stressing the non-necessity of divine action and thus

---

[42]Beginning with Scotus, he argues, medieval theology advocated a voluntarism in which God's absolute will transcends his revealed will; and this could "lead to the image of a capricious God, who is not even bound to truth and goodness. God's transcendence and otherness are so exalted that our reason, our sense of the true and good, are no longer an authentic mirror of God, whose deepest possibilities remain eternally unattainable and hidden beyond his actual decisions" (Benedict XVI, "Faith, Reason and the University: Memories and Reflections," September 12, 2006, Papal Archives, last accessed April 14, 2011, www.vatican.va/holy_father/benedict_xvi/speeches/2006/september/documents/hf_ben-xvi_spe_20060912_university-regensburg_en.html).

[43]Courtenay, "Nominalism and Late Medieval Religion," p. 26. See also his evaluation of this change: "The combined effect of the research of Hochstetter, Vignaux, Boehner, Moody, and Oberman has been to establish the orthodox non-radical character of the thought of Ockham and Biel, and, by extension, d'Ailly" (ibid., p. 50).

[44]Gilson, *Spirit of Mediaeval Philosophy*, p. 94. Gilson refers to God's self-appellation in Exodus 3:14, "I AM WHO I AM." The Hebrew could also be translated "I WILL BE WHO I WILL BE," but the Vulgate translation runs "ego sum qui sum" and medieval commentators, such as Aquinas, customarily interpreted this as an indication of God's metaphysical status as self-subsistent being (Aquinas, *Summa Theologiae*, 1.13.11).

[45]Gilson, *Spirit of Mediaeval Philosophy*, p. 39.

the quality of the world as a freely chosen gift of God."[46] The distinction between absolute and ordained power was, in short, "a statement about the created order, not the divine nature."[47] It was not used to explain divine miracles, where absolute power invaded ordained creation orders, nor did it contravene the conviction that God had bound himself by covenant and incarnation to his creation. Even in nominalists after Ockham, the distinction "excludes the idea of a capricious, arbitrary God who might change his mind and reverse the established laws that obtain in the orders of nature and salvation, and when he occasionally acts contrary to certain principles or laws that normally operate within that order, it is for reasons that are in keeping with the broader design of his established will."[48] Ockham was saddled with this view by theologians such as Luis de Molina (1535-1600), who took Ockham's hypothetical scenarios of God acting *de potentia absoluta* at face value.[49]

The traditional assumption that Ockham and nominalism engaged in the "wholesale destruction of metaphysics and disallowed natural theology in principle" is thus not the only defensible reading of nominalism.[50] While there were radical nominalist theologians, thinkers like Ockham and Biel did not argue against orthodox Christianity. Rather their positions developed as corrective moves against a perceived one-sided emphasis on universals and determinism in theology. When sacramental ontology was used to rationalize arbitrary papal authority by fusing the sacred and profane to bolster the pope's temporal power, for example, nominalists emphasized human freedom and individual cooperation with God.[51]

---

[46]Ibid., p. 42.

[47]In fact, the very idea of *potentia absoluta* as a hypothetical possibility of God having done otherwise in order to safeguard the *ex nihilo* nature of creation by definition excludes God's arbitrary circumvention of his ordained will. *Potentia absoluta* means that God could have but did not and now will no longer (once committed in faithfulness) change plans.

[48]Courtenay, "Nominalism and Late Medieval Religion," p. 43.

[49]Jacob Schmutz, "The Medieval Doctrine of Causality and the Theology of Pure Nature 13th to 17th Centuries," in *Surnaturel: A Controversy at the Heart of Twentieth-Century Thomistic Thought*, ed. Serge-Thomas Bonino, trans. Robert Williams and rev. Matthew Levering (Ave Maria, Fla.: Sapientia Press of Ave Maria University, 2009), p. 232.

[50]Ibid., p. 46. See also Henri de Lubac's recognition that Duns Scotus and William of Ockham, and even Gabriel Biel, maintained a "balance between extreme positions" that was later lost with Michael Baius (1513-1589). See Henri de Lubac, *Augustinianism and Modern Theology*, trans. Lancelot C. Sheppard, Milestones in Catholic Theology (New York: Herder & Herder, 2000), p. 12.

[51]Steven E. Ozment, *Age of Reform: (1250-1550): An Intellectual and Religious History of Late*

Moreover, Ockham, on closer inspection, is not really a conceptualist (who denies reality outside the mind) but a "realistic conceptualist," that is more of a critical realist.[52] And yet the theological stress on God's freedom did undermine a more traditional, incarnational view of God's relation to the world and eventually resulted in profound changes to how Christians viewed God and society. At its most basic level, the theological shift made possible by nominalism was this: until late medieval developments, Christianity had understood nature and human nature as dependent on God's grace.[53] The two theological indicators for the confluence of nature and grace were the relation of Adam to postlapsarian humanity and the relation of first and secondary causes in God's influence on the created order. Concerning anthropology, Augustine and Aquinas still argued for "the entire dependence, in all circumstances, of the rational creature on his creator."[54] Humanity had been created by God for communion with himself in true godlikeness, described in Western theology as the beatific vision and in Eastern thought as deification. The tradition generally agreed with the paradox that although humanity was created and thus naturally destined for this end, it was achievable only through divine grace. It is true that Adam's dependence on God was seen to be different, for unlike fallen humanity, Adam did not need extrinsic "remedial grace" to advance toward perfection,[55] but this did not imply in any way his self-sufficiency. The patristic tradition, including Augustine, to its medieval continuation in Aquinas, emphasized that Adam "in the state of innocence needed grace, he prayed, [and] had faith."[56]

Another important element in the discussion about nature and grace was the concept of causality, that is, the idea of God's continuing work in creation. Augustine and Aquinas still operated with a Neo-Platonic idea of causality, a kind of emanation of causal power (without, however, the

---

Medieval and Reformation Europe (New Haven, Conn.: Yale University Press, 1980), pp. 15-17.

[52]William Courtenay, "Late Medieval Nominalism Revisited: 1972-1982," *Journal of the History of Ideas* 44, no 1 (January-March 1983): 162.

[53]As Henri de Lubac puts it, nature exists for the supernatural and not the supernatural for nature (*Augustinianism and Modern Theology*, p. 6). Later, radically nominalist theologies, by contrast, "did not understand this created nature as wholly stepped in and supported by the loving action of the creator" (ibid., p. 12).

[54]Lubac, *Augustinianism and Modern Theology*, p. 86.

[55]Ibid., p. 100.

[56]Ibid.

pantheistic implications of Neo-Platonism),[57] so that the supernatural order of God is intricately involved in human action, without, however, controverting human freedom.[58] The nominalist emphasis on God's freedom laid the groundwork for profound changes in this traditional view. In essence, nature became uncoupled from grace. Nature itself came to be regarded as its own domain, operating according to laws set up by God but independent of his divine influence. As so often happens, good intentions paved the way for this development. For example, theologians such as Scotus were concerned that too direct an influence of God on human action raised the question of divine responsibility for human evil.[59] These negative limitations on divine influence on human causality did, however, mutate with theologians in the sixteenth and seventeenth centuries, such as Francisco Suarez, into the positive separation of the nature and grace. In part, this change stemmed from the uncritical adoption of Aristotelian causality. And in this instance Ockham bears at least some of the blame. Aristotle's axiom that organisms develop according to their potentiality was traditionally regarded by Christian theology as the limit of pagan philosophy because it could neither grasp nor explain the mystery that human nature was designed for communion with God but required divine grace to attain this "naturally" supernatural end. Human beings have the natural capacity for God, but this capacity is fulfilled only by God's work of grace. That, at least, is how the tradition from Augustine to Aquinas had seen the matter. Aquinas writes that "if man is ordered to an end which exceeds his natural capacity, some help must be divinely provided for him, in a supernatural way, by which he may tend toward this end."[60] Aquinas makes clear that Aristotle's principle—each organism contains within itself the power to achieve its end—must be modified for Christian anthropology. After all, "man is not able by his

---

[57]Schmutz, "Medieval Doctrine of Causality," p. 211.

[58]Jacob Schmutz provides an excellent summary of Aquinas's position: "Thomas Aquinas thus interpreted the notion of divine concurrence in such a way that God not only furnishes and conserves in every secondary cause the power to act, but he likewise acts on the secondary cause in order to produce its actual operations to a mode that is proper to the secondary cause. With respect to the will and freedom of choice of the secondary cause, this doctrine means that God orients the will toward such and such a direction freely, while with respect to natural causes, he does it naturally" (ibid., p. 209).

[59]Schmutz, "Medieval Doctrine of Causality," p. 247.

[60]Thomas Aquinas, *Summa Contra Gentiles,* Book Three: Providence, Part II (Notre Dame: Notre Dame University Press), chap. 147, p. 224.

own operation to reach his ultimate end, which transcends the capacity of his natural powers, unless his operation acquires from divine power the efficacy to reach the aforesaid end."[61]

While Aquinas saw the limits of Aristotelian logic for a biblical view of human nature, William of Ockham imposed Aristotle's axiom on theology to argue against the paradox that man could only attain his natural end with supernatural help. He argued in accordance with Aristotelian logic that if this desire was natural, humans should also have the means to attain it.[62] As a result of Ockham's view, human nature is no longer truly open to God, but becomes its own sealed-off compartment, to be endowed with its supernatural end only when God changes it by grace. In the sixteenth century, the Thomist Cajetan would claim just this kind of teaching as orthodox. For him, natural had to come to mean that human nature had no innate capacity for the divine; thus he defined the human spirit in opposition to the supernatural, creating, in effect, two mutually exclusive realms.[63] Once nature has become a separate, autonomous domain from grace, human nature has its own natural end that is then taken up and completed by grace (versus the older view that human nature in its entirety is oriented toward a single supernatural goal). Ockham can thus at least be said to aid the dissociation of the natural and supernatural orders.[64] Similarly, although one cannot demonize him as the inventor of theological naturalism, Duns Scotus's rejection of the analogy of being, and his attempt to include God within a univocal concept of being, did depart from the orthodox tradition by locating "transcendence within human intelligence and no longer beyond it,"[65] as the Christian tradition had done prior to nominalism. Henri de Lubac has shown how this separation of nature and supernature led to a more mechanical, even forensic, understanding of God's relation to humanity. Traditionally, organic, relational and participatory language

---

[61]Ibid. Based on this view, Aquinas, citing John 6:44 ("no man can come to Me, except the Father, Who hath sent Me, draw him"), sets "aside the error of the Pelagians, who said that man could merit the glory of God by his free choice alone" (ibid., p. 225).

[62]Laurence Renault, "William of Ockham and the Distinction Between Nature and Supernature," in Serge-Thomas Bonino, ed., *Surnaturel: A Controversy at the Heart of Twentieth-Century Thomistic Thought* (Naples, Fla.: Sapientia Press of Ave Maria University, 2009), pp. 191-202.

[63]Henri de Lubac, *Mystery of the Supernatural* (New York: Herder & Herder, 1998), pp. 140-41.

[64]Schmutz, "Medieval Doctrine of Causality," p. 218.

[65]Olivier Boulnois, "Reading Duns Scotus: From History to Philosophy," *Modern Theology* 21, no. 4 (October 2005): 605. For a more positive view of Scotus, see Richard Cross, *Duns Scotus* (Oxford: Oxford University Press, 1999), pp. 35-38. Even Cross concedes, however, that Scotus's univocity weakens divine ineffability.

of God's presence in and for us had been used to describe the Fall, restoration and elevation to divine likeness of humanity. This rich language of God's love for, and indwelling in, human beings changed to a more instrumental view of grace, according to which God, instead of "revivifying human being to its very depths,"[66] now merely restored our ability to keep the divine law. Colder, juridical categories now replaced the older relational ones.

As a result of this development, a number of divisions familiar to modern theology but foreign to the earlier tradition arose: the division between works and grace that still marks some forms of Protestantism, and between the self-contained realms of nature and supernature, with the latter becoming increasingly irrelevant.[67] Even the brief account of nominalism given here indicates that modernity is essentially the departure from the ancient worldview that saw a natural link between God and world. Severing this link also resulted in dividing a holistic view of human knowledge. The reduction of objective knowledge to empirically verifiable facts, extracted from a self-contained nature by science, or to rational truths discovered by philosophy, is now opposed to more subjective forms of knowledge. Art, literature and, along with them, revelation and theology are relegated to disciplines of soft knowledge that are informed by mere subjective beliefs instead of hard, objective facts. This weakening of realist metaphysics and of participatory ontology had far-reaching social and even political implications. As Jean Bethke Elshtain reminds us, nominalism "marks the shift from God as love and reason to God as command," and once we have an absolute God, the absolute monarch is not far behind.[68] In more general terms, radical nominalism purchased divine freedom and human autonomy at the cost of confidence in the intelligibility of the world. The synthesis of reason and faith, the conviction that a single intelligible universe and also a unified human nature could both be progressively understood—which is why Christians needed to read ancient authors— started to crumble as radical nominalism spread across the greater part of Europe.[69] The preceding discussion of nominalism reminds us how

---

[66]Lubac, *Augustinianism and Modern Theology*, p. 17.

[67]For an excellent summary of this development, see Louis Dupre's introduction to Henri de Lubac, *Augustinianism and Modern Theology*, pp. ix-xv.

[68]Jean Bethke Elshtain, *Sovereignty: God, State, and Self*, Gifford Lectures (New York: Basic Books, 2008), p. 38.

[69]David Knowles, *Evolution of Medieval Thought*, ed. David Edward Luscombe, Christopher

important it is to retain an incarnational balance that avoids identifying God with particular human structures on the one hand, but also remembers that his presence is mediated through human realities on the other.

Conclusion. Medieval humanism profoundly shaped Western culture and was, arguably, "the most important kind of humanism Europe has ever produced."[70] The essential contribution of this humanism to Western culture was an elaboration of the church fathers' view of humanity as God's rational, restorative agent—of the human person as made in God's image and thus as the uniquely privileged, cocreating link between the material world and its divine creator.[71] Scholastic humanism, and medieval theology in general, continued the church fathers' emphasis on knowledge and on self-understanding as assimilation to God. Like the fathers, Scholastic humanists viewed reason as an important support of faith, insofar as faithful reasoning, embedded in the pursuit of a life obedient to the Christian Logos, was thought to approximate, in a fallen world, the image and likeness of God. The driving force behind medieval theology was not an attempt to turn theology into analytic philosophy but to articulate and make the Christian faith applicable to a world with rapidly changing structures of social organization and knowledge dissemination, requiring increasing clarification of doctrine and a more regulated administration of society.[72] Even the briefest analysis of medieval intellectual culture demonstrates that humanism in Western culture has religious beginnings. The Western desire for education and progress begins with the Christian idea of the universal redemption of humanity through rational human activity. Journalistic atheism (along with much popular opinion) usually opposes religion and rational inquiry in order to present secularism as the liberation from religious irrationality and obscurantism. It may thus come as a surprise to learn that medieval humanism is the very root from which our modern scientific attitude and secular humanism developed. Contrary to popular belief about medieval scholarship, working within theological boundaries did not hinder but usually encouraged inquiry and speculation. In fact, the scholarly activity within medieval culture was indispensible for

---

Nugent and Lawrence Books, 2nd ed. (London: Longman, 1988), p. 335.
[70]Southern, *Foundations*, p. 44.
[71]Ibid.
[72]Ibid.

modern civilization. Scholars of medieval Scholasticism assure us that, contrary to popular depictions of medieval darkness, the age of reason in the West began in the Middle Ages, and not with secular humanism.[73] Both scholastic and secular humanism have a common desire to extend human powers of reasoning to their utmost.[74] Yet they differ completely in their presuppositions. In medieval humanism, reason did not become severed from its theological context but worked creatively within it. Secular humanism could not have come about without these theological roots.

Despite this noble motivation, Scholasticism as a method finally failed for two reasons. The first was, predictably, that the proliferation of knowledge and the differential drift of areas of public life simply rendered a unified body of knowledge impossible. The hope of accumulating an authoritative body of knowledge through the study of texts and nature proved to be unattainable, a realization that dawned on scholastics toward the end of the thirteenth century.[75] Moreover, producing handy compilations of authoritative texts could not but eventually become self-defeating. The proliferation of secondary texts and tertiary discussions of them in turn prompted the Renaissance call *ad fontes*, back to the sources themselves. The second reason was that despite Scholasticism's deep *theoretical* regard for nature as a source of knowledge,[76] its text-oriented exegetical method had no room for empirical discovery, and the rising new science scorned Scholasticism for its lack of empirical grounding. In addition, while Scholasticism deliberately separated theology and natural philosophy, an increasing ingress of logic and natural philosophy into theology eventually turned theology into an arid, logic-driven discipline, which effectively secularized it.[77]

RENAISSANCE HUMANISM

Introduction. A still tenaciously prevalent misconception perpetuated by Christians and non-Christians alike is the interpretation of Renaissance

---

[73]Grant, *God and Reason*, p. 289.
[74]Southern, *Foundations*, p. 22.
[75]Ibid., p. 12.
[76]Ibid., pp. 36-38.
[77]Grant, *God and Reason*, p. 289. Yet even when theology became an analytical subject, a generally acknowledged ecclesial and dogmatic framework kept theologians from drawing conclusions contrary to revealed truths and church dogma.

humanism as the progenitor of secularism. The following is a succinct summary of this distorted view:

> The Renaissance has been interpreted as chiefly responsible for the ensu-
> ing blasphemies of the Reformation, or as the inevitable consequence of a
> medieval Catholicism that departed from its evangelical origins and
> blended too promiscuously with the secular world. Or, from a non-reli-
> gious perspective, the Renaissance has been hailed, and is still hailed, as
> the harbinger of the Enlightenment, of the repudiation of the ecclesiastical
> domination of secular life characteristic of medieval society, as the first
> feeble expression of, if not an atheistic or agnostic view of the cosmos, a
> blithely irreligious outlook, as the first phase of modern secular culture
> and of a bourgeois community where ethics and politics have become fully
> secularized and human energies turned toward practical solution of purely
> earthly problems.[78]

As the following brief summary of Renaissance humanism demonstrates, however, not one element of this false interpretation is supported
by a thorough study of humanist writings. It is not surprising, therefore,
that a new wave of Renaissance studies during the 1970s and 1980s thoroughly discredited the traditional understanding of Renaissance humanism as a precursor to secular humanism.[79] The most likely explanation for
the continuing misunderstanding of this period is the tenacious hold of
what we earlier noted Charles Taylor labels a "subtraction narrative" that
accounts for the shift from devout humanism to secular humanism. If we
assume a story of human development in which departure from dependence on God indicates human progress toward maturity, then we will
naturally want to interpret Renaissance texts in light of this narrative. As
happens so often in intellectual history, any contrary evidence is easily

---

[78]Charles Edward Trinkaus, "The Religious Thought of the Italian Humanists, and the Reformers: Anticipation or Autonomy," in *The Pursuit of Holiness in Late Medieval and Renaissance Religion; Papers from the University of Michigan Conference,* ed. Charles Edward Trinkaus
and Heiko A. Oberman (Leiden: Brill, 1974), pp. 340-41.

[79]I am principally drawing on the scholarly effort spearheaded by Paul Oskar Kristeller, Charles
Edward Trinkaus and Albert Rabil, among many others, to show the continuity of Renaissance humanism with patristic and (despite many differences) even with scholastic nominalist
theology. See, for example, Paul Oskar Kristeller, *Renaissance Thought and Its Sources,* ed. Michael Mooney (New York: Columbia University Press, 1979). The three-volume collection of
conference papers on the relation of the patristic, medieval and Renaissance periods edited by
Albert Rabil also provides a solid overview of this trend: *Renaissance Humanism: Foundations,
Form and Legacy,* 3 vols. (Philadelphia: University of Pennsylvania Press, 1988).

suppressed, and once a false image is created that fits the subtraction narrative, it is not easily dislodged. Yet dislodge it we must if we want to prove faithful to the actual spirit of Renaissance humanism.

There is no question that Renaissance thought stressed the energy of the human will and mind. Yet the secular potential and triumphs of humanity were still viewed fully within a Christian worldview, a worldview that was, moreover, revived through a retrieval of patristic theology. It was, more precisely, the doctrines of the incarnation and human deification as the fulfillment of the *imago Dei* in man through Christ that animated Renaissance thought.[80] In the following depiction of Renaissance humanism as an essentially Christian humanism, keep in mind that language about human greatness loses its heretical flavor when seen in light of patristic affirmations of deification. Furthermore, it is important to grasp the essentially Christian spirit of Renaissance humanism rather than focus on any particular activity of humanists for defining what is essentially an initiative of Christian scholars. A proper understanding of Renaissance culture as a whole, of course, does require that we recognize humanism to be merely a certain, "well-defined sector" of this culture.[81] Nonetheless, this humanism cannot be adequately defined by focusing on its particular activities in scholarship or educational reforms. The reason for Renaissance humanists' study of classical antiquity, their passion for language and for moral education, was their essentially Christian vision of humans becoming like God, that is, the achievement of our full humanity in Christ.

The retrieval of patristic theology. Far from being a clear development away from Christianity toward modern secularism, Renaissance humanism was largely based on a recovery of patristic theology. Renaissance humanists argued for an incarnational focus on the *imago Dei*, for the compatibility of faith and reason in pursuing a Christian philosophy, and for the importance of a Christianized Neo-Platonism with its notion of deification. Like the church fathers, many humanists (who had much better access to original Platonic texts than had many of the Latin fathers) re-

---

[80]Charles Edward Trinkaus, *In Our Image and Likeness: Humanity and Divinity in Italian Humanist Thought* (Notre Dame, Ind.: University of Notre Dame Press, 1995), 1:xxiii-xxiv.

[81]Paul Oskar Kristeller, "Humanism," in *The Cambridge History of Renaissance Philosophy*, ed. Quentin Skinner and Eckhard Kessler, Cambridge Companions to Philosophy (Cambridge: Cambridge University Press, 2000), p. 114.

garded Platonism as the ideal philosophical means for pursuing the "two subjects of the renewed worship of God and the discovery of his image in the human soul."[82] The humanists' recovery and evaluation of ancient pagan art and letters were inseparable from their enthusiasm for patristic literature.[83] And along with patristic sources, Renaissance humanists read Plato and Aristotle as pagan authorities compatible with a Christian program of education.

To be sure, opponents pointed out the dangers of an all-too-easy adoption of pagan wisdom for Christian moral reasoning. Ironically, it was through the increasing access to source material that the differences between Plato's philosophy and biblical doctrines became more apparent. For example, some Renaissance humanists criticized the idea that God's love could be mediated through earthly loves and pleasures; the homosexual elements in Plato's dialogues were also used as ammunition against pagan intrusion into Christian thought.[84] Some Florentine humanists, Lorenzo Valla (c. 1406-1457) among them, even attacked the suggested synthesis of pagan and Christian wisdom, and came close to Protestant Reformers in asserting the singular validity of revelation for moral reasoning.[85] Indeed, most humanists, when pressed by critics, would assert the primacy of faith over natural reason. For this reason some scholars have denied a strong Pelagian current in Renaissance humanists and argued to the contrary that humanistic writings were motivated by a plea for "a renewal of a theology of grace as the acceptance that divine force alone was capable of reorienting the naturally egotistical motivations of mankind towards higher ethical and religious goals."[86] While most hu-

---

[82]Trinkaus, *In Our Image*, 2:465. Trinkaus also supports Renaissance scholars such as Ernst Cassirer and Paul Oskar Kristeller, who claimed that "the significance of Renaissance Platonism lay in its effort to consider the spiritual world of God and the human soul as one with the natural universe [using *natural* in a sense other than Ficino's application of it to the corporeal], and in its attempted conjoining of the subjective and objective realms" (ibid., 2:467).

[83]Eugene F. Rice Jr., "The Renaissance Idea of Christian Antiquity: Humanist Patristic Scholarship," in *Renaissance Humanism: Foundations, Form and Legacy*, vol. 1, *Humanism in Italy*, ed. Albert Rabil (Philadelphia: University of Pennsylvania Press, 1988), p. 17.

[84]James Hankins, *Plato in the Italian Renaissance*, Columbia Studies in the Classical Tradition (Leiden: Brill, 1990), 2:348-49.

[85]Jill Kraye, "The Humanist Moral Philosopher: Marc Antoin Muret's Edition of Seneca," in *Moral Philosophy on the Threshold of Modernity*, ed. Jill Kraye and Risto Saarinen, New Synthese Historical Library (Dortrecht: Springer, 2005), pp. 322-23.

[86]Trinkaus, *In Our Image*, 1:xx.

manists imitated Augustine in arguing for the compatibility of pagan moral philosophy with Christianity, they maintained the supremacy of the Christian faith.[87]

Renaissance humanism remained deeply indebted to Christian anthropology and its foundational claim that in Christ, the perfect image of God, godlikeness has been restored to humanity. At least in the case of the early Italian Renaissance, humanist anthropology is determined by incarnational theology. Writers such as Petrarch, Coluccio Salutati, Lorenzo Valla, Marsilio Ficino, Giovanni Pico della Mirandola and Pietro Pomponazzi (and many others) always discuss the idea of human nature in relation to the divine nature, and the central metaphor of this discussion is the creation of man "in our image and likeness," from the biblical account. Renaissance anthropology was in many ways a revival of Augustinian theology. Consequently, it stressed the superiority of the will over the intellect, and followed Augustine's exhortation to employ one's free will in subordinating one's passions in light of God's love, lest one succumb to a life governed by instinct alone and thus devolve into a beast. While not at all insensible to the brokenness of the divine image by sin and to consequent innate human selfishness, Renaissance humanism in general continued to propagate the view of human greatness espoused by the church fathers, offering "what is possibly the most affirmative view of human nature in the history of thought and expression. In making trial of his powers, man comes to be seen more as manifesting his inherent divinity than as risking the danger of transformation into a beast."[88]

***The incarnation and the* imago Dei.** Charles Trinkaus's work has convincingly shown that "the new vision of man in this period found its inspiration in a revival of the patristic exegesis" of the *imago Dei* in Genesis.[89] What image and likeness entail changes little from the view of the church fathers. The humanist Bartolomeo Facio's reprise of Augustine's interpretation of the *imago Dei*, in this case taken from Peter Lombard's *Sentences* (c. 1150), represents Renaissance humanism:

> The illustrious Master of the Sentences held that man is made in the image and similitude of God, hence it must be held that, as I have said, he is given

---

[87]Kraye, "Humanist Moral Philosopher," p. 321.
[88]Trinkaus, *In Our Image*, 1:xiv.
[89]Ibid.

a mind by which he excels all animals lacking in reason; and he thought that wisdom, memory and charity should be referred to the image, and innocence and justice to the similitude.[90]

Giovanni Pico della Mirandola, whose *Oration on the Dignity of Man* (1486) shows up in every Renaissance anthology, is usually interpreted as the humanistic Prometheus, paradigmatic for the general humanist tendency to bestow on humanity independence from God. Indicative of Pico's supposed inauguration of secular humanism are passages such as these, where God addresses Adam after the Fall:

> We have given you, O Adam, no visage proper to yourself, nor endowment properly your own, in order that whatever place, whatever form, whatever gifts you may, with premeditation, select, these same you may have and possess through your own judgement and decision. The nature of all other creatures is defined and restricted within laws which We have laid down; you, by contrast, impeded by no such restrictions, may, by your own free will, to whose custody We have assigned you, trace for yourself the lineaments of your own nature. I have placed you at the very center of the world, so that from that vantage point you may with greater ease glance round about you on all that the world contains. We have made you a creature neither of heaven nor of earth, neither mortal nor immortal, in order that you may, as the free and proud shaper of your own being, fashion yourself in the form you may prefer. It will be in your power to descend to the lower, brutish forms of life; you will be able, through your own decision, to rise again to the superior orders whose life is divine.[91]

Such passages are usually interpreted as foreshadowing secular humanism. Yet Pico's view of human nature is not radically different from how the church father Augustine describes humankind: "Thus man is an intermediate being, but intermediate between beasts and angels. A beast is irrational and mortal, while an angel is rational and immortal. Man is intermediate, inferior to the angels, and superior to the beasts; he is a rational and mortal animal, sharing mortality with the beasts, and rationality with the angels."[92] For Augustine too, the Christian life depends on moral rea-

[90]Bartolomeo Facio, *De hominis excellentia ad Nicolaum Quintum*, Bibl. Vatican Cod. Urb. lat. 227, f. 153r, quoted in Trinkaus, *In Our Image*, 1:217.

[91]Giovanni Pico della Mirandola, *Oration on the Dignity of Man*, Center for the Study of Complex Systems, last accessed April 18, 2011, www.cscs.umich.edu/~crshalizi/Mirandola.

[92]Augustine, *Concerning the City of God Against the Pagans* 9.12, trans. Henry Bettenson (New York: Penguin Books, 1984), p. 359.

soning and exercise of the free will with which God endowed his human creature. Augustine does not disparage passions as such, but the Christian is called to discipline the lower passions, lest his or her nature destined toward Godlikeness and "fellowship with the angels," become reduced to beastlike behavior, ruled by raw desire and biological instinct.[93]

When we read Pico's *Oration* in this patristic context of deification, his sentiments concerning human glorification can be seen to remain within the orthodox context of Genesis 1:26. After his *Oration*, Pico wrote a commentary on the first chapter of Genesis, in which he derives human dignity from prelapsarian man and from the incarnation. It is in Christ, the exemplar, that human nature is shown for what it truly is:

> just as the absolute consummation of all inferior things is man, so the absolute consummation of all men is Christ. . . . No one can doubt that from the Man, Christ, the perfection of all goodness in all men is derived; this is to say that the Spirit has been given to Him alone without measure, so that we all receive it from his plenitude. You may see beyond doubt that this prerogative is owed to Him as to God and man, and this is also peculiar to Him as man and is a fitting and legitimate privilege.[94]

If our ears are attuned to patristic theology, we recognize the language of a high Christology and of deification, that is, a Christian rather than a secular "apotheosis" in Pico's words. Pico celebrates humanity's God-given dignity, not human autonomy. Human beings are of central concern to God, who placed them as his image and representatives in charge of the earth. Moreover, Pico argues clearly within the Christian narrative of redemption, according to which Christ restores our full humanity:

> But just as all of us in the first Adam, who obeyed Satan more than God and whose sons we are according to the flesh, deformed from men degenerated into brutes, so in the newest Adam Jesus Christ, who fulfilled the will of the Father and defeated the spiritual iniquities with his own blood, whose sons we are all according to the spirit, reformed by grace we are regenerated by man into adoption as sons of God.[95]

Pico is not, as usually assumed, the Renaissance villain who proclaimed

[93]Ibid., 12.22, p. 502.
[94]Giovanni Pico della Mirandola, *Commentary on Genesis*, quoted in Trinkaus, *In Our Image*, 2:508-9.
[95]Ibid., 2:517.

the secularist sovereign self. The patristic scholar Henri de Lubac hits nearer the mark when he claims that Pico's Renaissance manifesto *Discourse on the Dignity of Man* is theologically not opposed to traditional Catholicism.[96] Like the church fathers and the medieval humanists, Renaissance thinkers regarded the ability and drive of humans to cultivate and shape their world as "an emulation of divinity, since it was in this respect that man was created in the image and likeness of God." Without question, Renaissance humanism strongly emphasized the individual and human creativity, and sometimes this focus gave rise to secular, nonreligious or even antireligious aspects. Yet these are neither central to nor typical of the Renaissance period, and should be "seen as incorporated into a new religious vision of *Homo triumphans* that found its inspiration in the patristic Christian tradition brilliantly combined with the non-rational aspects of the ancient rhetorical tradition and its ethics."[97] These "non-rational aspects" were the Christian-Augustinian notion of original sin and also the more pessimistic Stoic and Epicurean strands of ancient philosophy that subverted the Aristotelian naturalism of medieval times that had suggested a more mechanical and less volatile image of human nature. Renaissance humanists revived a more tragic picture of humanity that emphasized our human capacity for both sin and achievement on "a monumental scale."[98]

Humanistic education. It is generally acknowledged that education was a main concern of Renaissance humanists.[99] What is less well recognized is that humanistic education did not merely aim at character formation in a general sense but at the shaping of Christian virtues in particular. More specifically, humanist educators sought to inculcate a fully rounded, rational faith in their students. The humanist Pier Paolo Vergerio, for example, explains that "it is proper for a well-educated youth to respect and practice religion and to be steeped in religious belief from his earliest youth," for such faith ensures that we respect others.[100] Yet such faith should not be like "old

---

[96]Henri de Lubac, *Theology in History: The Light of Christ, Disputed Questions and Resistance to Nazism*, trans. Anne Englund Nash (San Francisco: Ignatius Press, 1996), p. 43.

[97]Trinkaus, *In Our Image*, 1:xx-xxi.

[98]Ibid., 1:xxi.

[99]Kristeller, "Humanism," pp. 13-14.

[100]Pier Paolo Vergerio, "The Character and Studies Befitting A Free-Born Youth," in *Humanist Educational Treatises*, ed. and trans. Craig Kallendorf, I Tatti Renaissance Library (Cambridge, Mass.: Harvard University Press, 2002), p. 25.

wives' tales," but one that is well reasoned and ably articulated. For this reason the student should "read and comprehend a great deal, and . . . bestow great pains on the philosophers, the poets, the orators and historians and all other writers."[101] The combination of literature and knowledge makes the well-rounded person, for "literary skill without knowledge is useless and sterile; and knowledge, however extensive, fades into the shadows without the glorious lamp of literature."[102] Yet a well-rounded mind is not the final goal. Rather, as the humanist Leonard Bruni asserts, "it is religion and moral philosophy that ought to be our particular studies, I think, and the rest studied in relation to them as their handmaids, in proportion as they aid or illustrate their meaning; and it is with this in mind that we must fix upon the poets, orators, and other writers."[103] Like patristic authors, the humanist teachers appreciated classical learning for its metaphysical, even religious, bent, and they believed that classical writings contained much truth that Christians could build on. Renaissance humanists also agreed with the patristic teaching that in Christ every moral human truth finds its fulfilment, wherefore the Christian should be spurned on to outdo the classical writer in moral virtue. As one humanist educator put it, if the Romans already knew about the importance of virtue and religion, "what must *we* do, who know the true God?"[104]

The study of language and poetry finds its place within this Christian humanistic education as that which orients the soul toward beauty and wisdom. For wisdom is nothing else but understanding oneself and the world in light of God's truth. With Plato, the humanists held that "the soul is ordered in special relation to the principles of Harmony and Rhythm," but more readily than Plato, they also believed that the study of language and especially poetry is important for attuning the soul to virtue.[105] Noble sen-

---

[101]Leonardo Bruni, "The Study of Literature To Lady Battista Malatesta of Montefeltro," in *Humanist Educational Treatises*, ed. and trans. Craig Kallendorf, I Tatti Renaissance Library (Cambridge, Mass.: Harvard University Press, 2002), p. 123.

[102]Ibid.

[103]Ibid., pp. 123, 125.

[104]Aeneas Sylvius Piccolomini, "The Education of Boys," in *Humanist Educational Treatises*, ed. and trans. Craig Kallendorf, I Tatti Renaissance Library (Cambridge, Mass.: Harvard University Press, 2002), p. 167.

[105]Leonardo Bruni, "Concerning the Study of Literature," in *Vittorino Da Feltre and Other Humanist Educators: Essays and Versions, An Introduction to the History of Classical Education*, ed. William Harrison Woodward, Renaissance Society of America Reprint Texts (Toronto: University of Toronto Press, 1996), p. 131.

timents require noble expression, and wisdom requires eloquence for its articulation. In the words of the English humanist Roger Ascham, "for good and choice meats be no more requisite for healthy bodies than proper and apt words be for good matters." Clear and sensible expression of truth— in other words, eloquence—is "one of the fairest and rarest gifts that God doth give to man."[106] Despite this ostensibly Christian platform for education and social reform, the humanists encountered plenty of fellow Christians who were rather suspicious of learning. One humanist warns his students that they "will be confronted by the opposition of the shallow Churchman," who will denounce classical learning as a waste of time.[107] The immediate defense against such ignorance in the disguise of religious piety is pointing to the church fathers' interest in pagan poetry. After all, Jerome, Augustine, Cyprian and Basil the Great "did not hesitate to draw illustrations from heathen poetry and sanctioned its study."[108] Moreover, they pointed out to their Christian critics that the Bible itself contains metaphors, poetry and analogies; indeed "theology is poetry about God."[109]

The humanists' more indirect but theologically deeper defense of reason and learning against their pious despisers was biblical anthropology. For the Christian humanists, this attitude amounted to a denial of our true human nature. After all, rather than to animals, "to man only is given the desire to learn." For this reason education, the training of human reason in the service of virtue and true humanity, is called "studia humanitatis."[110] While this term is drawn directly from Cicero, its meaning had taken on distinctly Christian overtones. Indeed, as English humanist Thomas Wilson believed, wisdom—reason coupled with eloquence—constituted part of humanity's original Godlikeness that was lost through sin in the Fall. The result was human crudeness and barbarism. Because God in his mercy had "repaired mankind," Christians are called "to persuade with reason all

---

[106]Roger Ascham, "The Schoolmaster," in *English Humanism: Wyatt to Cowley*, ed. Joanna Martindale (London: Croom Helm, 1985), p. 184.

[107]Aeneas Sylvius Piccolomini, "De Liberorum Educatione," in *Vittorino Da Feltre and Other Humanist Educators*, ed. William Harrison Woodward, Renaissance Society of America Reprint Texts (Toronto: University of Toronto Press, 1996), p. 149.

[108]Ibid.

[109]Trinkaus, *In Our Image*, 2:690.

[110]Battista Guarino, "De Ordine Docendi et Studendi," in *Vittorino Da Feltre and Other Humanist Educators*, ed. William Harrison Woodward, Renaissance Society of America Reprint Texts (Toronto: University of Toronto Press, 1996), p. 177.

men to society."[111] In other words, alienation of human beings from themselves and others in the Fall was to be remedied through education. Thus, the humanist love for language, rhetoric and education for the sake of wisdom stems from essentially the same eschatological drive that had motivated patristic and medieval humanism, namely, the restoration of creation through human transformation toward Godlikeness.

The importance of the incarnation. The incarnation held great theological and philosophical importance for Renaissance thinkers. Like the church fathers, Renaissance humanists such as Petrarch, Manetti and Ficino believed in a providential history of humankind for which the incarnation was the nexus or highpoint.[112] For this reason Christianity was indeed superior to other religions, because it was their culmination. Given that Christ was the world's Logos, this theology of fulfillment extended also to all the highest forms of philosophy that contained important truths and wisdom. Ficino, for example, held that the Christian incarnation is the specific way for all human beings to attain immortality. With Augustine he also believes that because human nature has both animal and divine characteristics, it is a mean between clay and divine spirit, and its redemption required a union between the divine and the earthly in the God-man Christ. On account of the incarnation, humanity can be lifted up to the divine, for "God in man renders man divine."[113] Christ is the fulfilment of all that is good in pagan philosophy: "What else was Christ but a certain living book of moral and divine philosophy, sent from heaven and manifesting the divine idea itself of the virtues to human eyes."[114] With the fathers, Renaissance humanists also saw clearly that the incarnation set Christian philosophy apart from pagan thought. As Petrarch put it, only Christianity truly joins heaven and earth. However close Platonic thought may have come to Christian truth, how the transcendent, the divine Word "became flesh, how joined to the earth it dwelt in us, this the learned Plato did not know."[115]

The incarnation also offered profound philosophical implications that

---

[111]Thomas Wilson, "The Art of Rhetoric," in *English Humanism: Wyatt to Cowley*, ed. Joanna Martindale (London: Croom Helm, 1985), p. 186.

[112]Trinkaus, *In Our Image*, 2:658.

[113]Marsilio Ficino (1433-1499), *On Christian Religion (De religione Christiana et fidei pietate*, 1476), quoted in Trinkaus, *In Our Image*, 2:740.

[114]Ibid., 2:741.

[115]Francesco Petrarch, *De Otio Religioso*, quoted in Trinkaus, *In Our Image*, 2:658.

went beyond the idea of deification, by focusing on the general idea of mediation. Few Renaissance thinkers have written as profoundly about the meaning of the incarnation for the nature of reality as Nicholas of Cusa (1401-1464). Cusanus (Cusa) was not technically a humanist in that his intellectual work focused explicitly on theological issues.[116] Nonetheless, he was an incarnational humanist in the best sense of the term because the peaceful union of humanity through religion was indeed the main goal of his thinking.[117] He was a Christian philosopher who worked out a synthesis of reason and faith that is reminiscent of patristic notions of the incarnation and of deification.[118] Cusanus's faith resembles the Christian Neo-Platonism of many Renaissance humanists: he presumes a natural religious sense and openness to the divine in human beings, the rational pursuit of which will lead one to the recognition of God, although the divine vision cannot be attained without divine grace.[119] Cusanus's vision of spiritual ascent to God through reason, faith and a life continually transformed into Christlikeness recalls also Clement of Alexandria and the patristic emphasis on deification. In his treatise *De filiatione Dei* (On Being a Son of God), Cusanus explains that "I consider filiation of God to be reckoned as nothing else than deification, which, in Greek, is also called *theosis.*"[120] As with the fathers, for Cusanus, knowledge, self-knowledge and human creativity arise from participation in the mind of God. Creation reflects the mind of God, but human spirit and reason are truly divine because we share with the divine mind the desire to assimilate things through knowledge and shape them in its own likeness.[121] Hence, as in the thought of Clement and other (especially Eastern) fathers, the fulfilment of one's humanity is conformity of the mind to God. The ultimate goal of Christianity is "one humanity in all, the humanity of Christ, and one spirit, that of Christ, in all spirits, and that each may dwell in him

---

[116]Caesare Vasoli, "The Renaissance Concept of Philosophy," in *The Cambridge History of Renaissance Philosophy*, ed. Charles B. Schmitt and Quentin Skinner (Cambridge: Cambridge University Press, 1988), p. 66.

[117]Nicholas Cusanus, *Of Learned Ignorance*, trans. Germain Heron, Rare Masterpieces of Philosophy and Science (Eugene, Ore.: Wipf & Stock, 2007), p. 171.

[118]Nancy J. Hudson, *Becoming God: The Doctrine of Theosis in Nicholas of Cusa* (Washington, D.C.: Catholic University of America Press, 2007), p. 193.

[119]Cusanus, *Of Learned Ignorance*, p. 160.

[120]Nicholas Cusanus, *Nicolai de Cusa Opera Omnia*, quoted in Hudson, *Becoming God*, p. 4.

[121]Nicholas Cusanus, *Idiota de Mente. The Layman: About Mind*, trans. Clyde Lee Miller (New York: Abaris, 1979), p. 67.

in such fashion that there is but one Christ in all."[122]

Cusanus's retention of Christian Platonism is remarkable given that he was more directly acquainted with Plato's original texts than were earlier generations of Christian Neo-Platonists. For this reason he understood the full force of the ontological separation between the forms and being, as well as the radical transcendence of the highest good that was beyond being.[123] By resurrecting with full force Plato's notion of otherness, Cusanus also posits again the Platonic question: How can universals participate in particulars? To put it in Neo-Platonic terms, how does the creation return to unity with its Creator? Cusanus, more clearly than any other Renaissance Platonist, proffers the incarnation as the solution to this problem. The finite and the infinite merge without any reduction, not in some principle but in the union of Creator and creation in the incarnation:

> First, then, stands God the creator. Next is God and man, whose created humanity has been assumed into the most intimate possible union with God, and, as being the universal limitation of all things, is hypostatically united with the absolute power behind the being of all things; that he may exist by the most absolute God through the universal limitation which is humanity.[124]

This convergence of transcendence and immanence is not an abstract principle, but "Jesus, ever blessed," who is "the image of the invisible God," the one in and by whom all things were created, are sustained and are now reconciled to God.[125]

Based on this incarnational Christology, Cusanus presents a christologically grounded cosmology in which all things find their unity in the God-man. Nature and human nature are thus raised up to God through the mediation of the divine humanity of Christ. One can see how this idea intrinsically validates nature and this world. The natural and supernatural are interrelated, universals and particulars are interpenetrated, and opposite aspects of knowledge are united through a humanity that is at once Creator and created.[126] Based on the union of

---

[122]Cusanus, *Of Learned Ignorance*, p. 167.
[123]Ernst Cassirer, *The Individual and the Cosmos in Renaissance Philosophy*, trans. Mario Domandi (Chicago: University of Chicago Press, 2010), p. 21.
[124]Cusanus, *Of Learned Ignorance*, p. 137.
[125]Ibid., pp. 138-39.
[126]Cassirer, *Individual and the Cosmos*, p. 40. See also Kurt Flasch on the importance of the in-

God and creation in the God-man, human beings can rise up to God through Christ, and they can do so through the pursuit of knowledge. For Cusanus there is, as one scholar puts it, no "rupture between seeking self and seeking God."[127] His emphasis on the incarnation as the human-oriented mediation of the sensible and the insensible, of the finite and the infinite, allows Cusanus to stress individuality and this-worldliness without, however, courting the nominalistic danger of denying universals. There are indeed patristic antecedents for this incarnational anthropology. Gregory of Nyssa, for example, in his *The Making of Man*, also refers to human being as the mediating middle between the spiritual and material aspects of this world: "While two natures—the Divine and incorporeal nature, and the irrational life of brutes—are separated from each other as extremes, human nature is the mean between them."[128]

While retaining a christological anthropology, Cusanus's view of human existence also exhibits the typical Renaissance emphasis on human beings as creative, historical agents. Human knowledge is no longer merely a representation of a divine idea, but a creative, historical working out of its content. Human action is, so to speak, the temporal unfolding of eternal truths. While human beings are finite and subject to time, *within time* they have the godlike freedom of creating and evaluating culture. Culture "confirms the freedom of the human spirit, which is the seal of its divinity."[129] Cusanus's emphasis on humanity's ability to create and evaluate culture continues, as we shall see below, in Giambattista Vico's humanism.

Opinions on the orthodoxy and significance of Cusanus's thought and his influence on other Renaissance thinkers remain divided. Some view him as a thinker basically in line with the patristic tradition of deification, particularly with the Eastern tradition's emphasis on the cosmic Christ.[130]

---

carnation for Cusanus's central belief in the coincidence of opposites (*Nikolaus von Kues: Geschichte einer Entwicklung: Vorlesungen zur Einführung in seine Philosophie* [Frankfurt am Main: Klostermann, 1998], p. 139).

[127]Hudson, *Becoming God*, p. 199.

[128]Gregory of Nyssa, "On the Making of Man," in *Gregory of Nyssa: Dogmatic Treatises*, vol. 5 of *Nicene and Post-Nicene Fathers*, Second Series, ed. Philip Schaff and Henry Wace, trans. William Moore and Henry Austin Wilson (Peabody, Mass.: Hendrickson, 1994), p. 405.

[129]Cassirer, *Individual and the Cosmos*, p. 44.

[130]Hudson, *Becoming God*, p. 200.

Others consider him to be a religious philosopher who mostly abandons orthodoxy and subordinates theology to reason and philosophy.[131] No scholar, however, doubts the centrality of the incarnation and the vision for a transformed humanity in Cusanus's effort to rearticulate a Christian version of Neo-Platonism for an emerging modern age. This Neo-Platonism influenced the spirit of Renaissance humanism, which guarded the transcendence of God but invested humanity with greater confidence in its abilities to rise to divinity through knowledge and action in this world.[132]

CHRISTIAN HUMANISM AFTER THE RENAISSANCE

I have argued that patristic incarnational anthropology, together with its concept of deification, that God became man so that man could become like God, provides the foundation for the educational idea of character formation in Western culture. Taking up the Platonic ontology of participation, the Christian humanistic ethos was essentially built on the idea of "faith seeking understanding." And even while this attitude gave precedence to divine revelation and theology, it nonetheless unified every area of human knowing under the umbrella of an intelligible cosmos within which human nature has a supernatural destiny of communion with God, as evidenced by his very nature as rational creature made in the image of God. Within our narrative of humanism the Renaissance continues this basic Christian tradition, albeit with important alterations. Renaissance humanism shifted anthropology decidedly toward an emphasis on individual creativity and a deeper sense of historical development, without, however, surrendering to either historicism or individualism. In Renaissance philosophy, the mind still participated in the forms, and nature did not yet stand opposed to the human spirit and culture. I have argued that medieval nominalism did not as a whole either begin or fully instantiate this dichotomy, so the question arises of when this split occurred. The following brief account suggests that a dualism between nature and supernature coincides with the demise of Platonic metaphysics, or, more broadly, with the breaking up of what Louis Dupré calls the onto-theological synthesis. Two main figures in the intellectual history of humanism will help us pinpoint this breakup, namely, the Italian humanist scholar Giambat-

---

[131]Flasch, *Nikolaus von Kues*, p. 645.
[132]Ibid., pp. 426ff.; Cassirer, *Individual and the Cosmos*, p. 63.

tista Vico (1668-1744) and the German intellectual historian Wilhelm
Dilthey (1833-1911). Both men may be regarded as fathers of the modern
human sciences.

Giambattista Vico, born into a book trader's family of modest means in
Naples, studied philosophy, history and law, and worked as an independent scholar until his appointment as professor of rhetoric (1699-1741). He
is best known for his work *The New Science* (*Scientia Nuova*), which is basically his blueprint for a universal humanistic science. Together with his
autobiography, his defense of humanistic education, *On the Study Methods
of Our Time*, and his annual university addresses on humanistic learning,
On Humanistic Education (Six Inaugural Orations 1699-1707), *The New Science* offers a decidedly Christian humanism in the Platonic mold that differs from earlier theological humanisms in two important respects. First,
it is clearly less christological, and, second, Vico already separates nature
from human nature, even though he retrains a Platonic sense of participation in a higher reality.

Vico's humanistic vision is squarely based on Christian Platonism.
With the church fathers and other Renaissance Christian humanists before him, Vico believed that "the archetypal *forms*, the ideal patterns of
reality, exist in God alone. The physical nature of things, the phenomenal
world is modeled after those archetypes."[133] Yet in Vico we can also observe the secularization of Christian humanism, even while echoes of
deification and incarnation remain discernible. Christ and his salvific,
redemptive significance for humanity are no longer mentioned at all. Nor
does the incarnation appear as an explicit mediator between transcendence and immanence. And even though God, "who is all reason,"[134]
often shows up, he no longer resembles the incarnate, personally encountered deity of earlier humanists; instead, his role seems reduced to a deistic, distant engine of providence. Nonetheless, the basic tenet of Christian humanism remains intact. True humanity, as well as a humane
society, depend on divine wisdom. They require "divine reason, which is
present throughout the universe and all its parts. It permeates all things

---

[133]Giambattista Vico, *On the Study Methods of Our Time*, trans. Elio Gianturco and Donald
Philip Verne (Ithaca, N.Y.: Cornell University Press, 1990), p. 23.
[134]Giambattista Vico, *The New Science of Giambattista Vico*, trans. Thomas Goddard Bergin and
Max Harold Fisch, 3rd ed. (Ithaca, N.Y.: Cornell University Press, 1988), p. 313.

and protects and sustains the world. This divine reason is in God, and it is called Divine Wisdom. In the pursuit of this wisdom lies the path to the unity of humankind: "What is it that brings man and God together? It is but truth, which only the man of wisdom can comprehend and that abides in God."[135] Human Godlikeness, says Vico, lies in the training of virtuous character and in the freedom bestowed by the authority of wisdom.[136] Human beings are designed for this kind of life; it is in accordance with their nature.[137] Knowledge derived from contemplating "divine things, the human mind, and the supreme God," will serve as the compass for navigating life.[138] All the human disciplines of knowledge are therefore a means to contemplate God and live a good life. Even without an explicit Christological foundation, Vico's Christian humanism retains the central idea of incarnational humanism that deification is the goal of all godly human striving, including education.[139]

Vico's Christian Platonism continues to provide a firm metaphysical foundation for human participation in the divinely ordained process of redemption through human progress. The same Platonism also makes Vico an early critic of the Enlightenment, particularly of the abstract, geometrical and mathematical reasoning propagated by Cartesian philosophy. Vico was initially fascinated by Descartes's emphasis on the mind and reason, but quickly altered his opinion when he realized that Descartes valued logic over eloquence and had little time for studies in language or rhetoric.[140] For Vico, Descartes's geometrical method for ascertaining firm knowledge had lost the most important foundation for wisdom, namely, the recognition that propositions and facts had to be integrated into a greater human context of knowledge.[141] True knowledge, as Vico understood, requires not mere bits of information but their meaningful integration into a whole for critical judgment and application. This is wisdom, and wisdom requires an interpretation of particulars within "the total life of the body politic," which

---

[135]Giambattista Vico, *On Humanistic Education: (Six Inaugural Orations, 1699-1707)*, trans. Giorgio A. Pinton and Arthur W. Shippee (Ithaca, N.Y.: Cornell University Press, 1993), p. 68.
[136]Ibid., p. 69.
[137]Ibid., p. 71.
[138]Ibid., p. 137.
[139]Ibid., p. 138.
[140]Donald Phillip Verene, introduction to Vico, *On Humanistic Education*, p. 26.
[141]Vico, *Study Methods of Our Time*, p. 13.

in turn should correspond to eternal moral laws. That is why Vico deems it "an error to apply to the prudent conduct of life the abstract criterion of reasoning that obtains in the domain of science."[142] While the moderns have much better scientific methods, the ancients were wiser in self-knowledge. In assessing the quarrel between the ancients and the moderns, Vico encourages his readers to follow the example of ancient philosophers in adjusting rational, physical and ethical doctrines "to the practical common sense that should govern human behaviour."[143]

Vico's term for this practical common sense based on universal moral laws that shine through all contingent legal codes is "*sensus communis.*"[144] The idea that eternal goals are realized through historical human agency forms the basic structure of the *New Science*. It is, as Vico puts it himself, "a rational theology of divine providence in history."[145] The basic historical assumption undergirding the new science is that successive stages in human history, each accompanied by the linguistic development of expression from mythological poetics to reasoned reflection, increasingly reveal God's eternal conception of humanity. Human nature is universal, but not a timeless essence. What it means to be human has to be gleaned from a careful scrutiny of history. The human actors of the cosmic drama of divine providence "can understand their parts—are their parts—and can, in principle, achieve self-understanding."[146] Self-understanding of our divinely ordained humanity thus requires a careful study of cultural history, or, as Vico would say, the history of the human spirit. For while Vico defines the new science in contrast to Descartes's rationalism, he betrays a certain affinity with modernity by setting human consciousness over against nature.[147] He does not, however, agree with the rising scientific confidence that reason will penetrate and conquer nature. And yet his final position does present a kind of duality between nature and culture: while nature remains a foreign, impersonal, inscrutable force, humans can understand culture, because it is a product of the human spirit.[148] As Vico

---

[142]Ibid.

[143]Ibid., p. 37.

[144]Stephan Otto, *Giambattista Vico* (Stuttgart: Kohlhammer, 1989), p. 85.

[145]Vico, *New Science*, p. 102; Otto, *Giambattista Vico*, p. 104.

[146]Isaiah Berlin, *Three Critics of the Enlightenment: Vico, Hamann, Herder* (London: Pimlico, 2000), p. 137.

[147]Berlin thus calls Vico "a dualist" (ibid., p. 145).

[148]Vico, *New Science*, pp. 22-23; Berlin, *Critics of the Enlightenment*, p. 42.

puts it, "for the first indubitable principle . . . is that the world of nations has certainly been made by men, and its guise must therefore be found within the modifications of our own human mind. And history cannot be more certain than when he who creates the things also narrates them."[149]

Vico's *New Science* makes the Renaissance emphasis on historical development the very basis for humanistic studies but retains wisdom and Godlikeness as the goal of education. Vico, as we have seen, already fought against the scientific rationalism arising with Descartes, and soon other developments, such as the philosophies of Thomas Hobbes and especially of David Hume, consummated the rupture of consciousness and being, thus sealing the end of Christian metaphysical realism. In the German tradition, and in the hermeneutic philosophies that will be vital for our understanding of incarnational humanism, it is not until the nineteenth century, with the thought of Wilhelm Dilthey, that this deepened historical consciousness becomes unmoored from the metaphysical realism of Christian Neo-Platonism. Dilthey, of course, is heir to both Kant and Schleiermacher, whose philosophies constitute important milestones in the debate about the link between human consciousness and a higher reality. Unlike British empiricists such as Hobbes and Hume, Kant does not outrightly deny such a link, but he complicates it. In order to distance himself from Hume's scepticism concerning objective universal truths, Kant tries to show that experience is never just neutral sense impression. Rather, the idea of "experience" already carries with it the objective reference that Hume denied (or at least Kant thought he did). According to Kant, experience contains within itself the features of space, time and causality (the so-called a priori categories of perception). Hence when we describe our experience, we always refer to an ordered perspective on an independent world. Kant named his conception of objective knowledge "transcendental idealism."

The term "transcendental" indicates ideas or categories that transcend experience and that make understanding (that is, correct judgments about the reality of things) possible. Transcendental idealism implies a harmony between the capacities of the knower and the known. In other words, "the world is as we think it, and we think it as it is."[150] Kant's position is that

---

[149]Vico, *New Science*, p. 104.
[150]Roger Scruton, *Kant: A Very Short Introduction* (Oxford: Oxford University Press, 2001), p. 34.

world and mind are not perhaps organically linked for immediate access, but that they are definitely (and perhaps wonderously) oriented toward one another. In this sense Kant retains the ancient insight that the mind is naturally adapted to perceive an intelligible world. As one commentator puts it, for Kant, "the order of the world is pre-established, and the internal principles of the substances are in harmony with their external relations. This means that he accepts a modified theory of pre-established harmony as the correct systematic account of the world as a whole."[151]

So if Kant does not outrightly deny a link between mind and being, what is the problem? Let us clear one other misreading of Kant out of the way before we answer this question. Commentators on Kant often, and mistakenly, refer to the famous phrase that we cannot know things in themselves as denial of objective truth. That phrase, however, was intended merely to reject any claims to totalizing viewpoints that could know something absolutely and without any reference to human experience.[152] No, from an incarnational humanist perspective, the problem with Kant's philosophy is his conflation of morality and religion. Kant's primary intent was to save morality from moral scepticism, by demonstrating its rational necessity. For Kant, morality is an expression of duty to the moral intuitions observable in us and in nature. Religion is itself merely an expression of this universal moral law. One wonders if Kant first construed religion in terms of duty and obedience and then found it easy to conflate relation and morality along those lines. Clearly for Kant, religion is defined in terms of duty and obedience. Thus he can think only of religion as moralism (deeds that please God) or confessionalism (confessing belief in creeds). For Kant, since religion is only about pleasing God through actions according to our deepest moral intuitions, particular religious faiths and experiences of God are delusions that will pass with humanity's increasing maturity.

Kant's rational faith undercuts one of the most important gains of Christianity, namely that the *imago dei* is not defined solely as rationality but also as participation in the personal being of God. Kant's moralism cannot really take account of personhood as a moral good. He does not believe that human beings are naturally moral beings but only that they

---

[151]Manfred Kuehn, *Kant: A Biography* (Cambridge: Cambridge University Press, 2001), p. 92.
[152]Scruton, *Kant*, p. 56.

become such when their "reason develop[s] ideas of duty and law."[153] Religion, in other words, is not needed to ground moral values that have now been severed from their former patristic goal of communion with God and divine likeness.

Schleiermacher, by contrast, advocates a less legalistic and more participatory approach to religion. He recalls the cultured despisers of religion to a higher reality, to their organic interconnectedness to a greater world order. Religion is essentially the recognition of this "World-All." By thus defining religion as God consciousness, Schleiermacher tends to reduce particular religions to respective expressions of this sense of utter dependence on something greater that binds all human beings together. Nonetheless, he still views religion as the very ground and goal of all human knowing. As he reminds the secularists of his day, the unity of knowledge and the idea of education as character formation depend on their religious, Christian origins:

> And so I was sure, you would see yourself what I wanted to show you, namely, that you are so completely rooted in the very form of religion, which you despise, i.e., in Christianity, that you cannot extricate yourself from it, and that you try in vain to imagine its destruction without at the same time destroying the things most dear and sacred to you, namely, your entire cultivation (*Bildung*) and way of being, indeed of your art and sciences.[154]

With Dilthey, participation in metaphysical realities is deliberately abandoned for a purely immanent framework for the interpretation of human experience. Dilthey is the first thinker who seeks to justify the human sciences for a postmetaphysical context. He is fully conscious that the ontological synthesis assumed by ancient philosophy and Christianity alike no longer appears valid for an age of science.[155] If transcendent, metaphysical realities no longer guarantee objective reality, the question becomes how objectivity is possible at all. Does human consciousness still

---

[153]Immanuel Kant, *On Education*, trans. Annette Churton, Dover Books on Western Philosophy (Mineola, N.Y.: Dover Publications, 2003), p. 108. The problem with this position is that, by implication, mentally handicapped individuals without this capacity are no longer human, no longer persons, and thus no longer worthy of human dignity.

[154]Friedrich Schleiermacher, *Über Die Religion: Reden an die Gebildeten unter ihren Verächtern (1799)*, ed. Günter Meckenstock (Berlin: Walter de Gruyter, 1999), p. 300.

[155]Wilhelm Dilthey, *Texte zur Kritik der historischen Vernunft*, ed. Hans-Ulrich Lessing (Göttingen: Vandenhoeck & Ruprecht, 1983), p. 40.

transcend biological matter or does it dissolve without remainder into the material world? This problem bears directly on the validity of the human sciences, which Vico had declared to be sciences of the human, culture-making spirit. Without metaphysics, is it not inevitable that the empirical sciences become the only true sciences? This is exactly the question Dilthey seeks to answer:

> The problem of the relation between the natural and human sciences is only solved when the opposition from which we proceeded, between the transcendental point of view, for which nature is ruled by the conditions of consciousness, and the objective empirical point of view, for which the development of Spirit is governed by the whole of nature, becomes resolved.[156]

Dilthey's dilemma shows clearly that what the incarnation had joined has now become separated. Unlike Cusanus, for example, he can no longer draw on the incarnation to explain the mediation between nature and supernature.

Rather than prove the objectivity of inner experience, Dilthey argues that the human sciences should assume that the inner life of spirit is anchored in reality and that universal traits of this life show up in this external reality.[157] In a way, Dilthey's foundation for the human sciences is a repristination of Vico's idea that spirit produces culture, but without Vico's belief in eternal ideals or moral laws. What the human sciences explore and interpret are the cultural expressions of the human spirit as it molds and shapes its material world into a meaningful history. The basic premise that sets the human sciences apart from the natural ones is the human scientist's full awareness and interpretation of the intrinsic connection between life and knowledge: "And thus beginning from life and staying constantly in touch with it forms the first foundational characteristic of the structure of the human sciences; they rest, after all, on experience, understanding, and life-experience."[158] Because of this intrinsic connection, the human sciences will ever struggle with the tension between particular experience, which forms an expression of culture and its interpretation on the one hand, and the attempt to arrive at universal insights on the other.[159]

---

[156]Ibid., p. 48.
[157]Ibid., p. 49.
[158]Ibid., p. 274.
[159]Ibid.

By making life experience the "firm ground" of knowledge, Dilthey overcomes the dualistic gap between perception and reality (and thus also between religion and the world) that earlier philosophies had opened up. He establishes the humanities as the particular science that pursues the meaningful connections of all particular insights in order to arrive at value judgments. Dilthey thus posits for the human sciences a hermeneutical circle. Its entirety consists of life experience and its expression in history, society and their cultural productions, which are then interpreted by dealing with a particular text or phenomenon. And so, "life and life-experience are the ever freshly flowing sources of understanding the socio-historical world; beginning with life, understanding advances into ever greater depths."[160] Neither the human self nor some metaphysical reality is the source of meaning, but rather life itself that "unfolds and forms itself in intelligible unities," which are understood by the careful interpreter. Like musical motifs that forge single notes into discernable melodies, so the unity of individual lives and societies organizes recognizable meanings in history.[161] Dilthey's strong emphasis on historical consciousness did not, at least for him, result in cultural relativism. What saves Dilthey from such historicism is his assumption of a common human nature, so that we can see ourselves in past historical experiences and learn to understand ourselves better through them. For this reason, too, Dilthey thought that the kind of reflections provided by the human sciences would impact life and society in turn, and would thus gain their highest importance.[162]

Dilthey's attempt to bridge the gap between self and world that was opened up by the loss of Platonic metaphysics has been judged unsuccessful by twentieth-century philosophy. Hans-Georg Gadamer, for example, argues that Dilthey is still too much influenced by the Cartesian opposition between mind and world. Dilthey still begins from a position of a private, doubting self that observes historical events. For Dilthey, "the realities of life, the tradition of morals, religion, and positive law" are worked on by human reason but do not really determine it.[163] It is still the private, autonomous self whose authority passes judgment on tradition and tries to

---

[160]Ibid., p. 275.
[161]Gadamer, *TM*, p. 223.
[162]Dilthey, *Texte zur Kritik*, p. 274.
[163]Ibid., pp. 238ff.

determine the meaning of history, rather than assume that history has intrinsic meaning. Dilthey's very effort to establish the objectivity of the human sciences in competition with the natural sciences indicates his continued dependence on Enlightenment rationalism. Thus, history becomes an object of examination, a text approached and deciphered by an ahistorical subject.[164] Gadamer, however, claims the opposite. We can understand history because human consciousness is itself historically determined, that is, carried by history and nourished by that which is handed down to us. Gadamer's criticism is motivated, of course, by his own belief that not until the philosophy of Martin Heidegger is the gap between human consciousness and the world genuinely overcome, because only Heidegger recognizes that the self is itself historically determined. The self can understand the past because it is itself determined by it. In the scientific or positivistic model of truth, the investigating researcher assumed an ahistorical mode of being, as if the observing consciousness floated above time and history. Heidegger claims to the contrary that the knowing subject has the same kind of mode of being as the object. Gadamer explains that Heidegger's claim has become common to "all contemporary criticism of historical objectivism or positivism, namely that the so-called subject of knowledge has the same mode of being as the object, so that subject and object belong to the same historical movement."[165] This "historically effected consciousness," no longer stands over against the realities of the world from which it has to wrest its secrets of meaning, but rather, as Heidegger explains in one of his early lectures, understanding and reflection are modes of human existing.[166] We always encounter things *as* something within a certain horizon of meaning, that is, within a certain context. In other words, understanding is not the bringing to bear of a free-floating consciousness on the raw material of the world, but "understanding is the original characteristic of the being of human life itself."[167] This modern hermeneutical philosophy attempts to do full justice to the historicity of human existence without falling into relativism.

---

[164]Ibid., p. 241.

[165]Gadamer, *TM*, Supplement I, p. 528.

[166]Martin Heidegger, *Ontologie. Hermeneutik der Faktizität*, vol. 63 of *Gesamtausgabe*, ed. Kate Bröcker-Oltmanns (Frankfurt am Main: Klostermann, 1995), p. 65. Hereafter all references to *Gesamtausgabe* are abbreviated *GA*.

[167]Gadamer, *TM*, p. 259.

More than anyone else, Hans-Georg Gadamer has built on Heidegger's philosophy to defend humanism in the twentieth century against "the universal claim of the scientific method" as the measure of truth.[168] Gadamer undertook this defense in the 1960s, but to this day his work constitutes a significant recovery of the importance of language, art and tradition, three old humanistic preoccupations. In describing "what the human sciences truly are,"[169] Gadamer essentially questions how the correspondence between ideas and their expression could be explained after the collapse of metaphysics. Gadamer finds the nexus of this correspondence in what he calls "the mid-world of language."[170] He contends that "our experience of the world is bound to language,"[171] so that language is the all-encompassing center from which we relate meaningfully to the world and to others. The world gives itself to us in language and concepts into which our tradition and historical context have placed us. Therefore, Gadamer can claim that "whoever has language, 'has' the world."[172] Thus like Heidegger, Gadamer opposes prior objectivist models of truth: we do not occupy a theoretical stance toward the world but we *belong* to it.[173] Here then is Gadamer's postmetaphysical revision of Plato's participation. He retrieves Plato's "transcendental relationship between being and truth," which "conceives knowledge as an element of being itself and not primarily as an activity of the subject."[174] For Platonic metaphysics, this correspondence was one between the mind and the forms. For Christians, it was between the human and the divine mind. Gadamer fully appreciates the impact of Christianity on the classical world. The incarnation, as the absolute moment of the saving act of God, contrasted sharply with classical views of

---

[168]Ibid., p. xxi.

[169]Ibid., p. xxii.

[170]Hans-Georg Gadamer, "Man and Language," in *Philosophical Hermeneutics*, ed. and trans. David E. Linge (Berkeley: University of California Press, 1976), p. 76. The English translation "medium" does not convey adequately the required double meaning of the German *Mitte*, as both center and conduit or medium of human existence. Gadamer calls language "the center that conjoins consciousness with existing things [*mit dem Seienden*]" and "the genuine center of human existence" (for German originals see "Die Natur der Sache und die Sprache der Dinge" and "Mensch und Sprache," in Hans-Georg Gadamer, in *Hermeneutik II: Wahrheit und Methode: Ergänzungen, Register*, vol. 2 of *Gesammelte Werke* [Tübingen: J.C.B. Mohr, 1993], pp. 146-54, 66-76; 72, 154, respectively).

[171]Gadamer, *TM*, p. 445.

[172]Ibid., p. 453.

[173]Ibid., p. 455.

[174]Ibid., p. 458.

history as mythical or cyclical, and made possible a true consciousness of history for the first time.[175] Of even greater importance for Gadamer's hermeneutic philosophy and his defense of humanism is the philosophical significance of the incarnation in establishing the centrality of language as the medium for our understanding of the world. The Christian transformation of Greek logic by means of incarnational theology gave birth to "the medium of language, in which the mediation of the incarnation event achieves its full truth."[176] Christianity, as Gadamer knows, solved the Platonic riddle on how the finite mind can participate in the eternal forms, namely, by establishing the "correspondence of soul and being" in the incarnate Word.[177] One could only wish that Christians would realize what Gadamer sees so clearly: "Christology prepares the way for a new anthropology, which mediates in a new way between the mind of man in its finitude and the divine infinity. Here what we have called the hermeneutical experience finds its own, special ground."[178]

Now it is true that Gadamer uses the incarnation and Christian theologies of the Word to go beyond classical Christian metaphysics. He wishes to ground the correspondence between the object of knowledge and the knowing subject, beings and consciousness, no longer in God but in language itself.[179] Gadamer deliberately radicalizes the historical and linguistic dimension, claiming that even Christian scholasticism failed to grasp "the enigma of the incarnation," but he still draws on incarnational insights to locate in language "that correspondence of world and soul" hitherto found by theologians in the infinite mind of God.[180] Precisely because of the incarnation, however, Gadamer's claim that language mediates the world to us is not adverse to theology and can easily be adopted by Christians to affirm the basically interpretive nature of human knowledge. Just because Gadamer lowers, as it were, the correspondence between word and thing to the level of tradition and interpreters does not preclude their ultimate correspondence in the eternal Word. Once such

---

[175]Supplement to ibid., p. 531.
[176]Ibid., p. 428. "Mediation" does not do justice to Gadamer's original term *Mittlertum*, which requires the clumsy English translation of "mediation function" or "mediation capability."
[177]Hans-Georg Gadamer, "The Nature of Things and the Language of Things," in *Philosophical Hermeneutics*, p. 75.
[178]Gadamer, *TM*, p. 428.
[179]Gadamer, "Nature of Things," pp. 75-76.
[180] Ibid., p. 78.

anxieties are laid aside, Gadamer's hermeneutic philosophy helps us to recover the sense that we inhabit an intelligible world. We are not standing over against a naked, indifferent reality, but we "belong" to this world as those who dwell linguistically in this world.

This belonging to an intelligible world through language also reinstates the essential role of tradition for understanding. Belonging is "brought about by tradition's addressing us. Everyone who is situated in tradition . . . must listen to what reaches him from it. The truth of tradition is like the present that lies immediately open to the senses."[181] Understanding has therefore an event character. Understanding something entails the recognition that one is taken up into the event of transmission of human self-understanding through language within a tradition. The "hermeneutical event proper consists in coming into language of what has been said in tradition: an event that is at once appropriation and interpretation."[182] Gadamer often draws on the analogies of play and art to convey the nature of this truth event. Play illustrates the impossibility of detached observation and thus the necessity of personal involvement in truth. In play, for example, a person cannot remain an observer if he or she wants to participate. Instead, one has to give up self-possession: "someone who understands is always already drawn into an event through which meaning asserts itself."[183]

Our experience of art also illustrates that understanding is participation in a truth event. Art, as Gadamer explains, transmits knowledge about our human condition that is historically dependent but also transcends its cultural origin toward universality. In art, something addresses us in the same kind of self-attesting manner that the beautiful does for Plato. The beautiful, Gadamer reminds us, was put forward by Plato to bridge the gap between the transcendent idea and its appearance in the material world. It was the link between being and becoming. Just as for Plato the idea incarnates itself in the appearance of form in the radiance of the beautiful, truth shines forth in art, a truth that we know we did not make and that seems true even though we cannot immediately reconcile it with our beliefs about things.[184] As Gadamer puts it, "when we under-

---

[181]Gadamer, *TM*, p. 463.
[182]Ibid., p. 463.
[183]Ibid., p. 490.
[184]Ibid., p. 485.

stand a text, what is meaningful in it captivates us just as the beautiful captivates us."[185] We feel taken up into an event of truth. What is it, however, that shines forth here? What kind of truth is conveyed? What we encounter are insights transmitted through human tradition that concern the great, perennial questions about human nature, together with possible answers about what it means to be human, without deciding the question of each respective truth in advance.[186]

If Christians find Gadamer's approach rather unsatisfying, we must remember that Gadamer never set out to determine the content of truth or meaning, but, rather, to provide an ontological explanation for *how* they occur. He draws attention, in other words, to the mediation of truth through language and tradition. In his later writings Gadamer sometimes goes beyond this description to assert the undecidability of truth in a way that has invited the charge of relativism.[187] Yet such statements have to be balanced with Gadamer's assertions of our common rationality and linguisticality as the foundation for truth's ability to transcend cultural boundaries. Gadamer is not, in other words, a historicist. His denial of a final interpretation rests rather on his emphasis on human finitude. We are not gods who have an absolute vantage point. Moreover, in effect, a final interpretation contradicts how transmission of truth through tradition works. Tradition, as he explains, "is not the vindication of what has come down from the past but the further creation of moral and social life; it depends on being made conscious and freely carried on."[188] Truth from the past is living truth that speaks to us precisely because its interpretation is the creative translation of past insights into our present horizon. It is for this reason "that interpretation must find the right language if it really wants to make the text speak."[189] Interpretation itself, while drawing on the creativity and meaningful content of language, requires the careful education of the interpreter to develop the tact and poise necessary for listening attentively to the voices of tradition. In this way, Ga-

---

[185]Ibid., p. 490.

[186]Ibid., p. 489.

[187]"It is by no means settled (and can never be settled) that any particular perspective in which traditionary thoughts present themselves is the right one. 'Historical' understanding, whether today's or tomorrow's, has no special privilege. It is itself embraced by the changing horizons and moved with them" (supplement to ibid., p. 535).

[188]Ibid., p. 571.

[189]Ibid., p. 397.

damer also properly links interpretation to virtue by insisting on a certain moral comportment toward tradition that is knowledgeable, respectful and competently attentive, even while critically appropriating its insights about our humanity.[190]

CONCLUSION

In this chapter I have traced the development of humanism after the Renaissance to modern hermeneutic philosophy. This brief survey omitted a detailed description of the rationalist challenge to the humanistic spirit that arose particularly with the work of Descartes and with the Euclidean mindset of Galileo that tended to objectify truth in terms of mathematics.[191] I have also not covered the well-documented loss of participatory metaphysics in the philosophies of Locke, Hume and Hobbes. My goal was rather to point out the continuity of themes within humanism and its educational ideal of character formation in which aesthetics and language play an important role. I have shown that Renaissance humanism was predominantly a Christian humanism, highly dependent on patristic, Platonic Christianity. Renaissance humanists shared with patristic authors a participatory metaphysic and an interest in the nourishment of our true humanity in light of an anthropology grounded in the *imago Dei*. Renaissance humanism continued the patristic and medieval projects of expressing Christianity through a transformative appropriation of the intellectual languages and themes of their day. These attempts were motivated by a deep conviction of a universal divine, personal, trinitarian Logos, on account of which faith and reason, philosophy and theology belonged together. The difference between the pagan Platonist and the Christian was, as Ficino (perhaps the foremost Renaissance Platonist) emphasized, that the latter was "wholly dependent on God's help."[192] Perhaps no one has as clearly formulated the spirit of Renaissance Christian humanism as its most illustrious representative, Erasmus of Rotterdam: "Our philosophy sinks easily into the human mind because it is so largely in accord with human nature. What else is this philosophy of Christ, which

---

[190]Ibid., p. 313.

[191]See my remarks in chap. 1, pp. 34-35.

[192]Marsilio Ficino, *Platonic Theology: Books I-IV*, ed. James Hankins and William Roy Bowen, trans. Michael J. B. Allen and John Warden, I Tatti Renaissance Library (Cambridge, Mass.: Harvard University Press, 2001), pp. 1, 13.

he himself calls being born again, but renewal of a human nature originally well formed?"[193]

Judged from the historical distance of our time, the Renaissance humanists' disdain of medieval culture in general and of scholasticism in
particular should not hinder us from seeing both manifestations of Christianity as pursuing essentially the same goal, namely, integration of reason and faith to show that all truth is God's truth. In attacking scholasticism, its syllogisms, dialectical method and reliance on secondary
compilations rather than on primary texts, Renaissance humanists asserted their own favorite disciplines of grammar, rhetoric, poetry and history, in short, the *studia humanitatis*.[194] The overall unity of all patristic,
medieval and Renaissance humanism is more easily perceived in light of
Étienne Gilson's "two-families" principle. Gilson argues that Christianity's history is marked by two approaches to the reason-faith relation, re-
sembling two families. The father of the first is Tertullian, who insists on
the primacy of revelation and its self-sufficiency.[195] The second is the
Augustinian family of "faith seeking understanding."[196] Clearly all three
Christian humanisms we have examined so far fall into this second family. All three believed in reason as an important element in attaining
Godlikeness, the basic goal of every genuinely Christian, incarnational
humanism. Based on this goal, all three Christian movements defined
education as training toward Godlikeness.

Probably the most significant, and indeed decisive, difference between
the medieval and the Renaissance mind was the dwindling importance of
the church as the main training ground for Godlikeness. In seeking reasons for this change, we cannot overlook the real social failure of the
church in the time leading up to the Protestant Reformation to maintain
its political and economical integrity, and its failure as an organization to
stand with the poor and disenfranchised rather than with the economic
powers of its day. It is for this reason that Luther and Erasmus, theologians
and humanists, could agree on the need for ecclesial reform. Even while
Renaissance Platonism ensured the humanists' adherence to a basically

---

[193]Desiderius Erasmus, "Paraclesis; or An Exhortation 1516," in *The Praise of Folly and Other
Writings*, ed. and trans. Robert M. Adams (New York: Norton, 1989), p. 123.
[194]Trinkaus, *In Our Image*, 1:23.
[195]Étienne Gilson, *Reason and Revelation*, p. 10.
[196]Ibid., p. 24.

sacramental ontology and a deep sense of human solidarity, [197] the deterio-
rated public image of the church must surely have contributed to their
dwindling interest in ecclesiology. Perhaps these conditions also served to
strengthen the noticeable individualization of the Christian faith among
Renaissance humanists,[198] a characteristic that remained deeply ingrained
in Protestantism.[199] This, however, is not our topic. What we do need to
emphasize is that the family resemblance of Christian humanisms across
different time periods depended on a philosophical realism of either Neo-
Platonic or Aristotelian variety.[200]

It is with the demise of this realism, with the breaking apart of the
ontological synthesis, that humanism profoundly changed from the time
of Schleiermacher, through Dilthey, to the time of Gadamer. The idea of
participation was retained, but no longer defined as sharing in an eternal
form or divine being. As Gadamer has shown us most clearly, the best
efforts at retaining humanism seek to correlate mind and matter in understanding the very structure of our historical existence. Gadamer's
philosophical hermeneutics offers incarnational humanism welcome new
perspectives on the nature of language and the role of tradition. He has
given us a thorough philosophical explanation of what Christians have
always claimed, namely, that meaning is never just discovered but
handed down to us (*paradosis*). The great value of Gadamer's hermeneutics for our recovery of incarnational humanism is his emphasis on
the historical nature of our consciousness, that is, of how we understand
ourselves by interpreting the world in light of tradition. Gadamer shows
us that meaningful knowledge about who we are and toward what end
we should live is always an act of translation. The same dynamics at
work in translating concepts from one language into another, the process of intuiting existing meaning and then clarifying and enlarging it
through research, contains "the whole secret of how human beings come
to an understanding of the world and communicate with each other."[201]

---

[197]Trinkaus, *In Our Image*, 2:646.

[198]Ibid., 1:309.

[199]For Luther's conscious attempt to separate divine spirit from church, see Jaroslav Pelikan, *Spirit Versus Structure: Luther and the Institutions of the Church* (London: Collins, 1968), pp. 6ff.

[200]Trinkaus, *In Our Image*, 2:23.

[201]Gadamer, supplement 2 to *TM*, p. 548.

Interpretation and dependence on tradition are conditions at play for every human being who seeks truth, whether in the natural sciences, in the humanities or in the context of religious faith.

Even in Gadamer, however, we see a resistance to the idea of divine transcendence. Something happened within intellectual history that made belief in divine revelation virtually impossible, which raises up important barriers to the recovery of a *Christian* humanism. Ironically, the changes that resulted from excluding revelation, indeed religion, from what counts as rational were caused by the loss of the church's incarnational theology, by the loss of the balance between immanence and transcendence that Gadamer still draws on to articulate his hermeneutic philosophy. This forgetfulness of the incarnation led to the reversal of the Christian synthesis of reason and faith and gives birth to anti-humanism, a cultural philosophy I discuss in the next chapter. First, beginning with Nietzsche's denunciation of metaphysics as Platonic invention that weakens love of life, metaphysics becomes a swear word, along with metanarratives, among postmodern thinkers. For postmodernists, universal concepts are abusive means of imposing limiting or even oppressive norms on the powerless by the powerful. Second, also beginning with Nietzsche, traditional Christianity becomes identified with metaphysics, and then devalued as onto-theology, that is, as the interpretation of God within the univocal categories of being, thus limiting God to human terms. When religion in general, and monotheisms like Christianity in particular, become equated with metaphysics by postmodern philosophers and also by scientists, the result is a deep-seated opposition between faith and reason in Western consciousness, an opposition that surfaces even in those who want to recover religion.

THE RISE OF
ANTI-HUMANISM

◆

Incarnational humanism with its foundational claim that God became a human being so that human beings could attain Godlikeness laid the foundation for the major ideals of Western culture. Our understanding of personhood (balancing the individual and social self), of human dignity and rights, of freedom conceived as responsibility, of the value of language, of the importance of literature and art for self-knowledge, of the correlation of faith and reason (indeed of the spiritual and the material), and, finally, of education as character formation were decisively shaped by the Christian doctrine of the incarnation. I have also argued that this humanistic outlook depended on a participatory ontology. Christians took the Platonic notion that the human mind knows things truly by the mind's participation in ideal forms and transformed it into the kind of illumination theory we find in Augustine.[1] On this account, any human recognition of truth occurs because of our participation in the divine light.

By claiming that universal reason, the cosmic Logos, was not an impersonal principle or world soul but rather a personal and communal being, Christianity added important new dimensions to human self-understanding. It combined the metaphysical realism of Platonic idealism with a personalism to create a true humanism. The theological and philosophical

---

[1]This theory goes beyond attesting to the "divinely instituted rationality of the universe" (Augustine, *De Doctrina Christiana: Teaching Christianity*, ed. John E. Rotelle, trans. Edmund Hill, Works of Saint Augustine: A Translation for the 21st Century [New York: New City Press, 1990], p. 154), but emphasizes the mind's participation in the divine light to discover truth. As Augustine puts it in his *Confessions*, "The mind needs to be enlightened by light from outside itself, so that it can participate in truth, because it is not itself the nature of truth. You will light my lamp, Lord" (4.15.25). Hence all truth is God's truth: "None other than [God] is teacher of the truth, wherever and from whatever source it is manifest" (5.6.10).

potential of this incarnational humanism was unfolded incrementally in the cultural periods we have already discussed. It still continues to provide an important resource for addressing contemporary issues concerning religion and culture. Our sketch of incarnational humanism so far should put to rest the tenacious rumor that Christian humanism is merely a bastardization of Platonic idealism. The church fathers did not create a dualistic worldview that denigrated the material body and disdained the present world for an immaterial existence with God. On the contrary, as I have argued, their belief in the incarnation as inaugurating the new humanity never allowed their uncritical acceptance of Platonism but effected its Christianization. In their incarnational Christology, the fathers emphasized that God "applied to us the similarity of his humanity to take away the dissimilarity of our iniquity, and becoming a partaker of our mortality he made us partakers of his divinity."[2] If the supposed patristic Platonizers had construed "participation in the Word . . . in that life which is the light of men" as a mere spiritual existence, they would have had to believe in the kind of resurrection liberal Protestantism invented in the nineteenth century. But they did not. Indeed, once again our modern linguistic habits betray the deeply ingrained dualism *we ourselves* inhabit, because we view what is spiritual as less substantial or real than the material.

Augustine's imagination is more fertile than our modern one, enabling him to envision that all material things that die or vanish from our human sight are not lost to God but will be restored one day, and, when deemed just, transformed into an imperishable state.[3] There was no question for Augustine that life after death was embodied. The real question we must ask ourselves is why modern readers of Augustine interpret him simply as a world-denying Platonist rather than an incarnational thinker. The reason, I suggest, is that our modern thinking is so deeply embedded in a nonparticipatory and immanent framework of reality, that we no longer really feel genuine kinship with Augustine's theological horizon. In this chapter I argue that Nietzsche's conscious inversion of Platonic metaphysics accounts for the modern inability to envision transcendence. It is with Nietzsche that

---

[2]Augustine, *The Trinity*, ed. John E. Rotelle, trans. Edmund Hill, Works of St. Augustine: A Translation for the 21st Century (New York: New City Press, 1990), p. 154.

[3]Augustine, *Instructing Beginners in Faith*, ed. Raymond F. Canning and Boniface Ramsey, Augustine Series (New York: New City Press, 2006), p. 156.

participatory ontology in the Platonic sense becomes incredible. Subsequent postmodern thinkers, such as Martin Heidegger, Michel Foucault, Jean-François Lyotard and Jacques Derrida, drunk so deeply at the well of Nietzsche's denial of transcendence that later attempts in continental philosophy to talk once again about transcendence, or about God and religion, fail to regain incarnational humanism's holistic view of reality.

THE BEGINNING OF THE END: THE UNITY OF MIND
AND BEING IN KANT AND HEGEL

It is not entirely clear when participatory metaphysics fell apart and along with it a holistic view of reality. We know, however, that the history of philosophy, especially from the Enlightenment onward, was more or less defined by the battle between idealism and realism, in which the question of God and religion always played an important role. The philosophical issue (a realistic versus an idealistic worldview) remained intertwined with the theological problem of how revelation or divine transcendence can exist within the realm of being.

As so often, the philosophy of Immanuel Kant (1724-1804) remains a watershed on this issue too. Kant, who had set out to circumscribe the boundaries of human reason, demonstrates quite clearly that the synthesis of reason and faith falls apart to the degree that we attempt to force our categories on the incarnation rather than allow its mystery to inform our patterns of thought. The treatment of the incarnation in his famous work *Religion Within the Limits of Reason Alone* illustrates this point. In this work, the incarnation is no longer a singular historical event whose peculiar features eventually gave rise to the only possible explanation: God became a human being in order to enable immortality and communion with God. Instead, Kant reinterprets the biblical idea of incarnation in idealist terms. The incarnation now refers to an archetypal idea of man as morally perfect being, an idea which, not unlike the idea of infinity in Descartes, we could not have made up ourselves. The Christian faith has now changed from an actual relational, communal participation in the divine nature to an attitude or disposition (*Gesinnung*).[4] Faith is "the well

---

[4]Immanuel Kant, *Die Religion innerhalb der Grenzen der blossen Vernunft. Die Metaphysik der Sitten*, vol. 5 of Immanuel Kant: Werke in Sechs Bänden, ed. Rolf Toman (Köln: Könemann, 1995), p. 68.

grounded confidence in oneself" to believe that even under trials one should unswervingly adhere to the moral ideal of Jesus as archetype (*Urbild*) of humanity.[5] Kant no longer describes a communion of divine and human spirit, but the contemplation of an *idea*, namely, the moral ideal of a life pleasing to God. Speculative reason has no need for the actual reality of the incarnation[6] or the intrinsic link of the incarnation with atonement and redemption. In short, Kant reduces the primarily communal and participatory nature of Christianity to a duty ethics for which Christ provides the inspiration. It is thus no surprise that he replaces the relational language of orthodox Christianity with duty language. Religion within the limits of reason alone is thus a "moral constitution" found "in the all-embracing and sincere maxim of conformity of conduct to the law."[7] This inner disposition requires a change of heart, but it is a change of attitude that "must be possible because duty requires it."[8]

As is well known, Kant's abstraction of Christianity into a moral ideal stems from his struggle to bridge the gap between being and consciousness. Kant wedged the filter of the transcendental categories between objects as they are in themselves and as they appear to our minds based on a certain mental grid. Kant is not an antirealist who denies the objective existence of things outside ourselves. He still assumes a natural congruence between mind and reality, but it is no longer direct. The thing in itself has no *meaningful* existence apart from the mind's role as a "synthetic unity of apperception" that presents an object as meaningful to us.[9] Kant deliberately narrows this activity of pure reason to the knowledge of empirical nature.[10] Within these limits, God can be known no more directly than the thing itself. He is not known by participation but rather through the detour of his moral law. It is indeed the limit of theoretical reason only

---

[5]Immanuel Kant, *Religion Within the Limits of Reason Alone*, trans. Theodore M. Greene and Hoyt H. Hudson (New York: Harper & Row, 1960), p. 55; Kant, *Die Religion*, p. 80.

[6]For Kant, such supernatural implications add nothing to the function of Christ as a moral ideal (*Religion Within the Limits*, p. 55).

[7]Ibid., p. 60.

[8]Ibid.

[9]Kant argues that we could not perceive order and regularity in nature had the nature of our mind not already placed them there. He calls this a "necessary, i.e. a priori natural unity" of the appearances, clearly arguing for the objective reality of the mind's correspondence to the world (Immanuel Kant, *Kritik der reinen Vernunft*, ed. Jens Timmermann [Hamburg: F. Meiner Verlag, 1998], A 125-26, 229). For the "transcendental-unity of apperception," see ibid., A 127-28.

[10]Immanuel Kant, "Die Transzendentale Dialektik," in ibid., p. 754.

to guess at the nature of God, not to see him. Through practical reason, however, through our intimations of the moral law, we get a sense of God.[11] Kant's ethic thus depends "on the motivational spring (*Triebfeder*) of pure practical reason" that grants us a sense of our sublime destiny.[12] As a result, Kant's religion, conceived within the bounds of reason, amounts to a moralism in which practical reason affirms the basic moral precepts of Christianity without the necessity of revelation or of divine grace.[13] This result is somewhat ironic in that Kant set out to prescribe the limits of reason, precisely in order to remove God from the grasp of rationalism.

Many of Kant's contemporary critics argued, however, that he destroyed the unity of reality and mind, so that his position ultimately amounts to skepticism and subjectivism. Such critics (including Friedrich Schlegel, Novalis, Friedrich Schelling and Georg W. F. Hegel) focused on passages in his work that seemed to deny any link between things as they are (things in themselves) and as they appear to us, so that perceptions are really only ideas in the mind.[14] Kant scholarship has shown that his "transcendental idealism" was actually meant to be a kind of empirical realism with an idealist twist. In other words, Kant did assume that the objects we encounter are real, but that our perception of them in the mind is not straightforward. Our perception of objects depends, instead, on formal categories in the mind that structure them, such as space and time, for example.[15] The most generous reading of Kant is that he sought to defend religion by denying theoretical reason direct access to divine reality. Much like the modern philosopher Derrida, Kant does not deny external reality or our mind's capacity to connect to it, but seeks to problematize this connection.[16]

Kant helps us to see what happens to the kind of critical realism made possible by the incarnation when an intrinsic connection between mind and reality begins to fall apart. For when the participatory ontology of

---

[11]Ibid., p. 463.
[12]Ibid., p. 386.
[13]Kant does refer to grace as that which compensates for the impossibility of adhering fully (on account of our finitude and mutability) to the moral ideal (Kant, *Die Religion*, pp. 93-94).
[14]Fredrick C. Beiser, *German Idealism: The Struggle Against Subjectivism, 1781-1801* (Cambridge, Mass.: Harvard University Press, 2002), pp. 48-49.
[15]Ibid., pp. 58-59.
[16]For Derrida's position on referentiality, see the interview "Jacques Derrida: Deconstruction and the Other," in *States of Mind: Dialogues with Contemporary Thinkers on the European Mind*, ed. Richard Kearney (New York: New York University Press, 1995), p. 173.

ancient metaphysics and its Christian transformation break down, the natural link between mind and being is severed. With this rupture, the age of epistemology begins. Subsequent thinkers in the modern age now have to wrestle with the relation of the mind to the object and ask how we can know things or other minds, including God. We have already seen how Schleiermacher tried to counter Kant's perceived dualism by arguing that human research into reality will ultimately point to the primordial unity of all things in a God. For Schleiermacher, each religion is merely a particular way in which this truth is expressed in history, and he fits the incarnation into this scheme. Christ does unite two otherwise disparate aspects, namely, the original image of our humanity (*das Urbildliche*) and the historical (*das Geschichtliche*). Yet Christ no longer is an actual incarnation of God himself but rather is of full God consciousness, that is of God's true presence in him.[17] Schleiermacher's emphasis on a sentiment of utter dependence or God consciousness shifts the weight from the doctrinal content of religions, and thus from their rational intelligibility to their value as an historical embodiment of God consciousness.[18]

It is not Schleiermacher the theologian but Hegel (1770-1831) the philosopher who tries to heal the breach between mind and reality by harnessing for his philosophical system the incarnation's ability to unite transcendence and immanence. Arguing explicitly from "a Christian point of view," Hegel draws on the incarnation to explain how an idea or concept (*der Begriff*) can be both universal and particular.[19] Just as in Christ, God's Spirit is particularized without loss of divine transcendence,[20] so a universal concept is incarnate in its concrete historical expressions.[21] For Hegel, this is not merely an analogy, because for him God really is the universal idea, and humankind participates in his "eternal history, the eternal movement" of divine self-revelation.[22] Hence Hegel can claim that Christianity reveals the true nature of reason. Just as God incarnates himself fully in

---

[17]Friedrich Schleiermacher, *Der christliche Glaube. 1821/22*, 2 vols., ed. Hermann Peiter (Berlin: Walter de Gruyter, 1984), vol. 2, § 116, p. 27.
[18]Gunter Scholtz, *Ethik und Hermeneutik: Schleiermachers Grundlegung der Geisteswissenschaften* (Frankfurt am Main: Suhrkamp, 1995), p. 196.
[19]Georg Wilhelm Friedrich Hegel, *Vorlesungen über die Philosophie der Religion* (Frankfurt am Main: Suhrkamp, 2003), 2:285, 533.
[20]Ibid., 2:336.
[21]Ibid., 2:533.
[22]Ibid., 2:298.

Christ, and our understanding of this revelation is a gradual unfolding through rational reflection while participating in this reality, so human reason unfolds the universal truths of ideas. This incarnational model allows Hegel, in contrast to Kant, to affirm without reservation the participation of human consciousness in the historical and material world, but also the simultaneous transcendence of human consciousness.[23]

For Hegel, the basic philosophical issue is the tension between the subjective pole of human consciousness and objective reality or being. Merely moral religions (Hegel's prime example is Islam, but he refers also to Judaism) tend to construe the relation of the self to a higher reality in voluntaristic terms. The will is central in these religions, which usually define reason and rational behavior as choosing to obey divine law. Even more moderate moralisms that define religion as a sense of utter dependence or of the need for salvation still postulate an abstract, general relation of consciousness and objective reality. Only in Christianity with its incarnation are subject and object united in a participatory way that retains the integrity of each. In the way Christianity determines the correlation between God (objective, transcendent reality) and the human consciousness (subjective pole of experience) as participation, we also detect how, in human knowing, general truths are expressed truly in the particular.

Hegel appeals to the Eucharist to demonstrate the conjoining without loss of objective reality and subjective perception. In the Eucharist, "the absolute content, the unity of the subject and the object is offered to the individual for immediate enjoyment, and insofar as the individual is reconciled, this achieved reconciliation is the resurrection of Christ."[24] For Hegel, the Lutheran understanding of the Eucharist represents particularly well how transcendent reality is present in the material. In the Eucharist, the receiving subject and the divine object are somehow united without either losing its identity or integrity. Hegel prefers the Lutheran to the Catholic mass, because the former emphasizes the spiritual presence of God. Hegel finds here a "transubstantiation" that sublimates the external. Here what is "other" becomes internalized without losing its identity. Moreover, the individual and church community necessarily experience and reflect the divine presence in their historical and cultured particular-

---

[23]Ibid., 2:299.
[24]Ibid., 2:327-28.

ity, and yet God is nonetheless fully present.[25] On this theological basis, Hegel develops his idea of the World Spirit (*Weltgeist*), whose self-realization through human beings determines the course of history.

It is unfortunate that Hegel eventually subordinated trinitarian, incarnational theology to his philosophical system. He takes the divine *kenosis* in the incarnation a step too far by turning God into the World Spirit who comes to consciousness through humanity in successive stages within the human disciplines of religion, art and philosophy. Orthodox Christianity defines kenosis as the condescension of God in the incarnation taking on sinful humanity with its limitations but without thereby ceasing to be God. This is a unilateral, downward movement from God whose love prompts this identification with humanity.[26] Hegel thus ultimately inverts the patristic idea of deification: "Hegel's God needs man, who becomes himself divine in this process."[27] The world, insofar as it corresponds to spirit, is the continual incarnation of God, who becomes himself through the other of humanity. This may indeed serve as an adequate ideal of how universal concepts appear to consciousness, but it remains an inadequate description of the incarnation in a biblical, theological sense.[28]

NIETZSCHE'S ANTI-PLATONISM AND THE BIRTH OF ANTI-HUMANISM

Hegel was the last great nineteenth-century philosophical thinker who tried to heal the breach of the onto-theological synthesis, and he did so explicitly on the basis of the incarnation. For him the incarnation of God still grounds the conjoining of the finite and the infinite, of being and mind.[29] There is, of course, another way of healing this breach, namely, by denying the existence of transcendence altogether. This is the path chosen by Friedrich Nietzsche (1844-1900), who, after undergoing a classical

---

[25]Ibid., 2:329-30.
[26]For a New Testament account of kenosis, see Gordon Fee, "The New Testament and Kenosis Christology," in *Exploring Kenotic Christology: The Self-Emptying of God*, ed. Stephen C. Evans (New York: Oxford University Press, 2006), pp. 25-36. For a theological account and the patristic view of kenosis together with its importance for atonement theology, see Kathryn Tanner, *Christ the Key* (Cambridge: Cambridge University Press, 2010), pp. 256-73.
[27]Eberhard Jüngel, *Gott als Geheimnis der Welt: Zur Begründung der Theologie des Gekreuzigten im Streit zwischen Theismus und Atheismus*, 3rd ed. (Tübingen: Mohr, 1978), p. 124.
[28]Wolfhart Pannenberg points this out in *Jesus—God and Man*, trans. Lewis L. Wilkins and Duane A. Priebe, Library of Philosophy and Theology (London: SCM Press, 2002), p. 362.
[29]Hegel, *Vorlesungen*, 2:480.

humanistic education, became one of Germany's most promising young philologists.[30] In Nietzsche's thought, universal reason, Platonism, metaphysics, indeed any kind of transcendence, are declared fundamental errors or illusions grown over time. To understand Nietzsche's philosophical interpretation of human existence requires that one grasp his resolute philosophical honesty in the pursuit of an immanent vision for human existence. Partially through his encounter with Arthur Schopenhauer, and partially through his work on ancient Greek tragedy, Nietzsche arrived at a vision of reality that he describes in his early work *The Birth of Tragedy from the Spirit of Music*.

According to Nietzsche, early Greek poets grasped an essential fact about human life, namely, its participation in the constant becoming of the world, the constant play of emerging entities and their eventual dissolution that gives way to new creations. They fully understood this play—nature's relentless fecundity and life within which human existence has no intrinsic meaning—to be the abyss of meaninglessness. This relentless force of life is captured by the Dionysian spirit of ecstasy and becoming, which proves bearable only when veiled by the Apollonian garb of rhythm and order. Apollo was the god of dreams and of order, and in Nietzsche's view Greek drama, music and art in general employ the beautiful as a veil to cover the abyss to render life livable. The genius of early Greek art, however, consisted in keeping this veil transparent enough to remind us of the primordial unity of all things in the eternal becoming of nature.[31] For this reason Nietzsche could claim that "only as aesthetic phenomenon are human existence and the world eternally justified."[32]

Nietzsche never fundamentally alters this basic, immanentist vision of the world.[33] For him, the remainder of Western philosophy, indeed of cul-

---

[30]For an exhaustive, detailed account of Nietzsche's life, see Curt Paul Janz, *Friedrich Nietzsche Biographie*, 3 vols. (Munich: Hanser, 1981).

[31]Friedrich Wilhelm Nietzsche, *Sämtliche Werke*, Kritische Studienausgabe, vol. 1, *Die Geburt der Tragödie. Unzeitgemässe Betrachtungen I-IV. Nachgelassene Schriften 1870-1873*, ed. Giorgio Colli and Mazzino Montinari, 2nd rev. ed. (Munich: Deutscher Taschenbuch Verlag, 1999), pp. 43-46. Hereafter references to *Sämtliche Werke*, Kritische Studienausgabe will use the abbreviation *KSA*.

[32]Ibid., 1:47.

[33]He did, however, shift his emphasis from working toward a renewal of Western culture through reviving this original Dionysian spirit in modern music, especially in the music of Beethoven and Wagner, to posing the more existential question about the meaning and stability of human existence in the absence of any metaphysical consolation. The change was occa-

tural history, is marked by successive attempts to make the Apollonian veil a permanent feature, so that the world becomes imbued with reason and order, and the mind becomes more important than the body. Nietzsche's summary term for this tendency is *metaphysics*. Religions are merely another variety of this tendency to find meaning beyond or behind this world. Nietzsche argues that in ancient Greece it was predominantly Plato and his mouthpiece Socrates who set this illusion of transcendent order in motion. Socrates "had taught that reason could penetrate reality to the point that it could correct reality's flaws. This had become the fundamental dream of Western culture, a dream that was later manifested in the modern approach to scholarship."[34] Plato is thus the first to objectify life and the world of experience, and therewith provides the platform for the measuring, calculating assessment of reality favored by the natural sciences. Nietzsche's rejection of Platonic idealism thus also leads him to argue against "contemporary culture's reliance on reason and its commitment to scientific optimism."[35] Science's overconfidence in reason, metaphysics and religion is dismissed by Nietzsche because these either overlook or deny the basic nature of reality as constant becoming. They all shy away, in other words, from the Dionysian dimension of life.

Religious types and metaphysical philosophers are thus classified by him as *Hinterweltler*, that is, those who suppose a world behind (*hinter*) the one we see.[36] Nietzsche's explanation for the invention of realities beyond this world varies, but he will increasingly argue from a biological (indeed, one might say, evolutionary) basis, as becomes evident if one keeps in mind that he, not unlike Richard Dawkins more recently, expands this term to include the transmission of cultural values as instincts that developed to ensure the survival of the human species.[37] Human

---

sioned by Nietzsche's own physical collapse in 1879, which ended his academic career and inaugurated a new, somewhat nomadic lifestyle in survival mode, characterized by the search for climate and diet that would ameliorate his physical ailments (Janz, *Friedrich Nietzsche Biographie*, 2:14ff.).

[34]Bernd Magnus and Kathleen M. Higgins, "Nietzsche's Works and Their Themes," in *The Cambridge Companion to Nietzsche*, ed. Bernd Magnus and Kathleen M. Higgins, Cambridge Companions to Philosophy (Cambridge: Cambridge University Press, 1996), p. 23.

[35]Nietzsche, *KSA*, 1:21.

[36]Friedrich Wilhelm Nietzsche, *KSA*, vol. 4, *Also Sprach Zarathustra, ein buch für Alle und Keinen*, ed. Giorgio Colli and Mazzino Montinari, 2nd rev. ed. (Munich: Deutscher Taschenbuch Verlag, 1999), p. 35.

[37]Friedrich Wilhelm Nietzsche, *KSA*, vol. 3, *Morgenröte. Idyllen aus Messina. Die fröhliche Wis-

beings, Nietzsche admits, cannot easily live without meaning. We need to know, from time to time, why we exist. We "cannot flourish without a periodic confidence in life! Without belief in reason in life."[38] Because of this human need for a purpose, the development of humanity follows a kind of "tidal law," alternating between setting up transcendent realities and then doubting them. Here we encounter a crucial dimension in Nietzsche that is later taken up by Foucault: any supposed objective truth is merely the interpretation of former interpretations without any anchor in anything permanent. In this radically immanent hermeneutic, truth *is nothing but* interpretation. Nietzsche thus goes beyond a hermeneutic view of truth, that is, beyond the claim that truth is always mediated through language and thus from a sociocultural and historical point of view. Rather Nietzsche claims that whatever we perceive as lasting insights into the human condition is destabilized by the continual becoming of life itself.

Life emerges as the cardinal category of Nietzsche's thought, and he classifies every philosophy or worldview as either life affirming or life denying. Metaphysics, and religions of any stripe—whether Christianity, Judaism or Buddhism—deny life and seek to escape life by positing another world.[39] Hence metaphysicians and the religious are "preachers of death."[40] The Christian idea of the incarnation itself, says Nietzsche, emphasizes a this-worldly orientation:

> That God became human points only to the fact that man should not seek his happiness in the eternal but establish his heaven on earth; the delusion of a celestial world produced a wrong attitude in the human spirit toward this earthly world: it was produced during humanity's childhood. . . . Only under difficult struggles and doubts does humanity become mature by recognizing the beginning, middle and end of religion.[41]

---

senshaft, ed. Giorgio Colli and Mazzino Montinari, 2nd rev. ed. (Munich: Deutscher Taschenbuch Verlag, 1999), 1.1., p. 372.

[38]Ibid.

[39]Nietzsche praised Islam for being more masculine, noble and life affirming than Christianity. See *Der Antichrist*, in Friedrich Wilhelm Nietzsche, *KSA*, vol. 6, *Der Fall Wagner. Götzendämmerung. Der Antichrist. Ecce homo. Dionysos-Dithyramben. Nietzsche contra Wagner*, ed. Giorgio Colli and Mazzino Montinari, 2nd rev. ed. (Munich: Deutscher Taschenbuch Verlag, 1999), secs. 59-60, p. 249.

[40]Nietzsche, *KSA*, 4:55.

[41]Friedrich Wilhelm Nietzsche, *Friedrich Nietzsches Werke*, Historisch-Kritische Gesamtausgabe (Munich: Beck, 1934-40), 2:54-61, quoted in Janz, *Friedrich Nietzsche Biographie*, 1.1:103.

Yet, as is well known, he soon dismissed this idea and condemned Christianity as life denying slave morality, a morality contrary to nature.[42] Natural morality is governed by "the instincts of life" and assures self-preservation and freedom. Christianity, however, introduces God as the enemy of life, who condemns human passions and instincts. Nietzsche summarizes and dismisses Christianity's nihilistic attitude with the words, "the Saint, in whom God delights, is the ideal castrate. Life stops where the kingdom of God begins."[43]

Nietzsche understands himself as a prophet who challenges the entire web of metaphysical and moral values woven by the amalgam of Christianity and Greco-Roman culture. He fights the "Christian-ecclesiastical pressure of thousands of years."[44] It is important, though, to notice that Nietzsche enters this struggle in the name of true humanity. A recurring refrain in his writings is that philosophy has to overcome traditional concepts of human being (der Mensch). Religious views of humanity, especially Christian ones, are rejected by Nietzsche because for the last eighteen hundred years European Christianity has turned man into a sublime monstrosity (Missgeburt) by subverting the human instinct toward greatness and self-fashioning.[45] Particularly, the Christian teaching that everyone is equal before God has papered over the differences in spirit and courage that exist between strong leaders and the common "rabble," thus reducing the modern European to a mediocre and ridiculous herd animal.[46] This decadent species aspires to tranquil mediocrity, remains satisfied with the opiates of a comfortable life, music, culture and education, and is afraid of facing the truth of life as suffering out of which something meaningful has to be fashioned by the creative and self-disciplined power of man. This is the task of the creative overman, who, like a mason, carves a meaningful existence out of the hard and ugly rock that is humanity.[47]

The new humanity exemplified by the overman is characterized by creative self-fashioning in the face of life's eternal becoming. I have already

---

[42]Christianity, argues Nietzsche, is "a negation of the will to life turned religion" (KSA, 6:359).

[43]Götzendämmerung in Friedrich Wilhelm Nietzsche, KSA, 6:85.

[44]Nietzsche, KSA, vol. 5, Jenseits von Gut und Böse. Zur Genealogie der Moral, ed. Giorgio Colli and Mazzino Montinari, 2nd rev. ed. (Munich: Deutscher Taschenbuch Verlag, 1999), 1.1., p. 372.

[45]Ibid., 5:83.

[46]Ibid.

[47]Nietzsche, KSA, 4:111.

mentioned that life and an affirmation of this world are central to Nietzsche's program. What however is life? Nietzsche's prophet, Zarathustra, reveals this secret to his disciples: life itself in its constant self-overcoming is the will to power: "Wherever I found living things, I found the will to power; even in the will of the servant I still found the will to be master. . . . Only where life is there also is Will: Not, however, will to life, but—this I teach you— will to power."[48] As will to power, life is "that which always has to overcome itself."[49] Every human endeavor and aspiration is part of this will to power, including the search for truth.[50] Everything we deem permanent achievements, including moral values, will be overcome by life itself in its constant becoming. Even good and evil become relative categories; they are mere phases in the eternal becoming of life itself. Life's creative force is beyond good and evil, and so should be those who recognize life for what it is. These are the overmen, the creative artists who, like life, are beyond good and evil.[51]

Nietzsche's antimetaphysical vision of being as becoming and his definition of becoming as the will to power have had far-reaching influences on seminal thinkers now classified as postmodern. Nietzsche is indeed the grandfather of postmodernism, and, more importantly for our topic, the progenitor of postmodern anti-humanism. For at least two major postmodern figures, Martin Heidegger and Michel Foucault, Nietzsche's critique of Platonism became a decisive factor in their thinking about humanity.

NIETZSCHE'S ANTI-HUMANIST HEIRS: MICHEL FOUCAULT AND MARTIN HEIDEGGER

For postmodern anti-humanists, Platonism, and by implication also Christianity, originated the modern view of truth as objectifying representation and the obsession with measuring truth according to eternal,

---

[48]Ibid., pp. 147-49.
[49]Ibid., p. 148.
[50]The view that the will to power can manifest itself as the will to truth and a rationally ordered world according to set universal laws connects Nietzsche's will to power with Michel Foucault's project in the *History of Madness* (ed. Jean Khalfa, trans. Jonathan Murphy and Jean Khalfa [London: Routledge, 2006]). For the discipline of the will to truth, all things are supposed to bend to the will of reason, so that reason becomes a recognizable deity that renders the world comprehensible (Nietzsche, *KSA*, 4:146).
[51]Nietzsche, *KSA*, 4:15-26; 4:99-101.

timeless and essential forms. Platonism, and by association humanism, signifies the arbitrary imposition of a reifying order on the dynamic and complex nature of reality. Clearly, Nietzsche is the father of anti-humanism, insofar as he already denounced the Platonic forms as a world-denying source of value, and linked Christianity to this form of Platonism in his famous line that "Christianity is Platonism for the people."[52] For Nietzsche, Plato's "invention" of pure spirit and the good beyond being is the beginning of metaphysical dogmatism in the West. The Platonic escape from the flux and complexity of this worldly history into a realm of fixed essences and ideals makes Platonism "the worst, longest-lasting and most dangerous error of all errors."[53]

Nietzsche's rejection of Platonic metaphysics resulted in two dominant strands of postmodern anti-humanism. Just like Nietzsche, these two successors provide some helpful elements for our recovery of incarnational humanism, but also counterproductive ones. On the positive side, they unmask any pretensions to a stable self whose rational powers can completely illuminate both self and world. They "decenter" the human subject by denying that the world revolves around an autonomous, sovereign "I" that stands over against an external world. On the negative side, however, they either deny transcendence altogether or declare it to be completely ineffable and unrepresentable. The first school of anti-humanism, exemplified by the French philosopher Michel Foucault, rejects transcendence altogether, and, as a result, reduces the human subject to a function within economic and political structures. Foucault's denial of transcendence and a rational order beyond the flux of history saddles human beings with the responsibility of becoming themselves divine artists who create meaning and fashion the self.

The second anti-humanistic adaptation of Nietzsche is Martin Heidegger's philosophy. Heidegger follows Nietzsche in rejecting Platonic metaphysics. Unlike Nietzsche, however, Heidegger retains transcendence, but shelters it from any possible objectification and hence from any totalizing control by any group or individual. In Heidegger's work, humanity is rightly denied the privilege of being the sole measure of things, but human dignity becomes wrongly subordinate to an indefinable trans-

---

[52]Nietzsche, *KSA*, 5:12.
[53]Ibid.

cendent beyond good and evil. In the following paragraphs we briefly examine each anti-humanism in turn.

Michel Foucault (1926-1984), who has become famous as a cultural historian with a focus on power relations and social structures, was influenced not only by Nietzsche but, in his structuralist phase, also by Marx and Freud. For example, the early Foucault advocated the "disappearance of the subject" because our supposedly stable self is actually governed by subconscious structures. Combining Freud's theories with structuralism, Foucault rejected the possibility of directly experienced meaning. Whatever we think of as a direct intuition or sense of truth actually depends on unconscious structures, which express "the formal conditions for the appearance of sense."[54] Along with the dissolution of the self, Foucault also advocates the dissolution of the idea of "history" as an ideal "evolutionary," linear process of consciousness.[55] Instead he favors the idea of "effective history," in which the self and its convictions are constituted by what he calls "discourses."[56] Discourses are a dominating cluster of linguistic, literary and scientific expressions that influence and strengthen one another to form an accepted paradigm that decides legitimate knowledge: "We are no longer inside truth but inside the coherence of discourses, no longer inside beauty, but inside complex relations of structures."[57] What we used to think of as a substantial self or a "proper name" is really nothing more than "one's voice in that great din of discourses which are pronounced."[58]

As much as these beliefs about the nature of human reality are shaped by Freud and Marx, however, the main determining influence on Foucault remains Nietzsche. Foucault himself admitted that his method "owes more to Nietzschean genealogy than to structuralism, so called."[59] When we survey the development of Foucault's thought from beginning to end, we find that each decisive phase was determined by Nietzsche, especially Nietzsche's anti-Platonic view that no essences or universals exist. Therefore, in keeping with Nietzsche's interpretations of cultural history, Fou-

---

[54]Hinrich Fink-Eitel, *Foucault: An Introduction* (Philadelphia: Pennbridge Books, 1992), p. 42.

[55]Ibid., p. 43.

[56]Interview with Michel Foucault, "On the Ways of Writing History," in *Aesthetics, Method and Epistemology*, ed. James D. Faubion, trans. Robert Hurley, vol. 2 of *Essential Works of Foucault* (New York: New Press, 1998), p. 289.

[57]Ibid., p. 290.

[58]Ibid., p. 291.

[59]Ibid., p. 294.

cault's historical method shows that supposedly timeless truths turn out to be favored interpretations that have stood the test of time.[60] In short, Foucault espouses a radically immanent hermeneutical approach in which signs no longer point to any transcendent reality. For him, semiology and hermeneutics are "two fierce enemies," for signs have no absolute existence, nor do they point to universal essences. In place of any transcendent realities to which signs can point, Foucault postulates that there are "only interpretations . . . the violence, incompleteness, the infinity of interpretations." Anything else results in rigid systems and arbitrary repression.[61]

Foucault's *History of Madness* provides another example of Nietzsche's influence. The work is evidently conceived in the spirit of Nietzsche's *Birth of Tragedy*. Foucault's history of reason reflects Nietzsche's sentiment that Western rationality is a repressive drive for Apollonian order that derives from a deep-seated will to power, whereby reason wants to suppress its Dionysian other.[62] This same sentiment continues into Foucault's poststructuralist phase. Foucault eventually follows Nietzsche's belief, in contrast to structuralism, that social practices, desire and the will to power shape discursive practices rather than the other way around.[63] This also remains the case when the will to power works through institutionalized discourses to control our lives, which is what Foucault terms "bio-power." Even Foucault's last ethical phase, in which he advocates self-fashioning or care of the self, follows Nietzsche's idea of self-overcoming.[64] It is thus fair to say that Foucault's research is a modern-day implementation of Nietzsche's philosophy.[65] It is a massive simplification of Foucault's thought but nonetheless true to claim that Nietzsche provided him with the two central themes: an absence of natural or essential meaning, and the overcoming of humanity in the name of creative self-fashioning. It remains for us to see how this Nietzschean philosophy influences Foucault's understanding of humanism.

---

[60]Hubert L. Dreyfus and Paul Rabinow, *Michel Foucault, Beyond Structuralism and Hermeneutics*, 2nd ed., with an afterword by and an interview with Michel Foucault (Chicago: University of Chicago Press, 1983), p. xii.
[61]Michel Foucault, "Nietzsche, Freud, Marx," in *Aesthetics*, p. 278.
[62]Fink-Eitel, *Foucault*, p. 17.
[63]Ibid., p. 42.
[64]Ibid., p. 61.
[65]Fink-Eitel notes that Foucault's "work repeats Nietzsche's philosophy under the influence of French conditions in our century" (ibid., p. 61).

Foucault rightly associates humanism with trust in human reason, but he shares Nietzsche's deep pessimism about human rationality. Reason, he argues, is nothing but a metaphysical ruse for justifying whatever the most powerful want to impose on the weak. Because of reason's moral indifference, Luther famously referred to reason as "the devil's appointed whore," and he criticized reason as an instrument of human self-assertion.[66] In his early work Foucault applies Luther's image to humanism, which he regards as a mask for human abuses of power. He concludes that "ultimately, this humanism has in a certain sense been the little whore of all thought, culture, morality, and politics of the last twenty years." Humanism is promiscuous enough to unite under one cover, so to speak, both "Stalinism and the hegemony of Christian democracy."[67]

For Foucault, humanism is only a substitute for religion; like god and religion, humanism is merely another myth we have invented to ensure and control society's functioning within a purposeful structure: "It is the possibility of control which gives rise to the idea of a purpose. But mankind has in reality no purpose[;] it functions; it controls its own functioning, and it continually creates justifications for this control. We have to resign ourselves to admitting that these are *only* justifications. Humanism is one of them, the last one." And therefore the posthumanist philosopher should demonstrate "that mankind is starting to discover that it can function without myths. No doubt the disappearance of philosophies and religions would correspond to something of that kind."[68]

What does functioning without myths look like? Foucault answers this question in the last, ethical phase of his thinking, in which he undertook to write a genealogy of ethics, that is, of how people thought about their selves.[69] His purpose was to change dangerous ideals of the self for better ones.[70] The governing idea of this "care of the self" is, again with Nietzsche, to achieve self-sovereignty, but to do so not in an essential way of discovering who one is, but of controlling and shaping one's self by certain

[66]Martin Luther, *Sämtliche Werke*, ed. Johann Conrad Irmischer and Johann Georg Plochmann (Erlangen: Heyder, 1826-1858), 16:142-48.
[67]Michel Foucault, *Religion and Culture*, ed. Jeremy R. Carrette, Manchester Studies in Religion, Culture, and Gender (New York: Routledge, 1999), p. 99.
[68]Ibid., pp. 102-3.
[69]Dreyfus and Rabinow, *Michel Foucault*, p. 240.
[70]Ibid., p. 236.

practices.[71] Foucault seems to prefer ancient Greek practices of self-mastery that were self-fashioning (self *poiēsis*) in the purest sense, because care of the self was not a means to an end. It was Christianity that introduced a crucial change into this picture by moving from a purely creative self to the self as a sign that had to be deciphered.[72] For this reason practices of self-mastery changed profoundly. Christianity "substituted an idea of a self which one had to renounce because clinging to the self was opposed to God's will, for the idea of a self which had to be created as a work of art."[73]

Foucault's view of Christianity is partially correct insofar as Christianity opposed a sovereign self. Yet his views that Christianity taught the renunciation of desire, was obsessed with deciphering the self and used ascetic techniques only to test one's dependence on God suffer from the same thin grasp of Christianity easily detectable in Nietzsche's writings.[74] Ancient Christians in fact warned against too much introspection. Nor was desire simply renounced, but, as we have seen in Augustine, was to be subordinated to love of God as the highest good. Finally, patristic Christianity especially evidences a strong tradition of fashioning the self in the image of the true humanity that is Christ. In contrast to Foucault's thought, Christianity knows of a self that ultimately escapes utter control or knowledge, but that is nonetheless more than a mere construct of time, culture and history. This concretely historical and yet transcendent self is based on the human relation to God, to the transcendent Thou, whose address establishes the infinite importance of the responding human "I."[75]

---

[71]Ibid., p. 250. The self "is constituted in real practices—historically analyzable practices. There is a technology of the constitution of the self which cuts across symbolic systems while using them."

[72]Ibid., p. 242. In Christianity "all this ethics has changed. Because the telos has changed: the telos is immortality, purity and so on. The asceticism has changed because now self-examination takes the form of self-deciphering" under divine law. And "even the ethical substance has changed, because it is not *apphrodisia*, but desire, concupiscence, flesh, and so on."

[73]Ibid., p. 245.

[74]Ibid., p. 249.

[75]The classical expression of this Christian self is literally and literarily embodied in Augustine's dialogue with God in the *Confessions*, especially when he talks about self-knowledge (10.5, p. 241). Bonhoeffer continues the Augustinian tradition of selfhood when trying to answer the question "Who am I" to himself during his imprisonment. Unable to decide between others' assessment of him as proud, unfazed and self-assured, and his own self-perception as weak, cowardly and faithless, he finally concluded: "They mock me, these lonely questions of mine. Whoever I am, Thou knowest, O God, I am Thine" (Dietrich Bonhoeffer, *DBWE*, vol. 8, *Letters and Papers from Prison*, ed. John W. de Gruchy, trans. Isabel Best et al., pp. 459-60).

Foucault's rejection of humanism stems from his total rejection of transcendence that he imbibes from Nietzsche. In the absence of transcendence, what remains is a purely functional view of human existence governed by power relations within which, according to the later Foucault, we must take care of the self. Foucault's anti-humanism does help to focus attention on economic and political structures that define what it means to be human. This recognition of "biopolitics," however, does not necessitate the rejection of transcendence. Nor is it at all clear how one can effectively resist structural injustice if functionality and immanence define reality. Self-assertion through countermanipulation seems to be the only remaining expression of human freedom. To be fair to Foucault, he follows his master Nietzsche in denying that an ethics of self-mastery automatically leads to the domination of others. Like Nietzsche, Foucault insists that one first has to take care of the self. And with Nietzsche, Foucault takes his cues from ancient Greek philosophy,[76] whose view of the self he favors over later Christian-Platonic views. At least he realizes that both ancient and Christian ascetic practices are united in their opposition to the Cartesian notion that truth can be had without any relation of the self to ethics. As Foucault puts it, after Descartes, "I can be immoral and know the truth."[77] Asked, however, whether the care of the self, when separated from care for others, runs the risk of becoming an absolute that will lead to the domination of others, he replies:

> No, because the risk of dominating others and exercising a tyrannical power over them arises precisely only when one has not taken care of the self and has become the slave of one's desires. But if you take proper care of yourself, that is, if you know ontologically what you are, if you know what you are capable of, if you know what it means for you to be a citizen of a city, to be a master of a household in an *oikos*, if you know what you should and should not fear, if you know what you can reasonably hope for and, on the other

---

[76]Foucault interprets the term *epimeleia heautou* as "taking care of oneself." This concept meant that from theoretical and scientific knowledge, one had to choose "only those kinds of things which were relative to him and important to life" (Michel Foucault, "On the Genealogy of Ethics: An Overview of a Work in Progress," in Dreyfus and Rabinow, *Michel Foucault*, p. 243). In the classical Greek view, this meant first of all "taking into account only oneself and not the other, because to be master of oneself meant that you were able to use others. . . . You should be master of yourself in a sense of activity, dissymmetry, and non-reciprocity" (ibid., p. 242).

[77]Dreyfus and Rabinow, *Michel Foucault*, p. 252.

hand, what things should not matter to you, if you know, finally, that you should not be afraid of death—if you know all this, you cannot abuse your power over others. Thus, there is no danger.[78]

There is no danger of abuse of others, because he who knows exactly what duties he has as husband, father and citizen "will find that he enjoys a proper relationship with his wife and children."[79]

Incredibly, Foucault argues that the ancient Greek idea of self-mastery did not entail the idea of abusing others; this idea only appeared on the cultural stage with Christianity's teaching of self-denial. According to him, the advent of Christianity profoundly changed the nature of self-mastery. The ethics of the self have changed because the *telos* of asceticism has changed from a kind of self-knowledge according to one's role and function in society and the world toward the more ethereal pursuits of one's spiritual purity and immortality.[80] In short, Foucault reverts to the old Nietzschean anti-Platonic accusation that Christianity's other-worldiness results in the neglect of this world. He does admit, of course, that Christianity, too, promotes self-fashioning, but the goal lies outside of this world. Greek ethics, by contrast, focus on the present life and society. If "the reputation one leaves behind is the only afterlife one can expect," the incentive for focusing on one's own life and on the place one occupies among others is much stronger.[81] Foucault also acknowledges that Christians seek to conquer the fear of death, but because of their belief in a life after death, they "rush through life" toward the next.[82]

Foucault's account of the self is problematic in two ways. First, he must surely know that the Greek concept of selfhood pertained predominantly to the ruling elite, for whom slaves were subhuman beings with, at best, a limited capacity for reason or virtue.[83] Aristotle shares this view, deeming friendship between slave and master impossible because it could never en-

---

[78]Michel Foucault, "The Ethics of the Concern for Self as a Practice of Freedom," in *Ethics: Subjectivity and Truth, Michel Foucault on Truth, Beauty & Power 1954-1984*, ed. Paul Rabinow (New York: New Press, 1997), p. 288.

[79]Ibid., p. 288.

[80]Ibid.

[81]Ibid., p. 289.

[82]Ibid.

[83]Trevor J. Saunders, "Plato's Later Political Thought," in *The Cambridge Companion to Plato*, ed. Richard Kraut (Cambridge: Cambridge University Press, 1992), p. 481.

tail a meeting of rational minds.[84] By not questioning the broader table of values according to which a society engages in self-mastery, Foucault seems to endorse inequalities modern society no longer tolerates. This problem raises the important question: beyond an assertion of freedom, according to *what image* ought the self be fashioned? Clearly, Foucault shares this problem with Nietzsche, whose move from an old to new table of values in *Zarathustra*, though freed from traditional Christian morality, cannot reach beyond mere self-affirmation.[85]

Even stranger is Foucault's second assertion that Christianity's idea of self-denial "disturbs the balance of the care of the self" because of its belief in another reality beyond this world. For Christianity, he claims, "the self was no longer something to be made, but something to be renounced and deciphered."[86] While ancient paganism advocated "an aesthetic of existence," Christianity advocated self-control for the sake of "renouncing the self and deciphering the truth."[87] Thus Christianity introduces a new inward turn together with the self-examination of conscience that was unknown to the ancient world.[88] Foucault refers in this context to Gregory of Nyssa's treatise on virginity as exemplary for the Christian renunciation of self and world.[89] And indeed, the chapter in which Foucault refers to Gregory, which bears the ominous title "That Release from Marriage Is the Beginning of Caring for One's Self," could be taken to signal Christianity's life-denying attitude.[90] At first glance Gregory's insistence on separating ourselves "from the life of the flesh" and embracing a life of im-

---

[84]In *Nicomachean Ethics,* Aristotle mentions the impossibility of friendship between master and slave on account of their inequality (1161a33-b5-10). The relation of master to slave is that of user to his tool. Aristotle does allow friendship on the basis of their mutual humanity, yet this is hardly possible, since he also declares slaves practically devoid of reason. For this discussion see C. C. W. Taylor, "Politics," in *The Cambridge Companion to Aristotle,* ed. Jonathan Barnes, Cambridge Companions to Philosophy (Cambridge: Cambridge University Press, 1995), p. 256.

[85]Just like Foucault, Nietzsche denounces Christianity as self-denial, but also wants to retain a sense of self-love in a nonnarcissistic sense, and a sense of community as his constant address to his "brothers" indicates. See "Von alten und neuen Tafeln," in Nietzsche, *KSA,* 4:246-69.

[86]Foucault, "Genealogy of Ethics," p. 248.

[87]Ibid.

[88]Ibid., pp. 248-49.

[89]Foucault, "Concern for Self," p. 288.

[90]Gregory of Nyssa, *Ascetical Works,* ed. Roy Joseph Deferrari, trans. Virginia Woods Callahan, Fathers of the Church (Washington, D.C.: Catholic University of America Press, 1999), p. 46. Hereafter shortened citations will use the abbreviation *AW.*

mortality does seem to indicate the kind of escapism which, along with an overscrupulous conscience, Foucault attributes to Christianity. The picture changes, however, when we read Gregory's treatise in light of the patristic incarnational theology described earlier.

The Christian idea of self-fashioning is indeed a poetics of the self, but it is *theopoēisis*, shaping oneself in the likeness of God. This is a participatory idea that involves soul, body and world, since God's purpose in that deification, the becoming fully human through participation in Christ the God-man, is itself part of creation's redemption by God. For Gregory at least, the body-soul relation has to be understood from their common creation by God and their ultimate goal of becoming like God.[91] For this reason Gregory argues that the human is made of body and soul, each nonexistent without the other.[92] And yet at the same time Gregory can claim that the true likeness of God only resides in the soul, which will be purged from all ungodly and merely material desire by God.[93] And yet for all his Platonic-sounding notions, Gregory, based on the New Testament teaching on the bodily resurrection, rejects reincarnation or a disembodied afterlife and maintains that the same body we possess in this life will be reassembled in glorified fashion around the purified soul for eternal communion with God.[94] In other words, Foucault's focus is unduly narrow and misses the bigger Christian framework within which self-fashioning finds its proper place. Without repeating in detail what I already described in earlier chapters, the briefest outline of Gregory's thought will suffice to expose Foucault's blind spot.

Gregory defines Christianity as "an imitation of the divine nature," a restoration of humanity's original creation in the divine image.[95] As Gregory explains, this restoration does not indicate our assumption of a divine nature but rather the conformity of our actions to the divine attributes. Godlike actions are "those that are free from all evil, purifying themselves

---

[91]Gregory of Nyssa, "On the Making of Man," pp. 420ff.

[92]Ibid., 30.29, p. 426.

[93]Gregory of Nyssa, "On the Soul and Resurrection," in *Gregory of Nyssa: Dogmatic Treatises*, vol. 5 of *Nicene and Post-Nicene Fathers*, Second Series, ed. Philip Schaff and Henry Wace, trans. William Moore and Henry Austin Wilson (Peabody, Mass.: Hendrickson, 1994), pp. 450-51.

[94]Ibid., p. 454. Gregory assumes that the soul possesses a kind of memory imprint of its former body, according to which matter will be reassembled around it (ibid., p. 448).

[95]"On What It Means to Call Oneself a Christian," in Gregory of Nyssa, *AW*, p. 85.

as far as possible in deed and word and thought from all vileness."[96] The central idea of deification, of becoming like God in thought and deed, is that one's soul and life radiate the beauty of God. The real experiential or participatory nature of this kind of Christianity is easy to miss. Gregory argues that "just as by participating in Christ we are given the title 'Christian,' so also are we drawn into a share in the lofty ideas which it implies. . . . If therefore someone puts on the name of Christ, but does not exhibit in his life what is indicated by the term, such person belies the name and puts on a lifeless mask."[97]

Life is the essential category for Gregory to describe communion with God. The life born from God necessarily must begin to show the features of this divine parentage. Gregory argues that every moral effort at virtue helps unearth the divine image that naturally belongs to human beings.[98] Yet no human effort can accomplish what is effected by communion with God. It is when God indwells the soul that the soul now wedded to actual life is nurtured by the Spirit. To the soul thus reborn, "participation in the Spirit restores to its nature its former beauty."[99] This process is a synergistic effort of grace and works: "For the grace of the Spirit gives eternal life and unspeakable joy in heaven, but it is the love of the toils because of the faith that makes the soul worthy of receiving the gifts and enjoying the grace."[100] There is no doubt in Gregory's mind that the gift of new life is by God's grace alone. God's gifts "are so great that it is not possible to find toils worthy of them."[101] Even in trying to achieve Godlikeness, that is, in establishing "himself as an honor to God," the Christian never thinks "for a minute that he has made himself worthy of God."[102] And yet toil is necessary. *Theosis* requires human effort to reflect the beauty of the God who is present in all creation. It is the life lived in communion with God in the pursuit of Christ's virtues

---

[96]Ibid., p. 87.

[97]Ibid., p. 85.

[98]For Gregory, Christ's saying "the kingdom of God is within you" shows "that the goodness of God is not separated from our nature, or far from those who choose to seek it, but it is ever present in each individual, unknown and forgotten when one is choked by the cares and pleasures of life, but discovered again when we return our attention back to it" ("On Virginity," in Gregory of Nyssa, *AW*, p. 44).

[99]Gregory of Nyssa, "On the Christian Mode of Life," in *AW*, p. 130.

[100]Ibid., p. 131.

[101]Ibid., p. 145.

[102]Ibid., p. 144.

that reflects the original beauty of the *imago Dei*.[103]

If all this is true, what does Gregory mean when he says "one must deny his own soul?"[104] What it does not mean is to perform inhuman feats of abstinence, self-flagellation or morbid scrutiny of conscience. Gregory actually warns against any ascetic excesses because such will fatigue and exasperate the soul, thus keeping it from its true goal of God-likeness.[105] Indeed, Gregory rejects as heretics those who would develop a hatred of creation and denounce marriage.[106] What self-denial does mean, however, is to fashion a self in the light of God's beauty through contemplation of God. By participating in and orienting oneself toward divine beauty, the spiritual eye is refocused and the soul becomes attuned to what makes us truly human.[107] Self-denial in this sense turns out to be rather a spiritual realism. Gregory soberly observes that our bodily growth is entirely due to nature's pleasure and entirely beyond our control. The measure of the soul, however, does depend on our judgment and efforts. Through the soul's participation in God, it is strengthened and participates in the divine virtues. Through the Spirit's presence, "the person is strengthened and has a share in and touches upon the other virtues we ask of God through a mystical holiness and a spiritual energy and an inexpressible disposition."[108] This disposition includes "redemption of the soul from the passions."[109]

Does not this denial of the passions at least confirm Foucault's assertion that on the "Christian model" of sexuality and of life in general, desire is accented in order to extinguish it?[110] Once again, Foucault fails to recognize the role of desire in Christian thought. From Gregory to Augustine, at least, pleasure and passions are sinful when they are *misdirected;* the task of self-fashioning is to eradicate base and dehumanizing passions, and to align one's pleasures with the love of God. "Evil passions" or "earthly passions" distort the beauty of the soul as the divine image.[111] It is evident that Greg-

---

[103]Gregory of Nyssa, "On Virginity," in ibid., p. 43.

[104]Gregory of Nyssa, "On the Christian Mode of Life," in *AW*, p. 145.

[105]Gregory of Nyssa, "On Virginity," in *AW*, p. 66.

[106]Ibid., p. 31.

[107]Ibid., pp. 39, 41, 51.

[108]Gregory of Nyssa, "On the Christian Mode of Life," in *AW*, p. 155.

[109]Ibid.

[110]Dreyfus and Rabinow, *Michel Foucault*, p. 243.

[111]Gregory of Nyssa, "On the Christian Mode of Life," in *AW*, pp. 155, 89, respectively.

ory uses these terms not to denote body or geography but to indicate that the entire human being, body and soul, should mirror the divine likeness.[112]

It is only by understanding Christian *theopoēisis*, or self-fashioning, as the inauguration and cultivation of the new humanity embodied in Christ and represented by his church, that Gregory's entire theology makes sense. In the end, far from simplistically denying the world, Gregory's ascetic writings end in ecclesiology, or better yet, in *koinonia*. Denying one's soul, then, has two goals, neither of which despises the world or the body when viewed from their eschatological destination as new creation in Christ. The first goal is deification, "transforming human nature and worth into the Angelic."[113] The second, however, is equally important, and intrinsically part of the first, because God is a God of community. In Gregory's words, "denying one's soul means to seek not one's own will but rather making one's will the established word of God and using this as a good pilot which guides the common fulfilment of brotherhood harmoniously to the shore of the will of God."[114] The idea of deification is linked to the idea of a new humanity that is enjoyed together with others. It is that for which Christ died, and the Christian is to follow the same way; such is the Christian mode of life:

> Knowing, then, the fruits of humility and the penalty of conceit, imitate the Master by loving one another and do not shrink from death or any other punishment for the good of each other. But the way which God entered upon for you, do you enter upon for Him, proceeding with one body and one soul to the invitation from above, loving God and each other. For love and fear of the Lord are the first fulfilment of the law.[115]

Perhaps Foucault's view of ancient Christianity would have improved with further research into the topic of self-fashioning. As it stands, however, he has not gone much beyond Nietzsche's own cliché of Christianity as a form of world-denying Platonism. It is remarkable, however, that Foucault, again like Nietzsche, also ends his career exploring his own kind of "hyper-humanism" by focusing on the human freedom for self-creation in

---

[112]As Gregory puts it, "For truly herein consists the real assimilation to the Divine; viz. in making our own life in some degree a copy of the Supreme Being" ("On the Soul and the Resurrection," in Gregory of Nyssa, *AW*, p. 449).

[113]Gregory of Nyssa, "On Virginity," in *AW*, p. 74.

[114]Gregory of Nyssa, "On the Christian Mode of Life," in *AW*, p. 145.

[115]Ibid., p. 147.

the absence of any universal rational order or natural law. For this reason some critics regard Foucault's work as a continuation of the Renaissance spirit with its emphasis on human autonomy. Michael Hardt and Antonio Negri, for example, see in Foucault's rejection of transcendence "the same revolutionary impulse that animated Renaissance humanism," especially when he extols "self-creation" in his later works. Anti-humanism, they claim, is a logical consequence of "Renaissance humanism's secularizing project, or more precisely, its discovery of the plane of immanence." Supposedly, both of these accomplishments "are founded on an attack on transcendence" and reject the false transcendence of liberal humanism, which simply transfers God's transcendence to man.[116] Yet for Hardt and Negri, this very refusal of any transcendence by anti-humanism is not some kind of resignation. For them the refusal of transcendence affords the wholly positive possibility of unleashing "the creative life force which animates the revolutionary stream of the modern tradition."[117] On this view, anti-humanism, or humanism after the demise of any transcendent conceptions of humanity, opens the space for self-fashioning.

The two main problems with the position taken by Hardt and Negri are historical and philosophical. Historically, Renaissance humanism did not "discover the plane of immanence" but rather built on the Christian discovery of this plane through the incarnation, and it is not evident that Renaissance humanism pursued a "secularizing project" with the goal of self-creation. Renaissance humanists were too Christian and too Platonic to endorse this modern idea of subjectivity.

The philosophical problem with anti-humanism is the disappearance of *any* transcendent *telos* for self-creation. In a way, of course, trusting the "creative powers that animate us as they do all of nature" hearkens back to the Aristotelian-Christian humanism of Thomas Aquinas and the developmental humanism of Giambattista Vico.[118] Without any conception of what humanity is to look like, however, how is anti-humanism not simply

[116]Michael Hardt and Antonio Negri, *Empire* (Cambridge, Mass.: Harvard University Press, 2000), p. 91.

[117]Ibid., p. 92.

[118]On Aquinas, see Étienne Gilson, *The Spirit of Mediaeval Philosophy* (Notre Dame, Ind.: University of Notre Dame Press, 1991), pp. 169-208. On the theological implications of Vico's *New Science*, consult John Milbank, *The Religious Dimension in the Thought of Giambattista Vico, 1668-1744*, 2 vols. (Lewiston, N.Y.: Edwin Mellen, 1991-1992).

an invitation for the powerful to trample the weak into submission? Without any transcendent standard of good or bad self-creations, how is anti-humanism not a "humanism" beyond good and evil?

MARTIN HEIDEGGER: FROM ANTI-HUMANISM TO HYPER-HUMANISM

The second philosophical anti-humanist strand actually champions transcendence, but refuses it any ethical contours because distinct forms of transcendence place them once again in the controlling hands of human beings. Martin Heidegger is the leading philosophical force behind the view that the humanist tradition in Western thought constitutes just such a reification of transcendence. Heidegger's view of humanism is, as is every other aspect of his thinking, determined by his account of the history of Being, or rather the alleged obfuscation of this history by philosophers from Plato onward, and by the need to recover humanity's relation to Being. Indeed, that Heidegger insists on defining human identity and self-knowledge in light of the history of Being poses the central ethical problem of his philosophy. Before we address this problem with the help mainly of Emmanuel Levinas's critique of Heidegger, we have to understand Heidegger's critical stance toward humanism. Heidegger does not reject humanism because it constitutes merely a negligible blip on the screen of intellectual history, but for the opposite reason: humanism is a central but disastrously wrong conception of human nature and has distorted human self-understanding. Heidegger's antipathy to humanism is based on his understanding of proper human reflection and his corresponding view of human subjectivity. Heidegger's philosophy constitutes another important attempt in the history of philosophy to construe in nonmetaphysical terms the intrinsic link between the mind and being, between "*logos* and *physis*."[119]

For Heidegger the best description of humanity's relation to Being, a relation he considers to be the very source of our reflections concerning our humanity, is found in the logos conception of the early Greek philosopher Heraclitus.[120] Logos should be understood with the early Greeks as

---

[119]Martin Heidegger, *An Introduction to Metaphysics*, trans. Ralph Manheim, vol. 40 of *GA* (New Haven, Conn.: Yale University Press, 1987), p. 135.

[120]Heidegger, without naming him as the inspiration, adopts Nietzsche's argument in *The Birth of Tragedy*, namely, that pre-Socratic philosophy had a more proper insight into the nature of reality, and that Plato and Socrates distorted this pretheoretical understanding.

"the original collecting collectedness which is in itself permanently dominant."[121] This sense of logos as original gathering and its importance for a historical understanding should reshape, according to Heidegger, the question about the nature of human being from "what is man" to "*who* is man."[122] According to Heidegger, beginning with Plato and Aristotle, Western thought has obscured this important insight and turned logos into logic, thus objectifying the essence of our humanity and turning the original Greek impulse of questioning into objectivistic obsession with verifiable answers.[123] However,

> the determination of human nature is *never* answer but *essentially* question. The asking of this question and our deciding of this question . . . is the very essence of history. The question about who a human being is always has to be asked in conjunction with the question how it stands with Being. The question of man is not an anthropological question but a historically metaphysical question.[124]

Nothing less is at stake for Heidegger in this question than the very essence of what it means to be human, and this essence depends on the human relation to Being. Any other definition of humanity constitutes an objectifying distortion of who we are. Along with Nietzsche, Heidegger regards the Christian religion, insofar as it has bought into metaphysics, as just such a distortion.

Heidegger argued in *Introduction to Metaphysics* that Christianity's Logos doctrine is another form of objectifying thinking that obfuscates the original Greek concept of logos as "gathering." He claims that the metaphysics behind the Christian Logos concept has obscured the openness toward Being of Heraclitus' logos with the distortive, objectifying lens of "whatness" by locating Being in *one* particular being, the son of God: "Logos in the New Testament does not, as in Heraclitus, mean the Being of beings, the gathering together of the conflicting; it means *one* particular being, namely the son of God. And specifically, it refers to him in the role of mediator between God and men. . . . A whole world separates

---

[121]Heidegger, *Introduction to Metaphysics*, p. 128.

[122]Ibid., p. 144.

[123]"Logic arose in the curriculum of the Platonic-Aristotelian schools. Logic is an invention of schoolteachers, not of philosophers" (ibid., p. 121).

[124]Martin Heidegger, *Einführung in die Metaphysik*, vol. 40 of *GA* (Tübingen: Max Niemeyer Verlag, 1998), p. 107. Cf. Heidegger, *Introduction to Metaphysics*, p. 140.

all this from Heraclitus."[125] Heidegger thus practically inverts a most basic conviction of Western humanism that originated with the Christian doctrine of the incarnation. The foundation for humanism and self-formation is no longer the incarnation, which was the archetypical interpretation of the *imago Dei*; rather, in a much more profound way than Nietzsche does, Heidegger claims that Christianity is indeed a form of Platonism and therefore essentially contributed to the decline of Western culture.

This decline consists in the inversion of early Greek epistemology. In early Greek anthropology—at least in Heidegger's view—humans experienced reality as something greater than themselves in which they participated and to the natural laws of which they should conform. Human reason (logos), as Heidegger puts it, was an intrinsic part of nature (physis) without being reducible to nature.[126] The result of this view was a participatory rather than detached conception of knowledge. Apprehension, claims Heidegger, was not yet viewed as an activity of the thinking self, but as an event: "Apprehension is not a function that man has as an attribute, but rather the other way around: apprehension is the happening that has man."[127] Human beings thus understand themselves as part of the history of Being, and thinking is the participation in Being. The mutual belonging of man and Being is

> for the West the crucial definition of being-human, and at the same time it embodies an essential characterization of Being. The separation between being and being-human comes to light in their togetherness. We can no longer discern this separation through the pale and empty dichotomy of "being and thinking," which lost its roots hundreds of years ago, unless we go back to its beginnings.[128]

The pre-Socratic roots show Heidegger that human identity is thus determined as the being which is open to the question of Being. According to him, neither biological definitions of humanity nor metaphysical anthropologies do justice to the question What is human being? Instead,

---

[125]Heidegger, *Introduction to Metaphysics*, p. 135. Translation slightly amended: "Logos meint im Neuen Testament von vorneherein nicht wie bei Heraklit das Sein des Seienden, die Gesammeltheit des Gegenstrebigen, sondern Logos meint ein besonderes Seiendes, nämlich den Sohn Gottes" (Heidegger, *Einführung in die Metaphysik*, p. 156).

[126]Heidegger, *Introduction to Metaphysics*, p. 135.

[127]Ibid., p. 141.

[128]Ibid.

Heidegger, decades before his *Letter on Humanism*, defines human identity as openness to Being. More overtly than he does later, his earlier work also links this identity to action, to the making of history. Heidegger scoffs at the spineless academic bookworms who discuss the question What is man? Instead, inserted into the tension between Being and thinking, man "must transform the being that discloses itself to him into history and bring himself to stand in it."[129] We can still hear in these words the ring of Heidegger's authentic existence from *Being and Time:* Man is neither "primarily an ego" or individual, nor is he primarily community. Rather, man's essence is determined "from out of the essence of Being itself."[130] According to Heidegger, it is only later with the rise of Platonism that the unity of Being and thinking is sundered, resulting in the distortion of humanity's self-understanding.[131] Plato's notion of the ideas constitutes the origin of objectifying the mystery of Being (and thus of its revelatory mode of disclosure) and is directly related to the humanistic notion of human formation (*Bildung*) or education.

It is important to note that for Heidegger the reification of Being initiates the forgetfulness of Being and thus the occlusion of humanity's true identity in its relation to Being. Platonism, scientific objectivity and humanism are all offshoots of this original alienation. In Heidegger's words,

> The beginning of metaphysics in the thinking of Plato is at the same time the beginning of "humanism." . . . Human being is thus determined within a metaphysical framework as the animal oriented toward the forms, toward logos thus defined, and becomes the rational animal. It is the basic thrust of all humanism to secure human flourishing by freeing him toward his potentialities and leading him toward the certainty of his destiny.[132]

Heidegger argues that in the various metaphysically oriented human-

---

[129]Ibid., p. 143.

[130]Ibid., p. 144.

[131]Heidegger argues that Greek and Christian metaphysics assume "a certain predetermined being as the archetype for all beings" (*Die Grundprobleme der Phänomenologie*, ed. Friedrich-Wilhelm von Herrmann, vol. 24 of *GA* [Frankfurt am Main: Klostermann, 2005], p. 210). Moreover, the notion that human being is first of all a "mental thing" that is only afterward placed in space and time has obscured that human understanding depends on embodied, existential modes of knowing (Martin Heidegger, *Being and Time: A Translation of Sein and Zeit*, trans. Joan Stambaugh [Albany: State University of New York Press, 1996], §12, 56).

[132]"Platons Lehre von der Warheit," in Martin Heidegger, *Wegmarken*, ed. Friedrich-Wilhelm von Herrmann, vol. 9 of *GA* (Frankfurt am Main: Klostermann, 1996), p. 236.

isms this calling is realized through the various means of "forming of moral comportment, as redemption of the immortal soul, as the unfolding of creative energies, as the training of reason, as the cultivation of character, as awakening of a sense for community, the disciplining of the body or the opportune combination of several or all of these humanisms."[133]

Heidegger concludes that the metaphysical idea of conformity to a certain eternal ideal has determined Western thought and only terminated when Nietzsche announced the demise of metaphysics. Yet this metaphysical attitude has been so firmly lodged in Western culture that it continues to determine modern history and our conceptions of humanity.[134] This history is also bound up with theology from the beginning, since Plato already posits the forms or archetypes for everything that exists. Heidegger explains that with Plato and Aristotle's definition of the highest and first cause as *to theion*, the divine, Being became reduced to an idea. And

> ever since the interpretation of Being as *idea* has thinking the Being of beings become metaphysics, and metaphysics is theological. In this context, theology is an interpretation of the cause of beings as God and the repositioning of Being into this cause which contains Being in itself, and from which it issues forth, because it is the Being of beings *(das Seiendste des Seins)*.[135]

According to Heidegger, our understanding of God, Being and human being has suffered as a result of this static metaphysical obsession with causal and normative thinking. God has become nothing more than the highest cause, and human beings as those who measure things have aspired to become independent and autonomous. Rather than participating in a higher reality, we have come to think of ourselves as masters of nature. Heidegger praises Nietzsche for having dethroned this overweening pride and trust in human reason. Nietzsche's criticism of Western rationalism and the autonomous self allows us to attune our ears once more to real thought, namely, the thinking of Being itself.[136]

Since Heidegger tries to expose stifling and reductive views of human

---

[133]Ibid.
[134]Ibid., p. 237.
[135]Ibid., p. 236.
[136]Ibid., p. 267.

rationality, it may be more accurate to call him a hyper-humanist rather than an anti-humanist.[137] For while Heidegger rejects traditional humanism as Platonism (and by implication also Christian humanism as another form of Platonism), he nonetheless suggests a *different* path of being truly human by returning to the ancient questions of why there is something rather than nothing, and of why humans are the only ones who really wonder about this at all. Because human beings ask this question, their very being is transcendence, a standing out from instinctual animal life. Heidegger insists that the question of our humanity is inevitably bound up with our recognition of the question of Being as the foundational question of philosophy. Our human freedom and dignity consist in our ability to care about the question of Being:

> Allowing the encounter with beings, comportment toward being in every way of openness is only possible where there is Freedom. Freedom is the condition for the possibility for the revealing of Being of beings, of the apprehension of Being. . . . The question about the nature of freedom is the foundational problem of Philosophy, when in turn the main question of Philosophy is determined by the question of Being.[138]

We are thus most essentially human, and most free, when we pursue the question of Being. The purpose of human existence is not the accumulation of knowledge, nor is it human progress through science and technology, not even through education. What defines our true humanity is our vocation as "Shepherds of Being."[139]

It is never quite clear what Heidegger means by Being, and the capitalization of this word in Heidegger translations tries to capture the sense that Being describes not merely the form of being of some existent thing, nor indicates the sum total of all beings, but points to that which lets

---

[137]Dominique Janicaud, "Du bon usage de la *Lettre sur l'humanisme*," in *Heidegger et la question de l'humanisme: Faits, concepts, débats*, edited by Bruno Pinchard and Thierry Gontier (Paris: Presses universitaires de France, 2005), p. 225.

[138]Martin Heidegger, *Vom Wesen der menschlichen Freiheit. Einleitung in die Philosophie*, ed. H. Tietjen, vol. 31 of *GA* (Frankfurt am Main: Klostermann, 1994), p. 303. For Heidegger authentic freedom and willing are determined out of our attunement to Being (ibid.).

[139]Heidegger asserts that his thinking, even in *Being and Time*, had always aimed at this conclusion: "Human being as the shepherd [*Hirte*] of Being. Toward this alone was the thinking of *Being and Time* directed, when ecstatic existence is experienced as Care" (Heidegger, *Wegmarken*, p. 331)

things appear and therefore transcends both beings and their being.[140] We should recall that Heidegger designates this transcendence precisely as mystery, and while we may not want to follow him into this mysticism of Being, we can agree with his essential point that human existence is determined by an openness to transcendence exterior to itself, something that cannot itself be objectified and thus brought under human control.

Whatever obstructs the pursuit of the human vocation to think Being, whether it be through prefabricated views or reductive, instrumental forms of reasoning, constitutes a barrier to our true humanity. For Heidegger, the obsession with objectifying and measuring knowledge in Western thinking has led to the fragmentation of knowledge. Research disciplines can no longer find a common purpose because they have lost a sense of their subservience to the question of Being. Given this view, it is no surprise that the nature of knowledge and the state of higher education were central, recurrent themes in Heidegger's work.[141] This concern is also evident in his installment as rector of the University of Freiburg and in his infamous inaugural address. The political context does raise many questions about this speech, but even this should not obscure the fact that unlike many modern university presidents, Heidegger at least understood that pragmatism and instrumental reason would be the death of the humanistic academy.

Why is all of this so important? Heidegger's existential analysis of human being recovers some important insights modern philosophy had lost. Catholic theologian Hans Urs von Balthasar argues, for example, that Heidegger recovers the mystery of existence, the wonder that something *is* at all.[142] Moreover, Heidegger rightly criticizes the anthropocentrism of

---

[140]Heidegger's point is that we are guided by an implicit understanding of Being that never becomes fully explicit; Being is something that does not exist like a thing but that *is* nonetheless. It is that which "makes our experience of beings possible." Our task is "to understand Being, Being that we may no longer call itself an existent, Being that does not appear as a being among other beings, but one that has to exist nonetheless [*das es aber gleichwohl geben muß*] and that does exist in our understanding of Being" (*Die Grundprobleme der Phänomenologie*, pp. 14-15). For a beginning definition, see Michael J. Inwood, *A Heidegger Dictionary*, Blackwell Philosopher Dictionaries (Malden, Mass.: Blackwell, 1999), pp. 27-28.

[141]Holger Zaborowski demonstrates the central importance of the developments of higher education in Heidegger's work. See Holger Zaborowski, *Ein Fall von Irre und Schuld? Martin Heidegger und der Nationalsozialismus* (Frankfurt am Main: Fischer Taschenbuch Verlag, 2010).

[142]Hans Urs von Balthasar, *Herrlichkeit: eine theologische Ästhetik,* vol. 3.1, *Im Raum der Metaphysik. Teil II: Neuzeit* (Einsiedeln: Johannes-Verlag, 1965), pp. 784-85.

Enlightenment humanism and rejects any form of rationalism. Ironically, he is very close to the Christian understanding of human reason that persisted from early Christianity through to the Renaissance when he argues that humans are essentially inclined to ask the questions about our existence, thus transcending a mere instinctual mode of being.

Another crucial contribution of Heidegger's philosophy to the idea of humanism is his reintroduction of meaning into philosophy. No doubt, Heidegger agrees with important Nietzschean claims; for example their assumption of the basic interpretive nature of human knowledge. Also, like Nietzsche and Foucault, Heidegger advocates "effective history" or what he would call a hermeneutic phenomenology: things always appear to us *as* something that we understand on account of a certain historical context and tradition. Already in his earliest lectures, now published as "Ontology—The Hermeneutics of Facticity," Heidegger explains that interpretation is not an intellectual tool employed by a disembodied mind but rather a mode of being characteristic of human beings. In contrast to Nietzsche and Foucault, however, Heidegger links this mode of human existence to a quintessential openness to transcendence, the urge to inquire after the *meaning* of being.[143] We recall that, for Heidegger, true thinking begins with wonder at the existence of things.[144] Every existing being appears, but what lets it appear as that which it is? What is this Being of beings? For Heidegger, human existence is determined by this question concerning the meaning of Being.[145] He defines *hermeneutics* as

---

[143]Martin Heidegger, *Sein und Zeit*, vol. 2 of *GA* (Tübingen: Max Niemeyer Verlag, 1993), §2, 5. This central question apparently came to Heidegger as early as 1907, when he studied the work of Franz Brentano (*Von der mannigfaltigen Bedeutung des Seienden* [On the Manifold Meaning of Existents]). In Heidegger's own account of this influence, Aristotle's statement *to on pollachos legetai* (being is expressed in manifold ways) triggered his life's work: "Concealed in this sentence is the *question* that determined the way of my thought: what is the simple, unitary determination of being that permeates all its manifold meanings? . . . What then does being mean?" (William J. Richardson, preface to *Heidegger: Through Phenomenology to Thought* [Fordham: Fordham University Press, 2003], p. x).

[144]Heidegger explains, "that which is [*das Seiende*] remains gathered in being [*Sein*], that which exists appears in the light of being; this caused the Greeks, and them alone, to wonder. Existing things [*Seiendes*] within being: this became the greatest wonder for the Greeks" ("Was ist das—die Philosophie?" in Martin Heidegger, *Identität und Differenz*, vol. 11 of *GA* [Stuttgart: Klett-Cotta, 2002], p. 14).

[145]Heidegger explains that *Being and Time* was meant to illumine the "meaning of Being" (*der Sinn von Sein*). Martin Heidegger, *Zur Sache des Denkens*, vol. 14 of *GA*, 3rd ed. (Tübingen: Max Niemeyer Verlag, 1988), p. 34.

the reflection on the ontological structures of our existence. Human thought and action are shaped by existential modes of being (being-in-the-world, being-toward-death, care etc.), existential structures (*Existenzialien*) that reveal our orientation toward Being,[146] wherefore they can provide clues about the meaning of Being.[147] The task of hermeneutics is to gain access to our own characteristic existence. This hermeneutic undertaking aims at existential knowledge of oneself. It is not an "artificially contrived" analysis by which we pretend to grasp ourselves as objects, but it is itself a way of being, namely, a kind of self-alertness.[148]

Heidegger's most important philosophical work, *Being and Time*, exemplifies what he thought to be an adequate approach to the meaning of human existence. In this work, he examines not scientific facts but the kind of things that determine our lives existentially, such as the circumscription of our lives by death, and the project-oriented nature of human life that determines the meaning objects will have for us. Therefore, academic disciplines such as history or philosophy are not abstract disciplines that collect factoids but are "modes of being" through which we can glimpse objectively who we are and how we exist. They are ways of gaining objective self-understanding and reveal modes of human existence in the light of being. Likewise, human moods such as curiosity or boredom are existential structures that reveal ontological truths about ourselves, about who and how we are as human beings.[149] His ultimate goal of this existential analysis is insight into the nature of Being itself,[150] and Heidegger will later largely abandon the hermeneutic phenomenology he pursued in *Being and Time* to think about Being without the circuitous route through beings.[151]

In addition to establishing the interpretive nature of human knowledge, Heidegger also recovers the importance of language. While rationalism and scientific objectivism had relegated language to a mere instrument of communication, Heidegger retrieves language and also art as the medium

---

[146]Heidegger, *Sein und Zeit*, §12, 54.
[147]Martin Heidegger, "Letter on Humanism," in *Basic Writings: From Being and Time (1927) to the Task of Thinking (1964)*, ed. David F. Krell (New York: Harper & Row, 1992), p. 207.
[148]"Das *Wachsein* des Daseins für sich selbst" (Heidegger, *Ontologie*, p. 15).
[149]Ibid., p. 65.
[150]Heidegger, *Sein und Zeit*, §2, 7.
[151]Heidegger, *Zur Sache des Denkens*, p. 35.

of human tradition and the embodiment of generational insights into the question of being. Especially in his later writings, Heidegger argues that the poet is the quintessential Shepherd of Being, who, harkening to the address of Being, proclaims its mystery and calls us back from fragmentation to view human existence in its wholeness as circumscribed by the four dimensions of earth, heaven, divine and mortal being by which we interpret the events of this world.[152] Speaking out of our relation to all that is, language does not merely convey facts but makes things appear, shows things to us in certain ways, ways that differ from language to language.[153] Since language speaks out of (and bespeaks) our existential context, we have to listen carefully to language, and no one does this better than the poet. The density of language in poetry, and to a lesser extent in literature, derives from the human relation to Being and throws light on it. In this sense language is "the house of Being,"[154] and the poet is most able to remind us that all human activity, especially artistic and creative activity from literature to the fine arts and architecture, should be in service to this transcendent relation.

Again, it is highly ironic that Heidegger's emphasis on language and poetry as vehicles for truth follows on the heels of his denouncement of humanism as Platonic distortion of truth. As Ernesto Grassi, a Renaissance scholar and former student of Heidegger, has shown, Heidegger is simply out of his depth when he defines Renaissance humanism as "moral aesthetic anthropology, that philosophical interpretation of man which explains and evaluates whatever is, in its entirety, from the standpoint of man and in relation to man."[155] Because humanism is for him merely a cipher for the Platonism that inaugurated Western culture's forgetfulness of Being,[156] Heidegger misrepresents Renaissance humanism and fails to

---

[152]Martin Heidegger, *Poetry, Language, Thought*, trans. A. Hofstadter (New York: Harper & Row, 1975), pp. 141-61.

[153]Martin Heidegger, *Unterwegs zur Sprache*, vol. 12 of *GA* (Pfullingen: Neske, 2001), pp. 254-55.

[154]Ibid., p. 267; "Language is the house of Being because as Saying language is event's way of being" (ibid.).

[155]Martin Heidegger, "The Age of the World Picture," in *The Question Concerning Technology and Other Essays*, trans. William Lovitt (New York: Harper Books, 1977), p. 133.

[156]Richard Bernstein has rightly identified Heidegger's use of the term *humanism* as an indicator of a certain mood: "The mood that I am seeking to elicit discloses itself in what might be called the 'rage against Humanism.' 'Humanism' seems to have become the signifier that names everything that is ominous, dark, and nihilistic in the modern age" (Richard J. Bern-

recognize the deep affinities between humanistic views on language and poetry and his own. Contrary to Heidegger, Renaissance humanists were not thoughtlessly anthropocentric but reflected very much on man's relation to Being and, much like he did himself, viewed poetry as an access to Being. Grassi argues that humanism provides us "in its interpretation of poetry and poetry's original 'revealing,' opening function, with a discussion of that original area in which Being confronts and makes a claim upon man."[157]

Grassi shows that Heidegger wrongly implicates humanism in a metaphysics that seeks a rational foundation for all that exists.[158] Heidegger erroneously reads back into the humanistic tradition what belongs to a later age. In fact, Heidegger's preference for poetic language as the medium of Being over the rational language of logic is already anticipated by a number of Italian humanists. Heidegger failed to recognize that "these problems are not dealt with in Humanism by means of a logical, speculative confrontation with traditional metaphysics, but rather in terms of the analysis and interpretation of language."[159] Italian humanists—like Dante, Leonardo Bruni, Giovanni Boccaccio, Cluccio Salutati and others—examined the relationship between word and subject matter (*verbum et res*) not in terms of logical relationships but "rather with the original dimension in which words permit the meaning of things to appear."[160]

Humanists realized long before Heidegger that the meaning of words is born from a living context and thus reveals the human relationship to being. Language was already interpreted as arising from a life world, and the semantic shifts of words revealed changing insights about human existence. Hence interpreting texts and following the changing meaning of words constituted "the essence of self-education: philology, love of the word."[161] Grassi's main point is that Italian humanists engaged in philo-

---

stein, "Heidegger on Humanism," in *Philosophical Profiles: Essays in a Pragmatic Mode* [Cambridge: Polity Press, 1986], p. 96).

[157]Ernesto Grassi, *Heidegger and the Question of Renaissance Humanism: Four Studies* (Binghamton: State University of New York, 1983), p. 51.

[158]Grassi summarizes this attitude, which Heidegger attacks in *Der Satz vom Grund*: "Every statement about nature, about man, about art, and so forth only proves to be justified and scientific if we are able 'to give the reason for it,' that is, if we can give a reason that explains it. Otherwise, our statements remain in the sphere of opinions (*doxa*)" (ibid., p. 41).

[159]Ibid., p. 17.

[160]Ibid., p. 19.

[161]Ibid., p. 20.

sophical interpretation of language and claimed that the poetic word permits reality to appear in concrete historical terms.[162] He rightly marshals
Vico's *New Science* as evidence that for humanists too poetry first gave rise
to an intelligible world. Moreover, as I have already shown, Vico was se-
verely critical of Cartesian rationalism and recognized the central importance of metaphor and its integrating work for a meaningful interpretation
of reality.[163] Without diminishing the value of Heidegger's philosophical
importance, when it comes to Renaissance humanism, he did not do his
scholarly homework but merely worked from a standard—but false—
stereotype of humanism as anthropocentrism.[164]

For an incarnational humanism, Heidegger's thought remains important
because of its insistence on embodied reasoning. Consciousness and thought
are determined by language, culture and history. Moreover, Heidegger's recognition of humanity's self-transcendence is also laudable, but the character
of this Heideggerian transcendence should worry Christian humanists—for
his transcendence is a relation between human being and Being, whereas
traditional Christian theology viewed this relation as itself determined by
the relation between Being and God. Heidegger's transcendence, in other
words, is closer to nominalist theology in excluding ontology from participation in God. As S. J. McGrath has argued, "Heidegger annuls the central
Thomistic hermeneutical principle of the analogical unity of the being of
God and the being of creation, the *analogia entis*."[165] In doing so, Heidegger
effectively destroys "the scholastic bridge between a rational philosophy and
revealed theology,"[166] and, I may add, the traditional Christian epistemological axiom of "faith seeking understanding." McGrath is quite right in
detecting a distinctly Lutheran flavor in Heidegger's later overtures to an
unknown god. God, unlike the human relation to Being, remains outside of
ontology and hidden from the realm of rational thought.[167]

---

[162]Grassi shows that Guarino Veronese, Dante and Lorenzo Valla held such positions (ibid., p.
21).

[163]Ibid., p. 76.

[164]Ibid., p. 29.

[165]S. J. McGrath, *The Early Heidegger and Medieval Philosophy: Phenomenology for the Godforsaken*
(Washington, D.C.: Catholic University of America Press, 2006), p. 20.

[166]Ibid., p. 17.

[167]Ibid., pp. 22-23. Like Luther, Heidegger and other postmodern disciples stress "the disconti-
nuity between the human and the divine and so compromise the integrity of the human
being, who remains an *imago Dei*, even in his fallenness."

CONCLUSION

In this chapter, we have seen that Nietzsche's work reflects most clearly the breakup of the natural link between consciousness and being taught by classical metaphysics. He deliberately breaks with classical thought and inverts Platonism to establish the unifying ground of reality in the will to power.[168] From this assumption that life is in essence a perpetual evolution without set goals arises his criticism of all positivistic epistemology.[169] Contrary to the classical Greek tradition and its Christian heirs, the world "lacks order, intentional arrangement, form, beauty, wisdom" and whatever other human conceptions of aesthetics we could come up with.[170] Nietzsche offers various sociobiological reasons for the illusory human need for transcendent reason and moral values, but ultimately roots this desire in the will to power. According to Nietzsche, a proper understanding of the will to power should acknowledge the world's constant becoming and our self-fashioning in light of this awareness. Yet the will to power can also manifest itself in a perverted fashion as "the will to truth." This is essentially an idolatrous apotheosis of reason, turning reason and order into a deity that renders the incomprehensible eternal becoming of reality comprehensible. For those obsessed with the will to truth, being is supposed to become "smooth and subject to the mind, as its mirror and reflection."[171] This is why these "wise men" talk about good and evil and about values—it is a manifestation of their will to power. They want to "create the world before which they can kneel. It is their last hope and intoxication."[172]

I have tried to show that Nietzsche's critique of Western rationality deeply influenced major postmodern thinkers such as Lyotard, Foucault, Derrida and even Heidegger, who accepts Nietzsche's verdict that the objectification of being began with Plato. In the place of Platonism, Nietzsche has bequeathed to postmodern philosophy three defining convictions: universals that transcend the material world do not exist; human

---

[168]Janz, *Friedrich Nietzsche Biographie*, 1:712.

[169]In some later writings, however, Nietzsche himself cannot resist the personification of nature. In the *Antichrist* (*KSA*, p. 6), for example, he speaks of a natural order (ibid., 6:242; unfortunately sanctioning the Indian caste system), the ascending movement of life toward power, beauty and self-affirmation (ibid., 6:192), and a "law of selection" as natural patterns of development (ibid., 6:173).

[170]Nietzsche, *KSA*, 3:468.

[171]Ibid., 4:146.

[172]Ibid.

knowledge is (nothing but) a matter of interpretation (i.e., perspectival-ism); and religion is at best, like metaphysics, an escapist illusion or thera-peutic coping mechanism, and at worst a seductive poison that keeps indi-viduals or humanity as a whole from self-fulfillment.

The latter aspect of Nietzsche's thought is unfortunate and misdirected. While Nietzsche's criticism of Christianity may apply to certain funda-mentalist variants of Protestantism, his designation of Christianity as life-denying asceticism and slave morality bears little resemblance to the greater Christian tradition.[173] Yet this shortcoming should not keep Chris-tians from appreciating Nietzsche's true insights into human nature. In fact, Nietzsche's own writings are marked by a resolute commitment to truth that is admirable. In his rejection of metaphysics, for example, he does not abandon truth as such, but only the kind of metaphysical truths that correspond to transcendent realities.[174] Nietzsche himself remains deeply committed to truth, even if he seeks it in strange places. His main, and probably impossible, agenda remains the affirmation of life outside the classical parameters of morality and truth set by Greek and Christian metaphysics. In his own estimation, Nietzsche's great work has been the overthrow of traditional metaphysics and ethics,[175] and his notions of the *Übermensch* and of recurrence of the same are metaphoric (rather than literal), tentative descriptions of life-affirming values in a new, postmetaphysical world.

The positive aspects of Nietzsche's philosophical labor are his criticism of the "idol worship of concepts" in rationalistic philosophies[176] and his insistence on the historical formation of human consciousness, an insight one can retain without reducing all thought either to biology or to con-flicting interpretations. Moreover, Nietzsche has indeed abolished dualis-tic thinking through his critique of rationalism.[177] His view that human judgments are radically contextual and inherently ambivalent has greatly

[173]Jorg Salaquarda, "Nietzsche and the Judeo-Christian Tradition," in Magnus and Higgins, *Cambridge Companion to Nietzsche*, p. 107.
[174]Maudemarie Clark, *Nietzsche on Truth and Philosophy* (Cambridge: Cambridge University Press, 1990), p. 21.
[175]Janz, *Friedrich Nietzsche Biographie*, 1:99.
[176]Nietzsche, *KSA*, 6:75.
[177]Reason has misled us, argues Nietzsche, to assume a true world of ideas and a less true world of appearances. He restates this insight in *Götzendämmerung. Der Antichrist* in Nietzsche, *KSA*, 6:75, which he had originally formulated in the *Birth of Tragedy*.

influenced (especially French) postmodern thinkers.[178] The ensuing per-
spectivalism, however, does not necessarily constitute "a life-enhancing
multiplicity," as Nietzsche's French heirs show.[179] As we will see in
chapter five, even postmodern thinkers who are committed to imma-
nentism cannot avoid transcendence altogether. Nietzsche's own work
shows that the options for thinking about human nature are indeed limited by the two great paradigms of pagan and Judeo-Christian thought.
Nietzsche derives most of his ideas concerning a new humanity in a postmetaphysical world of becoming directly from his studies in ancient Greek
philosophy: eternal recurrence of the same, the self-mastery of the overman, and his famous dictum from *Ecce Homo*, "become what you are."[180]

Because of this recurrence of ancient themes in Nietzsche, the very fact
that Christianity either transformed or explicitly refuted pagan conceptions of human nature inseparably ties his work to the Christian tradition.
Like Christianity, Nietzsche's philosophy focuses on a new humanity, and,
like Christianity, it believes that this new humanity is characterized by the
affirmation of life. Nietzsche's concept of the overman (der *Übermensch*),
for example, takes up the pagan idea of deification and thus remains tied
to its related idea of Christ formation in Christianity.[181] The radical differences between these two concepts remain, of course. In Nietzsche, the
new humanity rejects any stable being and affirms radical becoming, signing on with Dionysius and Heraclitus.[182] The Christian, by contrast, is not
beholden to such renewed binary opposites. Nietzsche's insistence that
only philosophy knows the true path to humanity links him not only with
Plato but also with Martin Heidegger, who also claims that philosophical
thought allows us to retrieve our true humanity in, indeed *as*, relation to
Being. Heidegger also carries forward Nietzsche's critique of objectivism,
of the desire to organize the world according to a fixed conceptual grid.
Like Nietzsche, Heidegger believes that after the pre-Socratics, Western
philosophy succumbed to this metaphysical reification of the world. Heidegger's wholesale and undifferentiated judgment of Western philosophy's

---

[178]Alan D. Schrift, "Nietzsche's French Legacy," in Magnus and Higgins, *Companion to Nietzsche*, p. 338.
[179]Ibid.
[180]*Ecce Homo* in Nietzsche, *KSA*, 6:257.
[181]Janz, *Friedrich Nietzsche Biographie*, 2:234-41.
[182]Nietzsche, *KSA*, 6:313.

forgetfulness of being blinds him to the similarities between his philosophical critique of modernity and traditional Christianity's own potential
for resisting modernity's epistemological poverty, a potential that was also
evident in the Christian humanism of the Renaissance, which Heidegger
failed to appreciate. Even if, in contrast to Nietzsche, Heidegger affirms
some kind of humanism, whatever this humanism might be, it cannot
build on Platonism or traditional Christianity. Religious or personal transcendence remains out of the question. It is precisely this absence of the
personal in Heidegger's thought that evokes severe criticism of his anti-
humanism by more ethically oriented thinkers. Heidegger thus remains
crucial for defining more recent postmodern discussions about humanism
and God that are marked by a strong ethical emphasis on the one hand,
and, for this very reason, by a reluctance to talk about God on the other.

STILL NO INCARNATION

From Anti-Humanism
to the Postmodern God

◆

The basic endeavor of what we usually label "postmodern" thought is the overcoming of dualism and the insistence on the interpretive nature of truth. In their own way, postmodern thinkers deal with the breakdown of the onto-theological synthesis, the rift between being and consciousness. Nietzsche and Foucault solved this issue by accepting the absence of meaning and embracing the idea of the self-creating individual or *Übermensch*, the existential artist who fashions a self for him- or herself. Essentially, they accept that meaning is *made*, created from preexisting traditions and discourses that are not subordinated to or participate in some kind of higher reality.

Another philosopher who embraces the absence of transcendent meaning is Jean-François Lyotard (1924-1998), whose *The Postmodern Condition* first made the term *postmodern* widely known in North America.[1] Like Nietzsche and Foucault, Lyotard accepts that meaning is not discovered but made, and he wonders by what means research can be justified under these conditions. Lyotard's analysis of knowledge and research in Western societies famously asked how scientific knowledge can legitimize itself in the absence of metanarratives. The postmodern researcher can no longer validate discourse by referring either to "the dialectic of the Spirit or even

---

[1]Perry Anderson has shown that Lyotard borrowed this term directly from Ihab Hassan, who had contributed essays on this subject to the critical journal *boundary 2*. Hassan enlisted Foucault's notion of an epistemic break to suggest that postmodernity's break with modernity lay in the play of indeterminacy and immanence, but he did not yet extend the label "postmodern" to social phenomena. See Perry Anderson, *The Origins of Postmodernity* (London: Verso, 1998), pp. 17-19.

to the emancipation of humanity."[2] Once again, Plato is blamed for wedding science to the need for a legitimizing authority outside of itself.[3] Without such external criteria, the scientist can only refer to rules immanent to scientific practices to justify the ultimate worth of his or her work.[4] Lyotard realizes that narrative is a fundamental feature of the human mind,[5] but now we have to be satisfied with "little narratives." Smaller stories are competing for a consensus among scientists and thus continue to generate new ideas. Pragmatism is one such "paralogy," or smaller story, that tries to set the rules for legitimate knowledge. Ideally, the free reign of competing stories will disallow any permanent regulatory system. Some new paradigm will always "disturb the order of reason," of an older system.[6] Lyotard also applies this postmodern condition of science to society.

Deprived of a grand narrative, society too must "reexamine its own internal communication and in the process question the nature of the legitimacy of the decisions made in its name."[7] Lyotard rejects resolutely any idea of universal reason. He permits not even rational debate for a social consensus on general norms of human emancipation that are acceptable across interest groups and language games.[8] For Lyotard, this kind of Habermasian consensus theory still yearns for unified meaning, a desire that will only lead back to total systems and "ideologies of legitimation."[9] Instead, Lyotard suggests that we pursue open societies without settled norms, in which new narratives compete for legitimation. The only admissible common denominator is "the desire for justice and the desire for the unknown."[10]

One may be tempted to ask what exactly postmodern justice might look

---

[2]Jean-François Lyotard, *The Postmodern Condition: A Report on Knowledge*, trans. Geoffrey Bennington and Brian Massumi, *Theory and History of Literature* (Minneapolis: University of Minnesota Press, 1984), p. 60. Consequently Jürgen Habermas's idea of rational consensus attained between knowing intellects and free wills through dialogue is also impermissible since it depends "on the validity of the [grand] narrative of emancipation" (ibid.).

[3]Ibid., p. 28.

[4]Ibid., p. 54.

[5]Anderson, *Origins of Postmodernity*, p. 54.

[6]Lyotard, *Postmodern Condition*, p. 16

[7]Ibid., p. 62.

[8]Ibid., p. 66.

[9]Ibid., p. 65.

[10]Ibid., p. 67.

like, but such a question already implies a transcendent goal and teleology, thus betraying the kind of Platonic leanings our Nietzschean heirs have already branded heretical. For these anti-humanistic thinkers, continuity and teleology are out; rupture and difference are in. Viewed positively, this posture might subvert any totalizing system, any structural inhumanities. Yet here is the rub: once rupture and difference are foundational, how can these thinkers legitimate their own "I," the continuous self that warns us about inhuman discourses? Is not this self itself merely a cog in the wheel of discourses accountable to no one?[11] Even more important, how does one define the human in the absence of a *telos*? Lyotard argues that the very notion of development espoused by classical humanism's notion of emancipation is in reality a death trap, leading to oppressive systems. Instead, he redefines development as a process of increasing complexity and differentiation with "no finality" or escape.[12] The only guard against inhuman practices (which, incidentally, he does not define) are fostering irrational elements that human reason cannot control, such as childhood, paganism and the stranger within the self.[13]

Perhaps the clearest illustration of Lyotard's anti-humanism comes from his discussion of art. He rejects realism in art for its inability to question or reexamine the rules of art. Traditional artists merely seek to conform their art to some kind of perceived norm and easy communicability for the sake of gratification. In a rather surprisingly reductionist statement, Lyotard argues that pornography is the "general model" for those arts that have not resisted the challenge of the mass media.[14] The postmodern is rather exemplified by an avant-garde that relentlessly questions realism and experiments with the rules of art. In fact, Lyotard's final point is that postmodernity is no longer embodied in art that seeks conformity with some kind of standard of the beautiful, but in art that manifests the sublime, the unrepresentable. Kant had already hinted at this possibility

---

[11]Alasdair MacIntyre has advanced this criticism in "Tradition Against Genealogy: Who Speaks to Whom?" in *Three Rival Versions of Moral Enquiry: Encyclopaedia, Genealogy, and Tradition*, Gifford Lectures Delivered in the University of Edinburgh in 1988 (Notre Dame, Ind.: University of Notre Dame Press, 1990), pp. 208-11.

[12]Jean-François Lyotard, *The Inhuman: Reflections on Time*, trans. Geoffrey Bennington and Rachel Bowlby (Stanford, Calif.: Stanford University Press, 1991), pp. 6-7.

[13]Martin Halliwell and Andy Mousley, *Critical Humanism: Humanist/Anti-Humanist Dialogues* (Edinburgh: Edinburgh University Press, 2003), p. 187.

[14]Ibid., p. 75.

with his notion of the sublime, but, according to Lyotard, even he was still too enamored with the idea of form and its correspondence to an idea or concept. The postmodern, by contrast, "denies itself the solace of good forms, the consensus of a taste which would make it possible to share collectively the nostalgia for the unattainable." The postmodern's business is "not to supply reality but to invent allusions to the conceivable which cannot be presented."[15] In short, we have arrived, once more, at the postmodern fear of objectification. Only that which is unrepresentable, the sublime without content, escapes the danger of the kind of totalizing ideologies that have led to the oppressive regimes of the past. Oppression is always the price we pay for our nostalgia for unified meaning, for "the reconciliation of the concept and the sensible." The postmodern answer is, "Let us wage war on totality; let us be witnesses to the unrepresentable; let us activate the differences and save the honour of the name."[16]

Lyotard's emphasis on the "unrepresentable" adds to the typically postmodern obsession with objectification expressed by the ethical elements of "otherness" and "difference." Subversion of totality and sameness is required to keep oppressive systems at bay. One may well ask the question, however, in what name should we wage a "war on totality"? The problem with the postmodern sublime is the very contourlessness Lyotard extols as necessary to oppose tyranny. In some postmodern thinkers, the potentially sinister connotations of this doctrine become rather obvious. Slavoj Žižek, for example, does not seem to care much *what* disrupts the self-satisfied subject and conscious will as long as "we derive energy from it."[17] A sublime that is beyond the moral categories of good and evil is indistinguishable from the inhuman or monstrous. Other postmodern thinkers have articulated the postmodern fear of objectification in more positive, ethical terms. Yet, as we shall see in the following, all too brief sketches of Emmanuel Levinas's ethical philosophy and Derrida's deconstruction, the fear of objectification continues to prevent even these ethical postmodern voices from bridging the gap between a radically transcendent ethical ideal and the ontological realities of language, social structures and institutions. These postmodern voices lack the philosophical and theological resources

---

[15]Ibid., p. 81.
[16]Ibid., p. 82.
[17]Slavoj Žižek, *The Plague of Fantasies* (London: Verso, 1997), p. 239.

historic Christianity had drawn from the incarnation. The resulting inability to bridge the gap between an ontology of immanence and transcendence haunts postmodern thought even when it returns to the themes of humanism and of God.

LEVINAS'S HUMANISM OF THE OTHER

Jewish philosopher Emmanuel Levinas (1906-1995) is especially important for our recovery of incarnational humanism because his entire ethical philosophy focuses on the irreducible dignity of each human being. Levinas develops his "humanism of the other" in dialogue with Martin Heidegger's philosophy and French structuralism.[18] The latter had loudly declared "the end of humanism, end of metaphysics, the death of man, death of God," slogans which Levinas rejects as Parisian fads that will soon be "reduced to bargain prices and downgraded."[19] Yet he detects in these announcements a general tendency of philosophy to measure human dignity by means of some greater theological or philosophical system or totality. Against any such attempts, Levinas resolutely affirms that all meaning takes its measure from our ethical responsibility. The human is indeed "holy" for Levinas, in the sense that we are human prior to any other consideration. To reflect on the human is to reflect "in a spirit which has been altered by the idea of holiness; that the meaningful appears and signifies and has its importance above all in my relation with another person."[20]

Levinas proposes a philosophical version of Judaism as "ethics of the other," to oppose the dissolution of the subject and of meaning in postmodern thought. Levinas denounces Heidegger's philosophy because it makes human dignity dependent on Being, thus defining our humanity as a relation to an "impersonal neutrality" rather than as a primordially ethical relation to another person.[21] Levinas argues that the genuine task of philosophy is to go beyond the objectifying layers of language and concepts toward an ethical relation prior to all ontology, toward a transcend-

---

[18]Richard Cohen, introduction to Emmanuel Levinas, *Humanism of the Other*, trans. Nidra Poller (Urbana: University of Illinois Press, 2003), p. xvi.

[19]Levinas, *Humanism of the Other*, p. 58.

[20]Emmanuel Levinas, *Is It Righteous to Be? Interviews with Emmanuel Lévinas*, ed. Jill Robinson (Stanford, Calif.: Stanford University Press, 2001), p. 56.

[21]Emmanuel Levinas, *Totality and Infinity: An Essay on Exteriority*, trans. Alphonso Lingis (Pittsburgh: Duquesne University Press, 1969), p. 298.

ence that is irreducible to anything within ontology. In short, Levinas pursues "a humanism of the other" in which the human subject is defined not primarily as rational animal but as recipient of an ethical demand to care for another fellow human being. According to Levinas, philosophy has inhumanly been more interested in contemplating truth than in being guided by this first ethical impulse.[22]

Levinas believed that philosophy, both modern and postmodern, is intrinsically unethical because it has always defined meaning as "contents given to consciousness." The main source of meaning thus remains the human intuition, whether what is given to consciousness are ideas, relations, or sense impressions. There is no difference in this regard between the idealist Plato and the sceptical empiricist Hume.[23] Even the German philosopher Edmund Husserl, whose phenomenological philosophy pays greater attention to *how* phenomena appear to the mind on their own terms, still enshrines intuition as the main source of intelligibility.[24] Only with the advent of Martin Heidegger's philosophy does the human experience of reality take a truly existential turn that takes into account how our perception of reality arises from our participation in the historical, linguistic, social and temporal structures of being. Now, "experience is a reading, an understanding of sense, an exegesis, a hermeneutic, and not an intuition."[25] Levinas appreciates that Heidegger's hermeneutic ontology manages to overcome the gap in earlier philosophies between consciousness and the world. No longer does a subject, defined as disincarnate consciousness, stand over against an objectified world. Rather, Heidegger recaptures a holistic, intelligible world, so that "everything remains within a language or within a world, a world whose structure resembles the order of language. . . . Objects become significant from language and not language from objects given to thought and designated by words that function as simple signs."[26] Meaning resides no longer merely in the human mind but

---

[22]"Philosophy is produced as a form that manifests the refusal of engagement in the Other, a preference for waiting over action, indifference toward others—the universal allergy of the first childhood of philosophers. Philosophy's itinerary still follows the path of Ulysses whose adventure in the world was but a return to his native island—complacency in the Same, misunderstanding of the Other" (Levinas, *Humanism of the Other*, p. 26).
[23]Ibid., p. 10.
[24]Ibid.
[25]Ibid., p. 13.
[26]Ibid.

permeates a world in which things are always given *as* something meaningful to us. This view fundamentally changes our understanding of art and culture. Linguistic and artistic expression is no longer merely the mediation of a prior, interior thought. Rather, "culture and artistic creation are part of the ontological order itself," and they reveal the meaning of its totality. Language and culture mediate the meaning of being. Levinas observes that in Heidegger "Being as a whole—signification—glows in the works of poets and artists."[27]

While Levinas appreciates Heidegger's critique of philosophical idealism, he also laments the absence of personal transcendence in his philosophy. Levinas had earlier criticized Platonic contemplation for its primary orientation toward abstract ideas rather than toward ethics. Now, however, he also warns that Heidegger's anti-Platonism collapses meaning into the immanent. For Plato, at least, "the world of significations precedes the language and culture that express it,"[28] so that any philosophical or even political interpretation of the transcendent order is better to the degree that it can remake the world in its image. The anti-Platonism of Heidegger's hermeneutic philosophy, by contrast, "lies in the subordination of intellect to expression."[29] Contrary to Plato, Heidegger finds the meaning of being in the ontological structures of our existence themselves. As Levinas puts it, "the intelligible is inconceivable outside the becoming that suggests it."[30] This immersion of meaning into existential-historical structures means that "signification is not separate from access leading to it. *Access is part of signification itself.*"[31]

One immediate problem is that without a transcendent unity of historical manifestations, the kind of unity given by Platonic ideal forms, every culture's interpretation of what it means to be human is equally valid. According to Levinas, the ensuing "multivocity of the sense of being, this essential disorientation, may well be the modern expression of atheism."[32] He argues that philosophical claims about language as universal medium of understanding, or about a generally meaningful world we explore from

---

[27]Ibid., p. 18.
[28]Ibid., p. 19.
[29]Ibid.
[30]Ibid., p. 18.
[31]Ibid., p. 20.
[32]Ibid.

equally valid perspectives, are insufficient grounds for governing human relations. The question is to what use do we put these insights? For example, the fact that I can translate one language into another still does not tell me why I should respect another language rather than consider it primitive. Indeed, says Levinas, the very impulse to see cultures as equally valid is already an ethical notion that transcends mere relativistic values. But from where do we derive "an unambiguous sense in which humanity stands"? Levinas presses on to the cardinal question:

> Must we not, therefore, distinguish significations in their cultural pluralism from the sense, orientation, and the unity of being, the primordial event where all the other procedures of thought and all the historical life of being are placed? . . . Do the significations not require a unique sense from which they borrow their significance?[33]

In Western philosophy this loss of unity is, ever since Nietzsche, experienced as the crisis of monotheism. For Levinas, this crisis was brought about because God became too implicated in the economic structures, so that his transcendence got mired in earthly matters and was eventually dismissed.[34] Now, Heidegger has tried to regain some sense of this former unity by arguing for humanity's orientation toward "Being," which is his word for the unrepresentable transcendent.[35] Levinas, however, dismisses this abstract concept because it is amoral; it is a unity that is neutral concerning the dignity of humanity, and thus inhuman. A true humanism of the other requires the kind of transcendence offered in the Scriptures. At least it does for Levinas, who concludes his criticism of anti-Platonism with these words: "We do not think that what makes sense can do without God, nor that the idea of Being, or the Being of beings, can substitute for God to lead signification to the unity of sense without which there is no sense."[36]

What then offers us a world that is both meaningful in its orientation to a transcendent meaning and also ethical? Levinas answers that the origin of meaning lies in human sociality.[37] For much of postmodern phi-

---

[33]Ibid., p. 23.
[34]Ibid., p. 24.
[35]Martin Heidegger, "Letter on Humanism," in *Basic Writings: From Being and Time (1927) to the Task of Thinking (1964)*, ed. David F. Krell (New York: Harper & Row, 1992), p. 217.
[36]Levinas, *Humanism of the Other*, p. 24.
[37]Levinas contrasts the primacy of human sociality with the neutrality of being: "the social is

losophy, transcendence remains an undefinable or impersonal entity—
what Levinas calls "a grand neuter"—but for him, transcendence cannot
be merely negative but "is thought positively in terms of the face of the
other person." Wherever we meet with transcendence, it indicates "the
absolute of the social, the *for-the-other*" which, for Levinas, defines our
humanity.[38] It is in "the desire for others that we feel in the most common
social experience" and where we should look for the ethical origin of
meaning. The other "is neither a cultural signification nor a simply given.
He is, primordially, *sense*, because he lends it to expression itself, because
only through him can a phenomenon such as signification introduce itself,
of itself, into being." Levinas, in short, reorients philosophy's preoccupation of meaning toward the meaning of the other human being. For him,
human freedom and responsibility are both founded on the relation to the
other human being, which points itself to a fundamental relation of human
beings to God.[39] It is, however, important to Levinas that this orientation
to God neither serve as a proof of God's existence nor reduce God to a
human Other. Rather, he wants to retrieve the Old Testament notion of
the *imago Dei* that focuses solely on the address by another.[40] For Levinas
the image of God founds human dignity, not in a sense of similarity but as
irreducible uniqueness. In contrast to an earthly stamp that mints innu-
merable coins that look alike, "God, succeeds, imposing His image with a
stamp, in creating a multiplicity of dissimilarities: selves, unique in their
genus."[41] Because the word image evokes the possibility of idolatry, of
making the other in the image of oneself, Levinas insists that "to be in the
image of God does not signify being the icon of God, but finding oneself
in his trace."[42] The trace of God in the face of the other is the ethical imperative to responsibility, "the proximity of God in the countenance of my

---

beyond ontology" (*Ethics and Infinity*, trans. Philippe Nemo, 1st ed. [Pittsburgh: Duquesne
University Press, 1997], p. 58). He argues that we have always construed knowledge as comprehension of facts by an individual self. Knowledge fails "to put us in communion with the
other; it does not take the place of sociality; it is still and always a solitude" (ibid., p. 60).

[38]"The Rights of Man and Good Will," in Emmanuel Levinas, *Entre Nous: On Thinking-of-the-
Other*, ed. Michael B. Smith, trans. Michael B. Smith and Barbara Harshav, European Perspectives (New York: Columbia University Press, 1998), p. 158.

[39]"Notes on Meaning," in Emmanuel Levinas, *Of God Who Comes to Mind*, trans. Bettina Bergo,
2nd ed. (Stanford, Calif.: Stanford University Press, 1998), pp. 170-71.

[40]Ibid., p. 149.

[41]Levinas, *Entre Nous*, p. 206.

[42]Levinas, *Humanism of the Other*, p. 44.

fellowman."[43] Wanting to preserve the infinite transcendence of the Ju-deo-Christian God, Levinas prefers *word* rather than *image* analogies to describe his ethical humanism. The ethical imperative is "the word of God and the verb in the human face."[44]

This ethical orientation from which all meaning begins cannot do without interpretation of language and cultural expression. Indeed, "com-prehension of the other is therefore a hermeneutic, and exegesis." Levinas's point is, however, that another human being is irreducible to his or her cultural expression and has significance prior and beyond "the inevitable paralysis of manifestation."[45] This ethical transcendence of the other human being is what Levinas calls "the face" or "naked form" or "absolute other."[46] Like Plato's form, the face is radically transcendent, but unlike Plato's idea, its otherness consists in an ethical demand that disrupts and unsettles any final interpretations of either myself or the other. In fact, it is the very quality of its incomprehensibility that marks it as a summons to responsibility. I am not asked to understand the other, but to obey the ethical summons radiating from the other. Levinas calls on the suffering servant in Isaiah 53 to describe how the ego is not merely affected but shaped by the summons of the other. The other is a challenge to con-sciousness, to any self-assertion or self-justification. In light of the ethical demand, the self becomes defined as "responsibility or diacony," as infinite responsibility for the other.[47]

True humanity, for Levinas, consists in being called toward ethical re-sponsibility. Modern philosophy has rightly decentered human being, but it has failed to recognize the self's origin in an ethical register that goes beyond philosophy's preoccupation with an immanent order.[48] Once again Levinas sees clearly the problem of modern philosophy: "There can be no

---

[43]"A Man-God?" in Levinas, *Entre Nous*, p. 57.

[44]Ibid., p. 199.

[45]Levinas, *Humanism of the Other*, p. 31.

[46]Ibid., pp. 32, 33. For a detailed description of Levinas's concepts, see my *Recovering Theologi-cal Hermeneutics: An Incarnational-Trinitarian Theory of Interpretation* (Grand Rapids: Baker Academic, 2004), pp. 187-229.

[47]Levinas, *Humanism of the Other*, p. 33.

[48]Levinas argues that "the social sciences and Heidegger" subvert the Judeo-Christian subject by denying a truly independent inner world of the subject. In Levinas's view, "The social sci-ences and Heidegger lead to the triumph of mathematical intelligibility, sending the subject, the individual, his unicity and his election back into ideology, or else rooting man in being, making him its messenger and poet" (Levinas, *Humanism of the Other*, p. 61).

sense in being except for sense that is not measured by being."[49] What is prior to being and to ontological categories, however, is the ethical responsibility to another human being. Modern anti-humanism of the Heideggerian or Foucauldian type is "wrong, in not finding for man, lost in history and in order, the trace of this pre-historic an-archic saying."[50] Levinas calls this relation the "saying" to emphasize the proximity of this personal appeal to our responsibility for our fellow human being, an appeal that is prior even to freedom,[51] but that necessarily occurs within ontological structures and its objectifying distortions. Levinas knows that we cannot negotiate life without objectifying others, but precisely because of this, philosophy's first task is to expose any such idols to clear the way toward ethics. For Levinas the task of philosophy is to seek out that which interrupts a set opinion of someone or something—an interpretation of a text, for example—and to make sure that no interpretive idol covers over the ethical responsibility evoked by voices different from our own. This is not to say that descriptions, concepts and interpretations are inherently bad; they become idols, however, when we believe ourselves to have isolated the essence of a thing and hence gained control over it. Often enough, the desire to understand is the desire to gain dominion over the object by completely capturing its essence in a definition. The popular kids' fantasy series *Eragon* illustrates this threat by introducing the notion of a proper name that contains the essence of its holder. Such a name is to be shared only with friends, for should an enemy get hold of it, he will be able to control the name's owner. Levinas's point is that seeking the essence of something is akin to the desire to create a distorting idol for the sake of controlling it. Truly humane philosophy counteracts this tendency by seeking out the "ethical interruption of essence."[52]

Levinas often invokes the biblical command against idolatry to illustrate his resolute opposition to any objectification of the other.[53] Levinas's tendency to equate image and idol is symptomatic of his entire philosophy.

---

[49]Ibid., p. 56.

[50]Ibid., p. 57.

[51]Ibid., p. 52.

[52]Emmanuel Levinas, *Otherwise Than Being, or, Beyond Essence*, trans. Alphonso Lingis (Pittsburgh: Duquesne University Press, 1998), p. 44.

[53]Emmanuel Levinas, "Reality and Its Shadow," in *Collected Philosophical Papers*, trans. Alphonso Lingis (Pittsburgh: Duquesne University Press, 1987), p. 11.

In advocating the irreducible uniqueness of every human being and a social, indeed ethical, conception of truth, he joins, albeit for deeply religious
reasons, the disincarnate sensibility of postmodernism. Neither God nor
the other can be fully implicated in ontological structures (be they language, conceptions of reason, economics or institutions), for this will result
in God's subordination to these structures. For Levinas "the unknown
God does not take shape in a theme."[54] At least in a theoretical sense, ontology is the enemy of religion for Levinas because ontology stands for
every theological and philosophical effort to squeeze both God and human
being into preconceived totalities.[55]

Nonetheless, Levinas does want to talk philosophically about religion
and ethics, precisely by defining religion as a humanism of the other. He
also acknowledges that talk about human being is intrinsically linked to
talk about God. Yet Levinas believes that if we talk about God, it should
be in a way that goes beyond either ontology or faith, beyond the typical
alternatives of a merely existential God "invoked without philosophy in
faith" on the one hand, and of a merely abstract God of the philosophers
on the other.[56] For Levinas, God is revealed in the ethical relationship to
another human being because "the very movement that leads to another
leads to God."[57] While Christianity bases human sociality and ethical obligation to one's neighbor on the incarnation, Levinas does not need this
doctrine for his ethics. Jewish spirituality pursues what the Christians call
imitatio Christi, but without the incarnation. Messianism for the Jew
means that everyone is called to be the suffering servant responsible for
every other: "I mean a Jesus without Incarnation, without the drama of the
cross." Levinas defines the difference between his religion and Christianity in this way: "you [the Christian] begin with 'God is love.' The Jew begins with obligation. And the *happy end* is uncertain."[58] In other words, for
Levinas the Messiah has not yet come, and certainly not as God incarnate
who has summed up in himself the destiny of humanity.

---

[54]Levinas, *Entre Nous*, p. 175.
[55]Ibid., p. 7: "The relation to the other is therefore not ontology. This bond with the other which
is therefore not reducible to the representation of the other, but to his invocation, and in which
invocation is not preceded by an understanding, I call *religion*."
[56]Levinas, *Of God*, p. 57.
[57]Ibid., p. 148.
[58]"Judaism and Christianity after Rosenzweig," in Levinas, *Righteous to Be?* p. 267.

Levinas's comments on the incarnation help Christians understand what this doctrine, this ultimate manifestation of God's presence in the world, provides. His statement that everything the Christian claims ethically occurs to the Jew without the incarnation should make Christians think about the value of this teaching. Levinas himself sees a convergence of Christianity and Judaism in the idea of divine *kenōsis*.[59] The idea, however, that God actually became a human being and entered into the ontological structures of the world remains suspect to him because this is what allowed God to become hijacked for political ends, such as the Crusades. Nor did the incarnation of God seem to help Christians to oppose the Nazis and prevent the Holocaust.[60] If, however, kenosis is conceived of without the incarnation, then Christianity basically means "to live and die for everyone."[61] Levinas has little time for the sacramental aspects of Christianity, but stresses that for the Jew what is important is not believing but doing.[62]

There is another reason why Levinas does not want God to become part of ontology. Aside from the danger of idolatry, of God's being subordinated to certain interpretations of reason or empire, Levinas does not like the ethical implications of a kenotic, defenseless God. "This powerless kenosis," he argues, forgets about justice and "has cost the lives of many suffering people."[63] In light of Auschwitz and the Holocaust, defenselessness comes too close to a divine justification of this event. Levinas finds it easier to understand the "meaning" of Auschwitz as God's demand for faithfulness "completely without promise."[64]

As we can see, there are deep historical and personal reasons for Levinas, who lost many loved ones in the concentration camps, to reject the incarnate presence of God. God's presence in ontology remains suspect to him. And yet this very presence is the heart of Christianity, which goes beyond ethics to insist on communion with God. As Catholic theologian Luigi Giovanni Giussani points out, Christianity takes from its Judaic roots the concept of salvation as essentially social and also the notion of a

[59]Ibid., p. 256.
[60]Ibid.
[61]Ibid., p. 257.
[62]Ibid., p. 258.
[63]Ibid., pp. 259-60.
[64]Ibid., p. 260.

universal human brotherhood.[65] The difference is that Christians believe that in Jesus God did indeed accomplish the redemption of humanity and that the church as the new people of God is an extension of his presence in the world through material means. All the former Jewish themes of election, universal vocation for true humanity and communal or social salvation remain, but they are transfigured by the presence of God through Christ and the work of the Spirit within the church as God's self-communication to the world in the incarnate, crucified and risen Christ.[66]

What is entirely missing from Levinas's account of religion is the presence of God through the work of the Spirit, whose workings effect and evidence humanity's communion with God by the "new birth" or "new creation" of each member. In line with the incarnational notion that the power of God is mediated through the material world, Christianity teaches that communion with God, initiated by his freely given elective grace, results in a new disposition that corresponds to the new creation God will ultimately usher in. In Guissani's words, because they have received the gift of the Spirit, Christians "are given the possibility of a new experience of reality" by which all human relations are transformed and reworked.[67] In contrast to Levinas's more legalistic ethic, Christianity suggests an organic new life from which ethical action flows. Without this empowering of the Spirit, granted to the church at Pentecost, without this pledge of the new age inaugurated by Christ, "it would prove very difficult—if not impossible, to acquire the conviction capable of building anything."[68] To be sure, Levinas's assertion that a subjectivity defined as responsibility for the other to the point of substitution without the promise of a happy ending has a certain heroic ring to it, a sternness that some may find appealing; nonetheless, it can itself become mere legalism and even a rational, intellectualist ethic, despite all its claims to be exactly the opposite of mere knowledge.

Levinas's dismissal of the incarnation is costly. The emphasis on the Other does, of course, reintroduce transcendence into the post-Nietzschean context of immanence. Yet as deeply rooted in the Jewish context, he can-

[65]Luigi Giovanni Giussani, *Why the Church?* (Montreal: McGill-Queen's University Press, 2001), p. 74.
[66]Ibid., p. 86.
[67]Ibid., p. 91.
[68]Ibid., p. 90.

not conceive of divine transcendence within being.[69] Without the union of transcendence and immanence the incarnation affords, however, ontology remains ever in the dark valley of the shadow of objectification by which the other becomes a distorted mirror of my consciousness and self-centeredness. God is not really "with" humanity, but the ethical demand, the face of the other, reveals a trace of his command that is all too easily ossified into ontological structures. As a result, the ethical human self is not shaped by communal relation to the divine but by an ethical demand to obedience; the weary and laden do not find rest and refreshment in a God who opens his arms, even when nails are driven through his hands and feet.

Perhaps the quickest and clearest way to understand the difference between Levinas's disincarnate religion and Christianity is by turning to the New Testament letter to the Hebrews, which focuses on the idea of mediation. The book's main point is that in Jesus the Messiah, who is identified as "the exact representation of his being" and as God's creating wisdom, who sustains all things, God himself has become the priest for humanity (Heb 1:1-3). While God could have chosen another way of rescuing creation from the Fall, the mystery of the incarnation demonstrates God's deep compassion for his creation.[70] When God becomes human and destroys sin and death from *inside of creation*, he reconciles being (ontology) and transcendence, but more than that, the incarnation effects an intimate bond between human beings and God that is most fully realized in the church. God, as the author of Hebrews puts it, did not come to help angels, "but Abraham's descendents. For this reason he had to be made like his brothers in every way, in order that he might become a merciful and faithful high priest in service to God" (Heb 2:16-17). As the writer makes clear, Jesus himself embodies and enacts the atonement, by which the Messiah not only defeats sin and death but also effects a hitherto impossible communion and intimacy between God and his people.[71]

---

[69]For Levinas, "the term 'transcendence' signifies precisely the fact that one cannot think God and being together" (*Ethics and Infinity*, p. 77). Ironically, the incarnation itself provides the perfect example of the kind of asymmetrical relationless relation Levinas seeks, the relationship with alterity that is "neither a struggle, nor a fusion, nor a knowledge" (ibid., p. 68).

[70]Basil the Great, *On the Holy Spirit*, trans. David Anderson, Popular Patristic Series (Crestwood, N.Y.: St. Vladimir's Seminary Press, 1980), p. 37.

[71]For the Christian meaning of atonement in a postmodern context, see Kevin Vanhoozer, "The Atonement in Postmodernity: Guilt, Goats, and Gifts," in *The Glory of the Atonement: Biblical, Historical, and Practical Perspectives, Essays in Honor of Roger R. Nicole*, ed. Charles Evan Hill,

When Levinas discusses the atonement, he characteristically stresses one's obligation to the neighbor. God can forgive, but real forgiveness depends on reconciliation with one's neighbor. Christianity retains this social element of forgiveness, but in contrast to Levinas, peace with God comes through participation in Christ's atonement, by which the community of God's people itself is established, and *from* which the issue of social relations, including forgiveness, is approached.[72] Without in the least diminishing the moral obligation to others, Christian incarnational theology avoids the almost traumatic pressure Levinas places on the ethical relation. It is not the other who has Godlike moral authority, but God's will in Christ. Our motivation comes from the *imago Dei* as sustained and redeemed by Christ in whom we participate.[73] Levinas is correct, of course, to draw attention to the importance of the face of the other. Christians can affirm that morality and human dignity depend on our mutual recognition as persons.[74] Yet for Christians, the face of the other is more than merely a moral demand; it is a revelation of the *imago Dei*, which God lovingly first created and has now restored to himself in Christ. Christianity is not first a moral demand but the "remembrance of the look of love that the Lord directs to man, this look that preserves the fullness of his truth and the ultimate guarantee of his dignity."[75] This focus on the incarnate love of humanity in Christ, this shifting of the relational pressure from its traumatic focus on me and the other to God as a third party, allows Christian ethics to avoid Levinas's language of "substitution" and being a "hostage" to the other.

And yet Levinas's ethical demand still resides firmly within a religious, Jewish framework, in which freedom and dignity are tied to a Creator God. His emphasis on human sociality before anything else remains a strong criticism of mere abstract philosophies of pure difference, which are

Roger R. Nicole and Frank A. James (Downers Grove, Ill.: IVP Academic, 2004), p. 298.

[72]Emmanuel Levinas, *Nine Talmudic Readings*, trans. Annette Aronowicz (Bloomington: Indiana University Press, 1990), p. 17.

[73]For a fuller discussion, see my *Recovering Theological Hermeneutics*, p. 278.

[74]Benedict XVI writes that "the other is the custodian of my own dignity. This is why morality, which begins with this look directed to the other, is the custodian of the truth and the dignity of man: man needs morality in order to be himself and not lose his dignity in the world of things." *Christianity and the Crisis of Cultures,* trans. Brian McNeil (San Francisco: Ignatius Press, 2006), p. 70.

[75]Ibid., p. 71.

even more paranoid about objectification and presence than is Levinas. The best known example of such detheologized postmodern ethics is the thought of French philosopher Jacques Derrida (1930-2004). Derrida once admitted the great influence of Heidegger, Nietzsche and Freud on his thought,[76] but the more he wrote on religious themes, such as forgiveness, hospitality and justice, the more he moved away from deconstructing texts and toward unfolding in his own way Levinas's ethics. Some scholars have argued that Derrida's criticism of Western rationality as logocentrism, of the privileging of an immediate present voice over the risks of interpretation in the written word, was inspired by Levinas.[77] On this reading, even Derrida's idea of deconstruction is the philosophical reduction, the rupturing, of ossified readings that Levinas called for. Derrida himself has acknowledged his debt to Levinas and clearly defines deconstruction as an ethical undertaking.[78] Deconstruction is

> vocation—a response to a call. The other, as the other than self, the other that opposes self-identity, is not something that can be detected and disclosed within a philosophical space and with the aid of a philosophical lamp. The other precedes philosophy and necessarily invokes and provokes the subject before any genuine questioning can begin.[79]

Like Levinas, Derrida dedicated himself to the task of the ethical interruption, of questioning essences and a plug-and-play approach to meaning.

Derrida's central critique of logocentrism, of the Western emphasis on reason as an immediate access to truth, is itself ethically motivated. "The critique of logocentrism," says Derrida,

> is above all else the search for the "other" and the "other of language." . . . Certainly, deconstruction tries to show that the question of reference is much more complex and problematic than traditional theories supposed. It even asks whether our term "reference" is entirely adequate for designating

---

[76]Jason Powell, *Jacques Derrida: A Biography* (New York: Continuum, 2006), p. 60.

[77]Simon Critchley, *The Ethics of Deconstruction: Derrida and Levinas* (West Lafayette, Ind.: Purdue University Press, 1999), pp. 11-12, 236ff.; James K. A. Smith, *Jacques Derrida: Live Theory*, Live Theory Series (New York: Continuum, 2005), pp. 76-80.

[78]Jacques Derrida, *Adieu to Emmanuel Levinas*, trans. Pascale-Anne Brault and Michael Nass (Stanford, Calif.: Stanford University Press, 1999), p. 5.

[79]Jacques Derrida, "Jacques Derrida: Deconstruction and the Other," in *States of Mind: Dialogues with Contemporary Thinkers on the European Mind*, ed. Richard Kearney (New York: New York University Press, 1995), p. 168.

the "other." The other, which is beyond language and which summons language, is perhaps not a "referent" in the normal sense which linguists have attached to this term.[80]

Yet going against the grain of traditional understandings of "referent" does not imply relativism. Derrida rejects any notion that deconstruction implies that everything dissolves into language, as if language were a prison house. Nor is questioning how we construe structures of reference and meaning the beginning of nihilism. No, the whole point of deconstruction is ethical: "Deconstruction is not a disclosure in nothingness but an openness towards the other."[81]

On account of his concern for ethics, and because of his painstaking, careful readings of texts, Derrida may also be counted among modern humanists.[82] Levinas even labels him a crypto-Platonist. Levinas believes that Derrida's notion of différance "attests to the prestige that eternity retains in his eyes, the 'great present,' *being*, which corresponds to the priority of the *theoretical* and the truth of the theoretical, in relation to which temporality would be a failure."[83] Levinas is not far off the mark with this accusation. In his remarkable tribute *Adieu to Immanuel Levinas*, Derrida distills from Levinas's work his own "structural or *a priori* messianicity."[84] This idea of a priori structures that prompts deconstruction has largely shaped Derrida's later writings on the messianic, on hospitality and on the gift. In each case, these religious themes are disincarnated, emptied of content in order to serve and protect difference and otherness. For example, in a seminar on the topic of hospitality Derrida first defines *hospitality* as unconditional welcome, expecting us "to say yes *to who or what turns up*, before any determination."[85] The remainder of the seminar is then spent on describing the gap between this uncondi-

[80]Ibid., p. 173.
[81]Ibid.
[82]Indeed, Richard Rorty has used this label to charge Derrida with a humanistic nostalgia (Richard Rorty, "Remarks on Deconstruction and Pragmatism," in *Deconstruction and Pragmatism*, ed. Chantal Mouffe (London: Routledge, 1996), p. 14.
[83]Emmanuel Levinas, *Alterity and Transcendence*, trans. Michael B. Smith, European Perspectives (New York: Columbia University Press, 1999), p. 173.
[84]Jacques Derrida, *Adieu to Immanuel Levinas*, trans. Pascale-Anne Brault and Michael Naas (Stanford, Calif.: Stanford University Press, 1999), p. 67.
[85]Jacques Derrida, *Of Hospitality*, trans. Anne Dufourmantelle, Cultural Memory in the Present (Stanford, Calif.: Stanford University Press, 2000), p. 77.

tional law of hospitality and the obvious sociopolitical restrictions reality imposes on this law.[86] The same pattern emerges in his treatment of forgiveness. For Derrida, true forgiveness must be unconditional, without any anticipation of changed behavior in the perpetrator: "In order for there to be forgiveness, must one not, on the contrary, forgive both the fault and the guilty as such, where the one and the other remain as irreversible as evil, as evil itself, and being capable of repeating itself, unforgivably, without transformation, without amelioration, without repentance or promise?"[87] Derrida understands, of course, that in society, forgiveness is necessarily mediated through language and institutions, but all these are compromises of pure forgiveness. He remains "torn" between this hyperbolical ethical vision and social realities.

Derrida's deconstruction basically amounts to a Levinasian ethic without God. Whereas Levinas refers clearly to the divine command "Thou shalt not kill," Derrida's a priori concepts point into the vague, nondescript place of otherness. In Levinas, the subject is defined by the inescapable ethical demand for responsibility behind which still stands a personal God, even if he remains remote. In Derrida, even this God is a big question mark. Like Heidegger, Derrida remains agnostic about who God is because he equates any claim to the presence of God with objectifying metaphysics. Theologian Kevin Hart once suggested to Derrida that the incarnation offers a way to talk about presence without falling into rational metaphysics. As Hart explained to Derrida, "the Christological claim that Jesus is fully human and fully divine does not erase difference. The two natures are neither fused nor dialectically related."[88] Derrida shows no real interest in following this lead. Given Derrida's learning and knowledge of intellectual history, it is hard to believe that he does not grasp the philosophical implications of Hart's important gesture toward the incarnation. More likely, the reason Derrida did not follow up on Hart's suggestion is that he simply is not interested in actually reconciling presence and differ-

---

[86]Ibid., p. 135.
[87]Jacques Derrida, *On Cosmopolitanism and Forgiveness*, Thinking in Action (London: Routledge, 2001), p. 39.
[88]Jacques Derrida, "Epoché and Faith: An Interview with Jacques Derrida," in *Derrida and Religion: Other Testaments*, ed. John D. Caputo, Kevin Hart and Yvonne Sherwood (New York: Routledge, 2005), p. 47.

ence, or at least not with the help of theology.[89] What interests him is God
and Christianity without the idea of presence, and, as he rightly surmises,
"If you insist only on difference that is without presence, or that is prior to
presence, you would have to erase a lot of things in the Christian corpus."[90]

Clearly, Derrida's understanding of faith, which so far continues to inform much talk about God in continental philosophy, remains nonparticipatory. For him, "it is only in the suspension of belief, the suspension of
God as a thesis, that faith appears." One can say "I am a believer" as little
as one can claim "I am an atheist," because such certain knowledge is impossible.[91] Derrida can imagine prayer or calling on God only within the
deconstructionist binary of presence and difference. God is either certainly
present, making calling on him unnecessary, or I am not sure about his
presence, whence I call. So, Derrida concludes, "if God were really present
to me, as a certain, a sure presence, why would I call?"[92] Derrida is right,
of course, to point out that every authentic faith includes an element of
doubt, of a kind of atheism, and that God's being cannot be reduced to a
metaphysical form of existence as essence or substance.[93] To say, however,
that the only possibility of faith lies with a God without presence is dogmatic refusal to entertain the idea of the incarnation, and also of the Holy
Spirit's power of presencing God. This position only takes us back to
Hart's earlier question: is not Derrida's rejection of divine presence based
on a definition of knowledge as merely theoretical, and of experience as
empty of content? Derrida has no problem with the private experience of
grace, which is inaccessible to deconstruction. He respects the possibility
of such grace because it is not publically accessible. In fact, he declares that
deconstruction itself is motivated by something that is "if not grace, then
certainly a secret, an absolute secret experience which I would compare
with what you call grace."[94] Unlike the Christian God, who has shown his
love for humanity and what it means to be human in the incarnation, Derrida's secret must remain nondescript.

For all the positive features that Heidegger, Levinas and Derrida have

---

[89]Ibid., p. 47.
[90]Ibid., p. 48.
[91]Ibid., p. 47.
[92]Ibid., p. 38.
[93]Ibid., p. 46.
[94]Ibid., p. 39.

brought to the discussion of meaning and humanism, from a Christian perspective their combined influence on the religious turn of continental philosophy raises serious problems. For example, Levinas and Derrida's ethics of otherness pay too little attention to the need for hermeneutic discernment. Levinas insists on the primordial ethical responsibility to the other, a relation he even describes with the hyperbolic images of "substitution" and "being hostage to the other."[95] Similarly, Derrida has called for radical hospitality that would even welcome the devil. Yet, "how can we tell the difference between benign and malign others? . . . How do we account for the fact that not every other is innocent and not every self is an egoistic emperor?"[96]

Richard Kearney, who has submitted the postmodern obsession with an unrepresentable other to a searching critique, concludes that the "suspicion of sameness" can easily become itself a new idolatry: "that of the immemorial, ineffable Other."[97] Kearney proposes a middle way he calls "a diacritical hermeneutics of alterity," along the lines of Paul Ricoeur's hermeneutic philosophy. This hermeneutic of discernment seeks a middle way beyond the dualisms created by the postmodern quest for an unrepresentable, absolute other. Instead of lining up insurmountable binaries of "anti-essentialism versus essentialism, alterity versus consciousness, silence versus speech, ineffability versus representation . . . [and] micro narratives versus master narrative," Kearney suggests a more realistic path. Between positivism and its postmodern flight into irrational otherness lies the way of interpretive discernment attainable through "a certain judicious mix of phronetic understanding, narrative imagination, and hermeneutic judgment."[98] Kearney is right. Why should one have to accept the overblown postmodern hyperboles of otherness with their rigid dichotomies?

Kearney does more, however, than merely expose the dangerous ambivalence of the postmodern fetish of otherness. He also rejects the postmodern denial of metanarratives as inhuman, because such narratives establish our identity and the purpose of our existence. Overarching stories

---

[95]Levinas, "A Man-God?" in *Entre Nous*, p. 58. "Subjectivity as such is initially hostage; it answers to the point of expiating for others" (Levinas, *Ethics and Infinity*, p. 100).

[96]Richard Kearney, *Strangers, Gods, and Monsters: Interpreting Otherness* (London: Routledge, 2003), p. 67.

[97]Ibid., p. 229.

[98]Ibid., p. 187.

are the very foundation of human solidarity and grant us cultural memory as well as the ability to deal with traumatic experiences.[99] Kearney insists that the dissolution of neither the self nor of meaning is necessary. He proposes with Ricoeur that we reconceive meaning and the self in narrative modes beyond either essentialism or postmodern absolutism. One may also say that Kearney, with Gadamer, recalls the basic linguisticality of human existence, the fact that we only have world, memory and meaning through language. Therefore, the meaning of suffering, of others, our individual and common history all depends on narration and interpretation.[100] Kearney realizes that this hermeneutic approach depends on some sense of hope, but he refuses to place this hope in one particular ultimate referent. Instead he offers a wager. A narrative hermeneutics is a risk worth taking because (1) we can and must try to negotiate the increasingly confusing disarray of a postmetaphysical, globalized world through the power of narrative, by clothing the fuzzy and unsayable in narratives; and (2) we may not have a transparent and unified self, but we "possess" a narrative identity that "persists through and is enriched by the stories we tell and receive from others."[101]

Kearney's approach is a vast improvement over much academic postmodernism, inspired, no doubt, by his own experiences with real suffering. When it comes to God, however, and especially the nature of revelation, his diacritical hermeneutic fails to capture the true nature of the Christian God's presence within the material world. In describing his "God who may be," who shows his face through a number of conflicting stories or religions, Kearney shares the general tendency in postmodern God talk to overlook the full implications of incarnational theology.

THE DISINCARNATE GOD OF CONTINENTAL PHILOSOPHY

Postmodern philosophy has smashed many idols of modernity, but the resulting vacuum has been filled with another idol. While God has become a popular topic among philosophers, especially within the so-called tradition of continental philosophy, this God is generally a disincarnate deity, a

---

[99]Richard Kearney, *On Stories,* Thinking in Action Series (London and New York: Routledge, 2002), pp. 61-62.
[100]Kearney, *Strangers, Gods, and Monsters,* pp. 188-89.
[101]Ibid., p. 231.

God without being, and not the Christian, incarnate, trinitarian God. The great mystery of the Christian religion is that God somehow includes the human through the incarnation and that our knowledge of God is mediated through this incarnation and therefore also through human history, language and other human beings.

The philosophical efforts of continental philosophers such as Heidegger, Gadamer, Derrida and Levinas have done much to free Western thought from the tyranny of rationalism and subjectivism,[102] and to reorient human knowledge toward an objective transcendent measure, whatever that measure might be. What unites all of these different thinkers who could broadly be captured under the umbrella term of "the phenomenological tradition" (and we should add Paul Ricoeur and Jean-Luc Marion to this tradition) is the fear of objectification, or, as Levinas would have it, the fear of conceptual idolatry.

God talk within this tradition is pursued by mainly three schools of thought: the theological phenomenology of Jean-Luc Marion and Michel Henry, the deconstructionism of Derrida and his theological disciple John Caputo, and the hermeneutical approach that draws on elements from both, as represented by Paul Ricoeur, Richard Kearney and, in a slightly different way, by the Italian Gianni Vattimo.[103] Of these three movements, theological phenomenology and hermeneutics are theologically more promising. For after deconstructing both God and self, the two central poles of human identity, postmodern ethics demands a critical recon-

---

[102]Philosophical hermeneutics, as begun by Heidegger and worked out by his student Hans-Georg Gadamer, understands itself as correcting the anthropocentrism of the modern era. Gadamer, for example, correctly labels Heidegger "a radical critic of modern conceptions of the subject" (Hans-Georg Gadamer, "Gibt es auf Erden ein Maß?" in *Neuere Philosophie I: Hegel, Husserl, Heidegger*, vol. 3 of *Gesammelte Werke* [Tübingen: J. C. B. Mohr, 1987], pp. 333-49, 370).

[103]I have not included Caputo in the hermeneutic camp because his own brand of "radical hermeneutics" is really a restatement of Derridean deconstruction in theological language. As many debates between the two thinkers have shown, Kearney's "diacritical hermeneutics," which shuttles back and forth between particular religious traditions and a universal idea of God, rightly criticizes the "masters of deconstruction" for neglecting the need for substantial notions of God and self to maintain ethics and deal with human suffering. I have also not mentioned Alain Badiou, Giorgio Agamben and Slavoj Žižek, who have recently written increasingly on Christian themes, but who do so mainly to supplement their own philosophies rather than to engage biblical theology or its interpretive tradition in a serious way. For a recent analysis of these thinkers, see Douglas Harink, *Paul, Philosophy, and the Theopolitical Vision: Critical Engagements with Agamben, Badiou, Žižek, and Others*, Theopolitical Visions (Eugene, Ore.: Wipf & Stock, 2010).

struction of both in order to respond discerningly and reasonably to human and divine actions.[104]

Unfortunately, however, this laudable concern against reification sometimes tends to produce another idol, namely, a God who "may be" or "a God without being." Insofar as these terms for God are understood as an antidote to fundamentalist appropriations of God, and as the cautious approach of philosophers who want to reintroduce God into philosophy without committing idolatry, Christians should welcome the religious turn in continental philosophy. Metaphysics, as Jean-Luc Marion points out, can easily become idolatry, and Christianity does not think God "within the theoretical space defined by metaphysics, or even starting from the concept, but indeed starting from God alone, grasped to the extent that he inaugurates by himself the knowledge in which he yields himself—reveals himself."[105] Marion's work, in fact, illustrates the problem of stressing conceptual idolatry to the point of distorting the Christian faith.

Marion is easily the most subtle and theologically sophisticated representative of French phenomenology. The importance of his work lies at least partially in his retrieval of the idea for phenomenology that certain phenomena we encounter confront our intuition with an inexplicable excess. These phenomena of "revelation" constitute "an appearance that is purely of itself and starting from itself," and one that escapes any prior determination or meaning.[106] The saturated phenomenon sets its own categories of meaning and is irreducible to our intuition of it. Marion hints that he is adapting Anselm's argument for God's existence (as that greater than which nothing can be thought) to phenomenology in which things appear that defy a priori intuition and a postiori explanation.[107] Just as these phenomena cannot be reduced to our expectations or understanding, so God also escapes our categories of understanding. Theologically, Marion recovers the classical Christian argument of *creatio ex nihilo* and God's independence of creation. Creation is a pure gift of God's love, and

---

[104]Kearney, *Strangers, Gods, and Monsters*, p. 188.

[105]Jean-Luc Marion, *God Without Being: Hors-Texte*, trans. Thomas A. Carlson, Religion and Postmodernism (Chicago: University of Chicago Press, 1991), p. 36.

[106]Jean-Luc Marion, "The Saturated Phenomenon," in *Phenomenology and the "Theological Turn": A French Debate*, ed. Dominique Janicaud, trans. Thomas A. Carlson, Perspectives in Continental Philosophy (New York: Fordham University Press, 2000), p. 215.

[107]Ibid., p. 216.

God therefore remains always prior to ontology and human categories.

Within the context of phenomenology, Marion argues against Heidegger that theology is an ontic subscience of the greater, broader investigation into ontology as such. Against Heidegger, and with Levinas, Marion argues for a liberation of God from being. Heidegger's vaunted ontological difference subordinates even God to its dynamic and thus creates another idol.[108] Marion seeks instead "another difference more essential to being than ontological difference itself,"[109] namely the "gift" of being, ceaselessly and gratuitously given by the God who is independent from the game of being, from the world's order, and whose revelation thus relativizes the self-affirming game of being.[110] Marion, in other words, turns Heidegger's subordination of theology to the ontological difference on its head by confronting it with the claim that God holds the ontological difference in his hand. Marion's retrieval of this Christian idea has a distinctly Barthian ring to it and shares Barth's conceptual problem of beginning with a rupture rather than with the reciprocity of ontology and transcendence in the incarnation. We can grant both Barth and Marion the necessity of this emphasis in light of intellectual contexts that are largely hostile to the concept of divine revelation. Both thinkers required a strong emphasis on exteriority in order to critique the liberal humanism of modern Protestant theology with its attendant historical-critical method and Husserl's "neutral" or Heidegger's existential-atheistic phenomenologies.

Yet what often gets lost in this approach is the biblical emphasis on participation in God and on the true knowledge we can have about God. In fairness to Barth, his model of revelation is distinctly trinitarian, and he recognizes the importance of God's "being for us" in Christ. Barth also acknowledges the importance of philosophical reflection for theology. His rejection of the *analogia entis* is not absolute but concerned the possible imposition of metaphysical prejudgments on theology. Nowhere does he intend or imply a faith-reason dualism.[111] Yet Barthian theologians such as Alan Torrance have acknowledged the lack of participatory quality in

---

[108]Marion, *God Without Being*, p. 68.

[109]Ibid., p. 85.

[110]Ibid., p. 94.

[111]Alan J. Torrance, *Persons in Communion: An Essay on Trinitarian Description and Human Participation, with Special Reference to Volume One of Karl Barth's Church Dogmatics* (Edinburgh: T & T Clark, 1996), p. 167.

Barth's concept of revelation as divine address by a wholly other God. Stressing the latter, Barth is never quite able fully to balance his emphasis on the presence of God in the preaching of the word with an equal emphasis on worship and the celebration of the sacraments.[112] Moreover, always concerned to guard God's otherness, Barth eschews the term *person* and opts for the descriptor "modes of being" (*Seinsweisen*) to designate the members of the Trinity.[113] Yet Barth's chosen terminology does not quite capture fully either the mutuality and relatedness of the trinitarian members, or our human participation in this divine communion through worship and the sacraments. Torrance argues that because of the incarnation, "the Trinitarian relations *ad intra* are to be conceived as open to us as creatures," and that they are open to us in worship when we "participate in the human priesthood of the Son through the presence of the Spirit."[114] There is no doubt about the high and central place Christ holds as mediator in Barth's theology.[115] Yet if by stressing Christ's mediating role Barth indeed aimed at recovering the trinitarian view of the Greek fathers,[116] then his understanding of our participation in God should have equally acknowledged the importance of sacramental mediation, to which Barth did not do justice, while Bonhoeffer did.

Barth, while sharing with postmodern theologians an emphasis on God's otherness, is much more conversant with the Bible and the Christian tradition than many postmodern advocates of a God after Christianity. By stressing the otherness of God and his distance from creation, postmodern theology, in rhetoric and substance, resembles fideism rather than biblical faith. For example, Pauline theology emphasizes human-divine participation by referring to the Christian's being "in Christ" (Rom 8:1) and the Spirit's living in us (Rom 8:9-11; 2 Tim 1:14). After all, the Christian message is Emmanuel, "God with us." The difference of Christian revelation from that of other religions is that the wholly transcendent God "is not a distant fact towards which man strives with great effort. Rather he is someone who has joined man on his path, who has become his

---

[112]Ibid., p. 118.

[113]Ibid., pp. 116-17.

[114]Ibid., p. 323.

[115]See for instance J. B. Torrance's assessment of Barth's theology in *Worship, Community and the Triune God of Grace* (Downers Grove, Ill.: InterVarsity Press, 1996), p. 28.

[116]Ibid., p. 24.

companion."[117] The central mystery of the Christian faith is that God has made himself a human presence without relinquishing his transcendence, and that this presence within history and time continues among believers as (and in) the church. It is our human tendency to reduce this presence of God with us "to the level of images we have of presence and absence."[118] Measured by the postmodern propensity to emphasize God's otherness to the detriment of his presence, Marion's theological work is actually quite nuanced, but he too seems uncomfortable with God's presence in ontological structures. Ever striving against idolatry, Marion argues, for example, that the divine logic of love does not provide any assurances for the Christian, whereas any relationship built on love does provide such assurances based on past experiences that certify the presence of love and encourage trust. Yet Marion balances the nonparticipatory tenor of his theology both by recognizing the importance of the church as a eucharistic community, whose diverse interpretation of the divine truly leads back to the Word, and by referring to God's love being poured out by the Spirit into the hearts of believers.[119]

Marion's thoughtful phenomenological appropriations of the Christian tradition have not made a noticeable impact on evangelical theology. Other representatives of postmodern theology have, however, and for this reason we will examine them in greater detail. Although well intentioned, the three following postmodern theologians within the continental tradition do not match Marion's knowledge of Christian source texts and lack his nuanced approach to theology. Our first example is Richard Kearney, a philosophical theologian, who introduced into continental philosophy's religious turn the notion of the "God who may be." The second is the theologian John Caputo with his deconstructionist theology. Finally, as a third example of postmodern theology, we will examine Gianni Vattimo's incarnational philosophy "after Christianity." We will briefly examine each thinker in turn.

Richard Kearny's philosophy of religion is an attempt to speak once again of God after the problematic deities of classical Christianity and of

---

[117]Giussani, *Why the Church?* pp. 14-15.
[118]Ibid., p. 15.
[119]Marion, *God Without Being*, p. 156. "And of love, the Christian never stands in need, since the Spirit pours love out into the hearts that receive it" (ibid., p. 195, citing Rom 5:5).

metaphysical philosophies have lost all credibility. His work is best understood as a philosophical apologetic for religion and the sacramental nature
of reality, as reflected in religions and in literary texts. In exploring philosophical approaches to God, Kearney employs the phrase the "God who
may be" to oppose fundamentalist claims of divine truth on the one hand
and amorphous postmodern claims of transcendence (or the sublime) on
the other. Against the fundamentalist who wants to possess God and insists on a certain interpretation of divine presence, Kearney upholds the
God who *may be*, whose possibilities always transcend human interpretation and control. Kearney concludes this argument with truly inspiring
images of the divine-human cooperative effort to transform the earth in
light of God's kingdom of neighborly love.[120] Kearney also opposes a prevalent postmodern tendency, evident in Derrida, Lyotard and Kristeva, to
stress a transcendent sublime beyond all human understanding and ethical
categories. In this "mystical Postmodernism," God is not tied to any identifiable ontological structure in order to overcome all conceptual idolatry
and established moral categories.

As Kearney points out, the problem with mystical postmodernism is
that God becomes now indistinguishable from the monstrous.[121] Eschew-
ing both the God of full presence and the nondescript God of the postmodern sublime, Kearney suggests an alternative path of "diacritical
hermeneutics." He rejects the iron cage of static tradition by which we
stunt our imagination and exclude others, and he also steers clear of the
radical openness exemplified by Derridean hospitality, a blind faith that
welcomes any guest whether good or evil. This undiscerning openness and
a God without a face, pried loose from any tradition or particular religion,
are neither feasible nor advisable.[122] Instead, Kearney wants to "reinterpret
the God of Exodus 3:14 as neither being nor nonbeing, but as something
before, between and beyond the two: an eschatological *may be?* Such a
third way might help us eschew the excesses of both *ecclesiastical mysticism*
on the one hand . . . and apocalyptic Postmodernism on the other."[123] No
doubt, Kearney is correct to suspect a one-sided metaphysical interpreta-

---

[120]Richard Kearney, *The God Who May Be: A Hermeneutics of Religion*, Indiana Series in the
   Philosophy of Religion (Bloomington: Indiana University Press, 2001), p. 110.
[121]Ibid., p. 34.
[122]Ibid., p. 76.
[123]Ibid.

tion of God's self-identification that equates God with being, and to emphasize that the Hebrew meaning contains the future tense, indicating a God who will be.[124] Kearney is also right to remind us that God's self-revelation to Moses indicates a divine commitment to a shared history with Israel.[125] Yet in his postmodern enthusiasm against *any* notion of divine being and sovereign, self-contained presence, Kearney pushes relentlessly toward a God *"who becomes with us"* someone "as dependent on us as we are on him."[126]

Kearney rightly reminds the Christian of the gospel's eschatological dimension, but his emphasis on a "new eschatology of God," what he terms "the God-who-may-be," ultimately ends up distorting the Christian faith. Our imagination about what God is or might be is no longer shaped by God's self-revelation in the incarnation, but rather God himself becomes shaped in the image of postmodern philosophy. It is one thing to alert believers to the eschatological dimension within Christianity and thus to combat fundamentalism (and also rationalism) with hermeneutics—this is what Kearney does very well; it is quite another matter, however, to rewrite the theological tradition without paying serious attention to its classical texts and teachings. To be sure, Kearney has a poet's soul, and poets are usually impressionist theologians, going for the overall effect rather than for theological precision. But when Kearney writes that we and God "carry each other within" and "give birth to each other," concluding that "we help God to become God," one no longer recognizes the language of Christian theology.[127] Is it stretching poetic license too much to claim that "God cannot become fully God, nor the Word fully flesh, until creation becomes a new heaven and a new earth"?[128] Kearney complains that classic theology's attempts to speak about God in metaphysical categories have

---

[124]It is not clear, however, who exactly commits this identification of God with Being. Thomas Aquinas certainly does not, for he claims that (1) "no created substance represents God in His substance" and that (2) the only "substance" that represents God is the incarnate Son. Thus Aquinas too knows that essence and substance of God are not static but relational ideas (*Summa Contra Gentiles. Book Four: Salvation*, trans. Charles J. O'Neil [Notre Dame, Ind.: University of Notre Press, 1975], 7.15, 58). See also Congar's understanding of the Exodus passage and Thomas in Yves Congar, *Fifty Years of Catholic Theology: Conversations with Yves Congar*, ed. Bernard Lauret, trans. John Bowden (Minneapolis: Fortress, 1988), p. 72.

[125]Kearney, *God Who May Be*, p. 29.

[126]Ibid., pp. 29-30.

[127]Ibid., p. 111.

[128]Ibid., p. 110.

reduced God to being, but are his own philosophical categories better? Is not Kearney too readily inverting analogy and forcing God into the narrow confines of the human imagination by dogmatically insisting that only the God who may be is a free God, beyond human categories? While we can appreciate Kearney's emphasis on eschatology, his overhasty rhetoric implies God's *need* for human synergy and thus departs from the spirit of classical orthodox theology.

On the one hand, Kearney is one of the sanest voices among continental philosophers who employ the postmodern emphasis on otherness to defend the freedom and creativity of both God and human beings. He does so, moreover, in opposition to Derrida and Caputo's exaggerated stress on otherness to the point of absurdity.[129] On the other hand, however, his philosophical claims about God are not borne out by the Christian tradition; this would not be problematic, of course, if Kearney did not frequently enlist orthodox theological figures, such as Gregory of Nyssa, in support of his project. For example, I submit that the following passage from Gregory with its participatory language of presence is much more representative of the Greek fathers than of Kearney's opposition of *posse* and *esse:*

> For all things depend on Him who is, nor can there be anything which has not its being in Him who is. If, therefore, all things are in Him, and he in all things, why are they scandalized at the plan of Revelation, when it teaches that God was born among men, that same God Whom we are convinced is even now not outside mankind? [God has always been present with and in nature,] only now, He Who holds together Nature in existence is transfused in *us;* while at that other time he was transfused throughout *our nature*, in order that our nature might by this transfusion of the Divine become itself divine, rescued as it were from death, and put beyond the reach of the caprice of the antagonist. For His return from death becomes to our mortal race the commencement of our return to the immortal life.[130]

Gregory defends the concept of the incarnation using the apostle Paul's christological interpretation of God's presence in creation. Nothing exists

---

[129]Ibid., p. 34.
[130]Gregory of Nyssa, "The Great Catechism" in *Gregory of Nyssa: Dogmatic Treatises*, vol. 5 of *Nicene and Post-Nicene Fathers*, Second Series, ed. Philip Schaff and Henry Wace, trans. William Moore and Henry Austin Wilson (Peabody, Mass.: Hendrickson, 1994), p. 495.

without participation in "Him who is." The deepest mystery of Christianity is that by becoming human, God infused his presence into human nature to ennoble it to the true image of God and to renew creation in the same breath. It is this vision of the continued presence of God with human nature that contradicts Kearney's caricature of classical theology as world-denying, Platonic metaphysics. In fact, Gregory points out that "heaven" is not a remote place somewhere in the cosmos but rather indicates the presence of God:

> It does not seem to me that the Gospel is speaking of the firmament of heaven as some remote habitation of God when it advises us to be perfect as your heavenly father is perfect, because the divine is equally present in all things, and, in like manner, it pervades all creation and it does not exist separated from being, but the divine nature touches each element of being with equal honor, encompassing all things within itself.[131]

This incarnational language of infusion, participation and presence has largely disappeared from Kearney's discourse, presumably because it might result in triumphalism. And yet in patristic texts it is the sovereign, omnipresent God, the God who alone is self-existing, who makes human freedom and choice possible. Possibility derives not from God's absence but from his presence. Moreover, it is the God who *is* in the incarnate Jesus, who is not merely an inspiring example but the very embodiment of what Christians are to emulate. Early Christian theologians believed that Christ is the true image of God, to whose likeness humanity is to be restored.

I want to be clear on this: Kearney is absolutely right in seeking a way beyond essentialism on the one hand and the radical alterity of deconstruction on the other. As Kearney puts it, "once the masters of deconstruction have done their necessary work, it is important to retrieve the notion of a responsible narrator committed to the task of historical and personal remembrance."[132] In other words, Kearney realizes that we need both tradition and an interpreting self to discern truth and live responsibly.

Yet Kearney's own engagement with theology lacks the important nuances that come from a deep familiarity with the Christian tradition. Perhaps the central problem with Kearney's reading of the Christian tradition

---

[131]Gregory of Nyssa, *AW*, p. 87.
[132]Kearney, *Strangers, Gods, and Monsters*, p. 188.

is his neglect of the "sacramental Christ," the divine Logos through whom all things were created and are sustained, who has become flesh and continues to be present with us.[133] In his most recent book on *Anatheism*, Kearney indeed seeks to recover a sacramental view of the world, especially as manifested in the incarnation of divine hospitality to others in modern saints such as Dorothy Day, Jean Vanier and Mahatma Gandhi,[134] and he is careful to describe their examples as a "testimony to the incarnation of divinity in the flesh of the world."[135] And yet he only talks about *their* incarnation of the divine, always construed as reflecting a God of hospitality rather than a God of sovereign power. There is really no discernable difference between Kearney's gospel of hospitality and the social gospel of liberal Protestantism, except for his added emphasis on the need for interfaith dialogue. Moreover, while Kearney rightly argues against the distillation of religions to their common denominator in order to arrive at world peace and insists on the specificities of each spiritual tradition, he seems to overlook that not all religions are equally sacramental, and that he is, in fact, borrowing from a Christian idea under which he gathers all religions.[136] The distinct Christian lens through which Kearney views other religions stresses similarities among religions and overlooks important differences. In particular, the orthodox Christian idea of Christ's incarnate and cosmic presence is largely absent from Kearney's construal of the Christian faith; Christ becomes more of an example who inspires and invites us to transform the world; the participatory language of Pauline theology, in which Christ has already achieved perfect humanity to which we are to be conformed by uniting with him, is no longer relevant. In short, Kearney's God, too, shrinks from concrete enfleshment in ontology, because Kearney, along with most of the French phenomenological tradition, regards being as the ossifying and totalizing oppressor of possibility.

The predictable result is that Kearney sets up his own oppositional categories. For example, he opposes the classical notion of God as pure act to

---

[133]Jeffrey Bloechl has pointed out this shortcoming of Kearney's eschatological reduction of theology in his essay "Christianity and Possibility," in *After God: Richard Kearney and the Religious Turn in Continental Philosophy*, ed. John Panteleimon Manoussakis, Perspectives in Continental Philosophy (New York: Fordham University Press, 2006), p. 136.

[134]Richard Kearney, *Anatheism: Returning to God After God*, Insurrections: Critical Studies in Religion, Politics, and Culture (New York: Columbia University Press, 2010), pp. 152-65.

[135]Ibid., p. 165.

[136]Ibid., p. 176.

the God of possibility. Yet the incarnation combines these two aspects of God, of being and becoming, and modern theologians such as Eberhard Jüngel have drawn attention to the theological potential of this correlation. Jüngel follows Karl Barth in claiming that God's self-revelation in the flesh (i.e., in Jesus the Messiah) enables a notion of his objective givenness whose event character unites being and becoming. The incarnation, in other words, could relieve Kearney of the need to oppose God's presence to his transcendence. God's objective presence with us is "an actuality proper to God's being," rather than merely something in the future.[137] This "sacramental presence of God with us," is, in the incarnation, an enduring "ontological connection" between God and humanity.[138] God, in other words, really *is* in the midst of being, whereas Kearney's categories are too one-sidedly invested in the eschatological.[139] To dichotomize God talk between onto-theology (the idolatrous construal of God in categories of being, with God as the highest form of being) and nonontological possibility is itself an act of idolatry. Moreover, contrary to Kearney's own hermeneutical beliefs, these stark alternatives are not borne out by the texts in question. Neither Anselm nor Aquinas is, as Kearney insinuates, beholden to a metaphysical framework that forces God into the procrustean mold of being. Rather these thinkers, standing in a long tradition of expressing biblical ideas through the conceptual language of philosophy, are well aware of the latter's limitations. Kearney often misses the radical transformation of Greek concepts along biblical lines. As chapter six on the origins of incarnational humanism will show, the very commitment to justice and hospitality Kearney argues for is found most profoundly in classical theology's sovereign God.

Failing to notice the faithfulness to biblical concepts of God in thinkers Kearney lists as God-distorting onto-theologians, he ultimately fails to provide a third way between onto-theology and the postmodern sublime of indiscernible otherness. The inevitable consequence is yet another set of dichotomies. For example, he stresses the conditionality of God's promises in order to ensure human participation, but fails to recognize that biblical

---

[137]Eberhard Jüngel, *God's Being Is in Becoming: The Trinitarian Being of God in the Theology of Karl Barth: A Paraphrase* (Grand Rapids: Eerdmans, 2001), p. 63.

[138]Ibid., p. 136.

[139]Kearney, *God Who May Be*, p. 100. Kearney's categories are the God who "will be," "can be" or "should be." Never really the God who fully "is" present with us.

texts also stress the unconditionality of God's acts.[140] God unilaterally establishes the covenant with Abraham (Gen 12:1-4; 15:1-6), and Paul argues in Romans that God fulfilled his covenant promise in the Messiah Jesus. In light of Isaiah's prophecies, especially Isaiah 63:5-6[141] and other similar passages, God responds to the failure of Israel to uphold the divine covenant and model true humanity to the nations by taking matters into his own hands. God himself will effect the salvation of humanity and usher in a new heaven and new earth (Is 65:17). And the whole point of New Testament theology is that God has already accomplished this in the Messiah Jesus. Jesus' life models kingdom living; in his death, creation is judged and sinfulness condemned; and in the resurrection, creation is redeemed and humanity reconciled to God. Paul's language is very much both present tense *and* eschatological. We "have been" set free from sin and Christ "is the end of the law," and we have "now received reconciliation" (Rom 6:22; 10:4; 5:11). It is because God has done these things that Paul's basic ethical message to the churches is "become who you *are* in Christ," so that you conform increasingly to the truly human-divine image of the Messiah (Rom 8:28). Kearney reads the Old Testament as if the incarnation had not taken place, while Paul reads the same text through the lens of Christ's incarnation, death and resurrection. Kearney's portrait of God is too one-sided. He overemphasizes the "God of the burning bush and the transfiguration," and neglects Emmanuel, the God with us.[142]

The difference between Judaism and Christianity is exactly this: that the glory and presence of God that led Israel in a cloud of fire and filled the Davidic temple during its dedication became present in Jesus and is even now present with God's people. Christians are, as Paul put it, "the temple of the living God" (2 Cor 6:16). For Paul and the majority of the Christian tradition, this transference of God's presence from the Davidic temple to Jesus and his church is the fulfillment of God's promise. Paul backs up his claim of divine indwelling by recalling the Old Testament prophecy:

---

[140]For these and related issues, see Merold Westphal's sympathetic but critical treatment of Kearney's *posse* in "Hermeneutics and the God of Promise" in Manoussakis, ed., *After God*, pp. 90ff.

[141]"I looked, but there was no one to help, I was appalled that no one gave support; so my own arm achieved salvation for me, and my own wrath sustained me." See also Is 59:16ff.: "[the Lord] saw that there was no one, he was appalled that there was no one to intervene; so his own arm achieved salvation for him, and his own righteousness sustained him."

[142]Kearney, *God Who May Be*, p. 4.

"As God has said: 'I will live with them and walk among them, and I will be their God, and they will be my people'" (2 Cor 6:16-17). Kearney, because he remains too suspicious of God's presence in the world, subtly changes the biblical language. Take, for example, his reinterpretation of classical Christian theology that the kingdom has come but not yet fully come.[143] He writes that "the kingdom has already come but is not yet here."[144] In saying this he persistently overlooks New Testament texts that speak of God's Spirit in our hearts, *guaranteeing* what is to come (2 Cor 1:22; 5:5). That Kearney nowhere talks about already present aspects of God's kingdom indicates once again that he inverts the biblical order of actuality and possibility. In Christian theology, "the actuality of the one who makes and keeps his promises both precedes and is the condition of the possibility that what is promised will actually occur."[145] To put it bluntly, God nowhere requires human beings to help him be God; instead, human beings are invited everywhere to participate in God's redemptive act of incarnation, death and resurrection, to preach and enact a new humanity, a mode of being-for-another. Kearney misses this because his supposedly "descriptive" phenomenological perspective is so focused on the opposition between the sovereign God of being and the incomprehensible kenotic God of hospitality that neither God's self-revelation in Jesus the Messiah nor God's abiding presence in individuals and his church through the Spirit is given much consideration. Thus Jesus becomes mere exemplar for divine presence, rather than its ongoing embodiment. For the same reason Kearney interprets Jesus' injunction to Mary "do not lay hold of me" and Jesus' appearance to his disciples not as the withdrawal of Christ's physical body before he is more powerfully and universally present through the Holy Spirit as indicated by Pentecost, but rather as another indication of the "God who may be," of a God who withdraws his presence for fear of being idolized.[146]

---

[143]See, for example, Luther's description of the kingdom as already in the Christian yet not realized in the world as a whole (interpretation of the Lord's Prayer in *Auslegung des Vaterunser, Sermon von den guten Werken*, vol. 3 of *Calwer Luther-Ausgabe*, ed. Wolfgang Metzger [Stuttgart: Hänssler, 1996], pp. 36-38). The church thus becomes the place in which kingdom manners and language ought to become ever more evident. The church then becomes a sacrament of the presence of God in the world.

[144]Richard Kearney, "In Place of a Response," in Manoussakis, *After God*, p. 374.

[145]Westphal, "Hermeneutics and the God of Promise," p. 89.

[146]Kearney, *God Who May Be*, pp. 49-50.

Nothing can be said, of course, against Kearney's basic enterprise insofar as it is a philosophical proposal. Yet his work, along with that of other postmodern apostles of God after God, is more than a modest philosophical proposal. These thinkers readily divide up the world of religious thought into "dogmatic theism and militant atheism" in order to propose a third way, usually by stressing one aspect of traditional theology to the breaking point. In Kearney's case it is the eschatological element of Christianity and the unknowability of God. Both aspects, eschatology and divine incomprehensibility, are well established in classical Christian theology, but they are not opposed, as they are by Kearney, to other aspects of God's concrete, albeit never controllable, presence. Isolating eschatology at the expense of presence inevitably distorts the Christian tradition and invents its own God. Postmodern Christians like Kearney are right, of course, in their insistence on social justice, and indeed social justice is a powerful manifestation of godlikeness. However, as we have argued already, for incarnational humanism, social solidarity and justice flow from the assurance of Christ's presence with us, as the one whose very being is a being for others, and who shapes his people in his image. Indeed, the incarnation ensures that the Christian faith unites spirit and flesh.[147] Faith without works is indeed dead. But these postmodern theologies buy this ethical emphasis at the cost of God's presence with his people because they are afraid of idolizing God.

A final example of Kearney's unorthodox, postmodern God is found in his description of the Trinity. Once again, Kearney sets out to revise an impersonal, faceless postmodern transcendence, the Derridean *chōra*, in personal terms. Derrida appropriates this Platonic idea of an impersonal neutral container of the forms as an image for the nonobjectifiable, impersonal, unnamable other of deconstruction. Kearney rightly wonders about this arbitrary choice, but rather than oppose *chōra* to God, Kearney integrates this concept into the Christian Trinity.[148] Yet this integration, once again, produces an unorthodox hybrid of the patristic *perichōrēsis*[149] rather

---

[147]Ibid., p. 51.

[148]Kearney, *Strangers, Gods, and Monsters*, pp. 204-5.

[149]*Perichōrēsis* and its Latin equivalent *circumcession* describe the intimate relation of the three "persons" within the Godhead as mutual indwelling without confusion. John of Damascus also uses this term for the interpenetration of the human and divine in the incarnation (John of Damascus, "Expositions of the Orthodox Faith" 4.13, in *Nicene and Post-Nicene Fathers*,

than allowing traditional and, arguably, more biblical descriptions of God to emerge. In Kearney's version, "different persons move endlessly around an empty center (*chōra*), always deferring one to the other, the familiar to the foreign, the resident to the alien. Without the *gap* in the middle there could be no leap, no love, no faith."[150] Aside from the fact that no such reference to empty space or gap is found in patristic literature, there are serious theological problems with this image. Trinitarian communion is usually described as involving the highest intimacy and trust without surrendering individuality. To propose an impersonal, "empty space" at the center of the Trinity[151] places something at the heart of divine communion that is nonpersonal and alien to God. To use creedal language, Kearney introduces another substance into the communion of persons of *homoousia*.

Contrary to Kearney's speculations, Andrei Rublev's icon of the Trinity does not depict three angels seated "around an empty chalice." Kearney interprets this "empty container" conveniently as "the gap in our time and space where the radically other may arrive."[152] Kearney knows, of course, that the icon derives from a long line of images depicting Abraham's hosting of God's messengers, indeed perhaps of God himself (Gen 18:1-21). But Rublev's icon, in contrast to Kearney, follows an ancient iconographic tradition that interprets this scene of hospitality christologically. The loaves and the calf offered by Sarah to the guests become a type for the sacrificial offering of Christ's body on the cross, and the meal therefore a type of the eucharistic feast.[153] Later icons have reduced the meal image to a single chalice containing a calf's head, and Rublev's icon has followed this tradition.[154] Thus, contrary to Kearney's claims, Rublev's chalice depicts the eucharistic *presence* of Christ and the indwelling of the Holy Spirit. The chalice does not indicate empty space, but "the self-offering of the Son," who reveals the Father's glory and makes possible humanity's communion with the divine, the ultimate heavenly hospitality.[155]

Second Series, vol. 9, *Hilary of Poitiers, John of Damascus*, ed. Alexander Roberts et al. [Peabody, Mass.: Hendrickson, 1994], p. 91).
[150]Kearney, *Anatheism*, p. 56.
[151]Kearney, *Strangers, Gods, and Monsters*, p. 207.
[152]Kearney, *Anatheism*, p. 25.
[153]Gabriel Bunge, *The Rublev Trinity: The Icon of the Trinity by the Monk-Painter Andrei Rublev*, trans. Andrew Louth (Crestwood, N.Y.: St. Vladimir's Seminary Press, 2007), pp. 27-28.
[154]Ibid., p. 87.
[155]Ibid., p. 97.

For a more christological and thus more humanistic interpretation of the *chōra*, we turn to the Italian poet Dante, who seems to have a better grasp of trinitarian theology than Derrida or Kearney. Dante's vision of the Trinity also includes a strange intrusion within the three divine persons, but in his case this is "our human effigy."[156] Seeking from God an interpretation of this oddity, the poet does not receive an answer but is moved by the *agapē* of the Trinity, pulsing with the rhythm of its love for humanity. This interpretation is also borne out by the many icons of the Trinity in which the three persons of the Godhead are grouped not around an "empty center" but around the sacrificial eucharistic cup, the symbol of divine love for humanity.

Even the few instances of postmodern theology we have discussed so far indicate that postmodern reinterpretations of classical Christian theology are not hermeneutic enough. Too often they do not reflect deeply enough on the historicity of their own interpretive framework, and unfortunately engage other traditions similarly. To some extent, of course, our understanding of God begins with cultural foreunderstandings. Yet, as Gadamer insists, interpreters have to become aware of their own historically effected consciousness and work hard to have their prejudices shaped increasingly by the subject matter. This would require a prolonged study of the Christian tradition and biblical texts, but unfortunately, in too many postmodern theologies, philosophical idols distort the Christian tradition. In each case the theologian claims to recover true religion from the "religious alienation and abuse" of dogmatic, established theology.[157] In the creed of postmodern theology, classical theology is invariably equated with the "strong" theology of reason, order, strict control, Platonic metaphysics and the oppression of difference.[158]

Ironically enough, postmodern theology, in its stated intention to overcome the dualistic, world-denying attitude of modernism, is itself riddled with dualistic oppositions unknown to classical Christian theology: actu-

---

[156]Dante Alighieri, *The Divine Comedy of Dante Alighieri: Paradiso*, with an introduction by Allen Mandelbaum (New York: Bantam Classics, 1986), p. 303.

[157]Kearney, *Anatheism*, p. 171.

[158]See, for instance, John Caputo's opposition of strong to weak theology, and of the God who is to the God who "promises, not from beyond but from below, without being or sovereignty." *The Weakness of God: A Theology of the Event* (Bloomington: Indiana University Press, 2006), pp. 38ff.

ality versus possibility, presence versus absence, immanence versus transcendence, the kenotic God of weakness versus the sovereign God of power, doctrine versus experience, and a host of other dichotomies. Moreover, postmodern proposals for the renewal of Christianity display the kind of reckless Protestant *sola scriptura* approach to biblical texts that evangelicals have mostly left behind. This curiously Protestant tendency to disregard tradition is compounded by an anti-authoritarian, anti-establishment slant that is itself the result of a certain (1960s?) historically effected consciousness.

John Caputo's recent discussion of the weakness of God, for example, customarily opposes the sovereign God with the kenotic God of the cross, to conclude with the same idea already advanced in earlier books, namely, that Christianity is partaking in an unnamable event, adhering to the promise of an unknown God. To ensure us against dogmatism and oppression, he insists that we cannot know anything definitive about either ourselves or God, so that faith becomes pure action, an anarchic resistance of power in the name of justice:

> For the truth of the event does not belong to the order of identificatory knowledge, as if our Life's charge were to track down and learn the secret name of some fugitive spirit. The truth of the event releases us from the order of names and transports us to another level where truth does not mean learning a name, but making it happen, *facere veritate*, letting the event happen, *sans voir, sans savoir, sans avoir*, praying and weeping for an unknown God.[159]

On the one hand, Caputo is simply stating the obvious, namely, that God cannot be comprehended by finite minds and that social justice, love of neighbor, is central to the Christian way of being. Both of these aspects are fully present in the tradition of "strong theology" that Caputo condemns in order to peddle his "radical" new theology of the event, which, as he admits, is merely another "theology of the cross."[160] On the other hand, his emphasis on blind faith marked by a fideistic prayer to "who knows who is calling" departs radically from the broad Christian tradition. For Caputo this is not a problem, since both tradition and Scripture have be-

---

[159]Ibid., p. 298.
[160]Ibid., p. 43.

come the proverbial wax nose in the hands of the impassioned event theologian. For example, the apostle Paul's understanding of Jesus' death as atoning sacrifice offends the theologian of the event and is cast aside, mainly because *any* atonement theology is *necessarily* complicit with worldly economic systems and with the grand inquisitors of ecclesial hierarchies.[161] This combination of holy ignorance with anarchy is heady stuff indeed, but it has little to do with Christianity.

Early treatises on Christian behavior always emphasize that we *do know* what God is like because he has revealed himself, incarnated himself, in Jesus the Messiah. At the same time, this self-revelation does not permit reason to comprehend the essence of God. After all, knowledge of God is found in a personal encounter and hence is irreducible to reason. And yet, there is an important difference between encountering God in Christ and encountering another human being in general. The difference is that Christ's divine love includes "its own conditions of recognizability," and therefore the possibility of recognizing and knowing a transcendent other.[162] God, in other words, wants us to know him. Because the influence of his grace alone makes this possible, knowledge of God is initiated by him and makes use of human rational ability; but it is never a grasping of God, let alone a comprehension of his essence. Postmodern insinuations that naming God encases God in idolatrous conceptions that allow us to domesticate God may stem from a genuine intention to respect God's otherness, but it is also merely the inversion (and hence still a reflection) of the belief that naming something grasps its essence. One would think that especially the hermeneutic branch of postmodern theology would know better. It is instructive that the alleged onto-theological, strong theology of Christian tradition provides a more subtle, indeed more hermeneutic, approach to knowing God. We turn once again to Gregory of Nyssa, who begins his argument for possible knowledge of God by asserting the limits of human reason: "knowing, then, how widely the Divine nature differs from our own, let us quietly remain within our proper limits. For it is both safer and more reverent to believe the majesty of God to be greater than we understand, than, after circumscribing his glory by our misconceptions, to suppose there is nothing beyond our conceptions

---

[161]Ibid., p. 234.
[162]Hans Urs von Balthasar, *Love Alone Is Credible*, trans. D. C. Schindler (San Francisco: Ignatius Press, 2004), p. 75.

of it."[163] This injunction, he argues, is imposed by Scripture itself, for "whosoever searches the whole of revelation will find therein no doctrine of the Divine nature."[164] Indeed, Scripture teaches us nothing about either the divine essence or about the essential nature of the human self.[165] Yet while Gregory asserts our human inability to grasp or articulate God's essence, he also refuses the opposite claim that nothing may be known about God. He argues that the history of Israel, as recorded in the Scriptures and Christian experience, testifies to the contrary. Creation itself and God's dealings with humankind, above all through his self-revelation in Jesus, enable a limited but true understanding of the divine nature. And yet even those who walked with the incarnate Word, the apostles and eyewitnesses, make no attempt to articulate the essence of God.[166] Gregory issues the apt warning against "dogmatizers of deceit, who seek to limit the Divine Being, and all but openly idolize their own imagination."[167] Pretensions to essential knowledge of God will inevitably result in the fabrication of idols of the human imagination, a warning that also applies to postmodern theology insofar as it advances the dogma that nothing definitive may be known about God, only to proffer its own conceptions of the divine.

While "Holy Scripture omits all idle inquiry into substance as superfluous and unnecessary," our God-given faculty of reason nonetheless provides a "dim and imperfect comprehension of the Divine nature," that is "sufficient for our limited capacity."[168] This knowledge works by analogy to human relations;[169] it does not grasp the divine essence, no more than naming people comprehends their essence, but it nonetheless provides a true *recognition* of who God is through his activity and evident properties.[170] It is not hard to recognize a basic philosophical realism in Gregory's position, a

---

[163]Gregory of Nyssa, "Answer to Eunomius's Second Book," in *Gregory of Nyssa: Dogmatic Treatises*, vol. 5 of *Nicene and Post-Nicene Fathers*, Second Series, ed. Philip Schaff and Henry Wace, trans. William Moore and Henry Austin Wilson (Peabody, Mass.: Hendrickson, 1994), p. 260.

[164]Ibid., p. 261.

[165]"For who is there who has arrived at a comprehension of his own soul? Who is acquainted with its very essence?" (ibid.).

[166]Ibid., p. 260.

[167]Ibid.

[168]Ibid., p. 263.

[169]"For if we have learned any names expressive of the knowledge of God, all these are related and have analogy to such names as denote human characteristics" (ibid., p. 260).

[170]Ibid., pp. 260-61.

strict refusal to view God as merely "a conception of the mind." Such nominalism (i.e., that God is merely a name) would be sheer madness and folly, a
verdict the ancients share with postmodern philosophy. The difference from
postmodern theorists lies in the greater subtlety of ancient metaphysicians to
see beyond the either-or of naive realism or agnosticism. For Gregory, concepts and names are neither mere inventions nor direct conduits to the essence of things. This critical realism is grounded in the conviction that God,
the creator and sustainer of reality, has designed human beings with a rational faculty capable of true intuitions, so that even with limitations, human
reason can still deduce true properties of God as evidenced in creation and
his dealings with humankind.[171] We can thus "transfer the thoughts that
arise within us about the Divine Being into the mold of a corresponding
name; so that there is no appellation given to the Divine Being apart from
some distinct intuition of him."[172] Yet these intuitions do not "grasp in
thought" the divine essence itself. Names, even while not groundless assig-
nations, nonetheless remain more or less accurate "speculations" about God.
For example, "since everything discoverable in the world is linked to the
Being Who transcends all existences and possesses there the source of its
continuance," we can perceive in the beauty of creation "a new range of
thoughts about the Deity."[173] These perceptions of God can be a true recognition of who he is without claiming to grasp his essence.[174]

Gregory's conception of nonessential but true knowledge of God is
grounded in the incarnation, by which God demonstrated true humanity
and its virtues in Jesus the Messiah. The Bible, both in the Old and New
Testament, is replete with injunctions to imitate God, a command that
requires substantive knowledge about God's character. In the words of the
apostle Paul, "Be imitators of God, therefore, as dearly loved children, and
live a life of love, just as Christ loved us and gave himself up for us as a fra-
grant offering and sacrifice to God" (Eph 5:1-2). This *imitatio Christi* is based
not on ignorance but on knowing how God revealed himself in Jesus the
Messiah, who can be known in the manner that persons are known. This is
why Basil of Caesarea can identify the goal of Christians as becoming "like

---

[171]Ibid., pp. 308-9.
[172]Ibid., p. 309.
[173]Ibid.
[174]Ibid., p. 308.

God, as far as this is possible for human nature," and then add that "we cannot become like God unless we have knowledge of him."[175] Moreover, this knowledge of God is both relational, or experiential, and cognitive. The main idea found in much early Christian theology is that the believer participates in the perfect humanity of God as manifested in Christ, and that the Christian life consists in understanding and living out this reality.

For example, Basil's brother Gregory, in his treatise *On the Christian Mode of Life*, assumes that doctrine and experience go hand in hand:

> we know very well that the rule of reverence in you is fixed by the right dogma of the faith which holds the Godhead of the blessed and eternal Trinity, never changing in any way, one in essence, one in glory, known by its will and worshiped under the three substances. On the grounds that we have received it from many witnesses, we make our confession by means of the Spirit which washes us in the stream of the mystery.[176]

Gregory explains that in the Christian the power of God is at work, an energy he calls "the Spirit's participation and the Spirit's activity with respect to those in communion with Him [Christ]." By this participation in Christ through the Spirit, the believer should become formed in the "habits" of the Lord's perfect Humanity.[177] This participatory knowledge of God is what postmodern apostles of the event and of God without being have completely overlooked, and yet this is the heart of incarnational humanism: to be human is participation in the incarnational mode of being. We recall once more Gregory of Nyssa's injunction to his parishioners to follow the pattern of the incarnation:

> imitate the Master by loving one another and do not shrink from death or any other punishment for the good of each other. But the way which God entered upon for you, do you enter upon for Him, proceeding with one body and one soul to the invitation from above, loving God and each other. For love and fear of the Lord are the fulfillment of the law.[178]

Much of postmodern philosophy and theology has obscured the true nature of the Christian faith by disregarding the centrality of the incarnation

---

[175]Basil the Great, *On the Holy Spirit*, trans. David Anderson, Popular Patristic Series (Crestwood, N.Y.: St. Vladimir's Seminary Press, 1980), p. 17.
[176]Gregory of Nyssa, "On the Christian Mode of Life," in *AW*, p. 128.
[177]Ibid., p. 150.
[178]Ibid., p. 147.

for Christian thought. From a merely philosophical point of view, the incarnation allows for the mediation of divine transcendence through matter. God can be within being without succumbing to its numbing effects. The postulation of an artificial chasm between the sovereign, onto-theological God who is and the contourless event God who may be that forms the mainspring of postmodern theologies is not necessary. The fear of idolatry or objectification of God is not resolved by the flight into fideism, into a blind faith that is being carried along by who knows what. Nor does Kearney's much needed call for hermeneutic discernment solve this false dichotomy as long as one remains trapped in the hermeneutic death spiral of opposing actuality and possibility, being and *posse*, revelation and ontology. Likewise, Caputo is not far off by inviting us to think of God as event, yet a close miss is still a miss. Caputo rightly claims that God (and truth for that matter) is an event, but he has no theological grounds for asserting the indeterminate nature of this event. God has revealed himself in a concrete, historically unique incarnation, witnessed by the disciples and recorded in the Scriptures. Christian theology has traditionally insisted that no matter how fertile the human imagination, it cannot reach behind God's own definition of the God event as *Christ* event. The Gospel of John is perhaps the clearest example of early Christian interpretations that proclaim the identity of Jesus the Messiah and the eternal Word and creative Wisdom of God in Genesis: *en archē ēn ho logos*—in the beginning was the Word. Speculative human thought cannot reach behind this beginning without distorting revelation. Christian conceptions of God must access God through the incarnate Word.[179] Christian orthodoxy wisely refused to venture behind this beginning and insisted that any interpretation of God cannot ignore "the fact that it is not possible to approach to a knowledge of the Father except through the Son."[180]

GIANNI VATTIMO: INCARNATION WITHOUT TRANSCENDENCE

Without a proper understanding of the incarnation, postmodern theologies overemphasize either transcendence or immanence. So far we have dis-

---

[179]Basil the Great, *On the Holy Spirit*, p. 30.
[180]Gregory of Nyssa, "Against Eunomius, Book I," in *Gregory of Nyssa: Dogmatic Treatises*, vol. 5 of *Nicene and Post-Nicene Fathers*, Second Series, ed. Philip Schaff and Henry Wace, trans. William Moore and Henry Austin Wilson (Peabody, Mass.: Hendrickson, 1994), p. 77.

cussed postmodern theologians whose preoccupation with God's transcendence lets them neglect his presence. We now turn to a philosopher who succumbs to the opposite extreme of losing God's transcendence by focussing too much on God's presence in the world. The Italian philosopher Gianni Vattimo has tried to articulate a postmodern, post-Christian Christianity on the basis of the incarnation. Vattimo's conflation of Heidegger's hermeneutic ontology with the central Christian doctrine of the incarnation justifies and requires a deeply theological response to his basic question: "Can we really argue, as I believe we must, that postmodern nihilism constitutes the actual truth of Christianity?" Assuming "we" refers to Christians, the short answer to this question is no, we cannot and must not.

Such a negative response to Vattimo's question still concedes that his general project of an incarnational ontology is philosophically bold—perhaps reminiscent more of Hegel than of Joachim de Fiore—a move that offers important insights for thinking through the West's current cultural crisis.[181] Our cultural situation, as I have argued, seems characterized by the exhaustion of secular reason on the one hand and the return of religion, accompanied by the fear of fundamentalism and religiously motivated violence, on the other. Vattimo tries to articulate Christianity within this context and rightly stresses the interpretive nature of the Christian faith to forestall dogmatism, escapism and the church's segregation from the world.[182] To this end, Vattimo tirelessly points out the need for herme-

---

[181]See here Anthony C. Sciglitano's excellent article that draws attention to this connection and claims that Vattimo, just like Hegel, seems just to know a little too much about the nature of the divine from an allegedly radically interpretive standpoint. Sciglitano argues that "to the extent that his system is Hegelian, Vattimo's philosophical theology falls well short of the criterion he sets for all theology: it falls short of love." This shortfall is the depersonalization of God that Sciglitano enumerates in seven similarities between Hegel and Vattimo: "(1) The Trinity is depersonalized; (2) the divine-world relation is given a modalistic and ultimately monistic reading; (3) Passibility is radical and history becomes a constitutive, or stronger, determinative of divine being; (4) Scriptural revelation is overcome by a "spiritual sense" reading that envisions a reconciliation between divine being and the being of the world, thus asserting some form of identity; (5) Jesus' historical existence becomes religiously insignificant; (6) Resurrection does not lead to exaltation and ends *kenosis*, and does not apply to Jesus as an individual, but rather continues *kenosis* as a general diffusion of divine Being into the secular or as the secular; (7) Divine will, election, missions are excised from theological reflection." Anthony C. Sciglitano, "Contesting the World and the Divine: Balthasar's Trinitarian 'Response' to Gianni Vattimo's Secular Christianity," *Modern Theology* 23, no. 4 (2007): 538.
[182]As the following citation makes clear, Vattimo's interpretation of Christianity is motivated by a rather one-sided impulse of accommodating Christianity to modern culture. One suspects that he is not so much opposed to "the literality" of the Catholic church's teaching, but any

neutic reflection not only within Christian belief but in all areas of political and civic life.

In equating weak thought with the essence of Christianity, Vattimo, much like his main sources Nietzsche and Heidegger, reacts against stifling cultural examples of Christianity, but fails to preserve the gift introduced into Western thinking by the Christian concept of the incarnation. This gift is the balanced correlation of transcendence with immanence, the alliance of divine otherness with human finitude, of radical difference with identity, and this gift has acted as a potent relativizer of absolute categories in Western thinking. Yet this relativizing—or as Vattimo might say "weakening" effect—depends on maintaining a careful balance of transcendence and immanence. Vattimo loses this balance because, as so often happens in postmodern theologizing, he twists the biblical mystery to suit a prior, postmodern framework. Of course, as we have learned from hermeneutic philosophy, any truth requires mediation through a particular language and its concepts, and neither Christianity nor the biblical text is an exception to this rule. There is no "pure" biblical message, free from particular historical context. Christianity has the essentially incarnational character of "a spiritual Reality becoming incarnate in the realm of sense" that matures in history.[183] The hermeneutic character of the Christian faith does, however, have a guiding measure for interpreting Christianity through particular language and concepts. This normative measure is Christ's claims about himself, his self-interpretation in light of the Jewish history his teachings passed on to the apostles, and their interpretations of his passion and resurrection as laid down in the New Testament writings. Unlike the church fathers, who were very alert to the tension between bib-

---

authority that requires repentance of cultural practices we find pleasing: "Above all, returning to the question of doctrine, it is not, for me (or for anyone else who has a similar trajectory through secularization in modernity), a matter of rediscovering the literality of the truths of faith as they are often so preached by the Church. I am persuaded, and not merely out of attachment to my passions, that if I have a vocation to recover Christianity, it will consist in the task of rethinking revelation in secularized terms in order to 'live in accord with one's age,' therefore in ways that do not offend my culture as, to greater or lesser extent, a man who belongs to this age. This is the exact opposite of returning to the father's house (as a Catholic discipline), filled with repentance, prepared to abase oneself and to mortify one's intellectual pride" (Gianni Vattimo, *Belief,* trans. Luca D'Isanto and David Webb [Stanford, Calif.: Stanford University Press, 1999], p. 75).

[183]Henri de Lubac, *Catholicism: Christ and the Common Destiny of Man,* trans. Lancelot C. Sheppard and Elizabeth Englund (San Francisco: Ignatius Press, 1988), p. 167.

lical ideals and the language of Greek philosophy by which they had to express them, postmodern theologies, despite their heightened hermeneutic sensibilities, are often less careful. Vattimo's post-Christian interpretation of the incarnation is a case in point. In his incarnational ontology, divine revelation becomes encapsulated in a certain postmetaphysical ontology and becomes a purely immanent, faceless, impersonal and monological principle without the transforming and emancipating power he desires.[184]

In other words, Heideggerian ontology determines his Christology to such an extent that Vattimo's end product, the weakening of all structures in the name of charity as the eventing of historical Being, loses the very transcendent quality that gives emancipation a charitable, human-divine face. To state this theologically, when faith in Christ becomes faith in a modalistic kenotic principle, *kenosis* is no longer Christian. Unless there is some room for real personal transcendence in hermeneutic ontology, Vattimo's brilliant adaptation of the incarnation for hermeneutic ontology risks slipping back into Heidegger's directionless *Seinsgeschichte* or Nietzsche's arbitrary affirmation of life with all the ethical impotency implied by such a move.[185] In the end, Vattimo's incarnational faith sacrifices transcendence on the altar of interpretation.

Weak thought or weak theology? Vattimo's Heideggerian Christianity. Vattimo's central idea, which he has developed in his four major publications, *The End of Modernity, Beyond Interpretation, Belief,* and *After Christianity,* is to read Heidegger's postmetaphysical philosophy of Being as

---

[184]Vattimo is familiar with this criticism: "Fine, one might say (among other things), won't this recovery of Christianity be an effort to give power to weak thought, that is, to a particular philosophy, thus legitimating and recommending it as authentic heir of the prevalent religious tradition which is dominant in Western society?" He realizes that critics must indeed wonder whether "from my perspective, the link between post-metaphysical thought, weak ontology and nihilism on the one hand, and Christian doctrine on the other, is in the end resolved in favour of one or the other term?" (Vattimo, *Belief,* p. 91). His answer boils down to a confession of faith in an event of kenotically benevolent quality without any other warrant for its existence than Vattimo's residual sympathy for the Christian religion (ibid., p. 92).

[185]This is, of course, not what Professor Vattimo wants. Indeed his entire project of an incarnational hermeneutic ontology follows Joachim of Fiore's inspiration of folding the kenotic quality of God into the historical process precisely to structure weakening as a *positive* force of charity rather than a completely arbitrary one. In this way the death of God weakens and eventually dissolves strong metaphysical and social structures for the benefit of humanity. Joachim of Fiore may not be, however, the best inspiration for a postmetaphysical Christianity, because in him one can already detect the Hegelian death trap of incarnational ontology: the depersonalization of God into a immanent, monological historical principle.

weak ontology or weak thought.[186] For Vattimo, the development of Western thought shows that Being manifests itself essentially as a weakening in theoretical and social structures:

> The recollective retracing of the history of Being is a philosophy of history too, which is directed by the idea of weakening: i.e., consummation of strong structures on the theoretical level (from the metaphysical metanarrative to local rationality; from the belief in the objectivity of knowledge to the awareness of the hermeneutic character of truth) and on the level of individual and social existence (from the subject centered on the evidence of self-consciousness to psychoanalysis' subject; from the despotic State to the constitutional state and so on).[187]

The latest development in Vattimo's thinking is his "discovery" that this weakening characteristic of Being is not accidental but was put in motion by Christianity itself, or, to be more exact, by the incarnation. Vattimo has rediscovered Christianity by realizing that the incarnation was the beginning of weak ontology and the end of metaphysics:

> I have begun to take Christianity seriously again because I have constructed a philosophy inspired by Nietzsche and Heidegger, and have interpreted my experience in the contemporary world in light of them. . . . The fact of the matter is at a certain moment I found myself thinking that the weak reading of Heidegger and the idea that the history of Being as a guiding thread to the weakening of strong structures . . . was nothing but the transcription of the Christian doctrine of the incarnation of the Son of God.[188]

---

[186]Gianni Vattimo, *The End of Modernity: Nihilism and Hermeneutics in Postmodern Culture*, trans. Jon R. Snyder, Parallax: Re-visions of Culture and Society (Baltimore: Johns Hopkins University Press, 1991). Gianni Vattimo, *Beyond Interpretation: The Meaning of Hermeneutics for Philosophy*, trans. David Webb (Stanford, Calif.: Stanford University Press, 1997). Gianni Vattimo, *After Christianity*, trans. Luca D'Isanto, Italian Academy Lectures (New York: Columbia University Press, 2002).

[187]Vattimo describes this weak ontology as follows: "Ontological hermeneutics replaces the metaphysics of presence with a concept of Being that is essentially constituted by the feature of dissolution. Being gives itself not once and for all as simple presence; rather, it occurs as announcement and grows into interpretations that list and correspond (to Being). Being is also oriented toward spiritualization and lightening, or, which is the same, toward *kenosis*. It is quite probable that ontological hermeneutics, which is generated from the dissolution of the metaphysics of presence, is not only a rediscovery of the Church but also, and mainly, the retrieval of Joachim of Fiore's dream" (*After Christianity*, p. 68). For Vattimo, the history of Being as the history of secularization *is* the history of salvation (ibid., p. 24). He states clearly that he is engaged in "a recovery of religion—summed up as the manifestation of Being as the destiny of weakening at the end of metaphysics" (ibid., p. 38).

[188]Vattimo, *Belief*, pp. 35-36. In a related passage Vatimo states: "This [Vattimo's weak ontol-

For Vattimo this discovery of a postmetaphysical faith has at least three liberating effects. The first is that weak ontology sounds the death knell of philosophical atheism. The end of metaphysics is the end of scientistic and historicist rationalism, and this means that "today there are no longer strong, plausible philosophical reasons to be an atheist, or at any rate to dismiss religion."[189] Vattimo concedes, of course, that philosophy is still conspicuously silent about God, but for him this is merely because most philosophers are habitual atheists whose "silence with respect to God has no basis in any philosophically relevant principle." Together with the metaphysical God of Christians announced by Nietzsche, his counterpart, the God of scientific objectivism which propped up naturalism and scientism has also died.[190] To put it simply: no metaphysics, no philosophical atheism.

The second salutary effect Vattimo finds in weak ontology is that far from opposing Christian revelation, the secularization of the West actually constitutes it. Vattimo argues that secularization is the inner and necessary development of the Judeo-Christian revelation, manifested in the weakening of Being and the consequent dissolution of metaphysics. Vattimo acknowledges as the main inspiration behind this idea, the medieval mystic and biblical commentator Joachim de Fiore, who suggested that a historical unfolding of revelation would eventually lead to an age of spirit without institutionalized religion under the rule of charity. Vattimo adopts this idea to argue that secularization, rightly understood, is not the Enlightenment's movement toward universal reason and the abandonment of God, but the historicizing kenotic force of the incarnation itself.[191] Because this weakening effect

---

ogy] approach emphasizes that the weakening of Being is one possible meaning—if not the absolute meaning—of the Christian message, through the radical reading of incarnation as *kenosis*. This message speaks of a God who incarnates himself, lowers himself, and confuses all the powers of this world" (Vattimo, *After Christianity*, p. 80).

[189]Vattimo, *Belief*, p. 28.

[190]"If the meta-narrative of positivism no longer holds, one can no longer think that God does not exist because his existence cannot be established scientifically. If the meta-narrative of Hegelian or Marxist historicism no longer holds, one cannot argue that God does not exist because faith in God belongs to an earlier stage within history of human evolution, or because God is just an ideological representation at the service of domination" (Vattimo, *After Christianity*, p. 86).

[191]Vattimo also acknowledges here his indebtedness to Rene Girard's religious anthropology: "In my view, Girard has persuasively demonstrated . . . that if a 'divine' truth is given in Christianity, it is an unmasking of the violence that has given birth to the sacred of natural religion, that is, the sacred that is characteristic of the metaphysical God" (ibid., p. 38).

was set in motion by God's self-abasement that culminated in the crucifixion, the weakening of all structures moves toward nonviolence:

> secularization is the way in which *kenosis*, having begun with the incarnation of Christ, but even before that with the covenant between God and "his" people, continues to realize itself more and more clearly by furthering the education of mankind concerning the overcoming of originary violence essential to the sacred and to social life itself.[192]

Vattimo's incarnational ontology can now assure us that the weakening of being follows a purposeful and somehow benign developmental trajectory issuing from a good event. With the incarnation as the driving principle of weak ontology, secularization is not the enemy of Christian revelation but its very substance.

The third advantage Vattimo gains from his equation of incarnation and weak ontology is a universal Christian message that avoids conflict and violence because it renounces any claims to positive doctrine. Vattimo argues rightly that the crucial task "facing the Christian world (the West) today is the recovery of its universalizing function without any colonial, imperialist, or Eurocentric implications. It is difficult to imagine that this task might be accomplished by stressing its [Christianity's] dogmatic, ethical, and disciplinary implications."[193] Vattimo follows a currently popular trend of equating any substantive religious doctrine with fundamentalism. For him, the church's obsession with positive doctrine stems from its fatal adoption of an onto-theological model of objective truth. This fall into objectifying metaphysics forces the church into the false choice between (1) either entrenching itself behind the walls of metaphysical claims to truth (fundamentalism) or (2) relinquishing all universal truth claims by retreating into communitarian cliques and fostering a tribal mentality. Vattimo's solution: rid ourselves of dogma, church discipline and moral teachings because they are at the root of religious conflict. Only when we give up the "dogmatic and fundamentalist forms that have characterized Christianity to date" can we avoid religious fanaticism and violence and fundamentally change the church's mission.[194]

According to Vattimo, the church's former perceived tasks of proclamation and mission were wrongly based on the universality of truth claims.

---

[192]Vattimo, *Belief,* 48.
[193]Vattimo, *After Christianity*, p. 110.
[194]Ibid., p. 102.

In today's spirit age of postmetaphysical existence, however, Christianity's universality consists not in doctrines but in the enactment of unfolding kenotic truth. Instead of finding confidence in the universality of its doctrinal claims, Christianity should move from "universality to hospitality," by rejecting a proclamatory role and limiting itself "almost entirely to listening, and thus giving voice to its guests," always assuming that the other may be right. Vattimo has learned from Heidegger that Christianity should not allow itself "to be defined by any positive content on the plane of faith or by any positive obligation on the moral plane."[195]

The church's participation in the universal kenotic weakening of Being thus requires what Vattimo calls a "reduced faith." With Heidegger he believes that faithfulness to the apostle Paul's teaching consists in "leaving aside the substantive elements of revelation"[196] and settling for a general feeling of dependence reminiscent of Schleiermacher's religious feeling.[197] From this follows the dissolution of doctrine and institutional Christianity according to kenotic weakening and its law of charity. Only when Christianity is prepared to historicize itself to the fullest extent of the law of weakening can it react properly to the current pluralist cultural climate and recover its missionary vocation.

What, however, are then to be the limits of the dissolution of doctrine, the limits of interpretation? To his credit Vattimo sees this problem clearly. He writes:

> If the relation between the history of salvation and the history of interpretation is understood in this way, will not salvation and interpretation be configured just as processes of drifting, in which there seem to be no limits, no criteria of validity, no risk of defeat, and finally, no space for freedom and responsibility?[198]

Vattimo has lived long enough to understand that "not every seculariza-

---

[195]Ibid., p. 135.

[196]Ibid.; for a fuller description see Vattimo, *Belief*, pp. 77ff.

[197]Vattimo, *Belief*, p. 78: "Is what Schleiermacher called the pure feeling of dependence the only sense left in the use of the term 'father'? Probably yes, and once again this is the kernel that, in my view, cannot be an object of reduction or demythification." Indeed, nor can it be the object of any qualification.

[198]Vattimo, *After Christianity*, p. 67. Earlier Vattimo had already asked, "But will the same secularization not be rather a 'drift' inscribed positively in the destiny of kenosis? As regards the meaning of dogmatic Christianity, it is to this question that the recognition of a 'substantial' relation with hermeneutics ultimately leads" (Vattimo, *Beyond Interpretation*, p. 50).

tion is good and positive, and neither is every interpretation valid; it must
be valid for a community of interpreters."[199]

How does this appeal to community help us? How is this not relativism
merely raised to a communal level?[200] Vattimo seeks to avoid this dilemma
by referring to the kenotic principle as the universal driving force of all
human history, and hence applicable to every community.[201] Jesus himself
already demonstrated this interpretive key: "The interpretation given by
Jesus Christ of Old Testament prophecies, or (better) the interpretation
which he himself *is*, reveals its true and only meaning: God's love for his
creatures."[202] In a beautiful passage Vattimo presents us with an Augustinian hermeneutic of charity as the irreducible limit of interpretation. Augustine's motto "love and do what you will" "expresses clearly the only
criterion on the basis of which secularization must be examined."[203] The
problem, however, with adopting Augustine's hermeneutic of charity as a
criterion of discernment is that—at least for Augustine and the early
church—Christian charity depends on participation in divine transcendence. Vattimo, however, has a decided allergy to transcendence.

Problems with Vattimo's incarnational ontology. The main problem
with Vattimo's incarnational ontology is his false equation of orthodox
Christian theology with metaphysics, and his consequent rejection of

---

[199]Vattimo, *After Christianity*, p. 67.

[200]This has always been the problem of Stanley Fish's interpretive approach.

[201]He insists, though, that we cannot appeal to this idea as the metaphysical ground of all being,
which we then wield as a club in our attempt to Christianize the nations.

[202]Vattimo, *Belief*, p. 65. This principle rather conveniently spiritualizes away the "hard sayings
of Jesus" as history progresses to overcome Jesus' upholding and sharpening of principles Vattimo does not endorse (for example, Jesus' affirmation of marriage and hatred for divorce).

[203]Ibid., p. 64. See also his understanding of the concern Christians may have with this stance:
"Aside from the positions that refute the very idea of modernity as secularization (such as
Blumenberg's)—and which seem untenable to us by virtue of the fact that they do not give
sufficient consideration to the historical roots of modernity in the ancient and medieval tradition—the objections that in general, above all by believers, are raised against this vision of the
secularization as a destiny 'proper' to Christianity concern the possibility of establishing a
criterion that permits the distinction of secularization from phenomena that confine themselves to applying the Christian tradition, often in a distorted fashion, yet which are themselves outside or indeed in opposition to it. Yet it is precisely here that one should rediscover
the 'principle of charity' which, perhaps not by accident, constitutes the point of convergence
between nihilistic hermeneutics and the religious tradition of the West. Secularization has no
'objective' limit: the Augustinian 'ama et fac quod vis' holds even for the interpretation of the
scriptures. For dogmatic Christianity (that is, the substance of New Testament revelation),
recognition of its relation with nihilistic hermeneutics means the emergence of charity as the
single most decisive factor of the evangelical message." Vattimo, *Beyond Interpretation*, p. 51.

transcendence as violence. Most likely he inherited this misunderstanding from Heidegger's false condemnation of the entire Christian theological tradition as an onto-theological adventure, deeply embroiled in the wrong, objectifying kind of Greek metaphysics, and therefore complicit in the forgetfulness of Being and in the birth of scientific objectivism. Indeed, Vattimo's equation of transcendence with metaphysics and metaphysics with Christianity is theologically and historically inaccurate. Further, his interpretation of secularization as the antimetaphysical substance of Christianity is unconvincing. A good case has been made that beginning with nominalism in the thirteenth century, secularism as the *disintegration* of theology is responsible for the rise of scientific objectivism.[204] It is false, in other words, simply to equate Christian theology with objectifying metaphysics and onto-theology. As Paul Ricoeur and many others have pointed out, such a view tends to forget that Greek metaphysics always underwent a radical transformation in their appropriation by Christian theologians.[205]

Perhaps the most important transformation of this kind is the incarnation's infusion of personal transcendence into ontology. In accordance with this innovation in Western thought, God can indeed be analogically described in ontological terms but remains irreducible to ontology. Heidegger's assertion in *Introduction to Metaphysics* that Christianity's identification of the person Jesus with the Greek logos signifies the fall into objectifying ontology either willfully or ignorantly misses the significant insertion of personal, social categories of transcendence into ontology.[206] This crucial shift has many philosophical implications and has prompted

---

[204]See, for instance, Henri de Lubac's assertion that the compartmentalization of natural and supernatural, as well as the abstraction of natural ends, was not part of traditional Christian doctrine. Not even for the scholastics, with their "absolute realism proposed such a thing." Lubac concludes that "Excessive naturalism and essentialism belong much more to the stream of modern philosophy—which has to some extent invaded the manuals of scholasticism, but in doing so has perverted the traditional teaching it was intended to transmit" (Henri de Lubac, *The Mystery of the Supernatural*, trans. Mary Sheed, Milestones in Catholic Theology [New York: Crossroad, 1998], p. 63). See also Philip Blond's review of Vattimo's *Belief*, titled "The Absolute and the Arbitrary," in *Modern Theology* 18, no. 2 (2002): 277-85.

[205]Paul Ricoeur, *Figuring the Sacred: Religion, Narrative, and Imagination*, ed. Mark I. Wallace, trans. David Pellauer (Minneapolis: Fortress, 1995), p. 268.

[206]Martin Heidegger, *An Introduction to Metaphysics*, trans. Ralph Manheim, vol. 40 of *GA* (New Haven, Conn.: Yale University Press, 1987), p. 134. The whole point of Heidegger's effort is, of course, to show how the wrong identification of the "essent" Christ is objectifying God and makes Christianity "Platonism for the People" (ibid., p. 106).

almost all great theologians within Christianity to define faith *primarily* (but not exclusively) as participation or relational trust in God rather than as objective knowledge.[207] As perceptive as Heidegger's criticism of onto-theology and scientific objectivism may be, Christians should be rather cautious in adopting his decidedly nonincarnational, impersonal ontology as an interpretive paradigm of Christianity.

The poverty of Heideggerian ontology for articulating an incarna-tional Christianity becomes particularly clear when Vattimo advocates a postmetaphysical, procedural ethic that would translate received ethical precepts into Heidegger's "language of overcoming metaphysics as obliv-ion of Being," to open up new ethical possibilities.[208] Vattimo rightly em-ploys Heidegger's stress on historical development against the disincar-nate and traumatic alterity of Derrida and Levinas,[209] yet he overlooks that, especially in Levinas, this flight into otherness is a flight from Hei-degger's impersonal ontology as much as from Nietzsche's arbitrary be-coming, or, for that matter, from Vattimo's own immanent view of the secular. Does not Levinas speak precisely to the problem raised by Vat-timo's conviction that interpretations of doctrine "change *in accordance with the becoming of history*"?[210]

Even when one shares Vattimo's passion for hermeneutics and applauds his incarnational critique of Levinas, can we simply dismiss Levinas's fear

---

[207]This is, for example, one of the reasons why Luther and Aquinas are actually a lot closer in their definition of faith than is often supposed, a fact that also modifies Aquinas's supposed Aristotelianism. "First truth, for Aquinas, is not an impersonal essence, but a personal God. . . . Faith, then, is not a simple agreement of our intellect with a supreme metaphysical truth, but is in the first place the hearing and acceptance of this word of his. . . . Thus it becomes clear that the import of *veritas prima* for Aquinas is completely new by comparison with the philosophical notion of the supreme metaphysical truth" (Stephan H. Pfürtner, *Luther and Aquinas on Salvation* [New York: Sheed and Ward, 1965], pp. 70-73). Thomas, therefore, "discovers a function of the intellect which the Greeks did not know in this express form. 'Reason' is no longer, as it was for them, more or less exclusively a capacity for knowing facts; it is also a power of the soul for knowing persons, able to grasp the truthfulness, the fidelity and the trustworthiness of the one whom I know. It is obvious that we are here concerned with a relationship of trust: *Intellegere* in faith is to base oneself on God's trustworthiness" (ibid., p. 77). It is therefore no accident that Luther's annoyance with Aristotelian terminol-ogy began with this very notion of apprehending truth as *intellegere* which did not, to him, convey the biblical notion of personal trust.

[208]Gianni Vattimo, *Nihilism and Emancipation: Ethics, Politics, and Law*, ed. Santiago Zabala, trans. William McCuaig, European Perspectives (New York: Columbia University Press, 2004), pp. 67, 69.

[209]Vattimo, *After Christianity*, p. 38.

[210]Ibid., p. 121, emphasis added.

that the becoming of history may opt for racial superiority? Opposition to the idols of race and capital usually grows from a strong sense of human dignity—what if that too is weakened by the becoming of history? Levinas's fears are shared by other theologians such as Karl Barth, Dietrich Bonhoeffer, Eberhard Jüngel, Hans Urs von Balthasar and Henri de Lubac, who were life witnesses to the fact that trinitarian theologies that leave divine transcendence behind often end up declaring some social or political developments or organization as absolute.[211] In effect, for all his dislike of mysticism and the ineffable, Vattimo's reduced faith is not very far from Levinas's otherness or Derrida's never arriving indeconstructible Messianic and justice. At least Levinas can root human dignity in a "place" outside of ontology that we can resort to in case negotiations in a procedural ethic turn ugly. It is not at all clear how Vattimo's own idea of *kenosis* as universal principle and its concomitant notion of hospitality are any more substantive or helpful than those of Levinas and Derrida.[212]

Perhaps Vattimo believes his appeal to the incarnation as kenotic teleology counters the ethical deficiencies of Nietzsche's arbitrary becoming and Heidegger's impersonal Being. Yet with his remark that the relationship between hermeneutics and faith means that secularization is inscribed positively as a "drift" in the notion of kenosis, Vattimo effectively allows Heideggerian ontology to shape traditional Christian trinitarian notions of transcendence rather than to consider at least a reciprocal influence—he thus stacks the interpretive cards in favor of becoming and of immanence.[213]

---

[211]This sentence is a paraphrase of the same statement by Sciglitano in "Contesting the World and the Divine," p. 546.

[212]Indeed as Marie L. Baird argues, Levinas actually borrows from Rabbi Haim a distinct notion of divine kenosis as incarnational ethics that is not onto-theological, does not ignore the incarnation (as Vattimo alleges) and which also collapses the distinction between profane and sacred history and even rejects negative theology. She concludes in her comparison of Vattimo and Levinas that for the latter "Ethical responsibility, hospitality, and charity are not mere philosophical abstractions, be they diachronic and transcendental or anchored in the recognition of Being as event. They refer to real relationships of love, fidelity, and the exercise of virtue. On this final point all three thinkers [i.e., Levinas, Derrida and Vattimo] would agree." Baird also wonders, as I have, why Vattimo does not see similarities between his own notion of the church's new universal vocation of hospitality and Derrida's idea. See Marie L. Baird, "Whose *Kenosis*? An Analysis of Levinas, Derrida, and Vattimo on God's Self-Emptying and the Secularization of the West," *Heythrop Journal* 48, no. 3 (2007): 433, 435.

[213]Vattimo, *Beyond Interpretation*, p. 50. Jüngel's concept of God's being as becoming may be helpful here, but even this requires a strong sense of Being that Vattimo would most likely reject.

Vattimo's exclusion of transcendence from his incarnational ontology results in a monological, immanent and flat conception of ontology that undermines some of the very things he desires. I can list only a few here. For example, his univocal interpretation of kenosis lacks any transcendence and thus conflates God and world, the incarnation and secularization.[214] Is not this simply the inverse of what fundamentalist Christians do when they confuse certain politics with true Christianity? In other words, while Vattimo seeks to weaken just such religiously motivated politics, his conflation of God and world actually removes divine transcendence as the authoritative counterforce that can subvert theocratic aspirations. In short, Vattimo's divine kenosis without transcendent remainder plays into the hands of religious radicals. Should we not rather insist on the distinction of God and world, of church and state? Moreover, how can Vattimo's univocity account for the relative autonomy of the secular we so desperately need if we ever want to sort out church-state relations in a pluralistic society? And, speaking of pluralism, how does his universal kenotic weakening not turn out to be exactly the kind of unifying straightjacket he wants to avoid? Immanence, after all, cannot account for new "revelations" that challenge the system; it cannot account for difference, but only such difference enables dialogue and makes plurality possible.[215]

I conclude this list of problems with a number of dualisms that spring up when transcendence is eradicated from ontology. Contrary to his intentions, Vattimo's immanent overdetermination of the incarnation leaves us with the opposition of Spirit to doctrine and ecclesial structures, of contemplation to action, of transcendence to ethics, of unity to difference. Vattimo's signature confession of faith, "I believe that I believe," arises it-

---

[214]Again, I am taking the term *kenosis* from Sciglitano, "Contesting the World," p. 549: "The secular describes not a reified entity, but a relationship the world has with God, that is, the world has been revealed in its creatureliness and gratuitousness through this relationship. In contrast to both Hegel and Vattimo, if there is no difference as Vattimo says, then the world in fact has no autonomy vis-à-vis the divine; instead, cultural movements will be tightly tied to revelation, thus distorting both salvation and secular history to make each fit a single vision of the other. Once again, monologue will trump dialogue."

[215]While we should appreciate Vattimo's emphasis on the historical and on interpretation in ethics, he makes it very clear that this "historical event of the incarnation" has no reality beyond its historical effect, which he has already determined as "a teleology in which every ontic structure is weakened in favor of ontological Being, namely, the Verbum, Logos, Word shared in the dialogue (*Gespräch*) that constitutes us as historical beings" (Vattimo, *After Christianity*, p. 112).

self from perhaps the most tragic dualism that characterizes not just Vattimo but also much of continental religious philosophy: either a substantial faith with real contours or a virtual fideism.

CONCLUSION

The problem with Vattimo's recovery of Christianity is the underlying suppositions running throughout his recovery of religion: substantive transcendence equals metaphysics, metaphysics equals doctrine, and doctrine equals conflict, which inevitably issues in oppression and violence.[216] Vattimo, like other Christians in a postmetaphysical world who still want to believe and desire to be active in politics, tries to counter the popular charge of fundamentalism against Christianity. Unfortunately, he does it by translating its incarnational essence into Heideggerian ontology. But the "languages" are simply too different. The very essence of the incarnation, the balance of transcendence and immanence, gets lost in this translation. Vattimo's otherwise welcome emphasis on the incarnation thus shares the general postmodern unease about objectification.

Postmodern theologies insist on an ineffable God without real presence, or, as we saw in Vattimo and Caputo, an incarnate God of the event. In the latter case kenosis becomes kenoticism, a principle of weakening to which God himself is subject. Unlike early Christian theology, postmoderns seem unable to hold together God's transcendence and sovereignty, and his suffering in his humanity. The ethical philosophy of Emmanuel Levinas provides the most striking example of the need of incarnational theology. Levinas almost single-handedly reintroduces a theologically grounded humanism into philosophy. Unafraid of universal truth claims or the secularism rampant in the philosophy of his day, Levinas proclaims human dignity and ethical responsibility as the trace of God in the face of our fellow human being. Yet the biblical, Old Testament roots of this

---

[216]Consider, for example, Vattimo's comment in the context of trying to reconcile peace and liberty: "What we really need to do—and this does not necessarily have to conflict with religiosity, especially Christian religiosity—is to say farewell to claims to absolute truth. In a society in which we are more and more likely to encounter ethical and religious positions and cultural traditions unlike the ones we were born into and grew up with, the best stance to adopt is that of a 'tourist' in a history park. The real enemy of liberty is the person who thinks she can and should preach final and definitive truth" ("Liberty and Peace in the Postmodern Condition," in Vattimo, *Nihilism and Emancipation*, p. 56). At the same time, Vattimo realizes that in his context, this "history park" is European, Western and Christian (ibid., p. 57).

ethical humanism reveal all the more the lacuna left by the disappearance
of incarnational theology from philosophical discourse: the transcendent
ethical demand of the other, just like the sovereignty and freedom of
God, remains threatened by their mediation through being. Ontological
structures such as language, art and institutions remain threats to, rather
than proper vehicles of, our humanity. The reason is clearly fear of objectification and the resulting suppression of others in the name of God.[217]
This postmodern dualism between ontology and transcendence, and the
consequent reduction of religion to ethics, stem ultimately from a divorce
of reason and faith that already characterized much of modernist thought.
It is, no doubt, the postmodern focus on criticizing theoretical, instrumental reason that has often resulted in the opposite extreme: if reason
has said bad and oppressive things about God, then now reason cannot
say anything about religion or God. There are, however, better theological ways of broadening rationality to include religion and to recover an
incarnational humanism that no longer separates reason and faith. This
will be our task in chapter six. We will see that Vattimo's opposition of
transcendence and ethics, or particular doctrine and hermeneutic openness, is unnecessary.

---

[217]See, for instance, Jacques Derrida's comment that "one has to dissociate God's sovereignty
from God, from the very idea of God" to avoid an onto-theological construct (Derrida,
"Epoché and Faith," p. 42).

INCARNATIONAL HUMANISM AS CULTURAL PHILOSOPHY

The human being itself, the concrete, real human being, exists insofar as the living God is for him and with him—his beginning and end. . . . That is the basis on which the Christian message can live in harmony with every other humanism, and perhaps also have to remain in opposition to them.

KARL BARTH, *HUMANISMUS*

♦

The purpose of this final chapter is to describe the kind of attitude incarnational humanism promotes as the basis from which Christians understand themselves and culture. It is not my intent to rehearse at length past and present models for Christianity's relation to culture.[1] Studying the various models of Christianity and culture is of course important for the church's self-understanding, but each of them also constitutes a particular Christian reaction to a specific cultural milieu. I am more concerned with the general outlook or, if you will, the basic attitude preserved in those approaches most faithful to incarnational thinking. The incarnation does not even allow the question of *whether* Christianity is related to culture. Especially Eastern Christianity, but also Roman Catholic and Reformational (Lutheran and Reformed) Christian confessions, have always maintained that because the triune God created the world in, through and for Jesus Christ, all of reality is oriented toward Christ. No autonomous realm

---

[1]The classic summary of these models is H. Richard Niebuhr's *Christ and Culture* (New York: Harper, 1956). More recent treatments of this topic that are concise and yet comprehensive are Graham Ward, *Christ and Culture*, Challenges in Contemporary Theology (Malden, Mass.: Blackwell, 2005), and the fine summary of theological models by Stephen D. Long, *Theology and Culture: A Guide to the Discussion* (Eugene, Ore.: Cascade Books, 2008).

of culture exists. As Stephen Long put it in his introduction to this topic, "this Jesus of Nazareth, a human creature born of Mary, nurtured in a culture, now mediated historically in and through every culture that has arisen, and will arise, is also no one less than God."[2] The same Christ that is Lord of history and culture is also mediated through the material-temporal world. This mediation is a dynamic process by which "Christ draws all people and all cultures into his own life, sanctifying them and preparing them as a new creation."[3] Reality and all human experience of it are thus unified in Christ. Incarnational humanism adopts without reservation Bonhoeffer's christological realism: "As reality is *one* in Christ, so the person who belongs to this Christ-reality is also a whole. Worldliness does not separate one from Christ, and being Christian does not separate one from the world. Belonging completely to Christ, one stands at the same time completely in the world."[4]

It is important for Christians to recover the full cosmic impact of the incarnation. Christianity, in agreement with Platonic philosophies, has always viewed the world as meaningful, but in contrast to pagan philosophies, Christianity believed the world was intelligible despite its confusion; the external order in nature, human moral conscience and the transcendent power of loving human relationships were pointers to a personal God.[5] The world, in a sense, was the "sacrament" of God's presence.[6] Yet this general sense becomes much more concrete with the incarnation. Christ, the creative wisdom of God and God's active Word in creation, is enfleshed in the temporal-historical dimension of our world as the concrete Jewish Messiah, Jesus the Christ. We should not forget the Old Testament connotations that John evokes in his Gospel. This is the Word through whom all things were made, the Word hid in the eternal bosom of God, the Word who spoke through the prophets, the Word whose mighty acts defined the history of Israel.[7] In Jesus the Christ this Word has become flesh, and the

---

[2]Long, *Theology and Culture*, p. 110.

[3]Ibid., p. 111.

[4]Dietrich Bonhoeffer, *DBWE*, 6:62.

[5]Kallistos Ware, *The Orthodox Way*, rev. ed. (Crestwood, N.Y.: St. Vladimir's Seminary Press, 1990), pp. 24-26.

[6]Alexander Schmemann, *For the Life of the World: Sacraments and Orthodoxy* (Crestwood, N.Y.: St. Vladimir's Seminary Press, 2004), p. 17.

[7]T. F. Torrance, *Incarnation: The Person and Life of Christ*, ed. Robert T. Walker, rev. ed. (Downers Grove, Ill.: IVP Academic, 2008), p. 60.

eternal enters the temporal, but without ceasing to be eternal. How often do we really think about not just the deep mystery of this event but also its full implications for reality as we now inhabit it? In Christ, temporality and eternity are conjoined. As one theologian reminds us,

> unlike other historical happenings that flow away into the past and tumble down into the dust, this historical happening *remains* [an] *eternally real* and alive happening, breaking through all the contingency and relativity of history in our fallen and decayed existence, a historical happening that is still accessible to us on the plane of history as well as in communion with the eternal.[8]

In the incarnation, creation, the world, time and history have been taken up into the God-man, who *is* the center of reality.

Reality is determined ultimately in personal terms as love and communion, by a life itself that is also the light of the world. Christianity is akin to Platonism insofar as it also advocates the basic unity and intelligibility of reality. This must ever be the Christian's response to any materialist or naturalist philosophy. In contrast to Platonism, however, the Christian holds to the unity of reality as Christ reality. Christians have to grasp the radical importance of the apostle John's claim that in Jesus, life itself (*zoē*) the true light (*to phōs to alēthinon*) that enlightens every human being has come into the world (Jn 1:4, 9).[9] John's Gospel gives theological expression to what I have argued earlier: not only does all human knowledge— whether scientific, secular or religious—takes the form of faith seeking understanding, but all human knowledge also ultimately tends toward the highest possible unity and purpose. Human curiosity, our tireless search for knowledge in all fields, always implies the search for the meaning of life.[10] Our deeply ingrained desire for truth cannot be satisfied by mere empirical or scientific knowledge, but strives toward an "ulterior truth" of ultimate purpose.[11] Faith and reason are inseparable because their unity is

---

[8]Ibid., p. 67.

[9]See also Jesus' assertion that he is life in John 14:6.

[10]John Paul II, *Veritatis Splendor*, August 6, 1993, Papal Archives, last accessed April 16, 2011, www.vatican.va/holy_father/john_paul_ii/encyclicals/documents/hf_jp-ii_enc_06081993_veritatis-splendor_en.html.

[11]John Paul II, *Fides et Ratio*, sec. 41, September 14, 1998, Papal Archives, last accessed April 17, 2011, www.vatican.va /holy_father/john_paul_ii/encyclicals/documents/hf_jp-ii_enc_15101998_fides-et-ratio_en.html.

in Christ, "the centre of the universe and of history."[12] Dietrich Bonhoeffer expressed the christological unity of reality most clearly: "Christ is the center and power of the Bible, of the church, of theology but also of humanity, reason, justice, and culture. To Christ everything must return; only under Christ's protection can it live."[13] With the incarnation the world is reconciled with God; humanity is invited into the trinitarian communion of God, joining the chorus of praise and thanksgiving of the new creation.

The incarnation has two important consequences for a Christian view of culture. The first is that the love displayed in Christ toward the world is the culmination and fulfilment of every philosophy and morality. The best in other religions and natural virtues will always point toward what is most meaningful and rational. Yet the Christian belief in the cosmic importance of the incarnation postulates that the determining center of any such insight is God's love as revealed in Christ. The importance of this first point is this: throughout this book I have argued for an "onto-theological synthesis." The incarnation makes clear that this synthesis *must be understood christologically.* There is no return to natural-supernatural harmony in classical, pre-Christian terms.[14]

Second, it is important to note where Christianity differs from other religions. The crucial difference is that the Christ reality is not primarily a religion, a certain cult or a body of laws. Rather, Christianity is the participation in the life of God and in his presence, a presence defined by Christ as true humanity. In Christ the cosmos regains its fundamental orientation toward the human: "it is through Christ that the world of things and values is given back its orientation toward human beings, as was originally intended in their creation."[15] Christianity is not to offer culture another religion but the gift of life, of true humanity. Truly, "in Christ life—life in all its totality—was returned to man, given again as a sacrament and communion, made Eucharist."[16]

---

[12]John Paul II, *Redemptor Hominis*, March 4, 1979, last accessed April 16, 2011, www.vatican.va/holy_father/john_paul_ii/encyclicals/documents/hf_jp-ii_enc_04031979_redemptor-hominis_en.html.

[13]Bonhoeffer, *DBWE*, 6:341.

[14]Hans Urs von Balthasar, *Love Alone Is Credible*, trans. D. C. Schindler (San Francisco: Ignatius Press, 2004), p. 134.

[15]Bonhoeffer, *DBWE*, 6:260.

[16]Schmemann, *Life of the World*, p. 20.

No doubt, such a tight, holistic view of reality raises many questions. For one, the problem of the modern Christian is exactly that she is modern, that her mental horizon has been shaped by the secularist opposition of nature and grace, reason and faith that determines modern life. Cultural pressures emanating from a technocratic and depersonalized world that even the virtual communities of Facebook and Twitter cannot rehumanize make it very hard not to feel that once the church doors close behind us, we step into a different world. Non-Christians, on the other hand, might well shudder at the thought of "one-Christ-reality." No matter how much we might emphasize that this center is the Christ of the cross who died for the life of the world, this emphasis on God's presence in the world may smack too much of theological imperialism for the secularist. The question thus becomes, how does incarnational humanism construe the presence of God in the world and in the church? And how does the Christian understand his or her existence within this context? I will try to answer these questions in the next two segments, and will do so mostly with the help of Dietrich Bonhoeffer's theology, which provides us with a blueprint for incarnational humanism.

GOD'S PRESENCE IN THE WORLD: SACRED AND SECULAR

Does the incarnational idea of one Christ reality mean that the world becomes the church? Does the rejection of a secular-sacred dualism in favor of one world under Christ strip the notion of the secular, public sphere of any real theological value? Do we inadvertently support some kind of Constantinianism, an undue conflation of church and state? Are we evoking the shadows of Christendom?[17] These questions are understandable in light of much contemporary unease about religion and politics, but in asking them, we have to avoid the popular opposition of secular and sacred for the simple reason that the Judeo-Christian tradition invented the very

---

[17]The words *Christendom* and *Constantinianism* have become bywords for many for undue Christian ambition and a compromise of the Christian gospel. Stanley Hauerwas is perhaps the best known advocate of this view. For a recent example, see Craig Carter's *Rethinking Christ and Culture: A Post-Christendom Perspective* (Grand Rapids: Brazos Press, 2006), which leaves us with the perhaps simplistic alternative of "Jesus or Constantine" (ibid., p. 207) and exhorts the modern church not to choose empire over Jesus (ibid., p. 211). The construction of Constantine as icon of religious imperialism and a state church has recently been questioned by Peter J. Leithart, *Defending Constantine: The Twilight of an Empire and the Dawn of Christendom* (Downers Grove, Ill.: IVP Academic, 2010).

concept of the secular in the first place. When the author of Genesis denies the reality of Egypt's nature gods by describing the sun as "great luminary" placed in the sky by God, the twilight of the gods has begun. God's power over his world is reasserted in the Christian gospel, but now this world is also placed within the overall eschatological trajectory of a new creation. Thus the secular, far from being an antireligious concept, "is originally a Christian event" and therefore testifies to the historical potency exerted by Christ's coming in our global world.[18]

In the Latin West, this tradition was clearly formulated by the church father Augustine in his book *The City of God*. In this work, he argues that the incarnation, death and resurrection of Christ have inaugurated a new era in the history of humanity, determined by Christ's rule already begun and fully realized with his return. Augustine holds with the apostle Paul that the Christian church constitutes the new humanity, a community in which one is called to order one's life according to three objects of love: "God, himself, and his neighbor."[19] Despite this new order of things, however, the citizens of the heavenly Jerusalem share with all others, until the full coming of the new creation, the temporal orders of government meant to preserve the kind of peace in which human beings can flourish. Christians, explains Augustine, "must make use of this peace also, until this mortal state, for which this kind of peace is essential, passes away." Christians "do not hesitate to obey the laws of the earthly city" because, "since this mortal condition is shared by both cities, a harmony may be preserved between them in things that are relevant to this condition."[20] Augustine does not, in other words, separate a sacred from a secular sphere. Rather, the heavenly and earthly cities both participate in the *saeculum*, in a shared penultimate era whose ultimate grounding in God upholds the relative autonomy of government, which, ideally, should further human life and prosperity. Augustine can speak of harmony between church and state within the *saeculum* because the life of *any human city*, whether heavenly or

---

[18]Johann Baptist Metz, *Zur Theologie der Welt* (Mainz: Matthias-Grünewald Verlag, 1968), p. 17.

[19]Augustine, *Concerning the City of God Against the Pagans* 19.14, trans. Henry Bettenson (New York: Penguin Books, 1984), p. 873. It is in fact not Constantine but Theodosius (347-395) who fully politicized Christianity (Charles Norris Cochrane, *Christianity and Classical Culture* [New York: Oxford University Press, 1957], p. 336).

[20]Augustine, *City of God* 19.17, p. 877.

earthly, "is inevitably a social life," and rational beings desire peace above all things.[21] And yet because of the Christian revelation, this harmony is never simple conformity to an established order. As R. A. Markus has rightly pointed out, "the clue to Augustine's distinctive view of the secular is his persistent eschatologism."[22] Both secular and sacred structures on this earth are relativized as transpiring within the *saeculum*, "that intermediate and temporary realm in which human affairs unfold before the end."[23] Hence secular values can neither simply be endorsed and ratified nor rejected: they must be given a more complex assessment in eschatological terms.[24] Even while the eschatological *telos* of society is revealed as the fulfilment of human nature in communion with God and one another, eschatological categories as such are not visible in historical realities. Thus, the penultimate realities of politics or history cannot be interpreted in ultimate terms; Augustine insists rather on "the ultimate eschatological ambivalence of all empirical human groupings."[25]

Augustine's view represents what has been called "Christian realism," a position that combines moral, theological and political realism.[26] Moral realism indicates the belief in a shared meaningful universe with objectively existing moral values. Theological (Christian) realism holds that this universe is grounded not in some vague idea of theism, but in the reality of the Judeo-Christian God as revealed in Jesus the Christ. This gives the secular its peculiar status of relative autonomy that demands the third element of Christian realism, namely, political realism. Dietrich Bonhoeffer's concept of "realistic responsibility" best describes a Christian incarnational hermeneutic that unites public and church life under the umbrella of a Christian humanism.

Bonhoeffer's idea of realistic responsibility begins with a christological view of reality unified in the world's reconciliation with God. God's self-

---

[21]Ibid., 19.17, pp. 878-79.

[22]R. A. Markus, *Christianity and the Secular*, Blessed Pope John XXIII Lecture Series in Theology and Culture (Notre Dame, Ind.: University of Notre Dame Press, 2006), p. 73. Markus defines Augustine's *saeculum* as "the realm in which the careers of the two Cities are inextricably intertwined" (ibid., p. 48).

[23]Ibid., p. 73.

[24]R. A. Markus, *Saeculum: History and Society in the Theology of St. Augustine* (Cambridge: Cambridge University Press, 1988), p. 168.

[25]Ibid., p. 151.

[26]Robert V. Lovin, *Reinhold Niebuhr and Christian Realism* (Cambridge: Cambridge University Press, 1995), p. 6. Lovin's book is one of the best descriptions of the Christian realist tradition.

revelation in Christ is an act of reconciling God and world. This means
that ultimate reality, that the most basic God-world relation, is not an
agonistic one of enmity but one of reconciliation. The notion of God's
incarnation, of God becoming human, is crucial here. God does not stand
apart from his creation and humanity, but identifies with them in the clos-
est possible way. And if God makes himself known incarnationally in the
world, that is the place where I encounter him: "The reality of God is
disclosed only as it places me completely into the reality of the world. But
I find the reality of the world always already borne, accepted, and reconciled in the reality of God. That is the mystery of the revelation of God in
the human being Jesus Christ."[27] The Christian question concerning public life is not, therefore, how to integrate faith and reason, but begins with
the question of how we embody in our actions, in every area of the life
called to true humanity, this one Christ reality of a world reconciled with
God in Christ. "It is not," as Bonhoeffer puts it,

> as if "our world" were something outside this God-world of reality that is in
> Christ, as if it did not already belong to the world borne, accepted, and
> reconciled in Christ. . . . Rather, the question is how the reality in Christ—
> which has long embraced us and our world within itself—works here and
> now or, in other words, how life is to be lived in it.[28]

We recall that for Bonhoeffer being a Christian is participation in
Christ. Consequently, if Christ "embraces the reality of the world in itself," any pious wish to have a religion without the world would be "a denial of God's revelation in Jesus Christ." However, the world does not have
any reality of its own; it is not independent from God's self-revelation in
Christ. To be realistic, to live authentically in the world and before God, is
to live as if "the whole reality of the world has already been drawn into and
is held together in Christ."[29] The unity of the world, however, is not something that is merely an intellectual conception taught by the Bible or theology books; rather, the same unifying power that determines reality determines the Christian self because faith is not primarily cognitive assent to
this reality but actual participation in it. The Christian interpretation of
the world has to follow the pattern laid down by the incarnation: "Just as

---

[27]Bonhoeffer, *DBWE*, 6:55.
[28]Ibid., 6:58.
[29]Ibid.

the reality of God has entered the reality of the world, in Christ, what is Christian cannot be had otherwise than in what is worldly, the "'supernatural' only in the natural, the holy only in the profane, the revelational only in the rational."[30]

An incarnational correlation of the natural and supernatural retains the integrity of each element. This is to say that the Christian experiences the one Christ reality as the eschatological dynamic Augustine had already argued for. Christian life itself, as participation in Christ, places one into this tension between, in Bonhoeffer's terms, the ultimate and penultimate:

> Christian life is the dawn of the ultimate in me, the life of Jesus Christ in me. But it is also always life in the penultimate, waiting for the ultimate. The seriousness of Christian life lies only in the ultimate; but the penultimate also has its seriousness, which consists to be sure, precisely in never confusing the penultimate with the ultimate and never making light of the penultimate over against the ultimate, so that the ultimate—and the penultimate—retain their seriousness.[31]

Bonhoeffer suggests a resolutely incarnational attitude toward life and culture. Christ came to heal and unify humanity, not to break it into private faith and public reason. The Christian lives in the eschatological age. In this era, the secular derives its full value and relative autonomy from the same God who will eventually renew it completely. Neither radically denying the world in light of the eschaton nor living as if this world were our only context of meaning corresponds to a properly Christian life. The Christian ethos does not dissolve the eschatological (ultimate-penultimate) tension into either fundamentalism or complacency. Christian ethics, to use Bonhoeffer's terms, should breed neither radicals nor compromisers.

The radicals have no patience with the world. They display "a hatred for creation" and an impatience with structure and procedure. In short, they are not satisfied with God's mediation within history and culture, but rather impose their own vision of an already-realized eschatology on their community. Radical Christians could, for example, be legalistic or antinomian;[32] they could be people advocating twelve rigid steps to suc-

---

[30]Ibid., 6:59.
[31]Ibid., 6:168.
[32]Note in this context Bonhoeffer's acute observation that "wherever a worldly and a Christian principle are set over against each other there the ultimate reality is the law," so that insofar as

cessful Christianity, but they could also be "anarchical" Christians who prefer private spirituality to the structure of church and community. A modern form of radical religiosity is fundamentalism, because fundamentalists do not appreciate that God's will is mediated through tradition and interpretation. They usually abandon critical reflection for a simplistic, pure communication from God that bypasses the ambiguities of thought that reality often demands.[33] Trying to think only within the artificially erected confines of a pure Christian theology inevitably "succumbs to the unnatural, the irrational, the undisciplined, and to willfulness."[34] Just as incarnational thinking is interpretive, Christian living does not entail a mere "aping" of Christ,[35] asking naively, "what would Jesus do," but a genuine interpretation—or even better, enactment—of the gospel for one's culture in the service of a common humanity. When the Christian says, "I am doing God's will," this is not a fundamentalist claim to realize a religious idea or cause, but a fundamentally hermeneutical claim to participate realistically and responsibly in the reconciliation of humanity in Christ.[36]

The compromisers represent the other extreme misjudgment of the ultimate-penultimate tension. Compromising Christians lack the relativizing perspective of the ultimate and tend to collapse the distinctions between Christ and the world. The compromisers Bonhoeffer had in mind were Lutheran theologians of the nineteenth century who defended the monarchy as the divinely instituted order of creation. More sinister compromisers were German theologians who legitimated Nazi ideology on the basis of natural order.[37]

Instead of these extremes, Bonhoeffer suggests that Christian faith, properly understood as participation in Christ, exhibits a hermeneutic structure of "realistic responsibility."[38] Christian realism proceeds from

evangelicalism pursues a dualistic worldview, legalism will inevitably dominate the church culture (ibid., 6:264).

[33]James Barr, *Fundamentalism* (Norwich: SCM Press, 1981), pp. xvi-xvii.
[34]Bonhoeffer, *DBWE*, 6:61.
[35]Ibid., 6:50.
[36]"From this perspective, to act responsibly means taking up human reality, as accepted by God in Christ, into the shaping of my action. The world has not stopped being the world, and any action which wants to exchange the world with the kingdom of God, is a denial of both Christ and the world" (ibid., 6:223).
[37]See Clifford Green's introduction to Bonhoeffer, *DBWE*, 6:19.
[38]Bonhoeffer, *DBWE*, 6:257.

the objective unity of reality in Christ, but understands this unity as shaped by the full Christ event. So the goal of our interpretation of a unified Christ reality is "life" or, to use an equally biblical term, a "new humanity." It is very important, however, to realize that the incarnation does not merely entail the affirmation of life and humanity as it *is* but also as it *should be*. This is why Bonhoeffer adds the all-important qualifiers that being human in Christ is participation in all three aspects of the Christ event. Bonhoeffer explains that

> in Jesus Christ we believe in the God who became human, was crucified, and is risen. In the becoming human we recognize God's love toward God's creation, in the crucifixion God's judgment of all flesh, and in the resurrection God's purpose for a new world. Nothing could be more perverse than to tear these three apart because the whole is contained in each of them.[39]

While the incarnation affirms and elevates the human, the cross also pronounces a double judgment on human being: "the absolute condemnation of sin and the relative condemnation of existing human orders," insofar as they are dehumanizing.[40] The crucifixion is God's judgment of the world, so that humanity lives "under this death-sign of the cross," where all autonomy, indeed all self-knowledge, stops. In light of the resurrection, however, the acceptance of this judgment turns into grace. For the resurrection "has broken into the midst of the world as the ultimate sign of its future, and at the same time as living reality."[41] Yet this new creation does not abolish the penultimate either, but through the church it occupies a space in it. Within this eschatological tension of affirmation, judgment and new creation, the Christian life unfolds as an essentially hermeneutic endeavor. The Christian has to employ reason to discern what is to be affirmed, what is under judgment and what already constitutes tokens of the new world.

Christianity is inherently interpretive because faith is participation in the Christ event, in God's encounter with the world. And therefore the Christian faith is in the truest sense an incarnational humanism because "Christian life means being human [*Menschsein*] in the power of Christ's becoming human, being judged, and pardoned in the power of the cross, living a

[39]Ibid., 6:157.
[40]Ibid.
[41]Ibid., 6:158.

new life in the power of the resurrection."[42] Because of the incarnation, "what is 'Christian' and what is 'worldly' are now no longer defined from the outset. Instead, both are understood in their respective uniqueness and their unique unity only within concrete responsibility of action that is based on the unity of the reconciliation in Jesus Christ."[43] Thus, when Christians think about the relation of their faith to the world, they no longer think about two competing realms between which they have to choose. Rather, the Christian's actions derive from the joy of a reconciled world and are motivated by this unity in every ethical decision. Christian ethics is not, therefore, the application of some divine law but the taking form (*Ausformung*) of Christ in us.[44] Such an ethic will not easily fall prey to the tormenting self-scrutiny of one's conscience, but rather orient itself toward Christ. A Christian ethic flows from "the already accomplished reconciliation of the world with God, from the peace of the already accomplished work of salvation in Jesus Christ, from the all-encompassing life that is Jesus Christ."[45]

For Bonhoeffer, this Christian responsibility is utterly concrete and cannot escape the ambiguities of human decision making. There are no templates for correct action, nor can we ever know on this earth in an ultimate sense whether we have done the right thing. Neither do we invent reality, but act within the "laws of nature" without submitting to deterministic views.[46] Our responsibility is not infinite but confined to our immediate area of social influence. But within these limits, responsibility encompasses the whole of reality. We cannot be naive. Christian responsibility is not merely concerned with good intentions or motives, but also with the outcome and consequences of the action. This is not to say that we can know the final outcomes of our actions, but that we cannot merely proceed on good intentions alone. One could also say that truly good intentions also consider the wider social and political consequences of actions. Yet we must also realize the limit of human possibilities. Bonhoeffer merely wants to take seriously human finitude and our propensity to selfishness: our human desire for absolute knowledge and absolute law, our

---

[42]Ibid., 6:159.
[43]Ibid., 6:266.
[44]Ibid., 6:101-2.
[45]Ibid., 6:253.
[46]Human relations and nature, says Bonhoeffer, have their intrinsic laws [*Wesensgesetze*], which we have to know and respect (ibid., 6:271).

wish to possess absolute clarity concerning the value and meaning of our action are really a grasping for Godhood. In contrast to ideologies that subordinate the human to a higher principle, "responsible [Christian] action renounces any knowledge about its ultimate justification."[47] Only God has true knowledge of good and evil from an absolute vantage point. In addition, when we strive to find timeless, surefire methods and principles of ethics, we often forget what the actual goal of good human action is: fully human life. Our tendency is to make the law ruler of humanity instead of placing law and principles in the service of humanity. Yet Christ died not to redeem the law but to restore humanity to life. Christ did not come to announce new ethical ideals; he became flesh out of love for humanity to free people from sin and guilt. The most basic goal (rather than a law or principle) of proper human reasoning and acting is determined by the incarnation: "Christ became human, and thus bore vicarious representative responsibility for all human beings. . . . It is through Christ that the world of things and values is given back its orientation toward human beings, as was originally intended in their creation."[48] The most basic goal of responsible action in interpreting the one Christ reality is therefore to live in the mode of the Christ event as "being-there-for-others."

Bonhoeffer is a Christian humanist because he regards full humanity as the ultimate goal of God's work in Christ. God sets us free because only free people can actually truly love and exercise genuine responsibility. Our responsible interpretation of a reality unified in Christ serves the same goal that prompted the incarnation, the restoration of humanity:

> Jesus Christ, the God who became human—this means that God has bodily taken on human nature in its entirety, that from now on divine being can be found nowhere else but in the human form. That is, in Jesus Christ, human beings are set free to be truly human before God. Now what is "Christian" is not something beyond the human, but it wants to be in the midst of the human. What is "Christian" is not an end in itself, but it means that human beings may and should live as human beings before God. . . . To live as a human being before God, in the light of God's becoming human, can only mean to be there not for oneself, but for God and other human beings.[49]

---

[47]Ibid., 6:268.
[48]Ibid., 6:260.
[49]Ibid., 6:400.

The task of the church is not to judge the world, but rather to proclaim and demonstrate to it that Christ died so that we could be fully human. The church exists, in effect, for the sake of humanity and not for itself. Christian engagement of culture and Christian responsibility are rooted in the certainty that "in the body of Christ all humanity is accepted, included, borne, and that the church-community of believers is to make this known to the world by word and life."[50]

In trying to live out this kind of realistic responsibility, albeit in the extreme context of Nazi Germany, Bonhoeffer knew the pain and personal cost of this incarnational theology better than anyone. Yet he did not despair, because he also knew how to surrender the ultimate evaluation of his responsible ethical action to God: "Permission to live through God's commandment includes the fact that the roots of human life and action are hidden in darkness, that doing and enduring are inextricably intertwined."[51] Moreover, "the motives of action are inscrutable. Everything we do is interwoven with something conscious and subconscious, natural and supernatural, with inclination and duty, with the egotistical and the altruistic, the intended and the inevitable, the active and the passive."[52] What the Christian has to do, after prayerfully considering God's Word and the intrinsic dynamics of the situation, is to surrender the decision to God and expect Jesus' gracious judgment. Responsible action has no recourse to some ultimate point of self-justification, no recourse to blaming others, no recourse to an ultimate knowledge of good and evil. Rather, it is a venture in which one takes risks and acts out of the freedom of participating in Christ. In this relation to God lies the total freedom that gives rise to initiative, creative obedience and responsible action in the first place. This freedom consists in not being ultimately bound by law or principle, and yet any danger of arbitrariness is curbed because participation in Christ is structured by his incarnation of obedience to the Father and love for humanity. Hence Christians act responsibly out of their relation with God for the sake of God and neighbor.[53]

What emerges from Bonhoeffer's discussion of the God-world relation

---

[50]Ibid., 6:54.
[51]Ibid., 6:385.
[52]Ibid., 6:384.
[53]Ibid., 6:297.

is his call for a unified existence in this world. How do we experience this unity of one Christ reality within the different institutions that shape our lives? In a way, of course, the person who participates in the unified reality of Christ on account of being in Christ already enjoys unity as an inward reality. Bonhoeffer, however, also addresses the unity of the various institutional realities that determine our existence in the world, such as marriage, government, the church, work and culture. One can see here how seriously Bonhoeffer takes his earlier proposal that ultimate reality is a world unified in Christ. If it is true, however, that "to speak about the world without speaking of Christ is pure abstraction,"[54] how is this relation of the world to Christ understood in terms of the institutions that determine our lives? Bonhoeffer answers this question by suggesting that government, work, marriage and church are mandated by God until Christ's return.[55] Thus, these institutions are autonomous in their own right but only relatively autonomous with respect to God's purpose for them. These mandates are given by God and reconciled to God through Christ, and hence not subject to arbitrary willful change.

The same ultimate-penultimate character of the world as held in Christ also applies to temporal institutions. Government, for example, is not merely an abstract notion but now concretely oriented toward Christ and meant to serve him by creating a space for a truly human life.[56] Yet the government itself is not the source of this life, but Christ is.[57] Since the church is the presence of Christ in society, it is its task to remind government of its calling to promote human flourishing and allow freedom of religion. The church reminds authority that Christ is the common head of church and government, but does not confuse the government with the church. The church is the conscience of the state. The church's role is to guard and proclaim the ultimate end of everything in Christ.[58] These

---

[54]Ibid., 6:68.

[55]Ibid., 6:68-74.

[56]"The mandate of the governing authorities (*der Obrigkeit*) to serve Christ is their inevitable destiny. They serve Christ whether knowingly or unknowingly, indeed whether they are faithful or unfaithful to this calling." For even if they unfaithfully suppress Christianity, it still serves Christ by highlighting the Christian witness of the suffering church (Dietrich Bonhoeffer, *DBW*, vol. 16, *Konspiration und Haft, 1940-1945*, ed. Jørgen Glenthøj, Ulrich Kabitz and Wolf Krötke [Gütersloh: Christian Kaiser Verlag, 1996], p. 521).

[57]Dietrich Bonhoeffer, "Staat und Kirche," in ibid., 16:524.

[58]Bonhoeffer speaks here of the church's "guardianship" to point out sin, to warn society of its effects and to call everyone to reconciliation in Christ (ibid., 16:531).

mandates preserve the relative autonomy of their appointed functions so that government does not meddle in church and the church does not exercise state authority. Yet at the same time, their common origin in God prevents our fragmentation as we operate within these mandates.[59]

The Christian who is at the same time churchgoer, worker, citizen and spouse sees all these mandates unified under God. As Bonhoeffer writes, "The divine mandates in the world are not there to wear people down through endless conflicts. Rather, they aim at the whole human being who stands in reality before God."[60] For the Christian, all of human life in its concreteness is addressed by God's commandments. Bonhoeffer follows an ancient Christian tradition in understanding God's commandments not as restrictions but as "permission" to live a fully human life: "God's commandment allows human beings to be human before God."[61] The commandment not to commit adultery, for example, does not define marriage as avoiding adultery, but permits people to live married life freely and confidently.[62] As a pastor, Bonhoeffer was well aware of our propensity to seek security in rules for the Christian life, which is probably why even today "how-to-do-Christianity" seminars prevail in evangelical churches over actual gospel proclamations. For Bonhoeffer, such an attitude is an abrogation of responsibility and a failure to enjoy the liberation effected by Christ to be fully human before God. Slaves need rules and lack initiative, but sons and daughters of God freely and responsibly enact what they know to be their Father's will: the reconciliation of the world with God for the sake of true humanity. For this reason, the evangelical tendency to establish Christian subcultures contradicts the incarnation if they are conceived as safety zones within which Christians move and grow up "protected" from secular culture. Bonhoeffer knew all too well that this sectarian strategy never works because these subcultures inevitably end up replicating culture—and often the worst of culture—in the name of Christianity. This is not to say, of course, that Christians should not take initiatives in education, for example, but Christian schools and universities are justifiable only insofar as they are conceived on the basis of a shared

---

[59]In the case of church and state, for example, "government and church are tied to the same Lord and tied to one another" but "separated by their differing tasks" (ibid., 16:533).
[60]Bonhoeffer, *DBWE*, 6:73.
[61]Ibid., 6:384.
[62]Ibid., 6:382.

humanity in a common secular sphere and meant to serve the world rather than withdraw from it. Christian institutions, insofar as they are necessary, should be about "creating islands of humanity" in our technocratic age that help society to become more human.[63] Christian and non-Christian citizens of this world are, or at least should be, united in their common pursuit of human flourishing.

The French philosopher and political thinker Jacques Maritain (1882-1973) has made more concrete suggestions than Bonhoeffer on this topic of a common secular sphere. Like Bonhoeffer, Maritain offers the incarnation as basis for the relative autonomy of the secular or temporal order,[64] as well as for a Christian attitude toward the world he describes as "theocentric" or "integral" humanism.[65] Like Bonhoeffer, Maritain holds that the guiding idea of this humanism is not the conversion of the world into the kingdom of God,[66] but the remaking of this world into "a field of a truly and fully human life."[67] The basis of this common life remains ultimately "the holy freedom of the creature whom grace unites to God." Finally, Maritain claims along with Bonhoeffer that this humanism fully takes into account that this spiritual reality is "refracted through the whole sinful and earthly substance of socio-temporal things."[68] Thus Maritain too realizes the interpretive risk of living out Christian convictions, and insists on the incarnational nature of Christianity: "The Christian is *part of* history, he *is* in history." Therefore acting out of the suprahistorical reality in Christ, Christians behave in the most gospel-like and circumspect way, but they cannot know the ultimate outcome of their deeds. After having done all he can, the Christian should "be at peace. The rest belongs to God."[69]

---

[63]Hans Urs von Balthasar, *Prüfet Alles das Gute Behalte: Ein Gespräch mit Angelo Scola*, ed. Angelo Scola, trans. Maria Shrady (Einsiedeln: Johannes Verlag, 2001), p. 50.
[64]For Maritain, "God so loved the world," implies "that the world is sanctified to the degree to which it is *not only* this world but is assumed into the universe of the Incarnation; and that it is reprobate in so far as it shuts itself up into itself . . . as it remains *only* this world, separate from the universe of the incarnation" (Jacques Maritain, *True Humanism*, trans. Margot Robert Adamson, 6th ed. [London: Geoffrey Bles, 1954], p. 102). In his own language, Maritain basically advocates the same ultimate-penultimate formation as do Augustine and Bonhoeffer.
[65]Ibid., p. 156.
[66]Ibid., p. 103
[67]Ibid., p. 104.
[68]Ibid., p. 156.
[69]Ibid., p. 243.

Bonhoeffer and Maritain carry forward the Augustinian tradition of a secular order founded on Christian principles. For them, Western society has "come of age" insofar as the temporal is no longer a mere springboard for the spiritual order, but has been saturated enough by Christian principles to search on its own for the common good of a secular commonwealth.[70] The common values pursued in such a secular society are "the vocation of the human person for spiritual accomplishment and the conquest of true freedom, and the reserves of moral integrity which this requires."[71] These values would provide the inner wellspring and motivation for the unity of an essentially pluralist society.[72]

What neither Bonhoeffer nor Maritain envisioned, however, is the ethnic diversity immigration has occasioned in European countries, for example. Maritain speaks of pluralism and a heterogeneous social groupings in modern society, but he assumes a generally Christian ethos. What would Maritain say, for example, in light of Europe's recent problems with immigration, particularly from Muslim countries, which imported a number of cultural differences that have proven so incompatible with Western society that a number of leading politicians have declared the death of a pluralist, that is, multiculturalist, society? Perhaps it is conceivable that at least the monotheistic religions could rally around a conception of society that is "in conformity with good reason and the common good."[73] It is a true that Christianity does not endorse or rely on any particular form of government. Yet it is also true that Western societies, and especially North America, have developed a democratic tradition that is carried by Christian values, albeit secularized ones.[74] As Jeffrey Stout rightly points out, civilization is "a matter of what kind of people we are going to be—a matter of self-definition and integrity. It is about what we care about most, of what we deem sacred or supremely valuable or inviolable."[75] As I have tried to show, many of these sacred values (human dignity, personhood, freedom, the reciprocal but independent relation of church and state, etc.) derive from the Chris-

---

[70]Ibid., p. 170.
[71]Ibid., p. 177.
[72]Ibid., p. 157.
[73]Ibid., p. 168.
[74]Jeffrey Stout's argument that Western democratic culture is a self-perpetuating tradition with a set of social practices that will remain humane seems rather unrealistic (*Democracy and Tradition* [Princeton, N.J.: Princeton University Press, 2005], p. 202; see also chaps. 9-10).
[75]Ibid., p. 200.

tian faith. Put differently, the humanizing of the world as it occurred in Western society is essentially indebted to the Spirit of Christianity.[76] Indeed, as we have seen, the very idea of the secular itself derives from the West's Christian history, and cannot simply be transplanted into another climate or unproblematically revitalized by different religions.[77]

Given all we have said about the humanistically and "other"-oriented nature of Christianity, the best way forward for Western societies is to abandon moribund attempts at pluralism and retrieve their Christian roots. The Judeo-Christian notion of humanity, culminating in the crucified and risen God, is the deepest spiritual source of the best so-called Western values.[78] Retracing these roots and a conscious adoption of humane values would best serve a modern secular and multicultural society. It is important to remember that governing authorities are never value neutral, but derive their values from a certain worldview. Western democratic societies can combine the need for historically grown and spiritually vital identities with a secular state by consciously adopting the kind of political construct Bonhoeffer and Maritain have suggested: a confessionally neutral state that nonetheless recognizes the derivation of its values from Christianity and therefore holds the mandate to pursue the most humane political course, including the freedom of other religions. The difficulty with such a nominally religious civic ethos is that the intellectual-spiritual forces that shape culture depend not on abstract ideals but require the inner motivational power of conviction, of sustained inner spiritual life.

This is, in fact, what Maritain rightly argues: no watered down, common profession of faith will work as "the source and principle of unity in society."[79] According to Maritain, Western culture requires nothing less than "a total and substantial reformation, a trans-valuation of its cultural

---

[76]Metz, *Zur Theologie der Welt*, pp. 62-63.

[77]That the concept of the secular and also the natural sciences have theological roots in the West is uncontested. See, for example, Bronislaw Szerszynski, "Rethinking the Secular: Science, Technology, and Religion Today," *Zygon* 40, no.4 (2005): 14.

[78]Christianity is not, as Pope Benedict has pointed out, a Western religion, but in Europe it took on its "most efficacious cultural and intellectual form," which gave rise to unique forms of rationality and morality, along with their pathological aberrations (Benedict XVI, *Christianity and the Crisis of Cultures*, trans. Brian McNeil [San Francisco: Ignatius Press, 2006], pp. 29ff.).

[79]Jacques Maritain, *True Humanism*, trans. Margot Robert Adamson, 6th ed. (London: Geoffrey Bles, 1954), p. 168.

principles." Western societies must change "to the primacy of quality over quantity, of work over money, of the human over technical means, of wisdom over science, of the common service of human beings instead of the covetousness of unlimited individual enrichment or a desire in the name of the State for unlimited power."[80] This is the common task for both Christians and non-Christians, but Christians will have to take the initiative because "it is only through the mystery of the redeeming Incarnation that a Christian sees the proper dignity of human personality, and what it costs."[81] In Christ are found the principles of personalism and integral humanism, that is, the freedom, dignity, and integrity of each individual human being and the orientation of all material things to human flourishing.[82] It is the divine love for humanity concretely revealed in Christ that "vivifies" human freedom in responsibility and "fixes the center of his life infinitely above the state."[83] For this reason Christians should actively participate in political life everywhere, but they have to resist the temptation to turn the secular into the church. Instead, as members of the human race and temporal society, they must act on society in the spirit of Christianity.[84]

Maritain and Bonhoeffer are right, of course. We need Christian humanists, believers who have a clear understanding of the world's value and who grasp fully that Christ did not come to pluck souls from the flames of hell and transport them to another world, but rather to give us life, to grant us our full humanity. It is for this that Christians ought to labor in the Spirit of Christ, and this "humanism of the incarnation . . . carries the sign of no theocracy other than the gentle dominion of God's love."[85] Christian concern for the world thus follows the incarnational pattern, as Bonhoeffer so rightly pointed out: "No one has the responsibility of turning the world into the kingdom of God, but only of taking the next necessary step to God's becoming human in Christ. . . . God became *human*.

---

[80] Ibid., p. 201.

[81] Ibid., p. 200.

[82] Ibid., p. 275.

[83] Ibid.

[84] Ibid., p. 265; See also Balthasar, *Prüfet Alles das Gute Behaltet*, p. 53: "We must not simply hand the political over to non-Christians." He suggests that Christians should live out faith, with the hermeneutic freedom proper to common citizenship and humanity, in politics and the professions.

[85] Maritain, *True Humanism*, p. 239.

That is why responsible action has to weigh, judge, and evaluate the matter within the human domain."[86] The training ground for this Christian understanding of the world and of humanity is the church, and it is to the presence of God in the church that we now turn.

GOD'S PRESENCE IN THE CHURCH

Bonhoeffer's pithy definition of the church as "Christ existing as community" shows that ecclesiology (what the church is) is always also Christology (who Christ is). Thus, every activity within the church—the sacraments, the liturgy, the interpretation of Scripture, preaching and prayer—receives its legitimation as a form of participation in Christ, as the making present of the incarnate, crucified and risen Christ. In this sense the church is itself a sacrament to the world, and every liturgical act a sacrament of Christ's presence in the church. Henri de Lubac has pointed out the close connection within the history of Christian theology between the words *sacrament* and *mystery*, to the effect that the sacrament is a visible sign of the mystery, that is, the mystery of God's salvation of humanity through Christ.[87] Lubac also reminds us that "in the thinking of the whole of Christian antiquity, the Eucharist and the Church are linked."[88] Just as the church is the body of Christ, a sacramental presence of Christ in the world, so the Eucharist is the central liturgical referent for Christ's presence in the church, drawing the participant up into the priestly sacrifice of Jesus, into his passion, death and resurrection. It is not that the sacrament of baptism or the preaching of the Word is any less essential to the life of the church, but in the Eucharist the salvific act of God and its universal import for all of humanity are most clearly imparted.

Before I delineate more clearly the special importance of the Eucharist for incarnational humanism, we have to address a fundamental problem: modern Christians have lost much of the sacramental realism that formed the consciousness of Christians from the church's inception well into the

---

[86]Bonhoeffer, *DBWE*, 6:224-25. More recently, Charles Mathewes has shown once more that Christians engage the world precisely because they believe in heaven as the destiny not only of the church but of the world as well (*A Theology of Public Life*, Cambridge Studies in Christian Doctrine [Cambridge: Cambridge University Press, 2007], p. 308).

[87]Henri de Lubac, *Corpus Mysticum*, ed. Laurence Paul Hemming and Susan Frank Parsons, trans. Gemma Simonds (Notre Dame, Ind.: University of Notre Dame Press, 2007), p. 49; Rom 16:25.

[88]Ibid., p. 13.

seventeenth century. The reason for this has already been explained. Somewhere in the history of ideas, the originally Platonic notion of the world as
an expression of a transcendent order, in which we participate and to which
the human mind corresponds, gave way to a disenchanted, inert, indifferent
world in which meaning is confined to the interior life of the human spirit.
This loss of metaphysical realism, of our participation in a higher, meaningful order of things, accounts for the modern Christian's inability to
imagine our actual participation in God and discern the mystery of church
and Eucharist. For early Christians, the idea that everything hangs together in Christ, in whom we live, move and have our being, is not merely
a metaphor but a spiritual reality; indeed, our modern propensity to view
metaphorical statements as mere adornments of straightforward, naked
truths is itself evidence of the continuing effect of this loss. Our modern
consciousness has been deeply affected by the loss of sacramental ontology.
We stand at the end of a long development within intellectual history,
through which nature has become defined in opposition to spirit. We have
already described the resulting dualisms of consciousness versus material
reality, faith versus reason, the natural versus the supernatural.

Yet nothing in philosophy or science necessitates that we assent to the
empty nonrealism of modernity or to its playful continuance under postmodernity. Scientific and philosophical developments in the last half of
the twentieth century have once and for all dislodged the pseudo-founda-
tions that formerly seemed to justify the segregation of science and faith.
Nothing stands in the way of asserting the possibility of God's interaction
with the world or of the mind's participation in an intelligible world. As
the theologian T. F. Torrance put it forcefully in 1970, "the axiomatic assumption of a radical dichotomy between phenomenon and idea" has become "as impossible for Christianity as it is for modern science."[89] Torrance explains that modern developments in science have moved us well
beyond a mechanistic universe and made possible once more a unity of
mind and reality. Along with this holistic experience of reality comes the
task of integrating reason and faith. Even while we must observe important distinctions and levels of activity among knowledge disciplines, our
integrative task is clear: Christian revelation and any other discourse of

---

[89]T. F. Torrance, *Space, Time and Incarnation* (Edinburgh: T & T Clark, 1997), p. 43.

human knowledge (i.e., the human and natural sciences) must be "co-ordinated in the same universe of knowledge."[90] Without some form of metaphysical realism, however, the incarnational truth that God's presence in the world is mediated through space and time makes no sense; thus, neither the church nor the sacraments as channels of God's presence in the world make sense.

Thankfully, adopting realism as the basic framework for theology can no longer be deemed a sacrifice of one's intellect. Indeed, we should emulate theologians like T. F. Torrance who go on the metaphysical offensive. Torrance argues that without dictating to the empirical sciences any particular scientific paradigm, the incarnation as revelation encourages us to return to Bonhoeffer's christological definition of reality. Rather than let science dictate the material space-time conditions under which God can show up in the world, "we must seek to build up a specifically theological interpretation, with its own apposite forms of thought and speech, within the unitary interaction of God with our world in creation and Incarnation, and within the unity of the rational structures that result from that interaction."[91] Such a conception of reality is not constructed *against* science, but on the grounds that science merely offers a partial and often reductive view of reality.

Exploring the longstanding debate about Christ's presence in the Eucharist, Torrance demonstrates the problems that ensue when preconceived categories of space and time dictate how we conceive of God's presence. When Aristotelian categories of space came to dominate late medieval theology, they narrowed the theological horizon by imagining God's presence exclusively in terms of space *apart* from time, imagining space as a static container into which God now had to pour his presence without becoming imprisoned.[92] This spatial model shaped all subsequent debates among Christians, For example, Reformed Christianity recognized the limitation this model placed on God's transcendence, and hence tried to define presence in such a way that God's utter freedom from creation would not be threatened. Yet because the container model of space still limited their imagination, Reformers struggled with articulating how God could be present in this world but not confined to a material container. This gave rise to the

---

[90]Ibid., p. 51.
[91]Ibid., p. 70.
[92]Ibid., pp. 26-29.

Reformed *hoc significat* (this points to) over Luther's *hoc est meus corpus* (this is my body), that is, the insistence that the eucharistic elements signify rather than constitute the presence of God in the church. Torrance argues rightly that the church fathers, not yet limited by such a narrow idea of space, had a much more dynamic view of God's presence in the world than did later theologians, a view to which we should return.[93]

We can return to this view by affirming for the sacraments the same workings of divine energy that occur in the incarnation. The incarnate God, in Jesus the Christ, is "the place of contact and communication between God and man in a real movement with physical existence, involving interaction between God and nature, divine and human agency."[94] This hypostatic union operates from within creation, drawing human nature up into the divine without compromising the integrity of either. God is not imprisoned or circumscribed by his becoming human, but really communicates himself as human while remaining divine. On account of this incarnation event, the human is now defined by the new pattern of human-divine working. Similarly, the relations of space and time, and of the transcendent and the material, are determined by the incarnation. Why then cannot God's presence in the Eucharist follow the same pattern? Rather than attempt to explain the divine presence through our a priori categories of reference (whether Aristotelian or otherwise), we should recognize that in the Eucharist as in the resurrection, God communicates himself through the elements "in such a way that through the material offerings we become aware of his majesty and transcendence that reaches infinitely beyond the created order."[95] We return, in other words, to the basic ultimate-penultimate relation Bonhoeffer already outlined. The ultimate coordinates by which we integrate all aspects of reality into a meaningful whole are from God, even while this ultimate reality does not destroy the referentiality of our worldly existence. Today we can affirm Luther's *hoc est* and assert that in the incarnation God made room for himself in the material world while maintaining his utter freedom and transcendence.[96]

---

[93]Ibid., pp. 77-79.
[94]Ibid., p. 78.
[95]Ibid., p. 79.
[96]Ibid., p. 76.

Once we understand the dependence of former theological views on outmoded Aristotelian views of physical processes, we can focus more ecumenically on the positive expressions of "full presence" in the Orthodox, Lutheran and Reformed traditions. This presence should be understood as spiritual presence in such way that spiritual no longer means virtual but real. We should seek neither a virtual nor a material presence, for what feeds the soul is not Christ's physical presence or proximity, but God's Spirit in us. Even in those who walked with Christ during his ministry, it was not his proximity but the Holy Spirit who revealed him as the Messiah. Augustine reminds us of this in a eucharistic sermon, when he says, "Don't let your gullet eat, but your mind. . . . [I]t is not what is seen but what is believed that will feed us."[97] We encounter Christ with the "inner sense of faith" through the mediation of external elements, such as bread and wine.[98] John Calvin, too, seeks to articulate Christ's presence in this way: "In his Sacred Supper, he bids me take, eat, and drink his body and blood under the symbols of bread and wine. I do not doubt that he himself truly presents them, and that I receive them."[99] For Calvin, it is by the incomprehensible power of the Holy Spirit that we are lifted up into the presence of God and "come to partake of Christ's flesh and blood."[100]

The preceding discussion of the divine presence in the church leads to this important conclusion: just as in the incarnation, it is in the church, the liturgy and the sacraments that the Christian is touched by and drawn into *reality in its fullest sense*.[101] Christians have to resist the modern con-

---

[97]Augustine, *Essential Sermons*, ed. Daniel Doyle, trans. Edmund Hill, Works of Saint Augustine: A Translation for the 21st Century (New York: New City Press, 2007), pp. 182-83.
[98]Ibid.
[99]John Calvin, *Institutes of the Christian Religion* 4.17.32, ed. John T. McNeill, trans. Ford Lewis Battles (Philadelphia: Westminster Press, 1960).
[100]Ibid., 4.17.31, 33. Calvin displays a certain ambiguity in how he defines *presence*. He clearly desires "real presence," but his anti-Catholic and anti-Lutheran polemic makes him emphasize the covenantal language of promise over ontological participation. With the Eastern Orthodox tradition, Calvin emphasizes that Christ is in heaven, and that we cannot "draw him away from there," down into the sacraments (ibid., 4.17.32). It often seems that because of the rather logico-mechanical way in which Calvinists understood flesh in this debate, it was often too crassly opposed to spirit, so that the term *spiritual participation*, which the fathers also used, appears "thinner" in Calvin than is necessary. See, for instance, this passage, where Calvin rejects Cyril of Alexandria's image of the transfusion of Christ's flesh into our soul: "For it is enough for us that, from the substance of his flesh, Christ breathes life into our souls—indeed, pours forth his very life into us—even though Christ's flesh itself does not enter into us" (ibid.).
[101]*Liturgy* is used here in the restricted sense of church service and its rites (call to worship,

notations of the term *spiritual* as that which is less real, and recover the
traditional Christian incarnational interpretation of *spiritual* as the *true*
reality, the *true* temporality and *true* materiality as determined by God
and embodied in the God-man Jesus. It is admittedly hard to imagine
this, but in the reality of the God-man, matter and temporality are taken
up into the divine reality of the new creation with its new, transformed
materiality. There is no reason, therefore, to doubt that through the elements of bread and wine, God's reality is present to us in a downward
movement, and we are drawn into this reality, in an upward movement.
As Augustine put it, we "feed on the body of Christ and the blood of
Christ" not in a merely imaginary way, but "we eat and drink to the extent
of a participation in the Spirit, staying in the Lord's body as members,
and being energized by his Spirit."[102] The whole point and focus of Christian worship is to draw us into the new creation, which is *not* the annihi-
lation of the material but its transformation into the new creation.[103] At
the center of worship is "the celebration of the Resurrection and of life"
and the expression of the new humanity, the abundant life made possible
through the paschal mystery.[104] According to the apostle Paul, each
Christian already possesses this eschatological reality within him- or herself through the indwelling of God's Spirit, "the divine agent that realizes
resurrection, 'eschatological existence,' the life of the age to come, in the
present" (cf. 2 Cor 1:22).[105] Yet this eschatological reality is ultimately
communion with the triune God, the fulfillment of our humanity, the
foretaste of a new state of being, whose expression is thanksgiving and
praise—Eucharist.[106]

---

prayer, communal singing, etc.). The Eastern church tends to reserve the term *liturgy* for the
eucharistic service.

[102] Augustine, "Homily 27," in *Homilies on the Gospel of John 1-40*, ed. Allan D. Fitzgerald, trans.
Edmund Hill, Works of Saint Augustine: A Translation for the 21st Century (New York:
New City Press, 1990), p. 475.

[103] Jean Daniélou tells us that "the life of ancient Christianity was centered around worship," and
in the sacraments "was inaugurated a new creation which introduced the Christian even now
into the Kingdom of God" (Jean Daniélou, *The Bible and the Liturgy* [Notre Dame, Ind.:
University of Notre Dame Press, 1956], p. 17).

[104] John Paul II, *Crossing the Threshold of Hope*, ed. Vittorio Messori, trans. Jenny McPhee and
Martha McPhee (New York: Knopf, 1994), p. 75.

[105] C. K. Barrett, *A Commentary on the Epistle to the Romans*, Harper's New Testament Commentaries (New York: Harper & Row, 1957), p. 80.

[106] Schmemann, *Life of the World*, p. 39.

While sensitivity to cultural context is important, of course, the point of Christian worship is not at all to make God palatable to people but to confront them with (and draw them into) ultimate reality. Among modern Protestant theologians, Thomas Torrance has expressed most clearly the theological reason why the actual purpose of the sacraments as mediating God's presence remains neglected in many mainline Protestant churches. According to Torrance, this reason is the failure to understand divine atonement as an incarnational act that happened in the very being of God himself. For Torrance, the crucial question is "whether we tend to regard atonement for sin as some external transaction between God and man, worked out by Jesus, or whether we think of it as having taken place within the Being of the Mediator."[107] If we do not regard incarnation and atonement as internally and essentially intertwined, then everything we do in church will reflect this external, merely forensic understanding of salvation. Our relation to Christ will be only in moral or juridical terms, and the sacraments will become "a means of grace merely in the sense that they help to cement moral relationships and promote Christian patterns of behaviour."[108] The entire tone of worship will be moralistic, legalistic and obedience driven. If we do believe, however, that the incarnation and the reconciliation of humanity to God through it fall within the very life of God, then through Christ we share in the inner relations of God's own life and love. Then the sacraments become means for drawing us into the divine life, "for in Christ our human relations with God, far from being allowed to remain on a merely external basis, are embraced within the Trinitarian relations of God's own being as Father, Son, and Holy Spirit."[109] It is in this sense that Eastern Orthodox theologians refer to the church as "heaven on earth."[110] In particular, the Eucharist as the reenactment of Christ's passion and resurrection celebrates the recapitulation of the world in Christ and its reconciliation to God. In the Eucharist we have a foretaste of the messianic banquet, which has nothing to do with a mystical experience of escaping the world and everything to do with opening one's eyes to the world as it really is in Christ.[111]

---

[107]Thomas Torrance, *The Mediation of Christ* (Colorado Springs: Helmers & Howard, 1992), p. 63.
[108]Ibid., p. 61.
[109]Ibid., p. 64.
[110]Schmemann, *Life of the World*, p. 30.
[111]Ibid., pp. 44-45.

The Christian church service is the portal, so to speak, into reality as taken up and transformed by Christ. When we enter the church and begin worship, every part of the liturgy should be a procession to the throne room of God, a procession into communion with the triune God. The sacraments, the order of worship, the liturgical calendar and sacred art are part of the church's sacramental activity of drawing history and meaning together in Christ.[112] Art, for example, demonstrates how worship takes up everything in creation into its ultimate meaning. Artistic expression, whether explicitly religious or secular, always constitutes a human interpretation of the world that beholds objects as participating in the mystery of being. The power of a picture, for example, lies in projecting an ideal world (or criticizing the present one), indicating human hope for the way the world should be. Art thus expresses the fundamental transcendence of the human spirit. Yet as Romano Guardini has rightly argued, human existence does not itself provide the ultimate meaning of this striving. Rather, the goal of all our striving, "this actual future, really has to come from outside of us, has to come from God as 'the new heaven and the new earth,' in which the true nature of things is revealed; as the 'new human being,' who is formed according to the image of Christ."[113] Art illustrates what the liturgy actually does: the liturgy draws the worshiper into the story of God's faithfulness to his people through a christological metaphor and shapes the community by this content.[114] Thus Luther rightly argues that the church service (*Gottesdienst*) should be modeled on Mary's willingness to serve God. Church and liturgy should be the place where we allow God to work in us.[115]

---

[112]Dietrich Bonhoeffer has expressed this notion of Christ as the center of reality: "In summary we can say that to call Christ the center of human existence, of history, and of nature—these are never abstract matters and are never to be distinguished from one another. It is a fact that human existence is both history and nature. Christ as the center means that Christ, as the mediator for the creation in its servitude, is the fulfillment of this law, the liberation from the servitude for the whole human being. Christ is all this only because he is the one who stands in my place, in my behalf before God, *pro-me*. Christ as the mediator is precisely the end of the old, fallen world and the beginning of the new World of God" (Dietrich Bonhoeffer, *DBWE*, vol. 12, *Berlin: 1932-1933*, ed. Larry L. Rasmussen, trans. Isabel Best, David Higgins and Douglas W. Stott [Minneapolis: Fortress Press, 2009], p. 327).

[113]Romano Guardini, *Über das Wesen des Kunstwerks*, 2nd ed. (Mainz: Matthias Grünewald Verlag, 1949), pp. 29-30.

[114]Robert Webber, *Ancient-Future Faith: Rethinking Evangelicalism for a Postmodern World* (Grand Rapids: Baker, 1999), p. 133.

[115]Martin Luther, *Das Magnifikat: Vorlesung über den 1 Johannesbrief*, vol. 9 of *Calwer Luther-*

It may be hard for our modern ears to hear and our modern imaginations to envision, but if we want to recapture the spirit that motivated patristic, medieval and Renaissance Christians to engage and transform culture, we have to recapture the idea that in worship we encounter the real world by encountering Christ. Surely, this happens in each individual Christian, but nothing can replace the gathering of God's people as they encounter together the presence of God in worship. For here, "the Christological concentration of all history is at the same time liturgical mediation of this history and expression of a new experience of time, in which past, present, and future touch each other because they are taken up into the presence of the risen one."[116]

This "new experience of time" has become possible because in the incarnation, human temporality and divine eternity have been united. We already have a record of God's entering into history through the Old Testament account of his covenant relation with Israel. From a New Testament, Christian point of view, the risen Christ fulfills this relation as an ongoing reality that constitutes the church, and a reality in which the church participates. Jesus' remarkably and intentionally public life[117] indicates that in him, God acted once more and now decisively on behalf of Israel and humanity by defeating evil, sin and death.[118] The universal implications of the incarnation are that in a concrete historical context, human history has been taken up into divine reality and becomes sacred history. In these events the ultimate reality and destiny of creation have been revealed, and through Christ the believer participates in this eschatological reality. The consequences of this view are what the theologian Yves Congar has termed "the sacramental nature of time in the Church."[119] Sacramental time is the eschatological time of God in which past, present and future are gathered into an eternal present in which the Christian

Ausgabe, ed. Wolfgang Metzger (Stuttgart: Hänssler Verlag, 1996), pp. 92-93.
[116]Benedict XVI, *Der Geist Der Liturgie: Eine Einführung,* 6th ed. (Freiburg im Breisgau: Herder, 2002), p. 101.
[117]See, for instance, John 18:20: "I have spoken openly to the world. . . . I always taught in synagogues or at the temple, where all the Jews come together. I said nothing in secret."
[118]See N. T. Wright, *The Climax of the Covenant: Christ and the Law in Pauline Theology* (Minneapolis: Fortress, 1992), p. 143 (but this is really the argument of the entire book).
[119]Yves Congar, *Tradition and Traditions: An Historical and a Theological Essay* (New York: Macmillan, 1966), p. 259. For a fuller account of sacramental time and its relation to tradition, see Hans Boersma, *Heavenly Participation: The Weaving of a Sacramental Theology* (Grand Rapids: Eerdmans, 2011), pp. 120ff.

participates by the power of the Spirit.[120] Congar argues that this sacred time is present in the sacraments of the church through which we are connected, in Christ, not only with past events of sacred history but with all other Christians both past and present. In this way the Spirit's power allows us a foretaste of the eschatological kingdom, where "God is all in all."[121] Moreover, this sacred time also gathers up into its sacred history the acts of Christians both past and present that are inspired by God's grace, by which "man goes beyond the limits of the merely temporal."[122] Sacred history and sacred time thus allow each Christian to participate, in Christ and by the power of the Holy Spirit, in the gradual building up of the City of God through living in the presence of God who is himself the center of history.[123]

Surely such a "heavenly ontology" or "sacred temporality" must appear strange to modern sensibilities,[124] but that is because we have grown too accustomed to viewing history as merely a succession of linear events. It is helpful to remember that any meaningful history, even in purely secular terms, requires a vantage point beyond the mere succession of events from which we integrate isolated facts into a meaningful whole. Thus our typically human desire for meaning and purpose requires, in a lesser sense perhaps, a kind of sacred time that allows us to relate to the past in a meaningful way. The sacred time of the church is another, much more comprehensive instance of meaningful integration of historical events into God's eschatological reality as brought forward into earthly time most fully by the incarnation.

The idea of sacred time also has important implications for the role of tradition as participation in and transmission of Christ's eschatological reality. The liturgy and the sacraments constitute the church's living memory or tradition, "the living transmission of lived realities."[125] For centuries, even while the scriptural canon was being formed, the liturgy communicated the teaching of the apostles and educated Christians in the faith. Indeed, church fathers often formulated doctrine by unfolding theo-

---

[120]Cf. Augustine, *Confessions*, bk. 11.
[121]Congar, *Tradition and Traditions*, p. 261.
[122]Ibid., p. 262.
[123]Ibid.
[124]Ibid., p. 259.
[125]Ibid., p. 79.

logically what was already practiced in the liturgy.[126] The liturgy thus exemplifies the important role of tradition in the formation of one's consciousness through history. Participating regularly in the liturgy that is itself a continuation of the first apostolic tradition shapes our theological imagination, and we form a sense of belonging within a meaningful world.[127] As Yves Congar explains, "Through the liturgy's special character, a mass of questions are resolved in a sane, Christian manner sometimes before they are even put, or at least without their being accompanied by tensions and difficulties; perhaps somewhat like the peaceful solving, within the calm of normal family circle, of questions full of discrepancies and conflicts, such as, example, authority and freedom, person and community, continuity and innovation, tension and relaxation, etc. It is the liturgy which gives to the Church the fullness of its family atmosphere; in this it rejoins Tradition, which is . . . very similar to what education is in the succession, the solidarity and the renewal of the generations."[128] Tradition also facilitates our participation in God's sacred history, because through tradition the Holy Spirit imparts to the Christian the realities of the incarnate Word of God through whom the Father's will and character are revealed.[129]

Congar holds that the liturgy is the principal instrument of the church's tradition.[130] If we accept Gadamer's account of how knowledge works in dependence on (but not servile obedience to) tradition, any residual Protestant squeamishness about the necessary role of tradition for scriptural exegesis should finally disappear. Unless we want to return to the myth of neutral, disinterested readings of Scripture, we have to concede that "there is not a single point that the Church holds by tradition alone, without any reference to Scripture; just as there is not a single dogma that is derived

---

[126]Basil the Great, for example, formulates the doctrine of the Holy Spirit by drawing on "all the witnesses available in scripture and in the baptismal and liturgical tradition of the Church" (Basil the Great, *On the Holy Spirit*, trans. David Anderson, Popular Patristic Series [Crestwood, N.Y.: St. Vladimir's Seminary Press, 1980], p. 10).

[127]Gadamer, *TM*, p. 262.

[128]Congar, *Tradition and Traditions*, p. 434. On the shaping of our self-understanding through social influences, see also Gadamer, *TM*, p. 276: "Long before we understand ourselves through the process of self-examination, we understand ourselves in a self-evident way in the family, society, and state in which we live."

[129]Congar, *Tradition and Traditions*, p. 265.

[130]Ibid.

from Scripture alone, without being explained by tradition."[131]

Given this important role of the liturgy as the medium for understanding our faith, the liturgical poverty that persists in many evangelical churches betrays a dangerous rootlessness. Anglican, Lutheran and Reformed churches have retained a rich liturgical heritage, and many evangelical churches have followed the call of Robert Webber to retrieve ancient worship traditions to revitalize postmodern Christianity[132] and to recognize the importance of a rule of faith for reading Scripture.[133] Whatever our Christian confession or denomination may be, Christians have to retrieve, and become conscious of, worship as participation in the heavenly dimensions of the new creation for two reasons. First, without such understanding, sacraments and liturgy as they have come to us through ancient tradition make no sense. On one level, a richer liturgy addresses the question of Christian identity and self-understanding. Second, and perhaps even more importantly, a fuller liturgy reminds us that we live in the age of eschatology, in the reality that is in tension with the world. To provide just one brief example: how many of us understand the significance of worship on Sunday? It is an understandable trend in churches that run out of space and are mindful of the frantic work schedules of many parishioners to offer services on Saturday nights. Yet this flexibility depends on treating each day as equal, whereas early Christians regarded Sunday as the day of resurrection and new creation, as the eighth day that represented everlasting rest:[134] Sunday was "the liturgical commemoration of this eighth day, and so at the same time a memorial of the

---

[131]Yves Congar, *The Meaning of Tradition*, trans. A. N. Woodrow (San Francisco: Ignatius Press, 2004), pp. 39-40.

[132]Webber, *Ancient-Future Faith*, especially chap. 16, contains the heart of Webber's project to retrieve christocentric, ecclesial and liturgical spirituality.

[133]Ibid., p. 185.

[134]The early Christian community deliberately adopted resurrection day, Sunday, as the primary day of worship to declare the fulfilment of the sabbath in Christ. Thus Sunday worship indicates the eschatological importance of the resurrection as inaugurating the new creation. See "Der Gottesdienst in der vornizänischen Kirche" in *Die Geschichte des Christentums*, vol 1. (Freiburg: Herder, 2000), p. 368. One of the earliest mentions of the "eighth day" is from the first century in The Epistle of Barnabas, who has God say, "Your present Sabbaths are not acceptable to Me, but that is which I have made, [namely this,] when, giving rest to all things, I shall make a beginning of the eighth day, that is, a beginning of another world. Wherefore, also we keep the eighth day with joyfulness, the day also on which Jesus rose again from the dead" (in Roberts and Donaldson, *Ante-Nicene Fathers*, vol 1., p. 146).

Resurrection and a prophecy of the world to come."[135] By going to church on this day, Christians participated visibly in the new divine economy inaugurated by Christ.

THE HEART OF THE CHURCH: THE EUCHARIST

Throughout the history of the church, the Eucharist has occupied a central place as the "sacrament of sacraments" to which all other sacraments are "ordered . . . as to their end."[136] The Eastern Orthodox, Anglican and Lutheran churches emphasize the interdependence of preaching and the Eucharist as sacramental acts, while the Roman Catholic Church focuses more on the Eucharist itself.[137] All can agree, however, that the Eucharist is the "source and summit of ecclesial life."[138] In the eucharistic celebration the worshiper enters into the heavenly liturgy, into the very reality of his joy.[139] The dimensions of heaven and earth meet, the worshiper's spirit and voice unite with those of the angels in worshiping the triune God, the maker of heaven and earth. It has been said that the Eastern eucharistic rite emphasizes the resurrection while the Latin celebration focuses more on the passion of Christ.[140] The underlying unity of both liturgies, however, is that the Eucharist represents the access to divine reality opened up by Christ. The worshiping community is drawn into and met by the eschatological reality of the new creation through the material elements of the Eucharist. This mediation of divine reality is grounded in God's divine action of assuming humanity in order to raise up humanity to the divine: "At the center of this worship is the priestly action of Christ in His Passion and Resurrection. It is this priestly action which, abstracted from time and place, constitutes the heart of the heavenly liturgy."[141] The "entire event of incarnation, Cross, resurrection and Christ's return is present as the form by which God draws human beings into co-operation with himself."[142] Our existence is

[135]Daniélou, *Bible and the Liturgy*, p. 37.
[136]*Catechism of the Catholic Church*, 2nd ed. (New York: Doubleday, 1997), p. 310.
[137]See Schmemann, *Life of the World*, p. 33, on the Orthodox position; compare *Catechism of the Catholic Church*, p. 334, where preaching is not even mentioned.
[138]*Catechism of the Catholic Church*, p. 334.
[139]Schmemann, *Life of the World*, p. 25.
[140]John Paul II, *Crossing the Threshold of Hope*, p. 75.
[141]Daniélou, *Bible and the Liturgy*, p. 136.
[142]Benedict XVI, *Der Geist der Liturgie*, p. 149.

drawn into the incarnation and the resurrection.

Recovering a sacramental view of church and the Christian life also opens up a more ecumenical understanding of the Catholic mass with its emphasis on Christ's passion and sacrifice. Especially during the Reformation debates about the Eucharist, Roman Catholic theology was criticized for advocating "cannibalism," the eating of the real flesh and blood of Christ, and also for offering again at each mass the atoning sacrifice of Christ. None of these criticisms was entirely without grounds.[143] However, we do not want to follow the aberrations but the correct theological insights that Roman Catholic theology preserved within the Christian tradition.[144] The main point of the mass is not the repetition of Christ's sacrifice but its *representation*,[145] in the same way that baptism imitates Christ's death, burial and resurrection to indicate participation in the new reality that resulted from them.[146] The term *representation* has to be taken sacramentally as "presencing." Liturgy is always "in the present tense." The historical past events of Christ's life become "a present presence that opens a new future."[147] The Eucharist as representation of Christ's passion draws us into the reality of Christ's high priestly role of mediator. The Roman Catholic understanding of the Eucharist focuses on this priestly function of Christ as explained in the epistle to the Hebrews. Christ is the "apostle and high priest" of our confession (Heb 3:1), whose blood sacrifice opened

---

[143]Benedict XVI concedes that in the twelfth century, an extreme understanding of divine presence did lead to expressions of eating flesh and blood (*Gott ist uns nah: Eucharistie: Mitte des Lebens*, ed. Stephan Otto Horn and Vinzenz Pfnür, 2nd ed. [Augsburg: Sankt UlrichVerlag, 2005], p. 85), and George Hunsinger has shown the ambiguities within the Council of Trent's statements that, while basically advocating the representation of Christ's sacrifice, also leave the door open to voices that suggest the resacrificing of Christ on the altar (*The Eucharist and Ecumenism: Let Us Keep the Feast*, ed. Iain Torrance, Current Issues in Theology [Cambridge: Cambridge University Press, 2008], p. 16 [but see the whole book for an excellent discussion of the Eucharist in ecumenical context]).

[144]For an excellent summary of Henri de Lubac's explanation for changes within the Roman Catholic understanding of the Eucharist, see Boersma, *Heavenly Participation*, pp. 115ff.

[145]Daniélou explains that for the fathers the sacrifice represented by the liturgy and the elements "is not a new sacrifice but the one sacrifice of Christ rendered present" (*Bible and the Liturgy*, p. 137).

[146]Robert Louis Wilken, *The Spirit of Early Christian Thought* (New Haven, Conn.: Yale University Press, 2003), p. 35, agrees here with Daniélou (*Bible and the Liturgy*, p. 136), that the Eucharist is a memorial not in the merely referential sense of Zwinglian theology, but as *anamnesis*, that is "of making present not in memory but in reality, under the sacramental signs, the unique sacrifice of Christ" (ibid., p. 137).

[147]Wilken, *Early Christian Thought*, p. 35.

up access not to a mere earthly sanctuary but to its heavenly original, in which Jesus the glorified Messiah officiates eternally as the "great priest over the house of God" (Heb 10:21). For Roman Catholics, the Eucharist is the center of the worship service because it makes present Christ's fulfillment of the Old Testament sacrificial economy. On account of Christ's death and resurrection, the Eucharist is the convergence of all promises in the old covenant, indeed of the history of religions in general.[148] The Christian is drawn into the priestly actions of Christ and thus into the new eschatological economy of God's love offered to humanity in Christ. Instead of the Old Testament temple, the Eucharist represents

> the universal temple of the risen Christ, whose cross-shaped arms are stretched out toward the world to draw everyone into the embrace of eternal love. The new temple already exists and therewith also the new, final sacrifice: the new humanity of Christ effected by the cross and resurrection; the prayer of the human being Jesus has now become one with the inner-Trinitarian dialogue of eternal love. Into this prayer Jesus draws human beings through the Eucharist, so that the always open door of worship and the true sacrifice, the sacrifice of the new covenant constitutes the "logos-shaped" liturgy.[149]

The Old Testament world with its ritual sacrifices has been fulfilled and spiritualized in Christ. Spiritualizing, however, does not mean that God's history with Israel and its record in the Old Testament have been abolished, but that they are fulfilled by and taken up into Christ. The incarnate God-man is indeed the living middle or nexus of all history and meaning. In this regard, too, modern Christians have to shed their rationalistic cast of mind and force themselves to understand that *spiritual* indicates a fuller, richer reality than the eye can perceive. In this full, spiritual sense, the Christian tradition claims that the entire old economy of animal sacrifices for cleansing and accessing God has been replaced by a new spiritual economy of the Word, the one Christ reality.[150] The Eucharist draws us into the reality of the "liturgy taking place in heaven,"[151] and this participation in Christ's sacrifice shapes the Christian being as com-

[148]Benedict XVI, *Der Geist der Liturgie*, p. 40.
[149]Ibid., p. 41.
[150]Daniélou, *Bible and the Liturgy*, p. 148.
[151]John Chrysostom, quoted in ibid., p. 137.

munal and sacrificial. Not merely the individual Christian's being and reasoning but the congregation "becomes 'logos-shaped,' like the *Logos* and
thus truly the body of Christ."[152]

The Eucharist is central to ecclesiology because it recalls us to the
christological foundation of reality itself. The Eucharist is "the efficacious
memorial of the Passion, the Resurrection and the Ascension," and calls us
to "participation in the sacrifice and the banquet of heaven."[153] Would not
the recovery of a sacramental mindset and of the Eucharist as participation
in Christ revolutionize modern worship? In the early church, the Eucharist was celebrated much more frequently, sometimes even daily.[154] What
would happen if once again we viewed the church as the place where
Christ makes himself present, and the Eucharist as the entrance into the
heavenly sanctuary, into the eschatological reality of communion with
God, the presence of angels and all the saints? How impoverished have
our traditions become when we treat the Lord's Table as if Christ were
observing from afar rather than presiding at the feast. Even if we concen-
trate only on the Western church, the tradition has insisted on the real
presence of Christ at the Table from Augustine all the way to Calvin and
Luther. As we have seen in the previous section, there are no metaphysical
reasons to prevent us from admitting Christ's presence through the elements; what really counts, however, is the renewal of our modern, stunted
theological imagination. However we might construe full presence, we
have to affirm with Augustine that at the eucharistic table, "we eat and
drink to the extent of participation in the Spirit, staying in the Lord's body
as members, and being energized by his Spirit."[155] Somehow, mysteriously,
as we drink and chew, we "eat in the heart" and our spirit is fed, in a
"spiritual" way by him who died for the life of the world. Too often we
abandon the central importance of the Eucharist as the encounter with
God that shapes us in the Christ image, turning it into a mere memorial
or pity party for Christ's death and our own sin. Confession of sin and appreciation for Christ's sacrifice are, of course, important elements in the

---

[152]Benedict XVI, *Der Geist der Liturgie*, p. 149.
[153]Daniélou, *Bible and the Liturgy*, p. 141.
[154]Augustine notes that "the sacrament of this reality, that is, of the unity of Christ's body and
blood, is placed on the Lord's table and received from the Lord's table—in some places every
day, in others at fixed intervals of time" (Augustine, *Homilies on the Gospel of John*, p. 463).
[155]Ibid., p. 475.

Christian life, but the Eucharist is much more than that: it is participation in the Christ event (passion, resurrection and ascension) and thus in the divine sacrifice by which we ourselves are shaped cruciformly.

The Eucharist is also the foretaste of the heavenly banquet with Christ, a sacrament of union with God and one another, and therefore "the source of spiritual joy."[156] In the Eucharist the Holy Spirit, who already indwells us as individual Christians, allows us to partake of Christ's flesh and body in a spiritual way that feeds the soul and energizes our community as the unified body of Christ.[157] I do not want to give the impression that the Eucharist can replace the individual Christian's dialogue with God in prayer, or to gainsay the importance of the preached Word. But I do want to emphasize the participatory, sacramental nature of the Eucharist that has strengthened the church from its apostolic beginnings. The apostle Paul tells us that the breaking of bread and drinking of wine is *koinonia*, that is, intimate communion with Christ. Because the incarnated and risen Christ becomes present to us at the eucharistic table, the early church drew on this presence of God for its engagement with culture. I will discuss the christological and ecclesial roots of incarnational humanism more fully in our final segment of this chapter. For now, we should acknowledge the importance of the Lord's Table as a special place within the church where we draw life from the Spirit of Christ. We should be able to exclaim with Augustine: "Oh sacrament of piety, O sign of unity, O bond of charity! The one who wants to live has somewhere to live, has something to live on. Let him approach, let him believe, let him belong to the body so as to be given life."[158]

THE SACRAMENT OF THE WORD

Christ becomes present not only in the Eucharist but also in the breaking of the bread of the Word of God. Bonhoeffer captures the sacramental nature of the sermon when he refers to preaching as the *sacramentum verbi*, the sacrament of the Word.[159] Bonhoeffer follows Luther's lead, who

---

[156]Daniélou, *Bible and the Liturgy*, p. 141.
[157]Augustine, "Homily 27," in *Homilies on the Gospel of John*, pp. 469-70.
[158]Augustine, "Homily 26," in ibid., p. 461.
[159]Dietrich Bonhoeffer, *Dietrich Bonhoeffer Werke*, vol. 14, *Illegale Theologenausbildung: Finkenwalde 1935-1937*, ed. Otto Dudzus and Jürgen Henkys in collaboration with Sabine Bobert-Stützel (Gütersloh: Gütersloher Verlag, 1996), p. 507. Hereafter all references to *Dietrich Bonhoeffer Werke* will use the abbreviation *DBW*.

taught that the proclamation of the word is the presencing of Christ.[160] The Orthodox tradition also grants the sacramental character of preaching and renounces "the false dichotomy between Word and sacrament."[161] Alexander Schmemann claims that "the proclamation of the Word is a sacramental act par excellence because it is a transforming act. It transforms the human words of the Gospel into the Word of God and the manifestation of the Kingdom. And it transforms the man who hears the Word into a receptacle of the Word and a temple of the Spirit."[162] All too often, however, modern evangelical Christianity does maintain a false dichotomy between Word and sacrament, which has proven detrimental to preaching. Too many sermons in evangelical churches are motivational speeches or moralistic, even legalistic exhortations that have lost any sacramental value. The sermon is no longer a proclaiming and making present of Christ by the power of the Spirit, but has become a vehicle for the preacher's own agenda and concerns.

Dietrich Bonhoeffer, once again, grasped this connection with characteristic clarity. The church is Christ existing as community, present in this church-community as Word and sacrament.[163] Bonhoeffer argues that the main question we must ask about the sacraments is not *how* Christ becomes present. The incarnation itself is the proof that Christ's very character, his very mode of being, is sacramental as the presence of God's transcendence through material means. Christ's "being sacrament is his being humiliated in the present."[164] The real question is not how but *"who* is the Christ who is present in the sacrament?" It is the incarnate God-man. The incarnation is God's gracious offering of himself to us in the human form we know, and this presencing continues to take place in the church through the bread and wine, as well as through the human address in the sermon. Once we understand that the church is all about Christ's becoming present as the incarnate, crucified and risen Lord through all channels of grace, the distinction between word and sacrament falls away: "What is the dis-

---

[160]Hans-Martin Barth, *Die Theologie Martin Luthers: Eine kritische Würdigung*, (Gütersloh: Gütersloher Verlag, 2009), p. 362; Luther says that Christ *is* in the baptism, in the Eucharist, and the oral Word, i.e., the sermon. See Luther, *Das Magnifikat*, p. 177.

[161]Schmemann, *Life of the World*, p. 33.

[162]Ibid.

[163]Bonhoeffer, *DBWE*, 12:323.

[164]Ibid., 12:322.

tinction between the Christ who is present *in* and *as* sacrament and the Christ who is present *in* and *as* Word? None."[165] The proclamation of the word is an encounter with the living Word.

Martin Luther summarizes the purpose of the sermon with the Latin phrase *nihil nisi Christus praedicandus*—nothing but Christ is to be preached.[166] Just as participation in the Eucharist conforms us to Christ, so the sermon is meant to form Christ in us. Luther vividly describes what God works through the preacher's human words: "I preach the gospel of Christ and with the corporeal voice I take Christ into your heart, so that he forms himself in you."[167] If a sermon does not proclaim the incarnate, crucified and risen Christ, and does not take the listener up into communion with the divine through making Christ present, then even an excellently crafted speech remains a mere lecture or entertainment. Evangelical Christians have to recover the sense that Christ *is* the living Word of God that should be present in preaching.[168] For Bonhoeffer, at least, the sermon is "the form of the present Christ to whom we are committed, whom we are to follow. If Christ is not wholly present in the sermon, the church breaks down."[169]

The Catholic Christian might respond that this is a uniquely Protestant problem that results from putting all the eggs of presence into the one basket of the sermon. Perhaps so, but one could equally argue that Catholics have neglected the sermon too much. The real issue, however, is that too many evangelical sermons have no sacramental character whatsoever. I can only reiterate that this paucity stems from a lack of christological reflection and consequently a shallow ecclesiology. The church is not a religious society, but rather partakes in Christ's incarnation of a new humanity; it is the place that calls the world to its true identity: "The church is nothing but a piece of the new humanity in which Christ has truly taken shape. . . . The church is the new human being [*der neue Mensch*] who has

---

[165] Ibid.

[166] *D. Martin Luthers Werke. Kritische Gesamtausgabe* (Weimarer Ausgabe) (Weimar: Verlag Hermann Böhlaus Nachfolger, 1883), 16:113; quoted in Barth, *Die Theologie Martin Luthers*, p. 362.

[167] WA 19:489, quoted in Barth, *Die Theologie Martin Luthers*. I have deliberately translated this awkwardly to keep the German idea of formation or *bilden:* "dass du ihn [Christus] in dich bildest."

[168] Bonhoeffer, *DBWE*, 12:317.

[169] Ibid., 12:318.

been incarnated, judged, and brought to new life in Christ."[170] Because the church is the new humanity,[171] it is sustained by preaching that makes the incarnate Word present. Bonhoeffer argues that, in a sense, the sermon is an incarnation of Christ: "The sermon derives from the incarnation of Jesus Christ and is determined through the Incarnation of Jesus Christ. It does not originate in any general truth or experiences. The word of the sermon is the incarnate Christ himself. The incarnate Christ is God." And therefore the sermon too is "God *as* human being, and Christ *as* Word. As Word he walks among his community."[172] The purpose of the sermon is not to lecture, not to inform, not to teach. The sermon is a sacrament, a gateway to God's presence through words. This presence is Christ's presence. And just as in Christ, in the incarnate eternal Word, all of humanity is taken up, so the sermon is directed toward the new humanity and toward community. The divine Word that is present through the human words of the preacher is the Word that carries all of humanity, its sin and its punishment. In Bonhoeffer's words, "The burden-carrying Christ, is the Word of the sermon."[173] For this reason a sermon should never lay a guilt trip on the listener but invite the weary and heavy laden to find rest. Clearly, the presence of Christ is also confrontation with sin, but ultimately the Word holds out reconciliation, offering new humanity and new creation. And because Christ the Word inaugurated and sustains the new humanity, his very being is oriented toward community. Bonhoeffer adds another vital insight for contemporary preaching: if a pastor desires deep community in his church, this goal cannot be achieved by small group meetings or other relation-building exercises. The primary way to community is to preach Christ. For Christ the divine Word creates and fosters community. Preach Christ, and community *will* happen. Christ, says Bonhoeffer, comes as the preached Word to the community, to accept and carry community. The preacher has to recognize the Word's own proper

---

[170]Ibid., 6:84.
[171]Bonhoeffer emphasizes the new humanity in Christ in many places through his works, a theme that continued through *Finkenwalde* into the *Ethics*. See, for example, Bonhoeffer, *DBW*, 14:435: "The space (*Raum*) of Christ in the world is taken by the *Church. She is the presence of Christ (der gegenwärtige Christus)*. The church has to be understood as as person, as a human being, not as multiplicity, but as unity . . . the church is the single [or 'only'] new human being."
[172]"Schreitet durch seine Gemeinde" (ibid., 14:502-03).
[173]Ibid., 14:504.

motion, and the preacher has to allow Christ himself to "climb out of the Bible to take shape."[174] Bonhoeffer is not naive, of course, and knows that a sermon requires a deliberate act of interpretation based on careful exegesis. But this interpretation should be guided by the preacher's and the community's desire to encounter the living God.

In preaching, the congregation encounters the cosmic, world creating Logos in whom all things co-inhere and in whom the church subsists. Just as the Eucharist unifies the body of believers and impresses on them the cruciform being of Jesus, so the sacrament of the Word draws the listener into Christlikeness. Since the same Christ is present in both sacraments, preaching and the Eucharist, both conform the believer to Christlikeness.[175] In other words, the ancient theme of deification resurfaces also in preaching: God became man so that man could become like God. Luther puts it this way: "You see that God pours himself and Christ, his beloved son, into us and, conversely, draws ourselves into him, so that he becomes completely human and we completely divinized."[176] The sacraments of the Word and of the Eucharist are thus both means for the believers' divinization and means for their becoming most fully human in the image of the God-man. The church, to put it in Bonhoeffer's terms, "is the place where the taking shape of Jesus Christ is proclaimed and where it happens. Christian ethics stand in service to this proclamation and event."[177] Bonhoeffer thus closes the circle of church life and public life. Christ has died to redeem creation and restore humanity to its intended glory. This restoration transcends any ethnic, racial or national boundaries and is aimed at all human beings. Yet it is in the body of Christ, the church, that the new humanity has its beginning and from which it grows outward. Thus "the church now bears the form that in

---

[174]Ibid.

[175]We know from lecture notes about Bonhoeffer's insistence on "the same measure of reality [that is of Christ's real presence] in preaching and the Lord's Supper" (*Predigt und Abendmahl*, in ibid., 14:508).

[176]The German terms are *vermenschet* and *vergottet* respectively. Martin Luther, *D. Martin Luthers Werke* (WA), 20:229, 30. Cited as a 1526 sermon in Kurt E. Marquart, "Luther and Theosis" *Concordia Theological Quarterly* 64, no. 3 (July 2000): 182-206, 185. Marquart also notes that there is quite a bit more of theosis language in Luther than one might assume based on the language usually cited from his theology of the cross. Marquart finds this little surprising, since "'Deification' is part of the church's traditional vocabulary, while that profound opposition, 'theology of the cross' versus 'theology of glory' is Luther's own coinage" (ibid., p. 187).

[177]Bonhoeffer, *DBWE*, 6:102.

truth is meant for all people. The image according to which it is being formed is the image of humanity."[178] The shape of this new humanity, however, its being, is cruciform. By participating in the Christ event of incarnation, cross and resurrection, the Christian's being is shaped in accordance with Christ's love for others, his humility and compassion. Defining Christian discipleship as cruciform humanity gives the Christian faith its concrete contours. For Christians, experiencing transcendence is not a religious relation to God, to a "highest, most powerful, most good being—that is not real transcendence—but our relation to God is a new life in 'being-there-for others,' through participation in the being of Jesus. The transcendent is not the infinite, unattainable tasks, but the neighbor within reach in any given situation. God in human form!"[179] Bonhoeffer has here articulated the very heartbeat and pulse of incarnational humanism. Just as Christ is the center of reality in the form of the new humanity desired by God, so the church is the center of every society that wishes to become more truly human. While the church is not the world, whenever the church is most focused on Christ and truly reflects the new humanity in Christ, it is of most service to society. Thus the sacraments of the Word and of the Eucharist remind us that Christianity is inherently a humanism, indeed an incarnational humanism.

Since the exegesis of Scripture is directly related to preaching as well as to the life of the individual Christian, we must briefly address this topic here. Once again, the basic christological principle, as articulated by Bonhoeffer, represents best the Christian tradition on the issue of interpretation: all of reality, all history and reason are oriented ultimately toward Christ, but without diminishing penultimate realities. Christ is "the center of human existence, of history, and of nature," and as this center Christ is "the new creation."[180] Christ is therefore also the unifying and transforming center of Jewish religious and national history as presented in the Old Testament and interpreted by the first Christians in the New Testament. When we keep in mind that Christ is the center of reality and not just of Christianity or the church, then biblical interpretation corresponds to reality to the extent that it is christological. Christianity, after all, is not a

---

[178]Ibid., 6:97.
[179]Bonhoeffer, *DBWE*, 8:501.
[180]Ibid., 12:327.

religion of the book. The text as such is not the living Word of God but only its sacrament, that through which God becomes present.[181] The Christian tradition, from the fathers onward, has argued that the two Testaments truly reflect one will of God as expressed in Christ. Therefore, the Bible requires theological interpretation or what Henri de Lubac has called "spiritual understanding."[182] Lubac argues that this is what early Christian theologians meant by allegorical exegesis. Lubac, however, prefers the term *spiritual interpretation* because we have come to define allegory as a nonliteral, even artificial, way of creating meaning that is imposed on the biblical text when the literal meaning does not fit a Christian's predetermined theological agenda. Lubac contests this notion. For, if "the present reality of the savior" is the unifying spirit of the Old and New Testament Scripture, then spiritual meaning is not "some tacked-on embroidery; it lies within the very texture of the fabric."[183] Thus, when the church fathers practiced spiritual interpretation, they did not abandon the historical narrative of Scripture, but claimed that the Scriptures have a sacramental quality through which Christ makes himself present. They thought that this view was faithful to the apostle Paul's hermeneutical clue that when reading the "old covenant" after turning to Christ, the "veil" covering its christological import is lifted. The church father Augustine, for example, carefully expresses the ongoing importance of the Old Testament and its harmony with the New:

> It is not the Old Testament that is taken away with Christ, but the veil over it. What is dark and hidden without Christ is understood, and as it were uncovered, through Christ. [Paul] does not say that the law or the Old Testament will be taken away. So it is not that they are taken away . . . but rather the cover that hides the good things there has been taken away.[184]

Theological interpretation means that the Scriptures are to be read ac-

---

[181]Congar, *Meaning of Tradition*, p. 102.
[182]Henri de Lubac, *Scripture in the Tradition*, trans. Luke O'Neill, Milestones in Catholic Theology (New York: Crossroad, 2000), p. 3.
[183]Ibid., p. 11.
[184]Augustine, *On Christian Belief*, ed. Boniface Ramsey, trans. Edmund Hill, Works of St. Augustine: A Translation for the 21st Century (New York: New City Press, 1991), p. 123. Because such reading depends on faith, Augustine also declaims a scholarly prerogative of interpretation and argues that anyone who draws from Scripture "in a spirit of devout respect" will find renewal and restoration of his soul (ibid., p. 127).

cording to the *sensus Christi* toward which they and God's providential ordering of history tend.

Spiritual interpretation is not, however, irrational or beyond verification. Indeed, modern assessments of patristic exegesis as arbitrary allegorizing are themselves anachronistic insofar as they fail to take account of the hermeneutic framework for ancient literary criticism. Before the rise of the modern historical consciousness, exegesis took place within a different metaphysical framework that embedded textual references in a meaningful spiritual world. The true difference between patristic and modern exegetes of Scripture lies not so much in contrasting methods as in divergent worldviews: "A culture which can conceive of the material universe as interpenetrated by another reality, which is transcendent and spiritual, will read the reference of scripture in those terms. That is far more significant for the differences between ancient and modern exegesis than any supposed 'method.'"[185] It was on the basis of this commonly accepted link between history, text and higher metaphysical realities that early Christian exegesis developed a sacramental view of language on the basis of the incarnation. Conforming to the pattern of the incarnation, the text of Scripture was a divine accommodation to human means of comprehension. This scaramental view of the text could trust the words to express God's self-revelation accurately, while equally acknowledging the limits of human language to do so.[186] Equally consonant with ancient literary practices was the fathers' assumption of a unifying transcendent reality "behind" the text. Similar to ancient rhetorical views on the connection between content and style, Christ provided the overall and unifying content of the Old Testament texts, or what Christian exegetes call "the mind of the text."[187] In short, given their cultural horizon, patristic spiritual exegesis of the Scriptures made perfect sense, and it was only normal that the

---

[185]Frances Young, *Biblical Exegesis and the Formation of Christian Culture* (Cambridge: Cambridge University Press, 2007), p. 139. Young goes on to show that the ancient world also operated on a different view of history, in which historical accounts were composed and read for moral instruction. Both allegory and typology are means to conduct such ethical criticism; wherefore the modern contrast between Alexandrian allegorizing and supposedly more historical Antiochene typologizing of Scripture is misleading. A better option is to say that Antiochene exegesis paid greater heed to the narrative coherence of the text, but both approaches assumed a greater, christological unity and meaning behind the text (ibid., pp. 181-83).

[186]Young, *Biblical Exegesis*, p. 160.

[187]Ibid., p. 129.

fathers' categories for scriptural reasoning were aesthetic rather than purely denotative or tied to a modern notion of historicity.

In trying to recover the spirit of premodern exegesis, Hans Urs von Balthasar has offered the notion of *Gestalt* as a helpful image for biblical interpretation. He argues that once Christ is accepted as the culmination of God's self-communication and the center of the Scriptures, one can discern an organic development of God's dealing with Israel and humanity that finds its completion in Christ. For those with "eyes enlightened by the light of faith," who are familiar with Christ, His form becomes the discernable whole to whom each part of the text is related and by whom everything is meaningfully integrated into a whole.[188] Balthasar's christological approach by no means excludes multiple interpretations. While he considers the scriptural canon closed, because Christ constitutes the highest point of God's self-revelation, the content of this revelation remains open to ever deeper understanding or varying understanding depending on our historical horizon.[189] This openness, however, cannot be boundless, because the same *Gestalt* that unifies the Scriptures also takes shape in the believer and the church.[190] The Scriptures themselves are part of God's basic incarnational *modus operandi*, the happy exchange, of making himself present among human beings so that they can become like God.[191]

This argument will hardly convince anyone who is not already a Christian, but, as hermeneutics rightly teaches, all human knowing proceeds in this circular fashion, moving from greater premise to the detail and back in a progressive spiral. It is never a question of avoiding this dynamic but of employing it rightly for increasing and perfecting our knowledge of a subject matter.[192] Within christological exegesis, historical-critical tools are highly useful. They become useless, however, or even destructive, when the form of Christ is not recognized as the whole that lends meaning to each individual part of Scripture. Spiritual interpretation does not oppose but employs tools of historical criticism, as long as they are in the service of Christ. Lubac sums up this relation as follows:

---

[188]Hans Urs von Balthasar, *Schau der Gestalt*, vol. 1 of *Herrlichkeit eine theologische Aesthetik* (Einsiedeln: Johannes Verlag, 1961), p. 530.
[189]Ibid.
[190]Ibid., p. 538.
[191]Ibid., p. 581.
[192]Martin Heidegger, *Sein und Zeit*, vol. 2 of GA (Tübingen: Max Niemeyer Verlag, 1993), §32, 153.

Spiritual understanding . . . does not disturb the scientific efforts of the
exegete, nor can it be replaced by such efforts. The true science of Scriptures, in the ancient sense of the expression, does not depend *wholly* on
science in the modern precise sense, even though it may derive much benefit from it. It is not separable from the sight through which Christ is recognized. Just as it is closely related to faith, it is also related to humility, the
purity of heart, the perfection of life.[193]

Spiritual exegesis, like the sacraments we discussed earlier, requires
participation in the divine. This in no way disparages scientific exegesis
or human effort. They play an important role, as they always have, in
God's work of salvation, but in terms of exegesis they can only lead to
better historical and textual knowledge. For example, we require a profound understanding of Old Testament in order to understand the New,
and surely modern scholarship has in many ways surpassed patristic exegesis in this area. But it then still remains "to recapture the Old Testament by an inverse movement and to reread it in the light of the New as
given to us by faith," and thus to lead it to the evangelical meaning of its
christological middle.[194]

The current term for spiritual interpretation is *theological interpretation*, though there are, as always, many differing views on what exactly
this term means.[195] Dietrich Bonhoeffer may serve again as a model for
what theological interpretation should mean, namely, a christological
hermeneutic.[196] Bonhoeffer's exegesis of the biblical text depends on his

---

[193]Lubac, *Scripture in the Tradition*, p. 153.
[194]Ibid., p. 155.
[195]For an overview of this issue, see Daniel J. Treier, *Introducing Theological Interpretation of
Scripture: Recovering a Christian Practice* (Grand Rapids: Baker Academic, 2008), pp. 22ff.,
and also Stephen E. Fowl, *Theological Interpretation of Scripture* (Eugene, Ore.: Cascade
Books, 2009).
[196]Modern evangelical theology increasingly advocates theological exegesis. If one takes, for
example, Kevin Vanhoozer's introduction to the recent *Dictionary for the Theological Interpretation of the Bible* as paradigmatic (ed. Kevin J. Vanhoozer, Craig G. Bartholomew, Daniel J.
Treier and N. T. Wright [Grand Rapids: Baker Academic, 2005]), this broadly evangelical
concern meshes with Bonhoeffer's understanding of the Scriptures rather well. Vanhoozer
writes that "we believe that the time is ripe for a resource that combines an interest in the
academic study of the Bible with a passionate commitment to making this scholarship of use
to the church" (ibid., p. 19). At the same time, theological interpretation does not want to
impose "a theological system or confessional grid onto the biblical text" (ibid.) (an openness
which Bonhoeffer also advocates, albeit always within a christological grid), but while appreciating historical critical exegesis, it also recognizes the hermeneutical necessity of the
interpreter's confessional involvement: "If exegesis without presuppositions is impossible, and

christological hermeneutics as defined by his incarnational Christology and ecclesiology. The basic goal of exegesis as the making present (*Vergegenwärtigung*) of Christ is defined by this framework.

We now have to deal with the most basic hermeneutical question this exegetical practice inevitably raises. Bonhoeffer himself was very well aware of this question that continues to excite heated debate between biblical scholars and theologians even today. This question concerns the legitimacy of an external criterion for textual interpretation. Traditional historical-critical exegesis rejects any such extrinsic christological or spiritual interpretive principle as a subjective illusion and shackle to interpretive freedom. For example, John Barton, in his review of historical-critical approaches, asserts that the basic underlying motivation of historical criticism is "to free the text to speak." Any other motivation goes against the critic's heroic stand against the shackles of tradition. For Barton, confessional exegesis attempts to seek "a place of refuge within safe 'interpretive communities' of faith," a cowardly retreat for those "who do not wish to be challenged by the biblical text, despite the honor they claim to give it."[197]

Philosophical hermeneutics has long exposed the fraudulency of presuppositionless exegesis, and hence the impossibility of "freeing the text to speak." One is compelled to ask, Speak of what? Is not, in fact, the presupposition of neutral, traditionless and purely inductive exegesis an invitation to exactly the kind of arbitrary readings Barton would like to avoid? Is not Hans-Georg Gadamer's basic insight correct that those who assert

---

if some of these presuppositions concern the nature and activity of God, then it would appear to go without saying that biblical interpretation is always/already theological. . . . Theological interpreters want to know, on the basis of Scripture and in light of contemporary concerns, what *we* should say and think about God" (ibid., pp. 21-22). Finally, another similarity to Bonhoeffer's exegesis is that "evangelical" theological interpretation links interpretation to the church's witness "through its language and life" (ibid., p. 22).

[197]John Barton, "Historical-Critical Approaches," in *The Cambridge Companion to Biblical Interpretation*, ed. John Barton, Cambridge Companions to Religion (Cambridge: Cambridge University Press, 2003), pp. 17-18. When Barton came to realize that historical criticism falsely pretends to be a neutral approach, he suggested renaming the discipline "biblical criticism," thus recognizing it as simply a literary operation concerned solely with making sense of the text's meaning, independent of its supposed references to an actual reality. As Michael Legaspi has argued, however, Barton's suggestion remains firmly within the pretensions to timeless meaning divorced from social references, and thus, in the context of biblical interpretation, equally firmly within a paradigm that reads the text as an academic Bible rather than Scripture—the book of the church. Michael C. Legaspi, *The Death of Scripture and the Rise of Biblical Studies* (Oxford and New York: Oxford University Press, 2010), p. 167.

radical freedom from tradition merely follow some tradition unconsciously and are therefore the true subjectivists?[198] Paul Ricoeur has argued that the kind of disinterested structuralist interpretation suggested by Barton is blind to a fundamental truth of human communication: "Discourse consists of the fact that someone says something to someone about *something*. 'About something' is the inalienable referential function of discourse."[199] For Christians this referent is Christ; thus, Luther's much ridiculed christological interpretive criterion "whatever promotes Christ" (*was Christum treibet*) gains renewed respectability in light of hermeneutic philosophy.[200] In the biblical text, God and the salvation of humanity through Christ are either directly or in some implied manner the subject matter of the text, a subject matter that necessarily narrows the context to a specific external referent that the text unfolds for us.

Hermeneutics, in other words, legitimates Bonhoeffer's christological reading of the biblical text, because hermeneutics recognizes the need for an integrative framework for interpretation. For Christians, the Christ event of incarnation, death and resurrection is the key to their understanding of who God is. Acknowledging this hermeneutic framework is not merely an issue of faith but an issue of intellectual integrity. If our knowledge is indeed always mediated through tradition and requires personal integration, then all human inquiry is a kind of faith seeking understanding. Again, "It is never a question," as Martin Heidegger once provocatively put it, "of avoiding the hermeneutic circle, but to enter it in the right way."[201] Gadamer clarifies Heidegger's statement by explaining that every human inquiry is motivated by questions, and these questions always originate in a tradition or worldview in which we already participate. Given

---

[198]Gadamer, *TM*, pp. 282-83, 299.

[199]Ricoeur, *Figuring the Sacred*, p. 220.

[200]This christological hermeneutic in no way requires the neglect of detailed and conscientious historical criticism, but makes this method subservient to the conviction that an objective reality, Christ, is mediated through the text. Francis Watson, for example, argues on this basis for "an *intratextual realism* which would understand the biblical text as referring beyond itself to extra-textual theological reality, while at the same time regarding that reality as accessible to us only in textual form, in principle, and not only in practice. . . . It is necessary to speak of the text as *mediating* the reality of Jesus, rather than *constructing* it" (*Text, Church, and World: Biblical Interpretation in Theological Perspective* [Grand Rapids: Eerdmans, 1994], pp. 224-25).

[201]Martin Heidegger, *Sein und Zeit*, vol. 2 of *GA* (Tübingen: Max Niemeyer Verlag, 1993), §32, 153.

the hermeneutical dynamic of human understanding, for the Christian to profess Christ as the center of scriptural exegesis is not a cowardly sheltering from radically open inquiry but rather acting with utter intellectual integrity in conformity with the workings of textual interpretation. Ingolf Dalferth has made this hermeneutical point clearly: "Jesus Christ," he writes, "constitutes the compass and destination of evangelical interpretation of the scriptures because he is also the compass and destination for the Christian interpretation of the self, of the world, and of God."[202]

Because all questions emerge from our human existence as an interpretation of the world, and are therefore never neutral or disengaged, the question concerning the center of biblical exegesis is already theological and emerges from a Christian experience of the world, and that is as it should be.[203] After all, the Christian faith rests not in the Scriptures but in an encounter with the One to whom they witness: "Faith is not directed to the scriptures but to Jesus Christ, and by attuning itself to this center of the scriptures, [faith] does not focus on a handed down 'once upon a time' or 'back then' but on the effective now and today of God's presence."[204]

Bonhoeffer practiced theological exegesis with his seminarians, and he published his Genesis commentary *Creation and Fall* deliberately as a sample of this theological approach to Scripture. Trained in the historical-critical method, he saw its great importance for biblical interpretation, especially since he insisted that spiritual exegesis does not impose subjective opinions on the text but follows its inner christological dynamic.[205] Bonhoeffer lamented, however, that historical critics often overlook the fact that biblical exegesis is not an individualistic exercise of the maverick scholar but belongs to the church as the body of Christ. Interpreting the Psalms, for example, requires an understanding of their historicity as expression of oriental piety because observing these human elements carefully is to follow the incarnational descent of God into the world.[206] Yet within a Christian reading, the

---

[202]Ingolf U. Dalferth, "Die Mitte ist außen. Anmerkungeg zum Wirklichkeitsbezug evangelischer Schriftauslegung," in *Jesus Christus als die Mitte der Schrift. Studien zur Hermeneutik des Evangeliums*, ed. Christof Landmesser, Hans-Joachim Eckstein and Hermann Lichtenberger (Berlin: Walter de Gruyter, 1997), p. 181.

[203]Ibid., p. 181.

[204]Ibid., pp. 193-94.

[205]The internal context that reveals Christ, he argued, is not a matter of *pneuma* but of *Logos*. All *logoi*, every passage, relates to Christ as truth (Bonhoeffer, *DBW*, 14:330).

[206]Ibid., 14:374-75.

results of the historical-critical method must be interpreted in light of Christ's reality; the piety and impieties of the Psalms have to be related to the coming of Christ as the fulfillment of God's covenant with Israel.[207] Because of Christ's real presence within the Christian community, the Psalms will have meaning. Neither they nor any other scriptural text has to be made artificially relevant. Any such attempt has already betrayed the Christ reality and does not approach the Bible christologically.

The incarnation, death and resurrection of Christ are the objective messages of the Bible for the Christian community (because it is founded on this reality), and current cultural realities have to justify themselves before Christ's presence—not the other way around.[208] The claim that the Bible has to be made relevant for the present already misunderstands that the Christ who is present in the Scriptures determines what reality actually is: "The criterion for actual reality is external to it, lies in the future, in the scripture and Christ's Word testified therein."[209] This also means, however, that the Christian interpreter does not know the meaning of a text for a concrete situation in advance. Such meaning, Bonhoeffer argues, is given by the Holy Spirit, and his work should not be usurped by the interpreter or preacher. It is wrong to read the Scriptures, including the New Testament, as templates for current actions or as a manual of wisdom. For the Scriptures proclaim the incarnation, death and resurrection of Christ, and the concrete issues besetting a congregation have to be transposed into the universal situation of humanity before God.[210] When in the exegesis of the Word Christ himself becomes present, "the one who formerly considered himself important as man, national socialist, or Jew, becomes someone who now considers himself important only as sinner, called one, or forgiven one."[211] In this way exegesis can reveal the true situation of a human being before God. Because of this Christ reality, the texts, when interpreted carefully, will become relevant all by themselves because they will speak out against abuses of humanity. Relying on this living presence and the power of Christ in the reading of his word will save us from trying to establish eternal norms on the basis of our own cultural

---

[207]Ibid., 14:376.
[208]Ibid., 14:403.
[209]Ibid., 14:405.
[210]Ibid., 14:411-12.
[211]Ibid., 14:410.

situation that might become unworkable for posterity.[212] For the same reason, the typical move of liberal theologians to reduce Christianity to its essence, stripped of mythological trappings is itself a misguided attempt to isolate the incarnation from history.[213] Bonhoeffer reminds us with these words that biblical exegesis is essentially "translation," that is, the making present in *our* particular circumstances of the one Christ reality.

Never should the sermon try to express some generally valid principles of living. For example, we do not find eternal norms and laws in the New Testament, but rather the call to obedient discipleship (*Nachfolge*), which only makes sense within the hearer's relationship to Christ.[214] Bonhoeffer realized that even this pressing call to obedient discipleship cannot itself become a template or principle, but has to be mediated through difficult decisions in the context of each person's life. His own decision to aid in Hitler's assassination is the most trenchant example of an interpretive Christian faith because it took Bonhoeffer to the extremes of committing a violent sin for the good of humanity. In the crucible of such circumstances, Bonhoeffer came to see that his former stance in *The Cost of Discipleship* of resolute obedience had to be qualified by a more hermeneutical view. Obedience to God's command to be fully human and to live out Christ's incarnation, death and resurrection is an intrinsically interpretive exercise of constant discernment. Earlier, Bonhoeffer admits, "I had thought, I myself could learn to have faith by trying to live something like a saintly life. I suppose I wrote [*The Cost of*] *Discipleship* as the end of that path."[215] Bonhoeffer continued to stand by this book, but now embraced a more interpretive view of the Christian life: "I discovered later, and am still discovering right up to this moment, that it is only by living completely in this world that one learns to have faith."[216] Bonhoeffer realized that the Christian life requires a profound this-worldliness, characterized by one's awareness of the Christ reality, expressed in disciplining oneself in light of his death and resurrection.

Bonhoeffer's christological hermeneutic grounded in a conception of faith as participation in the incarnation also provides an important link to his "re-

---

[212]Ibid., 14:415.
[213]Bonhoeffer, *DBWE*, 8:329.
[214]Ibid., 14:415.
[215]Ibid., 8:486.
[216]Ibid.

ligionless Christianity." As Eberhard Bethge has already argued, Bonhoeffer's religionless interpretation of the Bible is itself subordinate to his actual christological question, Who is Christ for us today? Consequently, Bonhoeffer is not offering a new hermeneutic, but "as he did in *Act and Being*, and in his Christology lectures, is asking about the person of Christ and how this person determines and meets us today."[217] Bonhoeffer concludes,

> By this-worldliness I mean living unreservedly in life's duties, problems, successes and failures, experiences and perplexities. In so doing we throw ourselves completely into the arms of God, taking seriously, not our own sufferings, but those of God in the world-watching with Christ in Gethsemane. That, I think, is faith; that is *metanoia* and that is how one becomes a human being and a Christian. How can success make us arrogant and failure lead us astray when we share in God's sufferings through a life of this kind?[218]

How could we be arrogant indeed? There is no room here for Christian triumphalism, but plenty of room for God's real presence in the world. Based on this presence in each believer and the strengthening imparted by the sacrament of the Word, Bonhoeffer suggests that the Christian life is an interpretive walk of faith in light of the Christ reality by which our new humanity takes shape. It is by continually living out "who Christ is for us today" that one becomes truly "a human being, a Christian."[219]

EUCHARISTIC HUMANISM: THE LINK BETWEEN CHURCH AND WORLD

Incarnational humanism is above all eucharistic humanism insofar as it views culture and humanity in light of the Christ's redemptive work. Christ, we emphasize with the church fathers, did not die to save individual souls from hell but to restore humanity to its full glory. Most modern evangelical Christians are by now critical of individualism and recognize the necessarily social nature of selfhood and belief. The church and its sacrament, rooted in the triune God, proclaim and effect the unity of the community that is Christ's body. Indeed, the church is the quintes-

[217]Eberhard Bethge, *Dietrich Bonhoeffer: Theologe—Christ—Zeitgenosse. Eine Biographie*, ed. Victoria J. Barnett, trans. Eric Mosbacher et al., rev. ed. (Gütersloh: Gütersloher Verlag, 2004), p. 969.
[218]Bonhoeffer, *DBWE*, 8:370.
[219]Ibid., 8:486.

sential expression of a common humanity, a communion whose rootedness in a personal, communal God founds a humanity that avoids either individualism or collectivism. Christ "is not only the bearer of an eternal message which he repeats to the astonished ears of successive individuals, but also he in whom humanity finds an unexpected answer to the problems of its organic unity."[220] Celebrating the Eucharist reminds us every time of this unity. This participation was believed to root the believer ontologically in the new humanity that Christ inaugurated and nourished as the church. Augustine, celebrating this unity, could say, "Clad as we are in Christ, we are all, together with our head in Christ. . . . It is therefore obvious that we belong to Christ and that being his members and his body we are, with our head, one human being."[221]

Indeed, the church is the very place in which the new humanity is born and nourished in the sacramental encounters of God's presence. Taking part in God's presence in the church through the sacraments and the preached word constitutes the church and shapes its members as the new humanity in Christ. The purpose of the Christian faith is humanity's communion with God as represented in the Eucharist. Therefore Christology, as Bonhoeffer realizes in following Luther, "here becomes truly Eucharistic Christology, i.e., Christology which thinks in accordance with the Eucharist."[222] In the Eucharist the church remembers not merely the atonement, but recalls its true vocation as the new humanity and is strengthened for this task. Via participation in Christ the character of the new humanity's originator, "being-for-another," is imparted to the new creatures in Christ:

> The being with each other of the church community and its members through Christ already entails their being for each other. Christ is the measure and standard of our conduct . . . and our actions are the actions of members of the body of Christ, that is, they possess the power of the love of Christ, through which each may and ought to become a Christ to the other.[223]

---

[220]Henri de Lubac, *Catholicism: Christ and the Common Destiny of Man*, trans. Lancelot C. Sheppard and Elizabeth Englund (San Francisco: Ignatius Press, 1988), p. 356. Lubac cites Canon Masure.

[221]Augustine, quoted in J. M. R. Tillard, *Flesh of the Church, Flesh of Christ*, trans. Madeleine Beaumont (Collegeville, Minn.: Liturgical Press, 2001), p. 55.

[222]Bonhoeffer, *DBWE*, 12:303.

[223]Bonhoeffer, *DBW*, vol. 1, *Sanctorum Communio: Eine dogmatische Untersuching zur Soziologie der Kirche*, ed. Joachim von Soosten (Munich: Christian Kaiser Verlag, 1986), p. 120; cf.

Bonhoeffer makes the important point that participation in Christ defines our humanity as a sociality and a solidarity of charity. Being a Christian means existing as beings in sociality founded on the love that flows from the triune communion of Father, Son and Spirit.

Yet at the same time, this ontological participation in Christ does not separate the church from the rest of humanity but rather establishes an intrinsic connection with it. At the very heart of the church, in the encounter with the incarnate Word of God through preaching and the Eucharist, we participate in Christ's humanity, which is ontologically structured as *being for others*. Without lapsing into a Neo-Platonic or Romantic panentheism, we can nonetheless affirm that eucharistic participation in the incarnation links us, in Christ, to all of humanity. In his summary of the Eastern and Western traditions on eucharistic theology, J. M. R. Tillard explains that in the church as the new humanity, God's

> salvation through *agapē* and communion is realized in this: in his historical work, the Son assumed everything in the human condition (by taking it on himself); at the same time, since the resurrection, he continues to live in his members the human tragedy in all its truth and all its reality. What this means is not a "continued incarnation" but the fulfillment (*teleiōsis*) of the work of the incarnation in the power of the Spirit.[224]

With these words, Tillard aptly summarizes the important patristic insight that the desire for unity and peace that should be filled through participation in Christ also extends to all of humanity "outside" the church at the very center of the church.

Joseph Ratzinger, standing in the same tradition, can therefore recover in the eucharistic theology of the church fathers a vision not only for the unity of the church but also for the nations: "The being of Jesus Christ and his message brought a new dynamic into humanity, the transitional dynamic from the ruptured being of many individuals into the unity of Jesus Christ, into the unity of God. And the church is basically nothing else but this dynamic, this setting into motion of humanity toward the unity of God."[225]

Dietrich Bonhoeffer, *DBWE*, vol. 1, *Sanctorum Communio: A Theological Study of the Sociology of the Church*, ed. Clifford J. Green, trans. Reinhard Krauss and Nancy Lukens (Minneapolis: Fortress, 1998), p. 182.
[224]Tillard, *Flesh of the Church*, p. 54.
[225]Benedict XVI, *Die Einheit der Nationen* (Salzburg, Munich: Pustet, 2005), p. 35.

And because in Christ this unity concerns not just Christians but the entire human race, the Communion Table emphasizes the common brotherhood of all human beings: while we feed on the body of Christ at the Communion Table, writes Ratzinger, we are at the same time participating in *human* intercommunication. For the church, the Eucharist represents the "melting of individuals into one new human being."[226] Augustine thought that Christ deliberately chose bread and wine to make himself present in the Eucharist, for in both elements one new thing is created from many ingredients.[227] While this unity refers first of all to the people of God, God's desire for unity applies to the entire human race. The Table, according to Ratzinger, is not a closed circle but the incarnated invitation of God to all human beings to participate in God's eternal wedding feast: "The ecclesial net of communion is in a way the concrete form of the same net God lowered into the world to catch humanity for himself and to guide it to the land of eternity."[228]

We can learn from this christological humanism of the church fathers and from Bonhoeffer that on account of the central importance of the incarnation, the sacrament and the liturgy form an intrinsic link between church and world. There are not two radically separate cities, the city of God and the city of man—rather, the new humanity and unity with God presented in Augustine's *civitas Dei*, this "city of living stones," is connected through the incarnation ontologically with all of humanity. By virtue of this link the Christian is called to labor for the good of humanity, to suffer with humanity in its common problems, not, however, to create heaven on earth but to proclaim the new humanity in Christ.[229] "The bride of Christ never ceases to be aware of that total humanity whose destiny she carries in her womb."[230]

---

[226]Ibid.

[227]Augustine, *Homilies on the Gospel of John*, p. 464.

[228]Benedict XVI, *Die Einheit Der Nationen*, p. 37.

[229]Tillard writes, "In virtue of its sacrificial nature, the church cannot be [simply] a servant of the world. It is the priest of the love of God in and for the world. Because the Spirit of the Lord Jesus the priest of God dwells in it, it offers 'in Christ,' its life, the sacrifice of humanity to the glory of the Father" (*Flesh of the Church*, p. 133). I read this to mean that the church guards its difference from the world; it does not just become a social club with love for everyone, a gathering of all humanity in a social sense, creating heaven on earth. In fact, Tillard states at the end of this paragraph that the church is a living eschatological mystery of union, not, however, an ethical program for global unity and peace (ibid., p. 133).

[230]Henri de Lubac, *The Splendor of the Church*, trans. Michael Mason (San Francisco: Ignatius Press, 1999), p. 184. Lubac cites Paul Claudel.

This connection between the individual Christian, the church as the body of Christ and humanity as a whole is crucial for incarnational humanism because its resulting ontology of solidarity should nullify any fear that Christianity is sectarian and elitist.[231] This link between church and world becomes particularly clear in Bonhoeffer's emphasis on the church as an embodiment of the new humanity in terms of the *imago Dei*. The Trinity, argues Bonhoeffer in *The Cost of Discipleship*, indwells each believer and therefore constitutes a new human self as part of the collective new humanity:

> It is indeed the holy Trinity who dwells within Christians, who permeates them and changes them into the very image of the triune God. The incarnate, the crucified, and transfigured Christ takes on form in individuals because they are members of his body, the church. The church bears the incarnate, crucified, and risen form of Christ. Within the body of Christ, we have become "like Christ."[232]

Bonhoeffer clearly describes the being of the Christian as participation in Christ: "We are *in him* in the power of his having become human."[233] Christ does not rest, says Bonhoeffer, until he has brought to completion in us the entire form of Christ (*Christusgestalt*), of the one who "has become human, crucified, and glorified." It is "in the becoming human of Christ" that the "entire humanity regains the dignity of being made in the image of God [*Gottesebenbildlichkeit*]."[234]

The true revelation of the *imago Dei* in Christ now requires the Christian to view all of humanity in the light of Christ, thus personalizing and intensifying the ethical imperative already contained in the Old Testament notion of *imago Dei:*

> Whoever from now on attacks the least of the people attacks Christ, who

---

[231]Bonhoeffer argues that Christ's nature is to be in the middle of things, of our existence, of history and of nature, with, obviously, important implications for church-state relations in *DBWE*, 12:307. Especially in the sections titled "positive Christology," he emphasizes the importance of keeping the mystery of the incarnation constantly before us as Christians in order to ensure a proper ecclesial understanding of the new humanity (ibid., 12:340-48).

[232]Dietrich Bonhoeffer, *DBWE*, vol. 4, *Discipleship*, ed. Geffrey B. Kelly and John D. Godsey, trans. Barbara Green and Reinhard Krauss (Minneapolis: Fortress Press, 2002), p. 287 (Dietrich Bonhoeffer, *DBW*, vol. 4, *Nachfolge*, ed. Martin Kuske and Ilda Tödt [Munich: Christian Kaiser Verlag, 2002], p. 303).

[233]Bonhoeffer, *DBW*, 4:273. The language of indwelling by God is routinely used by Bonhoeffer.

[234]Ibid., 4:301; cf. Bonhoeffer, *DBWE*, 4:285. Translation slightly altered to emphasize the "becoming human." The English translation has "incarnation" and "incarnate one."

took on human form and who in himself has restored the image of God for all who bear a human countenance. In community with the incarnate one, we are once again given our true humanity. With it, we are delivered from the isolation caused by sin, and at the same time restored to the whole of humanity. Inasmuch as we participate in Christ, the incarnate one, we also have a part in all of humanity, which is borne by him. Since we know ourselves to be accepted and borne within the humanity of Jesus, our new humanity now also consists in bearing the troubles and the sins of all others. The incarnate one transforms his disciples into brothers and sisters of all human beings. . . . The form of the incarnate one transforms the church community into the body of Christ upon which all of humanity's sin and trouble fall, and by which alone these troubles and sins are borne.[235]

The church thus clearly has a public responsibility, but it is not primarily to be political but rather to be a sacrament of God's new humanity in the world. The church truly is the center of reality, of true life and humanity, toward which every true human desire tends and in which true life should be offered to all who ask. As Bonhoeffer puts it, since Christ is the recapitulation of humanity and the head of the church, his body, all of humanity is "drawn proleptically as it were, into the church," and the church represents the world's reconciliation.[236] Following Christ himself, the church serves the world as representative of the new humanity. Bonhoeffer explains:

The concept of vicarious representative action [*Stellvertretung*] defines this dual relationship most clearly. The Christian community stands in the place in which the whole world should stand. In this respect it serves the world as vicarious representative; it is there for the world's sake. On the other hand, the place where the church-community stands is the place where the world fulfills its own destiny; the church-community is the "new creation," the "new creature," the goal of God's ways on earth.[237]

The church thus follows in the footsteps of its founder and head, "who was the Christ precisely in being there completely for the world and not for

---

[235]Bonhoeffer, *DBWE*, 4:285 (= Bonhoeffer, *DBW*, 4:301).
[236]Ibid., 6:98.
[237]Ibid., 6:404-5.

himself."[238] Rather than fighting or leaving the world, the church exists for the sake of the world.[239]

Even though Bonhoeffer carefully observes differences between world and church, between reason and revelation, he rightly emphasizes that the link between church and world is the common new humanity for which Christ died.[240] While not embodying this new humanity in any perfect way, the church points the world to the true human being, to Christ:

> We can only speak of the formation of the world in such a way that we address humanity in the light of its true form, which belongs to it, which it has already received, but which it has not grasped and accepted, namely, the form of Jesus Christ that is its own. . . . [W]here one talks about the formation of the world, only the form of Jesus Christ is meant.[241]

We may have to adjust our often rationalist and nonparticipatory views of the Eucharist and, perhaps, even of the Christian faith, but I hope to have made a plausible case for the intrinsic connection between Christology, ecclesiology and public life for the good of humanity. If the incarnation is the inauguration of a new humanity, God's offer of abundant life to everyone created in his image, then Christianity is indeed intrinsically a public faith that addresses every area of human existence.[242]

CONCLUSION

If you have come to the end of this book with a greater appreciation for the enormous theological, philosophical and social implications of the incarnation, my goal has been accomplished. In mixing with the material world, in

[238]Ibid., 6:405.
[239]Ibid., 6:63.
[240]That the church is not the world but exists for the world is the basic thrust of Bonhoeffer's ecclesiology in all of his works. In a sermon meditation from December 1940, Bonhoeffer writes: "Thirdly, if the death of the shepherd benefits the sheep, this does not deny that Jesus died for all human beings, but it points out that only the sheep of his fold will participate in the fruit of this dying. The focus is not on the world but solely on the merciful deed (*Wohltat*) of Jesus for his community (*Gemeinde*). The good shepherd and the community belong together" (Dietrich Bonhoeffer, *DBW*, vol. 15, *Illegale Theologenausbildung: Sammelvikariate, 1937-1940*, edited by Dirk Schulz [Gütersloh: Christian Kaiser Verlag, 1998], p. 561).
[241]Bonhoeffer, *DBWE*, 6:98.
[242]For a more detailed description of how professional activities, especially those of higher education, are integrated by this incarnational theology, see Norman Klassen and Jens Zimmermann, *The Passionate Intellect: Incarnational Humanism and the Future of University Education* (Grand Rapids: Baker Academic, 2006).

becoming flesh, God announces the redemption of creation and the unity of reality in him. The Christian knows that he or she participates in the personal Logos of the universe, in whom all reality has its being and by whom the cosmos is being redeemed. Because of the incarnation, God's transcendence, justice and otherness are intrinsically linked to the material world and brought to bear on life through human agency. The Eastern Church has often shown a more profound understanding of the sacramental reality inaugurated by Christ, but in principle the same view holds for both East and West: the sacramental element of the church's liturgy, including the Eucharist, points toward the unity of all reality in God.[243] The liturgy, and indeed the entire church service, are meant to provide an entrance into the new world begun by Christ's work and to make present "the One in whom all things are at their *end*, and all things are at their *beginning*."[244] The new creation inaugurated by the incarnation is above all the call to a new humanity Christians are to live out in the world. This vocation does not separate them from the world but sends them into it without reserve, not to create the kingdom of God but to humanize the world.

This incarnational humanism represents a vital part of the Western cultural heritage. Together with its secular offspring, liberal humanism, it has decisively shaped Western culture and its institutions. We need to recover this cultural ethos for a number of reasons. First, based on the belief that Christ is the incarnate Logos and new humanity, incarnational humanism unites church and culture based on a common humanity without blurring the church-world boundary. We find this unifying concept of humanity at the heart of the church, in the Eucharist. At this communal participation in Christ, the more we are drawn into him, the more we are pointed toward others, for this is the very pattern of Christ's work. As Pope Benedict put it in his apostolic letter on the Eucharist, "Our communities, when they celebrate the Eucharist, must become ever more conscious that the sacrifice of Christ is for all, and that the Eucharist thus compels all who believe in him to become 'bread that is broken' for others, and to the world."[245] Equally important is the Christian idea of the Logos,

---

[243]Ibid., pp. 218-19.

[244]Schmemann, *Life of the World*, p. 27.

[245]Benedict XVI, *Sacramentum Caritatis*, Papal Archives, last accessed April 14, 2011, www .vatican.va/holy_father/benedict_xvi/apost_exhortations/documents/hf_ben-xvi_ exh_20070222_sacramentum-caritatis_en.html.

which buries once and for all any possible enmity between reason and faith, for he through whom all things were created is also he who has given himself for the life of the world. While the world of things is different from the world of human relations, and scientific rationality differs to some degree from personal knowledge, both go back "to the same source in God's transcendent rationality, and they are both brought together in the incarnation of God's Word in Jesus Christ, for they are upheld and sustained by Him."[246] The relative autonomy of science and philosophy is in no way impeded by the fact that their ultimate foundation is Christ himself. This means that for the Christian the deepest mystery of the incarnation and the passions it evokes are intrinsically connected to all of our professional and everyday lives because we are to live in service to the humanity for whom Christ gave himself.

Second, because of this unity of a common reason and humanity in Christ, incarnational humanism stresses an interpretive Christian life in the common public sphere. Living out the incarnation is to follow Christ's own incarnational pattern in two ways. If the incarnation indeed determines reality, truth can be known only hermeneutically. As God made himself known to us through the material world in human form and language, so also all human knowledge both of things divine and human is a matter of interpretation. Even if we believe with Augustine that knowing the truth is participation in the divine light, we can also affirm with Gadamer that our human consciousness is historically effected. An incarnational model of knowledge thus acknowledges with hermeneutic philosophy the mediation of truth through tradition and language. For incarnational humanism, knowledge and indeed self-knowledge are tradition dependent; thus, Christians in particular are required to develop a historical consciousness and shape their self-understanding based on God's work within the Christian tradition. Reading the church fathers, and studying the creeds and other great theological works of the Christian tradition along with the Scriptures, are not a luxury but a hermeneutic necessity.

Third, incarnational humanism expects the Christian to apply hermeneutic reasoning in freedom and responsibility. As I said earlier, adoption

---

[246]T. F. Torrance, *God and Rationality* (London: Oxford University Press, 1971), p. 164.

by grace sets a person radically free from the slavery of sin, but becoming like God also means being shaped in Christ's character of "being-for-another." As Bonhoeffer puts it, participation in Christ sets us free for "realistic responsibility," that is, for realizing in an ongoing effort of discernment, both within the church and the public realm, the world's reconciliation to God in Christ.

A fourth reason for recovering incarnational humanism is the realization that it is not diluted Christian doctrine, but only the fullest Christology that brings out the humanistic nature of Christianity by reflecting God's passion for humanity in the sense of "suffering," empathic endurance. It is crucial, however, to begin with a high Christology that comprises the entire Christ event of incarnation, crucifixion and resurrection. None of these, as Bonhoeffer taught us, can exist without the others, and only if we keep all three elements together does our Christianity correspond to ultimate reality and therefore result in a proper attitude to the penultimate reality of this world. Neither a mere affirmation of creation, nor the single emphasis on suffering and *kenosis*, nor an overrealized eschatology do justice to orthodox Christology. We have seen how postmodern theologies often emphasize merely one aspect of the incarnation—the renewal of both church and culture, however, depends on Christians' recovery of a full Christology, for their understanding of the church stands or fall with it. Incarnational humanism emphasizes doctrine, but it also emphasizes the sacramental life of the church, especially (but by no means exclusively) the Lord's Table. The Eucharist serves as a reminder that our lives are to be sacraments, that all of our activities are a suffering with humanity in Christ: "by sharing the sacrifice of the Cross, the Christian partakes of Christ's self-giving love and is equipped and committed to live this same charity in all his thoughts and deeds."[247] Incarnational humanism thus addresses the public fear that religious dogma must be avoided at all cost in order to assure peaceful coexistence with those of other convictions. This fear has it backward. The more Christians understand their humanistic heritage correctly, the more they deepen their understanding of the mysteries of the faith and enrich their christological doctrine, the more they will contribute to the good of society. Evangelical

---

[247]Benedict XVI, *Sacramentum Caritatis*, p. 82.

theology may well have a long road to travel in recovering an ontology of participation in general and a deeper understanding of the Lord's Table in particular, but nothing less than a genuine religious renewal of Western culture is at stake.

Our current intellectual and cultural crisis demands a sense of solidarity and common humanity that is *intrinsic* to the Christian faith, and we should recover the early church's spirit of passionate engagement with culture based on the mystery of the incarnation. As Jacques Maritain puts it, we need a *new* Christian humanism, an

> integral or theocentric humanism in full autonomy of action. The guiding star in the supernatural world of this new humanism, the idea at its heart—not that it will claim to bring [the supernatural] down to earth, as if it were a product of this world and could be built up in this world as a basis for men's common life, but that it may be refracted through the whole sinful and earthly substance of socio-temporal things, and oriented to them on high—will not be that of God's *holy empire* over all things, but rather that of the *holy freedom* of the creature whom grace unites to God. Of this freedom liberalism is but a caricature, and even at times a mockery.[248]

This freedom to animate culture by "thinking, living, acting politically in a Christian way," has nothing at all to do with Christian triumphalism or fundamentalist theocratic leanings. Rather, it means to work within the political means of a common secular society, to promote and, if need be, suffer for the ideal of humanity embodied in the incarnational sacrifice whose participatory commemoration remains at the heart of the church.

Dante understood this well when he described his pilgrim's encounter with the Trinity:

> That circle—which begotten so, appeared
> In You as light reflected—when my eyes
> had watched it with attention for some time,
> within itself and colored like itself,
> to me seemed painted with our effigy,
> so that my sight was set on it completely.
> As the geometer intently seeks
> to square the circle, but he cannot reach,

---

[248]Maritain, *True Humanism*, p. 156.

through thought on thought, the principle he needs,
so I searched that strange sight: I wished to see
the way in which our human effigy
suited the circle and found place in it—
and my own wings were far too weak for that.
But then my mind was struck by light that flashed
and, with this light, received what it had asked.
Here force failed my high fantasy: but my desire and will were
    moved already—
Like a wheel revolving uniformly—by
the Love that moves the sun and the other stars.[249]

To see God is to be moved by the love whose goal is to reconcile the world to himself. Incarnational humanism is based on this divine love, but it also always remembers that God died to make us fully human. The social imagination of the early Christians was filled with this vision of Christ as the first true human being, to whose image we are molded by the work of God's Spirit, a Spirit that does not deny our own efforts. How gripped early Christians were by this vision is evident from the parting words of Ignatius of Antioch, who, before his fellow Christians, defends his unbridled enthusiasm for impending martyrdom with words that, while sounding strange to modern ears, contain the very vision through which Christians did not escape but shaped culture. Ignatius understood that Christianity is above all the path to true humanity: "Suffer me to obtain pure light: when I have arrived there, I shall indeed be a human being."[250] This is the heart of incarnational humanism, into which we are drawn every time the Lord invites us to the eucharistic table.

---

[249]Dante Alighieri, *The Divine Comedy of Dante Alighieri: Paradiso*, with an introduction by Allen Mandelbaum (New York: Bantam Classics, 1986), p. 303.

[250]Ignatius of Antioch, *Epistle of St. Ignatius to the Romans*, in in *The Ante-Nicene Fathers*, vol. 1, *The Apostolic Fathers, Justin Martyr, Irenaeus*, ed. Alexander Roberts and James Donaldson, rev. by A. Cleveland Coxe (Peabody, Mass.: Hendrickson, 2004), p. 76. The translators weaken this powerful statement of incarnational humanism by adding the words "a man *of God*." But the Greek simply has εκει παραγενομενος ανθcωπος εσομαι. Ignatius understands that in going to Christ, he will become most fully human, a human being indeed! See Erik Peterson, "Was ist der Mensch" in *Theologische Traktate*, Ausgewählte Schriften (Würzburg: Echter, 1994), p. 138. After I found this citation, I discovered the same point with the same reference made by John Behr in *The Mystery of Christ: Life in Death* (Crestwood, N.Y.: St. Vladimir's Seminary Press, 2006), p. 108.

BIBLIOGRAPHY

◆

Anderson, Perry. *The Origins of Postmodernity*. London: Verso, 1998.

Aquinas, Thomas. *Shorter Summa: St. Thomas Aquinas's Own Concise Version of His Summa Theologica*. Translated by Cyril Vollert. Manchester, N.H.: Sophia Institute Press, 2002.

———. *Summa Contra Gentiles. Book Four: Salvation*. Translated by Charles J. O'Neil. Notre Dame, Ind.: University of Notre Dame Press, 1975.

———. *Summa Theologiae*. 61 vols. Edited by Thomas Gilby. Translated by Jordan Aumann. Cambridge: Cambridge University Press, 2006.

Armstrong, A. H., and R. A. Markus. *Christian Faith and Greek Philosophy*. London: Darton, Longman & Todd, 1960.

Armstrong, John M. "After the Ascent: Plato on Becoming Like God." *Oxford Studies in Ancient Philosophy* 26 (summer 2004): 171-83.

Ascham, Roger. "The Schoolmaster." In *English Humanism: Wyatt to Cowley*, 179-84. Edited by Joanna Martindale. London: Croom Helm, 1985.

Athanasius. *On the Incarnation: The Treatise De Incarnatione Verbi Dei*. Edited and translated by a religious of C.S.M.V. Crestwood, N.Y.: St. Vladimir's Seminary Press, 1996.

Augustine. *Concerning the City of God against the Pagans*. 1972. Translated by Henry Bettenson. New York: Penguin Books, 1984.

———. *The Confessions*. Translated by Maria Boulding. New York: New City Press, 1997.

———. *De Doctrina Christiana: Teaching Christianity*. Edited by John E. Rotelle. Translated by Edmund Hill. Works of Saint Augustine: A Translation for the 21st Century. New York: New City Press, 1990.

———. *Essential Sermons*. Edited by Daniel Doyle. Translated by Edmund Hill. Works of Saint Augustine: A Translation for the 21st Century. New York: New City Press, 2007.

———. *Homilies on the Gospel of John 1-40*. Edited by Allan D. Fitzgerald. Translated by Edmund Hill. Works of Saint Augustine: A Translation for the 21st Century. New York: New City Press, 1990.

————. *Instructing Beginners in Faith.* Edited by Raymond F. Canning and Boniface Ramsey. Augustine Series. New York: New City Press, 2006.

————. *On Christian Belief.* Edited by Boniface Ramsey. Translated by Edmund Hill. Works of Saint Augustine: A Translation for the 21st Century. New York: New City Press, 1991.

————. *Psalms 99–120.* Edited by Boniface Ramsey. Translated by Maria Boulding. Vol. 5 of *Exposition of the Psalms.* Works of Saint Augustine: A Translation for the 21st Century. New York: New City Press, 1990.

————. *The Trinity.* Edited by John E. Rotelle. Translated by Edmund Hill. Works of Saint Augustine: A Translation for the 21st Century. New York: New City Press, 1990.

Baird, Marie L. "Whose *Kenosis?* An Analysis of Levinas, Derrida, and Vattimo on God's Self-Emptying and the Secularization of the West." *Heythrop Journal* 48, no. 3 (2007): 423–37.

Balthasar, Hans Urs Von. *Herrlichkeit: eine theologische Ästhetik.* Vol. 3.1, *Im Raum der Metaphysik. Teil II: Neuzeit.* Einsiedeln: Johannes-Verlag, 1965.

————. "Krisis: Gott Begegnen in der heutigen Welt." In *Spiritus Creator.* Skizzen zur Theologie 3. Einsiedeln: Johannes Verlag, 1967.

————. *Love Alone Is Credible.* Translated by D.C. Schindler. San Francisco: Ignatius Press, 2004.

————. "Person und Geschlect." In *Homo Creatus Est.* Skizzen zur Theologie 5. Einsiedeln: Johannes Verlag, 1986.

————. *Prüfet Alles das Gute Behaltet: Ein Gespräch mit Angelo Scola.* Edited by Angelo Schola. Translated by Maria Shrady. Einsiedeln: Johannes Verlag, 2001.

————. *Schau der Gestalt.* Vol. 1 of *Herrlichkeit eine theologische Aesthetik.* Einsiedeln: Johannes Verlag, 1961.

Barr, James. *Fundamentalism.* Norwich: SCM Press, 1981.

Barrett, C. K. *A Commentary on the Epistle to the Romans.* Harper's New Testament Commentaries. New York: Harper & Row, 1957.

————. *Paul: An Introduction to His Thought.* Louisville, Ky.: Westminster/John Knox Press, 1994.

Barth, Hans-Martin. *Die Theologie Martin Luthers: Eine kritische Würdigung.* Gütersloh: Gütersloher Verlag, 2009.

Barth, Karl. *Humanismus.* Theologische Studien. Zollikon-Zürich: Evangelishcer Verlag, 1950.

————. *Der Römerbrief.* 1922. Reprint, Zurich: TVZ Verlag, 1999.

Barton, John. "Historical-critical approaches." In *The Cambridge Companion to Biblical Interpretation.* Edited by John Barton. Cambridge Companions to Religion. Cambridge: Cambridge University Press, 2003.

Basil the Great. *On the Holy Spirit*. Translated by David Anderson. Popular Patristic Series. Crestwood, N.Y.: St. Vladimir's Seminary Press, 1980.

———. *On the Human Condition*. Translated by Nonna Verna Harrison. Popular Patristics Series. Crestwood, N.Y.: St. Vladimir's Seminary Press, 2005.

———. *On Social Justice*. Translated by C. Paul Schroeder. Popular Patristics Series. Crestwood, N.Y.: St. Vladimir's Seminary Press, 2009.

Battista Guarino. "De Ordine Docendi et Studendi." In *Vittorino da Feltre and Other Humanist Educators*, 185-90. Edited by William Harrison Woodward. Renaissance Society of America Reprint Texts. Toronto: University of Toronto Press, 1996.

Bauckham, Richard. *God Crucified: Monotheism and Christology in the New Testament*. Didsbury Lectures. Grand Rapids: Eerdmans, 1999.

Behr, John. *The Mystery of Christ: Life in Death*. Crestwood, N.Y.: St. Vladimir's Seminary Press, 2006.

Beiser, Fredrick C. *German Idealism: The Struggle against Subjectivism, 1781-1801*. Cambridge, Mass.: Harvard University Press, 2002.

Benedict XVI. *Christianity and the Crisis of Cultures*. Translated by Brian McNeil. San Francisco: Ignatius Press, 2006.

———. *Die Einheit der Nationen: Eine Vision der Kirchenväter*. Salzburg, Munich: Pustet, 2005.

———. "Faith, Reason and the University: Memories and Reflections." September 12, 2006. Papal Archives. www.vatican.va/holy_father/benedict_xvi/ speeches/2006/september/documents/hf_ben-xvi_spe_20060912_univer sity-regensburg_en.html.

———. *Der Geist der Liturgie: Eine Einführung*. 6th ed. Freiburg im Breisgau: Herder, 2002.

———. *Gott ist uns nah: Eucharistie: Mitte des Lebens*. 2nd ed. Edited by Stephan Otto Horn and Vinzenz Pfnür. Augsburg: Sankt Ulrich Verlag, 2005.

———. *Licht der Welt: Der Papst, die Kirche und die Zeichen der Zeit: Ein Gespräch mit Peter Seewald*. 2nd ed. Freiburg im Breisgau: Herder, 2010.

———. *Sacramentum Caritatis*. www.vatican.va/holy_father/benedict_xvi/apost _exhortations/documents/hf_ben-xvi_exh_20070222_sacramentum-carit atis_en.html.

Benedict XVI, and Marcello Pera. *Without Roots: Europe, Relativism, Christianity, Islam*. Translated by Michael F. Moore. New York: Basic Books, 2006.

Benson, Iain T. "Towards a (Re)Definition of the 'Secular.'" *UBC Law Review* 33, no. 3 (2000): 519-49.

Berlin, Isaiah. *Three Critics of the Enlightenment: Vico, Hamann, Herder*. London: Pimlico, 2000.

Bernstein, Richard J. "Heidegger on Humanism." In *Philosophical Profiles: Essays in a Pragmatic Mode*, 197-220. Cambridge: Polity Press, 1986.

Bethge, Eberhard. *Dietrich Bonhoeffer: Theologe—Christ—Zeitgenosse. Eine Biographie.* Edited by Victoria J. Barnett. Translated by Eric Mosbacher et al. Rev. ed. Gütersloh: Gütersloher Verlag, 2004.

Bloechl, Jeffrey. "Christianity and Possibility." In *After God: Richard Kearney and the Religious Turn in Continental Philosophy*, 127-38. Edited by John Panteleimon Manoussakis. Perspectives in Continental Philosophy. New York: Fordham University Press, 2006.

Blond, Philip. Review of *Belief*, by Gianna Vattimo. *Modern Theology* 18, no. 2 (2002): 277-85.

Boersma, Hans. *Heavenly Participation: The Weaving of a Sacramental Tapestry.* Grand Rapids: Eerdmans, 2011.

Bonhoeffer, Dietrich. *Dietrich Bonhoeffer Werke.* Vol. 1, *Sanctorum Communio: Eine dogmatische Untersuching zur Soziologie der Kirche.* Edited by Joachim von Soosten. Munich: Christian Kaiser Verlag, 1986.

———. *Dietrich Bonhoeffer Werke.* Vol. 4, *Nachfolge.* Edited by Martin Kuske and Ilse Tödt. Munich: Christian Kaiser Verlag, 2002.

———. *Dietrich Bonhoeffer Werke.* Vol. 14, *Illegale Theologenausbildung: Finkenwalde 1935-1937.* Edited by Otto Dudzus and Jürgen Henkys in collaboration with Sabine Bobert-Stützel et al. Gütersloh: Christian Kaiser Verlag, 1996.

———. *Dietrich Bonhoeffer Werke.* Vol. 15, *Illegale Theologenausbildung: Sammelvikariate, 1937-1940.* Edited by Dirk Schulz. Gütersloh: Christian Kaiser Verlag, 1998.

———. *Dietrich Bonhoeffer Werke.* Vol. 16, *Konspiration und Haft, 1940-1945.* Edited by Jørgen Glenthøj, Ulrich Kabitz and Wolf Krötke. Gütersloh: Christian Kaiser Verlag, 1996.

———. *Dietrich Bonhoeffer Works.* Vol. 1, *Sanctorum Communio: A Theological Study of The Sociology of the Church.* Edited by Clifford J. Green. Translated by Reinhard Krauss and Nancy Lukens. Minneapolis: Fortress Press, 1998.

———. *Dietrich Bonhoeffer Works.* Vol. 4, *Discipleship.* Edited by Geffrey B. Kelly and John D. Godsey. Translated by Barbara Green and Reinhard Krauss. Minneapolis: Fortress Press, 2002.

———. *Dietrich Bonhoeffer Works.* Vol. 6, *Ethics.* Edited by Clifford J. Green. Translated by Reinhard Krauss, Charles C. West and Douglas W. Stott. Minneapolis: Fortress Press, 2005.

———. *Dietrich Bonhoeffer Works.* Vol. 8, *Letters and Papers from Prison.* Edited by John W. de Gruchy. Translated by Isabel Best et al. Minneapolis: Fortress Press, 2010.

———. *Dietrich Bonhoeffer Works*. Vol. 12, *Berlin, 1932-1933*. Edited by Larry L. Rasmussen. Translated by Isabel Best, David Higgins and Douglas W. Stott. Minneapolis: Fortress Press, 2009.

Boulnois, Olivier. "Reading Duns Scotus: From History to Philosophy." *Modern Theology* 21, no. 4 (October 2005): 603-8.

Bruni, Leonardo. "Concerning the Study of Literature." In *Vittorino da Feltre and Other Humanist Educators*, 119-34. Edited by William Harrison Woodward. Renaissance Society of America Reprint Texts. Toronto: University of Toronto Press, 1996.

———. "The Study of Literature To Lady Battista Malatesta of Montefeltro." In *Humanist Educational Treatises*, 92-126. Edited and translated by Craig Kallendorf. I Tatti Renaissance Library. Cambridge, Mass.: Harvard University Press, 2002.

Brunner, Emil. *Christianity and Civilization*. Vol. 2, *Second Part: Specific Problems*. Gifford Lectures. New York: Scribner's, 1949.

———. *The Mediator: A Study of the Central Doctrine of the Christian Faith*. Translated by Olive Wyon. Lutterworth Library. Philadelphia: Westminster Press, 1947.

Buck, August. *Humanismus: seine europäische Entwicklung in Dokumenten und Darstellungen*. Freiburg: Karl Alber, 1987.

Bunge, Gabriel. *The Rublev Trinity: The Icon of the Trinity by the Monk-Painter Andrei Rublev*. Translated by Andrew Louth. Crestwood, N.Y.: St. Vladimir's Seminary Press, 2007.

Calvin, John. *Institutes of the Christian Religion*. Vol. 1. Edited by John T. McNeill. Translated by Ford Lewis Battles. Philadelphia: Westminster Press, 1960.

Caputo, John D. *The Weakness of God: A Theology of the Event*. Bloomington: Indiana University Press, 2006.

Carter, Craig. *Rethinking Christ and Culture: A Post-Christendom Perspective*. Grand Rapids: Brazos Press, 2006.

Casanova, José. *Europas Angst vor der Religion*. Edited by Rolf Schieder. Berliner Reden zur Religionspolitik. Berlin: Berlin University Press, 2009.

Cassirer, Ernst. *The Individual and the Cosmos in Renaissance Philosophy*. Translated by Mario Domandi. Chicago: University of Chicago Press, 2010.

Catechism of the Catholic Church. 2nd ed. New York: Doubleday, 1997.

Chadwick, H. Article on Augustine's doctrine of deification. *Revue des Sciences Religieuses* (forthcoming).

———. "Justin Martyr's Defense of Christianity." *Bulletin of the John Rylands Library* 47 (1965): 275-97.

Christensen, Michael J., and Jeffery A. Wittung, eds. *Partakers of the Divine Nature: The History and Development of Deification in the Christian Traditions.* Madison, Wis.: Fairleigh Dickinson University Press, 2007.

Clark, Mary T. *"De Trinitate."* In *The Cambridge Companion to Augustine,* 91-102. Edited by Eleonore Stump and Norman Kretzmann. Cambridge Companions to Philosophy. Cambridge: Cambridge University Press, 2001.

Clark, Maudemarie. *Nietzsche on Truth and Philosophy.* Cambridge: Cambridge University Press, 1990.

Clement of Alexandria. *Exhortation to the Heathen.* In *Ante-Nicene Fathers,* Vol. 2, *Hermas, Tatian, Athenagoras, Theophilus, Clement of Alexandria.* Edited by Alexander Roberts and James Donaldson. Revised by A. Cleveland Coxe. Peabody, Mass.: Hendrickson, 2004.

———. *The Instructor.* In *Ante-Nicene Fathers,* Vol. 2, *Hermas, Tatian, Athenagoras, Theophilus, Clement of Alexandria.* Edited by Alexander Roberts and James Donaldson. Revised by A. Cleveland Coxe. Peabody, Mass.: Hendrickson, 2004.

———. *Stromata, Or Miscellanies.* In *Ante-Nicene Fathers,* Vol. 2, *Hermas, Tatian, Athenagoras, Theophilus, Clement of Alexandria.* Edited by Alexander Roberts and James Donaldson. Revised by A. Cleveland Coxe. Peabody, Mass.: Hendrickson, 2004.

Cochrane, Charles Norris. *Christianity and Classical Culture: A Study of Thought and Action from Augustus to Augustine.* New York: Oxford University Press, 1957.

Cohen, Richard. Introduction to Emmanuel Levinas, *Humanism of the Other.* Translated by Nidra Poller. Urbana: University of Illinois Press, 2003.

Colish, Marcia L. *Stoicism in Classical Latin Literature.* Vol. 1 of *The Stoic Tradition from Antiquity to the Early Middle Ages.* Leiden: Brill, 1985.

Congar, Yves. *Fifty Years of Catholic Theology: Conversations with Yves Congar.* Edited by Bernard Lauret. Translated by John Bowden. Minneapolis: Fortress Press, 1988.

———. *The Meaning of Tradition.* Translated by A. N. Woodrow. San Francisco: Ignatius Press, 2004.

———. *Tradition and Traditions: An Historical and a Theological Essay.* New York: Macmillan, 1966.

Cooper, John M. "Justus Lipsius and the Revival of Stoicism in Late Sixteenth-Century Europe." In *New Essays on the History of Autonomy: A Collection Honoring J. B. Schneewind.* Edited by Natalie Brender and Larry Krasnoff. Cambridge: Cambridge University Press, 2004.

Courtney, William J. "Nominalism and Late Medieval Religion." In *The Pursuit of Holiness in Late Medieval and Renaissance Religion: Papers from the University of Michigan Conference,* 26-58. Edited by Charles Edward

Trinkaus and Heiko A. Oberman. Leiden: Brill, 1974.

———. "Late Medieval Nominalism Revisited: 1972-1982." *Journal of the History of Ideas* 44 no. 1. (January-March 1983): 159-64.

Critchley, Simon. *The Ethics of Deconstruction: Derrida and Levinas.* West Lafayette, Ind.: Purdue University Press, 1999.

Cupitt, Don. "The Christ of Christendom." In *The Myth of God Incarnate*, 133-47. Edited by John Hick. London: SCM Press, 1977.

Cusanus, Nicholas. *Idiota de Mente. The Layman: About Mind.* Translated by Clyde Lee Miller. New York: Abaris, 1979.

———. *Of Learned Ignorance.* Translated by Germain Heron. Rare Masterpieces of Philosophy and Science. Eugene, Ore.: Wipf & Stock, 2007.

Dalferth, Ingolf U. "Die Mitte ist außen. Anmerkungen zum Wirklichkeitsbezug evangelischer Schriftauslegung." In *Jesus Christus als die Mitte der Schrift. Studien zur Hermeneutik des Evangeliums*, 173-98. Edited by Christof Landmesser, Hans-Joachim Eckstein and Hermann Lichtenberger. Berlin: Walter de Gruyter, 1997.

Daniélou, Jean. *The Bible and the Liturgy.* Notre Dame, Ind.: University of Notre Dame Press, 1956.

———. *A History of Early Christian Doctrine Before the Council of Nicaea.* Vol. 2, *Gospel Message and Hellenistic Culture.* Edited and translated by John Austin Baker. London: Darton, Longman & Todd, 1973.

Dante Alighieri. *The Divine Comedy of Dante Alighieri: Paradiso.* With an introduction by Allen Mandelbaum. New York: Bantam Classics, 1986.

Derrida, Jacques. *Adieu to Emmanuel Levinas.* Translated by Pascale-Anne Brault and Michael Naas. Stanford, Calif.: Stanford University Press, 1999.

———. "Epoché and Faith: An Interview with Jacques Derrida." Edited by John D. Caputo, Kevin Hart and Yvonne Sherwood. In *Derrida and Religion: Other Testaments*, 27-52. Edited by Yvonne Sherwood and Kevin Hart. New York: Routledge, 2005.

———. "Jacques Derrida: Deconstruction and the Other." In *States of Mind: Dialogues with Contemporary Thinkers on the European Mind*, 156-76. Edited by Richard Kearney. New York: New York University Press, 1995.

———. *On Cosmopolitanism and Forgiveness.* Thinking in Action. London: Routledge, 2001.

———. *Of Hospitality.* Translated by Anne Dufourmantelle. Cultural Memory in the Present. Stanford: Stanford University Press, 2000.

Dilthey, Wilhelm. *Texte zur Kritik der historischen Vernunft.* Edited by Hans-Ulrich Lessing. Göttingen: Vandenhoeck & Ruprecht, 1983.

Dostoevsky, Fyodor. *Brothers Karamazov.* New York: Bantam, 1981.

Dreyfus, Hubert L., and Paul Rabinow. *Michel Foucault, Beyond Structuralism and Hermeneutics.* 2nd ed. With an afterword by and an interview with Michel Foucault. Chicago: University of Chicago Press, 1983.

Dupré, Louis. *Religion and the Rise of Modern Culture.* Erasmus Institute Books. Notre Dame, Ind.: University of Notre Dame Press, 2008.

Eagleton, Terry. *After Theory.* Art of Mentoring Series. London: Allen Lane, 2003.

————. "Lunging, Flailing, Mispunching." Review of *The God Delusion*, by Richard Dawkins. *London Review of Books* 28, no. 20 (2006): 32-34.

Elshtain, Jean Bethke. *Sovereignty: God, State, and Self.* Gifford Lectures. New York: Basic Books, 2008.

Engberg-Pedersen, Troels. "Stoicism in the Apostle Paul." In *Stoicism: Traditions and Transformation*, 52-75. Edited by Steven K. Strange and Jack Zupko. Cambridge: Cambridge University Press, 2004.

Erasmus, Desiderius. "Enchiridion militis Christiani." In vol. 1 of *Ausgewählte Schriften.* Edited by Werner Welzig. 8 vols. Darmstadt: Wissenschaftliche Buchgellschaft, 1967-1980.

————. "Paraclesis; Or, An Exhortation (1516)." In *The Praise of Folly and Other Writings*, 118-26. Edited and translated by Robert M. Adams. New York: Norton, 1989.

European Union. Preamble to "Treaty Establishing a Constitution for Europe," 9-16. October 29, 2004. http://news.bbc.co.uk/2/shared/bsp/hi/pdfs/09_01_05_constitution.pdf.

Facio, Bartolomeo. *De hominis excellentia ad Nicolaum Quintum.* Bibl. Vatican Cod. Urb. lat. 227.

Fee, Gordon D. *The First Epistle to the Corinthians.* The New International Commentary on the New Testament. Grand Rapids: Eerdmans, 1987.

Ferry, Luc. *Man Made God: The Meaning of Life.* Chicago: University of Chicago Press, 2002.

Ficino, Marsilio. *Platonic Theology: Books I-IV.* Edited by James Hankins and William Roy Bowen. Translated by Michael J. B. Allen and John Warden. I Tatti Renaissance Library. Cambridge, Mass.: Harvard University Press, 2001.

Fink-Eitel, Hinrich. *Foucault: An Introduction.* Philadelphia: Pennbridge Books, 1992.

Finlan, Stephen, and Vladimir Kharlamov, eds. *Theōsis: Deification in Christian Theology.* Princeton Theological Monograph Series. Eugene, Ore.: Pickwick, 2006.

Fish, Stanley Eugene. *The Trouble with Principle.* Cambridge, Mass.: Harvard University Press, 2001.

Flasch, Kurt. *Nikolaus von Kues: Geschichte einer Entwicklung: Vorlesungen zur Ein-führung in seine Philosophie*. Frankfurt am Main: Klostermann, 1998.

Foucault, Michel. *Aesthetics, Method and Epistemology*. Edited by James D. Fau-bion. Translated by Robert Hurley et al. Vol. 2 of *Essential Works of Foucault*. New York: New Press, 1998.

———. "The Ethics of the Concern for Self as a Practice of Freedom." In *Ethics: Subjectivity and Truth, Michel Foucault on Truth, Beauty & Power 1954-1984*, 281-302. Edited by Paul Rabinow. Translated by Robert Hurley et al. Vol. 1 of *Essential Works of Foucault*. New York: New Press, 1997.

———. *History of Madness*. Edited by Jean Khalfa. Translated by Jonathan Mur-phy and Jean Khalfa. London: Routledge, 2006.

———. "Nietzsche, Freud, Marx." In *Aesthetics, Method and Epistemology*, 269-78. Edited by James D. Faubion. Translated by Robert Hurley et al. Vol. 2 of *Essential Works of Foucault*. New York: New Press, 1998.

———. "On the Genealogy of Ethics: An Overview of a Work in Progress." In Hubert L. Dreyfus and Paul Rabinow. *Michel Foucault, Beyond Structuralism and Hermeneutics*, 229-52. 2nd ed. Chicago: University of Chicago Press, 1983.

———. "On the Ways of Writing History." In *Aesthetics, Method and Epistemol-ogy*, 279-96. Edited by James D. Faubion. Translated by Robert Hurley et al. Vol. 2 of *Essential Works of Foucault*. New York: New Press, 1998.

———. *Religion and Culture*. Edited by Jeremy R. Carrette. Manchester Studies in Religion, Culture, and Gender. New York: Routledge, 1999.

Fowl, Stephen E. *Theological Interpretation of Scripture*. Eugene, Ore.: Cascade Books, 2009.

Gadamer, Hans-Georg. *Die Aktualität des Schönen: Kunst als Spiel, Symbol und Fest*. Stuttgart: Reclam, 1977.

———. *Hermeneutik II: Wahrheit und Methode: Ergänzungen, Register*. 1986. Vol. 2 of *Gesammelte Werke*. Tübingen: J. C. B. Mohr, 1993.

———. "Man and Language." In *Philosophical Hermeneutics*, 59-68. Edited and translated by David E. Linge. Berkeley: University of California Press, 1976.

———. "The Nature of Things and the Language of Things." In *Philosophical Hermeneutics*, 69-81. Edited and translated by David E. Linge. Berkeley: Uni-versity of California Press, 1976.

———. *Neuere Philosophie I: Hegel, Husserl, Heidegger*. Vol. 3 of *Gesammelte Werke*. Tübingen: J. C. B. Mohr, 1987.

———. *Philosophical Hermeneutics*. Edited and translated by David E. Linge. Berkeley: University of California Press, 1976.

———. *Truth and Method*. Translated by Joel Weinsheimer and Donald G. Mar-shall. 2nd rev. ed. London: Continuum, 2004.

German Bundestag. Constitution of the Federal Republic of Germany. May 23, 1949, as amended by the Unification Treaty of August 31, 1990. www.bundestag .de/dokumente/rechtsgrundlagen/grundgesetz/gg_00.html.

Gilson, Étienne. *Reason and Revelation in the Middle Ages.* New York: Charles Scribner's, 1938.

———. *The Spirit of Mediaeval Philosophy.* Notre Dame, Ind.: University of Notre Dame Press, 1991.

Giussani, Luigi Giovanni. *Why the Church?* Montreal: McGill-Queen's University Press, 2001.

Gorman, Michael J. *Inhabiting the Cruciform God: Kenosis, Justification, and Theosis in Paul's Narrative Soteriology.* Grand Rapids: Eerdmans, 2009.

Grant, Edward. *God and Reason in the Middle Ages.* Cambridge: Cambridge University Press, 2001.

Grassi, Ernesto. *Heidegger and the Question of Renaissance Humanism: Four Studies.* Binghamton: State University of New York, 1983.

Green, Joel B. *Body, Soul and Human Life: The Nature of Humanity in the Bible.* Studies in Theological Interpretation. Grand Rapids: Baker Academic, 2008.

Gregory of Nyssa. "Against Eunomius, Book 1." In *Gregory of Nyssa: Dogmatic Treatises.* Vol. 5 of *Nicene and Post-Nicene Fathers.* Edited by Philip Schaff and Henry Wace. Translated by William Moore and Henry Austin Wilson. Peabody, Mass.: Hendrickson, 1994.

———. "Answer to Eunomius's Second Book." In *Gregory of Nyssa: Dogmatic Treatises.* Vol. 5 of *Nicene and Post-Nicene Fathers.* Edited by Philip Schaff and Henry Wace. Translated by William Moore and Henry Austin Wilson. Peabody, Mass.: Hendrickson, 1994.

———. *Ascetical Works.* Edited by Roy Joseph Deferrari. Translated by Virginia Woods Callahan. The Fathers of the Church. Washington, D.C.: Catholic University of America Press, 1999.

———. "The Great Catechism." In *Gregory of Nyssa: Dogmatic Treatises.* Vol. 5 of *Nicene and Post-Nicene Fathers.* Edited by Philip Schaff and Henry Wace. Translated by William Moore and Henry Austin Wilson. Peabody, Mass.: Hendrickson, 1994.

———. *Gregory of Nyssa: Dogmatic Treatises.* Vol. 5 of *Nicene and Post-Nicene Fathers.* Second Series. Edited by Philip Schaff and Henry Wace. Translated by William Moore and Henry Austin Wilson. Peabody, Mass.: Hendrickson, 1994.

———. "On the Making of Man." In *Gregory of Nyssa: Dogmatic Treatises.* Vol. 5 of *Nicene and Post-Nicene Fathers.* Edited by Philip Schaff and Henry Wace. Translated by William Moore and Henry Austin Wilson. Peabody, Mass.: Hendrickson, 1994.

————. "On the Soul and Resurrection." In *Gregory of Nyssa: Dogmatic Treatises*. Vol. 5 of *Nicene and Post-Nicene Fathers*. Edited by Philip Schaff and Henry Wace. Translated by William Moore and Henry Austin Wilson. Peabody, Mass.: Hendrickson, 1994.

Guardini, Romano. *Über das Wesen des Kunstwerks*. 2nd ed. Mainz: Matthias Grünewald Verlag, 1949.

Gunton, Colin E. *Act and Being: Towards a Theology of the Divine Attributes*. Grand Rapids: Eerdmans, 2003.

Halliwell, Martin, and Andy Mousley. *Critical Humanism: Humanist/Anti-Humanist Dialogues*. Edinburgh: Edinburgh University Press, 2003.

Hallosten, Gösta. "Theosis in Recent Research: A Renewal of Interest and Need for Clarity." In *Partakers of the Divine Nature: The History and Development of Deification in the Christian Traditions*, 281-93. Edited by Michael J. Christensen and Jeffery A. Wittung. Madison, Wis.: Fairleigh Dickinson University Press, 2007.

Hamerton-Kelley. *Pre-existence, Wisdom, and the Son of Man: A Study of the Idea of pre-Existence in the New Testament*. Cambridge: Cambridge University Press, 1973.

Hankins, James. *Plato in the Italian Renaissance*. 2 vols. Columbia Studies in the Classical Tradition. Leiden: Brill, 1990.

Hardt, Michael, and Antonio Negri. *Empire*. Cambridge, Mass.: Harvard University Press, 2000.

Harink, Douglas, ed. *Paul, Philosophy, and the Theopolitical Vision: Critical Engagements with Agamben, Badiou, Zizek, and Others*. Theopolitical Visions. Eugene, Ore.: Wipf & Stock, 2010.

Harnack, Adolf Von. *What Is Christianity?* Translated by Thomas Bailey Saunders. Minneapolis: Fortress, 1986.

Harris, Sam. *The End of Faith: Religion, Terror, and the Future of Reason*. New York: W. W. Norton, 2005.

Hart, David Bentley. *Atheist Delusions: The Christian Revolution and Its Fashionable Enemies*. New Haven, Conn.: Yale University Press, 2009.

Hebblethwaite, Brian. *The Incarnation: Collected Essays in Christology*. Cambridge: Cambridge University Press, 1987.

Hegel, Georg Wilhelm Friedrich. *Vorlesungen über die Philosophie der Religion*. 2 vols. Frankfurt am Main: Suhrkamp, 2003.

Heidegger, Martin. "The Age of the World Picture." In *The Question Concerning Technology and Other Essays*, 115-54. Translated by William Lovitt. New York: Harper Books, 1977.

————. *Being and Time: A Translation of Sein und Zeit*. 1927. Translated by Joan Stambaugh. Albany: State University of New York Press, 1996.

———. *Einführung in die Metaphysik.* 1935. Vol. 40 of *Gesamtausgabe.* Tübingen: Max Niemeyer Verlag, 1998.

———. *Die Grundprobleme der Phänomenologie.* 1927. Vol. 24 of *Gesamtausgabe.* Edited by Friedrich-Wilhelm von Herrmann. Frankfurt am Main: Klostermann, 2005.

———. *Identität und Differenz.* 1955-57. Vol. 11 of *Gesamtausgabe.* Stuttgart: Klett-Cotta, 2002.

———. *An Introduction to Metaphysics.* 1935. Vol. 40 of *Gesamtausgabe.* Translated by Ralph Manheim. New Haven, Conn.: Yale University Press, 1987.

———. "Letter on Humanism." In *Basic Writings: From Being and Time (1927) to the Task of Thinking (1964).* Edited by David F. Krell. New York: Harper & Row, 1992.

———. *Ontologie. Hermeneutik der Faktizität.* Vol. 63 of *Gesamtausgabe.* Edited by Kate Bröcker-Oltmanns. Frankfurt am Main: Klostermann, 1995.

———. *Poetry, Language, Thought.* Translated by A. Hofstadter. New York: Harper & Row, 1975.

———. *Sein und Zeit.* 1927. Vol. 2 of *Gesamtausgabe.* Tübingen: Max Niemeyer Verlag, 1993.

———. *Unterwegs zur Sprache.* 1950-1959. Vol. 12 of *Gesamtausgabe.* Pfullingen: Neske, 2001.

———. *Vom Wesen der menschlichen Freiheit. Einleitung in die Philosophie.* 1930. Vol. 31 of *Gesamtausgabe.* Edited by H. Tietjen. Frankfurt am Main: Klostermann, 1994.

———. *Wegmarken.* 1967. Vol. 9 of *Gesamtausgabe.* Edited by Friedrich-Wilhelm von Herrmann. Frankfurt am Main: Klostermann, 1996.

———. "What Calls for Thinking?" In *Basic Writings,* 345-67. Edited by David F. Krell. New York: Harper & Row, 1992.

———. *Zur Sache des Denkens.* 1962-64. Vol. 14 of *Gesamtausgabe.* 3rd ed. Tübingen: Max Niemeyer Verlag, 1988.

Hirsi Ali, Ayaan. *Nomad.* Toronto: Knopf Canada, 2010.

Hudson, Nancy J. *Becoming God: The Doctrine of Theosis in Nicholas of Cusa.* Washington, D.C.: Catholic University of America Press, 2007.

Hunsinger, George. *The Eucharist and Ecumenism: Let Us Keep the Feast.* Edited by Iain Torrance. Current Issues in Theology. Cambridge: Cambridge University Press, 2008.

Husserl, Edmund. *Die Krisis der europäischen Wissenschaften und die transzendentale Phänomenologie: Eine Einleitung in die phänomenologische Philosophie.* Edited by Elisabeth Ströker. Hamburg: Meiner, 1996.

Ignatius of Antioch. *Epistle of St. Ignatius to the Romans.* In *Ante-Nicene Fathers.* Vol. 1, *The Apostolic Fathers, Justin Martyr, Irenaeus.* Edited by Alexander

Roberts and James Donaldson. Revised by A. Cleveland Coxe. Peabody, Mass.: Hendrickson, 2004.

Inwood, Michael J. *A Heidegger Dictionary*. Blackwell Philosopher Dictionaries. Malden, Mass.: Blackwell, 1999.

Irenaeus. *Irenaeus Against Heresies*. In *Ante-Nicene Fathers*, Vol. 1, *The Apostolic Fathers, Justin Martyr, Irenaeus*. Edited by Alexander Roberts and James Donaldson. Revised by A. Cleveland Coxe. Peabody, Mass.: Hendrickson, 2004.

Jaeger, Werner Wilhelm. *Early Christianity and Greek Paideia*. Cambridge, Mass.: Belknap Press of Harvard University Press, 1985.

———. *Humanism and Theology*. Milwaukee: Marquette University Press, 1943.

———. *Paideia: The Ideals of Greek Culture*. Vol. 1, *Archaic Greece: The Mind of Athens*. 2nd ed. Translated by Gilbert Highet. New York: Oxford University Press, 1945.

Janicaud, Dominique. "Du bon usage de la *Lettre sur l'humanisme*." In *Heidegger et la question de l'humanisme: Faits, concepts, débats*, 213-26. Edited by Bruno Pinchard and Thierry Gontier. Paris: Presses universitaires de France, 2005.

———. *On the Human Condition*. Thinking in Action. New York: Routledge, 2005.

Janz, Curt Paul. *Friedrich Nietzsche Biographie*. 3 vols. Munich: Hanser, 1981.

Jenkins, Philip. *God's Continent: Christianity, Islam, and Europe's Religious Crisis*. Oxford: Oxford University Press, 2007.

———. *The Next Christendom: The Coming of Global Christianity*. Oxford: Oxford University Press, 2007.

John of Damascus. "Exposition of the Orthodox Faith." In *Nicene and Post-Nicene Fathers*. Second Series. Vol. 9, *Hilary of Poitiers, John of Damascus*. Edited by Alexander Roberts et al. Peabody, Mass.: Hendrickson, 1994.

John Paul II. *Crossing the Threshold of Hope*. Edited by Vittorio Messori. Translated by Jenny McPhee and Martha McPhee. New York: Knopf, 1994.

———. *Fides et Ratio*. September 14, 1998. Papal Archives. www.vatican.va/ holy_father/john_paul_ii/encyclicals/documents/hf_jp-ii_enc_15101998_fi des-et-ratio_en.html.

———. *Redemptor Hominis*. March 4, 1979. Papal Archives. www.vatican.va/ holy_father/john_paul_ii/encyclicals/documents/hf_jp-ii_enc_04031979_ redemptor-hominis_en.html.

———. *Veritatis Splendor*. August 6, 1993. Papal Archives. www.vatican.va/ holy_father/john_paul_ii/encyclicals/documents/hf_jp-ii_enc_06081993_ veritatis-splendor_en.html.

Jüngel, Eberhard. *God's Being Is in Becoming: The Trinitarian Being of God in the Theology of Karl Barth: A Paraphrase*. Grand Rapids: Eerdmans, 2001.

———. *Gott als Geheimnis der Welt: Zur Begründung der Theologie des Gekreuzigten im Streit zwischen Theismus und Atheismus.* 3rd ed. Tübingen: Mohr, 1978.

Justin Martyr. *Dialogue with Trypho.* In *Ante-Nicene Fathers,* vol. 1, *The Apostolic Fathers, Justin Martyr, Irenaeus.* Edited by Alexander Roberts and James Donaldson. Revised by A. Cleveland Coxe. Peabody, Mass.: Hendrickson, 2004.

———. *The First Apology of Justin.* In *Ante-Nicene Fathers,* vol. 1, *The Apostolic Fathers, Justin Martyr, Irenaeus.* Edited by Alexander Roberts and James Donaldson. Revised by A. Cleveland Coxe. Peabody, Mass.: Hendrickson, 2004.

———. *Hortatory Address to the Greeks.* In *Ante-Nicene Fathers,* vol. 1, *The Apostolic Fathers, Justin Martyr, Irenaeus.* Edited by Alexander Roberts and James Donaldson. Revised by A. Cleveland Coxe. Peabody, Mass.: Hendrickson, 2004.

———. *The Second Apology of Justin.* In *Ante-Nicene Fathers,* vol. 1, *The Apostolic Fathers, Justin Martyr, Irenaeus.* Edited by Alexander Roberts and James Donaldson. Revised by A. Cleveland Coxe. Peabody, Mass.: Hendrickson, 2004.

Kallendorf, Craig, ed. and trans. *Humanist Educational Treatises.* I Tatti Renaissance Library. Cambridge, Mass.: Harvard University Press, 2002.

Kant, Immanuel. *Kritik der reinen Vernunft.* Edited by Jens Zimmermann. Hamburg: F. Meiner Verlag, 1998.

———. *On Education.* Translated by Annette Churton. Dover Books on Western Philosophy. Mineola, N.Y.: Dover Publications, 2003.

———. *Die Religion innerhalb der Grenzen der blossen Vernunft. Die Metaphysik der Sitten.* Vol. 5 of *Immanuel Kant: Werke in sechs Bänden.* Edited by Rolf Toman. Köln: Könemann, 1995.

———. *Religion within the Limits of Reason Alone.* Translated by Theodore M. Greene and Hoyt H. Hudson. New York: Harper & Row, 1960.

Kearney, Richard. *Anatheism: Returning to God After God.* Insurrections: Critical Studies in Religion, Politics, and Culture. New York: Columbia University Press, 2010.

———. *The God Who May Be: A Hermeneutics of Religion.* Indiana Series in the Philosophy of Religion. Bloomington: Indiana University Press, 2001.

———. "In Place of a Response." In *After God: Richard Kearney and the Religious Turn in Continental Philosophy,* 365-88. Edited by John Panteleimon Manoussakis. Perspectives in Continental Philosophy. New York: Fordham University Press, 2006.

———. *Strangers, Gods, and Monsters: Interpreting Otherness.* London: Routledge, 2003.

Kelly, J. N. D. *Early Christian Creeds.* London: Longmans, Green, 1950.

Kharlamov, Vladimir. "Rhetorical Application of *Theosis.*" In *Partakers of the Divine Nature: The History and Development of Deification in the Christian Traditions,* 115-31. Edited by Michael J. Christensen and Jeffery A. Wittung. Madison, Wis.: Fairleigh Dickinson University Press, 2007.

Klassen, Norman, and Jens Zimmermann. *The Passionate Intellect: Incarnational Humanism and the Future of University Education*. Grand Rapids: Baker Academic, 2006.

Knowles, David. *Evolution of Medieval Thought*. Edited by David Edward Luscombe, Christopher Nugent and Lawrence Books. 2nd ed. London: Longman, 1988.

Körtner, Ulrich. *Wiederkehr der Religion? Das Christentum zwischen neuer Spiritualität und Gottvergessenheit*. Gütersloher: Gütersloher Verlag, 2006.

Kovacs, J. L. "Divine Pedagogy and the Gnostic Teacher According to Clement of Alexandria." *Journal of Early Christian Studies* 9, no. 1 (2001): 3-25.

Kraye, Jill. "The Humanist Moral Philosopher: Marc Antoin Muret's Edition of Seneca." In *Moral Philosophy on the Threshold of Modernity*, 307-30. Edited by Jill Kraye and Risto Saarinen. The New Synthese Historical Library. Dortrecht: Springer, 2005.

Kristeller, Paul Oskar. "Humanism." In *The Cambridge History of Renaissance Philosophy*, 113-37. Edited by Quentin Skinner and Eckhard Kessler. Cambridge Companions to Philosophy. Cambridge: Cambridge University Press, 2000.

———. *Renaissance Thought and its Sources*. Edited by Michael Mooney. New York: Columbia University Press, 1979.

Küng, Hans. *Der Islam: Geschichte, Gegenwart, Zukunft*. Munich: Piper, 2004.

Lawrence, Fred. "Gadamer, the Hermeneutic Revolution, and Theology." In *The Cambridge Companion to Gadamer*, 167-200. Edited by Robert J. Dostal. Cambridge Companions to Philosophy. Cambridge: Cambridge University Press, 2002.

Leaman, Oliver. *Introduction to Classical Islamic Philosophy*. 2nd ed. Cambridge: Cambridge University Press, 2002.

Leithart, Peter J. *Defending Constantine: The Twilight of an Empire and the Dawn of Christendom*. Downers Grove, Ill.: IVP Academic, 2010.

Levinas, Emmanuel. *Alterity and Transcendence*. Translated by Michael B. Smith. European Perspectives. New York: Columbia University Press, 1999.

———. *Entre Nous: On Thinking-of-the-Other*. Edited by Michael B. Smith. Translated by Michael B. Smith and Barbara Harshav. European Perspectives. New York: Columbia University Press, 1998.

———. *Ethics and Infinity*. Translated by Philippe Nemo. Pittsburgh: Duquesne University Press, 1997.

———. *Humanism of the Other*. Translated by Nidra Poller. Urbana: University of Illinois Press, 2003.

———. *Is It Righteous to Be? Interviews with Emmanuel Levinas*. Edited by Jill Robbins. Stanford: Stanford University Press, 2001.

————. *Nine Talmudic Readings.* Translated by Annette Aronowicz. Blooming-ton: Indiana University Press, 1990.

————. *Of God Who Comes to Mind.* Translated by Bettina Bergo. 2nd ed. Stanford: Stanford University Press, 1998.

————. *Otherwise Than Being, or, Beyond Essence.* Translated by Alphonso Lingis. Pittsburgh: Duquesne University Press, 1998.

————. "Reality and its Shadow." In *Collected Philosophical Papers*, 1-23. Translated by Alphonso Lingis. Pittsburgh: Duquesne University Press, 1987.

————. "The Rights of Man and Good Will." In Emmanuel Levinas, *Entre Nous: On Thinking-of-the-Other*, 155-58. Edited by Michael B. Smith. Translated by Michael B. Smith and Barbara Harshav. European Perspectives. New York: Columbia University Press, 1998.

————. *Totality and Infinity: An Essay on Exteriority.* 1961. Translated by Alphonso Lingis. Pittsburgh: Duquesne University Press, 1969.

Long, A. A. "The Scope of Greek Philosophy." In *The Cambridge Companion to Early Greek Philosophy*, 1-21. Edited by A. A. Long. Cambridge Companions to Philosophy. Cambridge: Cambridge University Press, 1999.

Long, Stephen D. *Theology and Culture: A Guide to the Discussion.* Eugene, Ore.: Cascade, 2008.

Lovin, Robert V. *Reinhold Niebuhr and Christian Realism.* Cambridge: Cambridge University Press, 1995.

Lubac, Henri. *Augustinianism and Modern Theology.* Translated by Lancelot Sheppard. Milestones in Catholic Theology. New York: Herder & Herder, 2000.

————. *Catholicism: Christ and the Common Destiny of Man.* Translated by Lancelot C. Sheppard and Elizabeth Englund. San Francisco: Ignatius Press, 1988.

————. *Corpus Mysticum: The Eucharist and the Church in the Middle Ages: A Historical Survey.* Edited by Laurence Paul Hemming and Susan Frank Parsons. Translated by Gemma Simonds. Rev. ed. Notre Dame, Ind.: University of Notre Dame Press, 2007.

————. *The Mystery of the Supernatural.* Rev. ed. Milestones in Catholic Theology. Translated by Rosemary Sheed. New York: Crossroad, 1998.

————. *Scripture in the Tradition.* Translated by Luke O'Neill. Milestones in Catholic Theology. New York: Crossroad, 2000.

————. *The Splendor of the Church.* Translated by Michael Mason. San Francisco: Ignatius Press, 1999.

————. *Theology in History: The Light of Christ, Disputed Questions and Resistance to Nazism.* Translated by Anne Englund Nash. San Francisco: Ignatius Press, 1996.

————. *Über Gott Hinaus: Tragödie Des Atheistischen Humanismus*. Translated by Edith M. Riley. Einsiedeln: Johannes Verlag, 1984.

Luther, Martin. *Auslegung des Vaterunser, Sermon von den guten Werken*. Vol. 3 of *Calwer Luther-Ausgabe*. Edited by Wolfgang Metzger. Stuttgart: Hänssler Verlag, 1996.

————. *Das Magnifikat: Vorlesung über den 1 Johannesbrief*. Vol. 9 of *Calwer Luther-Ausgabe*. Edited by Wolfgang Metzger. Stuttgart: Hänssler Verlag, 1996.

————. *Sämtliche Werke*. Edited by Johann Conrad Irmischer and Johann Georg Plochmann. 68 vols. Erlangen: Heyder, 1826-1858.

Lyotard, Jean-François. *The Inhuman: Reflections on Time*. Translated by Geoffrey Bennington and Rachel Bowlby. Stanford: Stanford University Press, 1991.

————. *The Postmodern Condition: A Report on Knowledge*. Translated by Geoffrey Bennington and Brian Massumi. Theory and History of Literature. Minneapolis: University of Minnesota Press, 1984.

MacIntyre, Alasdair. "Tradition Against Genealogy: Who Speaks to Whom?" In *Three Rival Versions of Moral Enquiry: Encyclopaedia, Genealogy, and Tradition: Being Gifford Lectures Delivered in the University of Edinburgh in 1988*, 196-215. Notre Dame, Ind.: University of Notre Dame Press, 1990.

Magnus, Bernd, and Kathleen M. Higgins, eds. *The Cambridge Companion to Nietzsche*. Cambridge Companions to Philosophy. Cambridge: Cambridge University Press, 1996.

————. "Nietzsche's Works and Their Themes." In *The Cambridge Companion to Nietzsche*, 21-70. Edited by Bernd Magnus and Kathleen M. Higgins. Cambridge Companions to Philosophy. Cambridge: Cambridge University Press, 1996.

Mann, Nicholas. "The Origins of Humanism." In *The Cambridge Companion to Renaissance Humanism*, 1-19. Edited by Jill Kraye. Cambridge Companions to Literature. Cambridge: Cambridge University Press, 1996.

Manoussakis, John Panteleimon, ed. *After God: Richard Kearney and the Religious Turn in Continental Philosophy*. Perspectives in Continental Philosophy. New York: Fordham University Press, 2006.

Marcus Aurelius. *Meditations*. Translated by A. S. L. Farquharson. New York: Knopf, 1992.

Marion, Jean-Luc. *God Without Being: Hors-Texte*. Translated by Thomas A. Carlson. Religion and Postmodernism. Chicago: University of Chicago Press, 1991.

————. "The Saturated Phenomenon." In *Phenomenology and the "Theological Turn": A French Debate*, 176-216. Edited by Dominique Janicaud. Translated by Thomas A. Carlson. Perspectives in Continental Philosophy. New York: Fordham University Press, 2000.

Maritain, Jacques. *True Humanism*. Translated by Margot Robert Adamson. 6th ed. London: Geoffrey Bles, 1954.

Markus, R. A. *Christianity and the Secular*. Blessed Pope John XXIII Lecture Series in Theology and Culture. Notre Dame, Ind.: University of Notre Dame Press, 2006.

———. *Saeculum: History and Society in the Theology of St. Augustine*. Cambridge: Cambridge University Press, 1988.

Mathewes, Charles T. *A Theology of Public Life*. Cambridge Studies in Christian Doctrine. Cambridge: Cambridge University Press, 2007.

Maximus the Confessor. "Letter 2: On Love." In *Maximus the Confessor*, 81-90. Edited by Andrew Louth. The Early Church Fathers. London: Routledge, 1996.

McGrath, S .J. *The Early Heidegger and Medieval Philosophy. Phenomenology for the Godforsaken*. Washington, D.C.: Catholic University of America Press, 2006.

Metz, Johannes Baptist. *Zur Theologie der Welt*. Mainz: Matthias-Grünewald Verlag, 1968.

Milbank, John. *The Religious Dimension in the Thought of Giambattista Vico, 1668-1744*. 2 vols. Lewiston, N.Y.: Edwin Mellen, 1991.

Morgan, Michael. "Plato and Greek Religion." In *The Cambridge Companion to Plato*, 227-47. Edited by Richard Kraut. Cambridge Companions to Philosophy. Cambridge: Cambridge University Press, 1992.

Moule, Charles F. D. *The Origins of Christology*. Cambridge: Cambridge University Press, 1977.

Naldini, Mario. Introduction to *De Doctrina Christiana: Teaching Christianity*, by Augustine. Edited by John E. Rotelle. Translated by Edmund Hill. Works of Saint Augustine: A Translation for the 21st Century. New York: New City Press, 1990.

Nauert, Charles Garfield. *Humanism and the Culture of Renaissance Europe*. 2nd ed. New Approaches to European History. New York: Cambridge University Press, 2006.

Niebuhr, H. Richard. *Christ and Culture*. New York: Harper, 1956.

Nietzsche, Friedrich Wilhelm. *Friedrich Nietzsches Werke*. Historisch-Kritische Gesamtausgabe. 5 vols. Munich: Beck, 1934-1940.

———. *Sämtliche Werke*. Kritische Studienausgabe. 15 vols. Edited by Giorgio Colli and Mazzino Montinari. 2nd rev. ed. Munich: Deutscher Taschenbuch Verlag, 1999.

———. *Sämtliche Werke*. Kritische Studienausgabe. Vol. 1, *Die Geburt der Tragödie. Unzeitgemässe Betrachtungen I-IV. Nachgelassene Schriften 1870-1873*. Edited by Giorgio Colli and Mazzino Montinari. 2nd rev. ed. Munich: Deutscher Taschenbuch Verlag, 1999.

———. *Sämtliche Werke*. Kritische Studienausgabe. Vol. 3, *Morgenröte. Idyllen aus Messina. Die fröhliche Wissenshaft*. Edited by Giorgio Colli and Mazzino Montinari. 2nd rev. ed. Munich: Deutscher Taschenbuch Verlag, 1999.

———. *Sämtliche Werke*. Kritische Studienausgabe. Vol. 4, *Also Sprach Zarathustra, ein buch für Alle und Keinen*. Edited by Giorgio Colli and Mazzino Montinari. 2nd rev. ed. Munich: Deutscher Taschenbuch Verlag, 1999.

———. *Sämtliche Werke*. Kritische Studienausgabe. Vol. 5, *Jenseits von Gut und Böse. Zur Genealogie der Moral*. Edited by Giorgio Colli and Mazzino Montinari. 2nd rev. ed. Munich: Deutscher Taschenbuch Verlag, 1999.

———. Sämtliche Werke. Kritische Studienausgabe. Vol. 6, Der Fall Wagner. Götzendämmerung. Der Antichrist. Ecce homo. Dionysos-Dithyramben. Nietzsche contra Wagner. Edited by Giorgio Colli and Mazzino Montinari. 2nd rev. ed. Munich: Deutscher Taschenbuch Verlag, 1999.

O'Daly, Gerald J. P. *Platonism Pagan and Christian: Studies in Plotinus and Augustine*. Surrey: Ashgate, 2001.

Origen. *Commentarii in Epistolam ad Romanos: Origenes Römerbriefkommentar*. Vol. 4. Freiburg: Herder, 1990.

Osborn, Eric Francis. *Irenaeus of Lyons*. Cambridge: Cambridge University Press, 2001.

Otto, Stephan. *Giambattista Vico*. Stuttgart: Kohlhammer, 1989.

Ozment, Steven E. *Age of Reform (1250-1550): An Intellectual and Religious History of Late Medieval and Reformation Europe*. New Haven, Conn.: Yale University Press, 1980.

Pannenberg, Wolfhart. *Jesus—God and Man*. Translated by Lewis L. Wilkins and Duane A. Priebe. Library of Philosophy and Theology. London: SCM Press, 2002.

Pelikan, Jaroslav. *Christianity and Classical Culture: The Metamorphosis of Natural Theology in the Christian Encounter with Hellenism*. New Haven, Conn.: Yale University Press, 1993.

———. *Spirit Versus Structure: Luther and the Institutions of the Church*. London: Collins, 1968.

———. *What Has Athens to Do with Jerusalem? Timaeus and Genesis in Counterpoint*. Ann Arbor: University of Michigan Press, 2000.

Peterson, Erik. "Was ist der Mensch." In *Theologische Traktate*. Ausgewählte Schriften. Würzburg: Echter, 1994.

Pfürtner, Stephan H. *Luther and Aquinas on Salvation*. New York: Sheed & Ward, 1965.

Piccolomini, Aeneas Sylvius. "The Education of Boys." In *Humanist Educational* Treatises, 126-259. Edited and translated by Craig Kallendorf. I Tatti

Renaissance Library. Cambridge, Mass: Harvard University Press, 2002.

———. "De Liberorum Educatione." In *Vittorino da Feltre and Other Humanist Educators*, 134-58. Edited by William Harrison Woodward. Renaissance Society of America Reprint Texts. Toronto: University of Toronto Press, 1996.

Pico della Mirandola, Giovanni. *Oration on the Dignity of Man.* Center for the Study of Complex Systems. November 21, 1994. www.cscs.umich.edu/~crshalizi/Mirandola.

Pieper, Josef. *Scholasticism: Personalities and Problems of Medieval Philosophy.* Translated by Richard Winston and Clara Winston. New York: McGraw-Hill, 1964.

Polanyi, Michael, and Harry Prosch. *Meaning.* Chicago: University of Chicago Press, 1996.

Powell, Jason. *Jacques Derrida: A Biography.* New York: Continuum, 2006.

Puchniak, Robert. "Augustine's Conception of Deification Revisited." In *Theōsis: Deification in Christian Theology*, 122-33. Edited by Stephen Finlan and Vladimir Kharlamov. Princeton Theological Monograph Series. Eugene, Ore.: Pickwick, 2006.

Rabil, Albert. *Renaissance Humanism: Foundations, Form and Legacy.* 3 vols. Philadelphia: University of Pennsylvania Press, 1988.

Rahman, Fazlur. *Major Themes in the Qur'an.* Minneapolis: Bibliotheca Islamica, 1989.

Rice, Eugene F., Jr. "The Renaissance Idea of Christian Antiquity: Humanistic Patristic Scholarship." In Albert Rabil, *Renaissance Humanism.* Vol. 1, *Humanism in Italy*, 17-28. Philadelphia: University of Pennsylvania Press, 1988.

Ricoeur, Paul. *Figuring the Sacred: Religion, Narrative, and Imagination.* Edited by Mark I. Wallace. Translated by David Pellauer. Minneapolis: Fortress, 1995.

Roberts, Alexander, and James Donaldson, eds. *The Ante-Nicene Fathers: The Writings of the Fathers down to A.D. 325.* 1885. 10 vols. Revised by A. Cleveland Coxe. Peabody, Mass.: Hendrickson, 2004.

Robinson, Marilynne. *Absence of Mind: The Dispelling of Inwardness from the Modern Myth of the Self.* Terry Lectures. New Haven, Conn.: Yale University Press, 2010.

Roehr, Sabine. *A Primer on German Enlightenment.* Translated by Karl Loenhard Reinhold. Columbia: University of Missouri Press, 1995.

Rorty, Richard. "Remarks on Deconstruction and Pragmatism." In Simon Critchley, Jacques Derrida, Ernesto Laclau and Richard Rorty, *Deconstruction and Pragmatism*, 13-18. Edited by Chantal Mouffe. London: Routledge, 1996.

Russel, Norman. *The Doctrine of Deification in the Greek Patristic Tradition.* Oxford Early Christian Studies. Oxford: Oxford University Press, 2004.

Salaquarda, Jorg. "Nietzsche and the Judeo-Christian Tradition." In *The Cambridge Companion to Nietzsche*, 100-29. Edited by Bernd Magnus and Kathleen

M. Higgins. Cambridge Companions to Philosophy. Cambridge: Cambridge University Press, 1996.

Saunders, Trevor J. "Plato's Later Political Thought." In *The Cambridge Companion to Plato*, 464-92. Edited by Richard Kraut. Cambridge Companions to Philosophy. Cambridge: Cambridge University Press, 1992.

Sayre, Kenneth M. *Plato's Late Ontology: A Riddle Resolved*. Princeton, N.J.: Princeton University Press, 1983.

Schleiermacher, Friedrich. *Der christliche Glaube. 1821/22*. 2 vols. Edited by Hermann Peiter. Berlin: Walter de Gruyter, 1984.

———. *Über die Religion: Reden an die Gebildeten unter ihren Verächtern (1799)*. Edited by Günter Meckenstock. Berlin: Walter de Gruyter, 1999.

Schmemann, Alexander. *For the Life of the World: Sacraments and Orthodoxy*. Crestwood, N.Y.: St. Vladimir's Seminary Press, 2004.

Schmutz, Jacob. "The Medieval Doctrine of Causality and the Theology of Pure Nature 13th to 17th Centuries." In *Surnaturel: A Controversy at the Heart of Twentieth-Century Thomistic Thought*, 203-250. Edited by Serge-Thomas Bonino. Translated by Robert Williams. Translation revised by Matthew Levering. Ave Maria, Fla.: Sapientia Press of Ave Maria University, 2009.

Scholtz, Gunter. *Ethik und Hermeneutik: Schleiermachers Grundlegung der Geisteswissenschaften*. Frankfurt am Main: Suhrkamp, 1995.

Schrift, Alan D. "Nietzsche's French Legacy." In *The Cambridge Companion to Nietzsche*, 323-55. Edited by Bernd Magnus and Kathleen M. Higgins. Cambridge Companions to Philosophy. Cambridge: Cambridge University Press, 1996.

Schweitzer, Albert. *Kultur und Ethik*. Munich: Beck, 1990.

Sciglitano, Anthony C. "Contesting the World and the Divine: Balthasar's Trinitarian 'Response' to Gianni Vattimo's Secular Christianity." *Modern Theology* 23, no. 4 (2007): 525-59.

Sheiman, Bruce. *An Atheist Defends Religion: Why Humanity Is Better Off with Religion Than Without It*. New York: Alpha Books, 2009.

Smith, James K. A. *Jacques Derrida: Live Theory*. Live Theory Series. New York: Continuum, 2005.

Sokolowski, Robert. *Eucharistic Presence: A Study in the Theology of Disclosure*. Washington, D.C.: Catholic University of America Press, 1994.

———. *The God of Faith and Reason: Foundations of Christian Theology*. Washington, D.C.: Catholic University of America Press, 2006.

Sommerville, John. *The Decline of the Secular University*. Oxford: Oxford University Press, 2006.

Southern, R. W. *Foundations*. Vol. 1 of *Scholastic Humanism and the Unification of Europe*. Oxford: Blackwell, 1995.

———. *Medieval Humanism and Other Studies*. Oxford: Blackwell, 1970.

Stark, Rodney. *The Victory of Reason: How Christianity Led to Freedom, Capitalism, and Western Success*. New York: Random House Trade Paperbacks, 2006.

Steenberg, M. C. *Of God and Man: Theology as Anthropology from Irenaeus to Athanasius*. London: T & T Clark, 2009.

Stout, Jeffrey. *Democracy and Tradition*. Princeton, N.J.: Princeton University Press, 2005.

Szerszynski, Bronislaw. "Rethinking the Secular: Science, Technology, and Religion Today." *Zygon* 40, no. 4 (2005): 793-800.

Tatian. *Tatian's Address to the Greeks*. In *Ante-Nicene Fathers*. Vol. 2, *Hermas, Tatian, Athenagoras, Theophilus, Clement of Alexandria*. Edited by Alexander Roberts and James Donaldson. Revised by A. Cleveland Coxe. Peabody, Mass.: Hendrickson, 2004.

Taylor, C. C. W. "Politics." In *The Cambridge Companion to Aristotle*, 233-58. Edited by Jonathan Barnes. Cambridge Companions to Philosophy. Cambridge: Cambridge University Press, 1995.

Taylor, Charles. *A Catholic Modernity? Charles Taylor's Marianist Award Lecture, with Responses by William M. Shea, Rosemary Luling Haughton, George Marsden, and Jean Bethke Elshtain*. Edited by James L. Heft. New York: Oxford University Press, 1999.

———. *The Malaise of Modernity*. Concord, Ont.: House of Anansi Press, 1992.

———. *Sources of the Self: The Making of the Modern Identity*. Cambridge, Mass.: Harvard University Press, 1989.

Tillard, J. M. R. *Flesh of the Church, Flesh of Christ: At the Source of the Ecclesiology of Communion*. Translated by Madeleine Beaumont. Collegeville, Minn.: Liturgical Press, 2001.

Torrance, T. F. *God and Rationality*. London: Oxford University Press, 1971.

———. *Incarnation: The Person and Life of Christ*. Edited by Robert T. Walker. Rev. ed. Downers Grove, Ill.: IVP Academic, 2008.

———. *Space, Time and Incarnation*. Edinburgh: T & T Clark, 1997.

Treier, Daniel J. *Introducing Theological Interpretation of Scripture: Recovering a Christian Practice*. Grand Rapids: Baker Academic, 2008.

Trinkaus, Charles Edward. *In Our Image and Likeness: Humanity and Divinity in Italian Humanist Thought*. 2 vols. Notre Dame, Ind.: University of Notre Dame Press, 1995.

———. "The Religious Thought of the Italian Humanists, and the Reformers: Anticipation or Autonomy." In *The Pursuit of Holiness in Late Medieval and Renaissance Religion; Papers from the University of Michigan Conference*, 336-66. Edited by Charles Edward Trinkaus and Heiko A. Oberman. Leiden: Brill, 1974.

Vanhoozer, Kevin J. "The Atonement in Postmodernity: Guilt, Goats, and Gifts." In *The Glory of the Atonement: Biblical, Historical, and Practical Perspectives: Essays in Honor of Roger R. Nicole*, 367-404. Edited by Charles Evan Hill, Roger R. Nicole, and Frank A. James. Downers Grove, Ill.: IVP Academic, 2004.

———. Introduction to the *Dictionary for the Theological Interpretation of the Bible*, 19-25. Edited by Kevin J. Vanhoozer, Craig G. Bartholomew, Daniel J. Treier and N. T. Wright. Grand Rapids: Baker Academic, 2005.

VanKooten, Georg H. *Paul's Anthropology in Context*. Wissenschaftliche Untersuchungen zum Neuen Testament 23. Tübingen: Morh Siebeck, 2003.

Vasoli, Caesare. "The Renaissance Concept of Philosophy." In *The Cambridge History of Renaissance Philosophy*, 55-74. Edited by Charles B. Schmitt and Quentin Skinner. Cambridge Companions to Philosophy. Cambridge: Cambridge University Press, 1988.

Vattimo, Gianni. *After Christianity*. Translated by Luca D'Isanto. Italian Academy Lectures. New York: Columbia University Press, 2002.

———. *Belief*. Translated by Luca D'Isanto and David Webb. Stanford: Stanford University Press, 1999.

———. *Beyond Interpretation: The Meaning of Hermeneutics for Philosophy*. Translated by David Webb. Stanford: Stanford University Press, 1997.

———. *The End of Modernity: Nihilism and Hermeneutics in Postmodern Culture*. Translated by Jon R. Snyder. Parallax: Re-visions of Culture and Society. Baltimore: Johns Hopkins University Press, 1991.

———. *Nihilism and Emancipation: Ethics, Politics, and Law*. Edited by Santiago Zabala. Translated by William McCuaig. European Perspectives. New York: Columbia University Press, 2004.

Verbeke, Gérard. *Presence of Stoicism in Medieval Thought*. Washington, D.C.: Catholic University of America Press, 1983.

Verene, Donald Phillip. Introduction to Giambattista Vico. *On Humanistic Education (Six Inaugural Orations, 1699-1707)*,1-16. Translated by Giorgio A. Pinton and Arthur W. Shippee. Ithaca, N.Y.: Cornell University Press, 1993.

Vergerio, Pier Paolo. "The Character and Studies Befitting A Free-Born Youth." In *Humanist Educational Treatises*, 2-91. Edited and translated by Craig Kallendorf. I Tatti Renaissance Library. Cambridge, Mass: Harvard University Press, 2002.

Vico, Giambattista. *The New Science of Giambattista Vico*. Translated by Thomas Goddard Bergin and Max Harold Fisch. 3rd ed. Ithaca, N.Y.: Cornell University Press, 1988.

———. *On Humanistic Education (Six Inaugural Orations, 1699-1707)*. Translated by Giorgio A. Pinton and Arthur W. Shippee. Ithaca, N.Y.: Cornell University Press, 1993.

————. *On the Study Methods of Our Time.* Translated by Elio Gianturco and Donald Phillip Verene. Ithaca, N.Y.: Cornell University Press, 1990.

Ward, Graham. *Christ and Culture.* Challenges in Contemporary Theology. Malden, Mass.: Blackwell, 2005.

Ware, Kallistos. *The Orthodox Way.* Rev. ed. Crestwood, N.Y.: St. Vladimir's Seminary Press, 1990.

Watson, Francis. *Text, Church, and World: Biblical Interpretation in Theological Perspective.* Grand Rapids: Eerdmans, 1994.

Webber, Robert. *Ancient-Future Faith: Rethinking Evangelicalism for a Postmodern World.* Grand Rapids: Baker, 1999.

Westphal, Merold. "Hermeneutics and the God of Promise." In *After God: Richard Kearney and the Religious Turn in Continental Philosophy,* 78-93. Edited by John Panteleimon Manoussakis. Perspectives in Continental Philosophy. New York: Fordham University Press, 2006.

Wilken, Robert Louis. *The Spirit of Early Christian Thought: Seeking the Face of God.* New Haven, Conn.: Yale University Press, 2003.

Wilson, Thomas. "The Art of Rhetoric." In *English Humanism: Wyatt to Cowley,* 185-90. Edited by Joanna Martindale. London: Croom Helm, 1985.

Woodward, William Harrison, ed. *Vittorino da Feltre and Other Humanist Educators.* Renaissance Society of America Reprint Texts. Toronto: University of Toronto Press, 1996.

Wright, N. T. *The Climax of the Covenant: Christ and the Law in Pauline Theology.* Minneapolis: Fortress Press, 1992.

————. *Justification: God's Plan and Paul's Vision.* Downers Grove, Ill.: IVP Academic, 2009.

————. "The Letter to the Romans: Introduction, Commentary, and Reflections." In *The New Interpreters Bible: A Commentary in Twelve Volumes,* 393-770. Edited by Leander E. Keck. Vol. 10. Nashville: Abingdon, 2009.

————. *Paul: In Fresh Perspective.* Minneapolis: Fortress Press, 2005.

————. *What Saint Paul Really Said: Was Paul of Tarsus the Real Founder of Christianity?* Grand Rapids: Eerdmans, 1997.

Yoder, John Howard. "The Christological Presuppositions of Discipleship." In *Being Human, Becoming Human: Dietrich Bonhoeffer and Social Thought,* 127-51. Edited by Jens Zimmermann and Brian Gregor. Princeton Theological Monograph Series. Eugene, Ore.: Wipf & Stock, 2010.

Young, Frances. *Biblical Exegesis and the Formation of Christian Culture.* Cambridge: Cambridge University Press, 2007.

Zaborowski, Holger. *Eine Frage von Irre und Schuld? Martin Heidegger und der Nationalsozialismus.* Frankfurt am Main: Fischer Taschenbuch Verlag, 2010.

Zimmermann, Jens. *Recovering Theological Hermeneutics*: *An Incarnational-Trinitarian Theory of Interpretation*. Grand Rapids: Baker Academic, 2004.

Zimmermann, Jens, and Brian Gregor, eds. *Being Human, Becoming Human: Dietrich Bonhoeffer and Social Thought*. Princeton Theological Monograph Series. Eugene, Ore.: Wipf & Stock, 2010.

Zink, Jörg. *Sieh nach den Sternen—gib acht auf die Gassen: Erinnerungen*. Stuttgart: Kreuz, 1992.

Žižek, Slavoj. *The Plague of Fantasies*. London: Verso, 1997.

Zizioulas, John. *Communion and Otherness: Further Studies in Personhood and the Church*. Edited by Paul McPartland. London: T & T Clark, 2006.

Name Index

Subject Index

Scripture Index